TWENTY-FOUR LAYS
FROM THE FRENCH MIDDLE AGES

EXETER STUDIES IN MEDIEVAL EUROPE

History, Society and the Arts

Twenty-Four Lays from the French Middle Ages

Translated by
Glyn S. Burgess
and
Leslie C. Brook

LIVERPOOL UNIVERSITY PRESS

First published 2016 by
Liverpool University Press
4 Cambridge Street
Liverpool
L69 7ZU

British Library Cataloguing-in-Publication data

A British Library CIP record is available

ISBN 978-1-78138-336-0 cased
ISBN 978-1-78138-337-7 paperback

Typeset by Carnegie Book Production, Lancaster
Printed and bound in Poland by BooksFactory.co.uk

Contents

Passion and Tears

Romance and Realism

The Lay as History

General Introduction

The genre of the narrative lay (or *lai*) in Old French is predominantly associated with an author traditionally known as Marie de France. Her twelve surviving lays, known collectively as the *Lais*, have often been regarded as the model of the genre, and Marie herself as its creator. Often known as the Breton lay – because of its perceived links with Brittany in terms of origin and the presence, in some cases but not all, of Breton locations and personages – the narrative lay is to the modern short story what the genre of the romance is to the modern novel.

It would be wrong, however, to think that the lay as a genre is restricted to Marie's twelve poems. No definitive list has been established, and the boundaries between genres are never clear-cut, but in the present volume we provide translations of twenty-four further poems that possess all, or at least many, of the characteristics that define the lay. Some of them (e.g. *Espine* and *Guingamor*) have over the years been attributed to Marie de France, some (e.g. *Espervier* and *Ignaure*) have features that are associated with the comic tales known as the *fabliaux*, and the *Chastelaine de Vergi*, despite its marked similarities in form and content to the lay, has, especially in more recent times, been regarded as a short romance. Taken as a whole, these lays are often referred to as 'the anonymous lays' but the expression is inappropriate, even if it does help to differentiate them from the lays of Marie de France, as five of these twenty-four works provide us with the name of their author: *Amours* (Girart), *Aristote* (Henri), *Cor* (Robert Biket), *Ignaure* (Renaut) and *Ombre* (Jehan Renart). But the fact that far more of our lays do not name their authors is in no way surprising, as many writers at the time regarded it as their task to pass on to their public stories composed by others rather than to emphasise or flaunt their own individuality.[1]

[1] In MS H of the *Lais* the author's name is given as Marie (not Marie de France), but in MS S, which contains nine of her lays, she is not named (see the Manuscripts section below).

Just as it is impossible to date the *Lais* of Marie de France with any degree of precision (the 1160s are often mentioned, but the work could have been completed a couple of decades later), so it is with the dating of the lays in this volume. There is some evidence that the *Lai de l'Ombre*, definitely one of the later lays, was composed in the period 1217–22, and that *Graelent* was composed before *Guingamor*. But, although the classical lays of *Piramus* and *Narcisus* may have been composed as early as the 1150s, the best we can do for the remaining works is to suggest a date between the end of the twelfth century and the first decades of the thirteenth.[2] Some of our lays, especially those in the last section, 'Romance and Realism', give the impression that the genre has moved on somewhat, with clever dialogue or everyday matters, rather than compelling action or supernatural events, at the centre of the story.[3]

When more than one manuscript is concerned, the length of the surviving lays varies. The shortest lay in this volume is *Nabaret* at forty-eight lines and the longest *Haveloc* at 1,099 lines, the average length being 621 lines (Marie's shortest lay is *Chevrefoil* at 118 lines and her longest *Eliduc* at 1,184 lines, her average being 476 lines). A typical lay, whether by Marie de France or another author, opens with a prologue and these also vary greatly in length. Elements commonly found in these prologues are the use of the term *lai*, as an indication of the nature of the tale to be told, and the notion of *aventure*, that is, something that has happened in the past and is so remarkable that in the author's view it deserves to be the subject of a new work. The names of the protagonists are frequently given in the prologues and reference is sometimes made to the Bretons, who are said to have composed a lay on the subject at stake. The lays sometimes indicate their title, and occasionally we learn about the original composition and transmission of the lay in question or of lays in general (e.g. *Espine*, *Lecheor*, *Tyolet*). Sometimes mention is made

[2] In her editions of *Piramus* and *Narcisus*, Eley dates both texts to the 'classicising' period 1155–70 (pp. 11, 10 respectively), but she goes on to suggest that *Piramus* could be dated to 'before 1170' and *Narcisus* to 1160–65 (p. 11).

[3] A number of lays, by Marie and other authors, seem to be based on Celtic themes or plots. If there seems to be a specific Celtic source, we point this out in our individual introductions. On the whole, the lays in our Magic and Mystery section have a strong Celtic connection, as do the lays of Marie de France, and could have been composed at a fairly early stage. For a recent study of the Celtic origins of Marie's lays in particular (including Irish, Welsh and Breton sources), see Bernard Sergent, *L'Origine des Lais de Marie de France* (Geneva: Droz, 2014).

of a musical element involved in the performance of the lay (e.g. *Doon*, *Graelent*). Almost all the lays conclude with an epilogue that reinforces the observations made in the prologue, often reminding the audience that they have been listening to an account of an *aventure* in the form of a *lai*. Sometimes the Bretons are mentioned in the epilogue as the original composers of the poem and, as in the prologues, there can be allusions to the poem's title or to the melody of the lay.

The stories themselves, inserted within this prologue-epilogue framework, usually treat of a relationship between a brave and handsome knight and a wise and beautiful woman. In an ideal world, love would blossom and these perfect lovers would be able to marry and live happily ever after. But in feudal society young males, thanks to their chivalric skills, were expected to acquire fame and fortune and to fight wars on behalf of their lords. When it came to marriage and inheritance, the expectation of society was that knights and ladies would form a marital alliance that, rather than being based on their personal feelings, would be of advantage to their families and to aristocratic society in general. It was not anticipated that love would be a significant factor in these marriages. But in the lays, as in the case of the courtly romances of the day, love is of considerable importance to the authors and their characters. This is especially true of Marie de France, who depicts the passions of love with a remarkable intensity, but in the stories translated in this volume, too, the plot usually revolves around love, sexuality and the search for personal fulfilment.

Both the lays composed by Marie de France and those included in the present volume can be grouped in different ways. The difficulty we all have in finding fulfilment in real life may in part explain the authors' recourse to non-realistic figures, whose astonishing beauty and magic powers make them attractive as lovers. We open our collection with a group we have entitled 'Magic and Mystery'. In *Melion*, the first lay in this group, both the hero and the heroine have supernatural powers, the predominant element of which is Melion's ability, thanks to a magic ring, to transform himself into a werewolf. Graelent, Guingamor and Desiré all enter into a passionate relationship with stunningly beautiful fairy-type figures who have the capacity to make their lovers rich and joyful but also to cause them considerable anguish. In *Doon* the hero has extraordinary powers (especially his ability to predict the birth of a son), as does his lady, who can kill men as they sleep in the bed she has prepared for them. But the tournament and the 'happy-ever-after' marriage are perfectly realistic.

Also ending up happily married within the real world are the lovers in *Espine*, but they inhabit a world in which a hawthorn bush forms the frontier between the real world and the Other World, where on the eve of the feast of St John mysterious knights appear, on this occasion ready to do battle with the young hero of the lay. *Tydorel* fits into several of these categories. He is capable of living in the deepest part of a lake, that is, in the Other World (the lake itself is magical in that those who succeed in swimming across it will have all their desires satisfied), and of informing a lady who has given him her heart and her body that she will bear a son to him and that he will not be able to sleep and will need to be entertained with stories all night long. When the son discovers that he is of non-human origin, he makes an abrupt departure from the real world in order to join his father in his lake. In a world filled with horses, nothing could be more realistic than the difference between the painful act of trotting and the pleasing act of ambling, but in the lay of *Trot* this distinction is coupled with an Other World or afterlife experience. The joy or sorrow of the female riders is determined by the god of Love: has he been well served or scorned?[4]

An important aspect of our collection of lays, one that is less pronounced in the *Lais* of Marie de France, is that some authors like to present love as blending into lust, amorous relationships thus descending either into farce or disaster. In the Arthurian lay of *Mantel*, the ladies at court are obliged to try on a mantle that will be too long or too short if they have in any way been unfaithful to their beloved. Unsurprisingly, the results are calamitous for all the ladies, including the queen. Humour is created by the dashing of the male courtiers' expectations that their beloved will be free of any trace of infidelity, and a deeper level of comedy is produced when the audience realises that, far from being a model of social behaviour, the court is a hotbed of pretensions, jealousies and self-delusion. Similar tensions and infidelities are revealed in the lay of *Cor*, in which Arthur and his knights are presented with a horn from which no one can drink without

[4] In the tales in this collection, and in other contemporary works, Love is sometimes referred to as masculine, sometimes as feminine (i.e. as the god or goddess of Love). This was no doubt partially because of the varying gender of the term for 'love' (*amor*), which was masculine in Latin and largely, but not consistently, feminine in Old French (note the expression 'la fine amor'/'pure love'). *Amour* is masculine in Modern French, except when used in the plural, and this fluctuation reflects the situation that existed in the Middle Ages.

the contents pouring over him if he is cuckolded or jealous, or if his wife has had lewd thoughts about another man.

Comedy in *Mantel* and *Cor* arises to a great extent from the incongruity of a highly sophisticated and successful court becoming embroiled in petty squabbling, envy and sexual peccadilloes. Incongruity is found again in *Aristote*, this time on a more superficial level, when the renowned philosopher Aristotle is captivated by the beauty of his master Alexander's mistress and ends up being persuaded to carry her around the garden on his back. In *Lecheor* knights and ladies meet ostensibly to talk about love and chivalry and end up talking about women's sexual organs. The motif of sexual organs reappears in *Ignaure*, in which the eponymous hero's remarkable success in juggling relationships with twelve women, without any of them being aware of the existence of rivals for his affections, is brought to an abrupt end when he is captured by one of the husbands and suffers the posthumous indignity of having his genitals fed to his former mistresses. In these lays the total commitment of a Tristan and Iseut or a Lancelot and Guinevere is parodied by the figure of Ignaure with his twelve-strong cohort of mistresses and by the realisation of a group of Brittany's finest women that they would be nothing without their cunts.

Different forms of comedy are also found in this group. The entire edifice of courtliness is predicated on the superiority of aristocratic values and lifestyle. As the wealthy owners of lands and castles, the members of the nobility were wont to exert power over peasants or *vilains* with their uncouth habits and impoverished lives. In a move that must have sent shock waves through the landowning gentry, a new class of 'riches vilains' was beginning to appear. This happens in *Oiselet*, which tells of a clash between a peasant, who has purchased a magnificent estate and garden formerly owned by a noble knight, and a little bird, which represents both tradition and courtly values and gives its name to the lay. When the bird finally flies away for good, the garden fades and withers and the fountain dries up. If not entirely defeated, the peasant is revealed as ignorant, foolish and covetous. Another group of people constantly under attack in the Middle Ages are women. In medieval short narrative, misogyny is associated in particular with the genre of the *fabliau*, but even our courtly lay of *Melion* concludes with the comment that anyone who believes his wife completely will be ruined in the end. But there is sometimes a twist in that the dubious actions of a woman can also be regarded as impressive and ingenious. In *Espervier* a woman who has just disported with her lover and, unbeknown to him, has his squire hiding in her bedroom, is faced with a dangerous situation when her husband comes knocking on the door. The question in such narratives is not whether she will survive but how she will effect her escape. The lady in *Nabaret* is likewise faced with a threat to her way of life and well-being, from both her husband and her parents. But a finely tuned barb aimed at her husband saves the day.

Ovid's *Metamorphoses* being their principal source, the lays of *Piramus and Thisbe* and *Narcisus and Dané* are often known as 'classical lays'. They are associated with other texts from the 1150s and 1160s (e.g. the romances of antiquity: the *Roman de Thèbes*, the *Roman d'Eneas* and Benoît de Sainte-Maure's *Roman de Troie*) that brought pagan antiquity to the attention of a new vernacular audience. In these classical lays there is no Breton element, no humour and no supernatural characters. But symbolism is present in *Piramus* in the form of a change in the colour of the fruit of the mulberry tree, from white to black or blood red. This symbol of death and tribulation is in keeping with Ovid's concept of metamorphosis but also demonstrates how lives can be transformed by Love, in this case from joy to sorrow but elsewhere from despair to elation. *Piramus* and *Narcisus* are noteworthy for the poignancy of their monologues and for the nature of the deaths they describe. Grief-stricken at the loss of their beloved, Piramus and Thisbe take their own lives, and once Narcisus's heart has given out he dies beside Dané, who then embraces him so tightly that she forces the soul from her body.

It was tempting to include the *Chastelaine de Vergi* in our 'Passion and Tears' section for a similar sadness pervades the ending of this work: the *châtelaine* dies of heart failure, her lover kills himself and the duchess is murdered by her husband. As seems be the case in *Piramus*, the two lovers are buried in the same tomb. Seven deaths occur in these three lays, all caused by some form of misunderstanding. Tragedy and frustration seem to hover over the narrative and the characters leave nothing but grief in their wake. But, despite their dissimilar endings, the *Chastelaine* seems to be to be closer to the *Lai de l'Ombre*, with which it not only shares a number of episodes and motifs but also the general sense of the struggle to find love within a world that the public would recognise as their own. Hence the section 'Romance and Realism'. The relationship that is formed between the knight and the lady in the *Lai de l'Ombre* can be seen as one part of a diptych, the other part being the way in which a similar relationship, such as that found in in the *Chastelaine de Vergi*, can be destroyed by the lovers' own decisions and the values of the society in which they live. There is no sign in these two lays of supernatural beings, symbolic objects, otherworldly encounters or anything that one could describe as an *aventure*, there is just the intense search for happiness in a world that can be devastated by one wounded ego, such as that of the duchess in the *Chastelaine.*

The lays of *Amours* and *Conseil* share with the *Chastelaine de Vergi* and the *Lai de l'Ombre* this sense of characters finding their way in a down-to-earth world. Love is still the fundamental theme, but the power of argument and eloquence are key here, rather than fairy-type figures and magic mantles or horns, thus producing a different tone from that found in our other sections. In *Conseil* the narrative moves from the lady's request for advice regarding her three suitors to her happy marriage with her advisor. In itself this could be regarded as quite dull, but in fact the audience is being treated to what John Beston calls 'a sophisticated mutual seduction'.[5]

But other lays have different thematic structures. *Haveloc*, with its pseudo-historical hero, concentrates on feudal themes such as kingship, inheritance and power and it seems to merit a category of its own. *Haveloc* is in fact the only one of our lays that is not dominated by love or matters relating to the courtly world. On the one hand, this lay does have a magic horn, an enigmatic dream and a rags-to-riches transformation as the hero discovers his true identity but, on the other hand, more space is devoted here to warfare and other forms of fighting than in any other lay. Haveloc's wife Argentille is an important figure, and after being forced into a marriage of convenience the couple come to love each other, but the narrative ends not with love's quest fulfilled, with the hero's departure to another land (in or outside the real world) or even with suffering or death, but with lands recovered and the promise of new conquests to come during twenty years of successful kingship.

The twenty-four works in this collection demonstrate the wide-ranging possibilities of the lay as a literary form. Some of them seem to have close ties with one or more of the lays of Marie de France and may have been influenced by her (*Melion* with *Bisclavret*; *Doon* with *Milun*; the *Deus*

[5] John Beston, 'The Psychological Art of the *Lai du Conseil*', *French Studies Bulletin*, 33 (2012), 26–28. Beston also make comparisons between *Conseil* and the *Lai de l'Ombre*: for example, the knight in former lay does something similar with the belt to what the knight in the latter does with the ring, both actions sealing their relationship with a beloved. Both authors have a keen understanding of the games their characters play with one another as they interact.

Amanz with *Yonec*; *Graelent*, *Guingamor* and the *Chastelaine de Vergi* with *Lanval*; *Conseil* with *Chaitivel*). But among our lays are some that are a good distance away from a typical Marie lay, whether it be *Oiselet*, which hints at a crisis in aristocratic landholding but has a perspicacious little bird as it star performer; the *Chastelaine de Vergi*, in which the duchess complains to her husband that no landholder can recognise a loyal servant from a traitor (vv. 114–19); or *Ignaure*, where the philandering hero bequeaths his heart and his genitals to his fasting lovers as a highly praised evening meal.

The present volume constitutes the culmination of a project aimed at making the surviving narrative lays (besides the twelve by Marie de France, which over the years have been published on numerous occasions) available for the purposes of research, while at the same time making a contribution to the enjoyment of the short story tradition in medieval France. A more specific aim was to stimulate work on MS S Paris, Bibliothèque Nationale de France, nouv. acq. fr. 1104, a manuscript containing twenty-four lays, far more than any other, fifteen from the present volume intermingling with nine usually attributed to Marie de France (see note 1 above and the section 'Manuscripts' below). Our first publication appeared in 1999 as the first title in the Liverpool Online Series, Critical Editions of French Texts (http://www.liv.ac.uk/cultures-languages-and-area-studies/french/liverpool-online-series/). It provides new editions of three lays, *Trot*, *Lecheor*, *Nabaret*, with parallel English translations and substantial introductions. In 2005 the lays of *Doon* and *Tyolet* were published as item 9 in this series and *Aristote* in 2012 as item 16. Eleven of the lays in the present volume are included in our *French Arthurian Literature IV: Eleven Old French Narrative Lays*, published in 2007 by D. S. Brewer (in the order *Desiré*, *Doon*, *Espine*, *Graelent*, *Guingamor*, *Lecheor*, *Tydorel*, *Tyolet*, *Melion*, *Nabaret*, *Trot*). The choice of these eleven poems, which we have arranged in a different order for the purposes of the present collection, derived from our decision to begin our project by re-editing and translating the lays found in Prudence Tobin's *Les Lais anonymes des XIIe et XIIIe siècles: édition critique de quelques lais bretons* (Geneva: Droz, 1976). Three further lays are found in our *The Old French Lays of Ignaure, Oiselet and Amours*, published in 2010, and our editions and translations of the lays *Mantel* and *Haveloc* that appeared in 2013 and 2015 respectively.[6]

[6] The *Mantel* volume includes a prose translation of the lay of *Cor*, which is thematically associated with *Mantel* but is not, in our view, in need of a new edition. In the case of *Haveloc*, our edition with parallel translation is of MS H, whereas the

In 2012 Glyn Burgess published an edition and translation of the lay *Espervier* in *The Medieval Imagination: Mirabile Dictu. Essays in Honour of Yolande de Pontfarcy Sexton* (pp. 17–46). The present volume includes our own translations of three further lays available in the Liverpool Online Series: the editions of *Piramus and Thisbe* (item 5, 2001) and *Narcisus and Dané* by Penny Eley (item 6, 2002) and the edition of Jehan Renart's *Le Lai de l'Ombre* by Alan Hindley and Brian J. Levy with a translation and introduction by Adrian P. Tudor (item 8, 2004). In the case of the lay of *Conseil*, edited in 2013 for the Liverpool Online Series by Brînduşa Elena Grigoriu, Catharina Peersman and Jeff Rider and translated by Grigoriu and Rider (item 18), we have translated the version of the lay in MS S not that in MS A, the base manuscript for the online edition.

Each translation in this volume is accompanied by a brief introduction that provides information on the surviving manuscript or manuscripts of the lay, any available information about the author or date of the lay, a summary of the plot, some general observations on the characters, themes and structure, and a section on further reading. For more details concerning manuscripts, see our section 'Manuscripts' below. When given, designations of manuscripts as A, B, C, etc., which can vary from editor to editor, are those used in the editions on which we have based our translations. More extensive bibliographies for individual lays can be found in the introductions to the editions cited in our Bibliography or in Glyn S. Burgess, *The Old French Narrative Lays: A Critical Bibliography* (Cambridge: D. S. Brewer, 1995). Items of general interest for our corpus of lays are listed in the Bibliography. Tenses in Old French move frequently between past and present, perhaps to provide an added sense of drama or impact, but as this can be somewhat disconcerting for a modern reader, we tell the stories in the past tense. We have endeavoured to provide straightforward prose translations of the Old French verse texts, rendering their meaning if not their poetic rhythm.

We would like to acknowledge the help and encouragement we have received for our project from friends and family, especially Jane Bliss, Steve Brook, Janet McArthur and Sarah Peverley.

Liverpool University Press and the present authors are grateful to Boydell and Brewer for permission to publish prose translations of those lays for which, as part of the present project, they have published editions with facing line-by-line translations.

prose translation found in the present volume is taken from MS P.

Manuscripts

I. The two most important manuscripts relating to the genre of the lay are S and H

S: Paris, Bibliothèque Nationale de France (hereafter BNF), nouv. acq. fr. 1104.
This manuscript is of particular importance. It contains twenty-four lays, far more than any other manuscript, in the following order: *Guigemar, Lanval, Desiré, Tyolet, Yonec, Guingamor, Espine, Espervier, Chevrefoil, Doon, Les Deus Amanz* (vv. 1–169), *Bisclavret* (the final 84 lines), *Milun, Le Fresne, Lecheor, Equitan, Tydorel, Mantel, Ombre, Conseil, Amours, Aristote, Graelent, Oiselet*. Fifteen of the lays in the present volume are found here, eight of which (*Aristote, Conseil, Desiré, Espine, Graelent, Mantel, Oiselet* and *Ombre*) are also found in at least one other manuscript (see below). Our translations are based on S in all relevant cases. Nine of the lays of Marie de France are also included in S, in a different order from that found in H: *Guigemar, Lanval, Yonec, Chevrefoil, Les Deus Amanz, Bisclavret, Milun, Le Fresne, Yonec* (from v. 396).

H: London, British Library, Harley 978.
By far the best known manuscript of the *Lais* of Marie de France, H contains her twelve lays in the order: *Guigemar, Equitan, Le Fresne, Bisclavret, Lanval, Les Deus Amanz, Yonec, Laüstic, Milun, Chaitivel, Chevrefoil, Eliduc*.[1]

[1] The titles of Marie's lays vary. They are based here on the edition of the *Lais* by Alfred Ewert (Oxford: Blackwell, 1944; repr. with introduction and bibliography by Glyn Burgess, London: Bristol Classical Press, 1995). Besides S, only two other manuscripts contain both one or more of Marie's lays and a lay included in our collection, both in Paris: BNF, fr. 2168 and BNF, fr. 24432. MS London, Cott. Vesp. B XI contains *Lanval*. For further information on MS S, see Rupert T. Pickens,

II. Manuscripts containing between one and seven of the lays in our collection

Berlin, Staatsbibliotek, Preußischer Kulturbesitz, Hamilton 257 (*Chastelaine de Vergi*, *Narcisus and Dané* (incomplete), *Piramus and Thisbe*).[2]

Berne, Bibliothèque de Berne 354 (*Mantel*).

Cologny-Genève, Bibliotheca Bodmeriana, Codex Bodmer 82 (*Desiré*, *Haveloc*, *Nabaret*).

London, College of Arms, Arundel XIV (*Haveloc*).

Oxford, Bodleian Library, Digby 86 (*Cor*).

Paris, BNF, fr. 353 (*Mantel*).

Paris, BNF, fr. 837 (*Aristote*, *Chastelaine de Vergi*, *Conseil*, *Mantel*, *Narcisus and Dané*, *Oiselet*, *Ombre*, *Piramus and Thisbe*).

Paris, BNF, fr. 1553 (*Espine*, *Ignaure*, *Ombre*).

Paris, BNF, fr. 1593 (*Aristote*, *Conseil*, *Mantel*, *Oiselet*, *Ombre*).

Paris, BNF, fr. 2153 (contains a sixteenth-century version of *Mantel*).

Paris, BNF, fr. 2168 (*Graelent*, *Narcisus et Dané*). Also contains Marie de France's *Guigemar*, *Lanval* and *Yonec* (from v. 396).

Paris, BNF, fr. 12603 (*Ombre*).

Paris, BNF, fr. 14971 (*Ombre*).

'Marie de France in the Manuscripts: *lai*, fable, fabliau', in *The Old French Fabliau: Essays on Comedy and Context*, ed. Kristin L. Burr, John F. Moran and Norris J. Lacy (Jefferson, NC and London: McFarland, 2008), pp. 174–86; 'BnF, nouv. acq. fr., 1104: Marie de France and "Lays de Bretagne"', in *'Li premerains vers': Essays in Honor of Keith Busby*, ed. Logan E. Whalen and Catherine Jones (Amsterdam and New York: Rodopi, 2011), pp. 341–55.

2 Manuscripts of the *Chastelaine de Vergi* are included here only when they contain another lay. There are in all twenty-two manuscripts which contain this work, twelve of which date from the fifteenth century or later; for a full list, see the edition by R. E. V. Stuip, pp. 32–33. Three manuscripts containing *Piramus and Thisbe* as a separate work are included in this list, but see also the nineteen manuscripts in which this work forms part of the *Ovide moralisé*, a fourteenth-century adaptation of Ovid's *Metamorphoses*. The full list is included in the edition of *Piramus and Thisbe* by Francesco Branciforti, pp. 79–99; see also the edition by Penny Eley, pp. 7–10.

Paris, BNF, fr. 19152 (*Aristote, Narcisus and Dané, Ombre, Piramus and Thisbe*).

Paris, BNF, fr. 24432 (*Oiselet*). Also contains Marie de France's *Yonec.*

Paris, BNF, fr. 25545 (*Chastelaine de Vergi, Oiselet*).

Paris, BNF, Moreau 1727 (eighteenth-century copy, made by La Curne de Sainte-Palaye, vv. 1–335 only).

Paris, BNF, Rothschild 2800 (*Conseil*).

Paris, Bibliothèque de l'Arsenal 2770 (a partial eighteenth-century copy, made by La Curne de Sainte-Palaye, of Paris, BNF, fr. 2168, containing *Graelent* and *Narcisus and Dané*). Also contains Marie de France's *Guigemar* and *Lanval.*

Paris, Bibliothèque de l'Arsenal 3516 (*Aristote, Melion, Trot*).

St Omer, Bibliothèque Municipale 68 (*Aristote*).

Turin, Bibliotheca Municipale L.iv.33 (contained *Melion*, but was largely destroyed by fire in 1904).

Magic and Mystery

1. *Melion*

Introduction

Melion is currently preserved in only one manuscript (S). A second manuscript was in existence in Turin but it was largely destroyed by fire in 1904.[1] As a werewolf tale, *Melion* is often compared with Marie de France's *Bisclavret* and with other tales such as the French verse romance *Guillaume de Palerne* and the Latin prose romance *Arthur and Gorlagon*.[2] *Melion* is one of five Arthurian lays in this collection, the others being *Cor*, *Mantel*, *Trot* and *Tyolet*.

Melion swears he will never love a woman who has ever loved another man. Ostracised by the ladies at Arthur's court, he loses all interest in chivalry and retires to one of Arthur's castles on the coast. One day, out hunting, he meets an Irish princess who seems to be his perfect match: she has never been, and never will be, loved by anyone other than himself. They marry and have two children, but one day, when they are hunting together, she demands a piece of meat from a stag he has spotted. Melion then tells her his secret: his ring can transform him into a wolf. However, when he returns bearing the meat for his wife, he finds she has fled, together with his squire, and the ring. He follows her back to Ireland and with ten wolves as companions causes havoc among the local livestock. When a peasant spots the wolves and reports this to the king, Melion's companions are killed. Hope comes when Arthur arrives in Ireland, as Melion is able to secure his protection. When he sees the squire at court, he attacks him. The squire confesses and Melion retrieves his ring. In the privacy of the king's chamber, he resumes his

[1] For textual variants from this manuscript, see the edition by W. Horak (for this and all other editions, see the Bibliography).

[2] See Amanda Hopkins, 'Sources and Analogues: *Melion* and Other Medieval Werewolf Tales', in Burgess and Brook, 2007, pp. 417–21.

human shape but wants his wife to be transformed into a wolf. Arthur recommends mercy for the sake of the children and Melion returns home cursing all women.

Looked at from the perspective of 'magic and mystery', or from the contrasting poles of realism and the supernatural, both the principal protagonists in *Melion* have non-realistic elements in their make-up. If, on the one hand, Melion's somewhat extreme view that his love can only be bestowed on a woman who has never loved, or even spoken of, any other man, merely confirms that he is different from the other knights at court, on the other, his ability to metamorphose into a wolf while retaining his human intellect clearly places him in a category apart from other human beings. Moreover, his wife comes to him while he is out hunting in a way that is reminiscent of the fairy figures in Marie de France's *Lanval* and the anonymous lay of *Desiré*. Her statement that she has never loved another man, and will never do so, thus fulfilling Melion's vow, points to her status as a supernatural figure. This is confirmed once more when the unusual size of a stag causes her to faint and to experience a sudden desire to partake of the beast's flesh. We are not told how she came to love Melion, or why she deserts him (in so doing she displays the ruthlessness of a fairy-type figure), and another mystery is the author's failure to tell us why Melion's squire goes off with her to Ireland.

It has often been suggested that *Melion* is based on Marie de France's *Bisclavret*. Similarities certainly exist, but there are also differences. In both lays the heroes become wolves through a specific agent of transformation: in *Bisclavret* it is the removal of clothing and in *Melion* the use of a magic ring with colour-coded stones (Melion also removes his clothes, but here nudity seems less important than in *Bisclavret*). Bisclavret is alone when he becomes a beast, whereas Melion requires assistance in order to be transformed. However, both heroes are betrayed by their wives, who retain the clothing and the ring respectively, and in both cases restoration of human form occurs in the privacy of a king's chamber. Both men use wolf-type violence after their transformation and both retain human reasoning (Melion in particular plots his escape from bestiality, working out that his wife has gone to Ireland, finding a boat and making the crossing, recognising Arthur and his knights and realising that Arthur is his only hope). At the outset, Bisclavret already has experience as a werewolf, as for some time he has been spending three days each week in wolfish form and has established a pattern for his transformations. But Melion throws off his human identity for a specific purpose and there is no evidence that this is a regular occurrence in his life, if indeed it has happened before. Thus, as she loses her husband for a considerable period each week, the wife in *Bisclavret* has the semblance of an excuse for her disloyalty, whereas no similar justification could be proffered in the case of Melion's wife (when she hears that one of the wolves has escaped her father's hunters, her remark that the survivor will be the cause of further grief suggests that she is aware of the wolf's identity, yet she does nothing to save her husband from his pursuers). All in all, *Melion* is an intriguing story, albeit one with a number of loose ends relating to the nature and the sometimes curious behaviour of the principal protagonists. The balance of realistic and supernatural events is, however, carefully maintained and the tightly organised plot moves at a good pace.

Further Reading

Boyd, Matthieu, 'Melion and the Wolves', *Neophilologus*, 93 (2009), 555–70.

Ménard, Philippe, 'Les Histoires de loup-garou au Moyen Age', in *Symposium in honorem Prof. M. de Riquer* (Barcelona: Universitat de Barcelona, Quaderns Crema, 1984), pp. 209–38.

Milin, Gaël, *Les Chiens de Dieu: la représentation du loup-garou en Occident (XIe–XXe)* (Brest: Centre de Recherche Bretonne et Celtique, Université de Bretagne Occidentale, 1993).

Translation

In the time when Arthur reigned – he who conquered lands and gave sumptuous gifts to his knights and barons – there was in his entourage a young knight whose name, I have heard, was Melion. He was very courtly and brave, and he was loved by all.[3] He was highly distinguished in feats

[3] The Old French adjective *corteis* (feminine *corteise*) and the substantive *corteisie* appear frequently in these lays. A person who is described as *corteis(e)* is someone who understands the workings of the court and displays such characteristics as politeness, sophistication, wisdom, sensitivity to the needs of others, eloquence of speech and, on occasion, a good grasp of the law. Neither the term 'courteous' ('polite, respectful, considerate') nor 'courtly ('very polite and dignified') in modern English provides a satisfactory translation, but we prefer the term 'courtly' (cf. the frequently used expressions courtly romance and courtly love). See Glyn S. Burgess, 'Le Terme

of arms and a most courtly companion. The king had a magnificent household, esteemed throughout the world for its courtliness and prowess, its excellence and generosity. (1–14)

One day the knights made their vows, and I can assure you that they kept to them. But Melion made one that brought him great harm: he said he would love no maiden, however noble or beautiful she was, who had loved any other man, or spoken of one. Things remained like this for some while. Those who had heard the vow related it in many places and told the maidens about it. When they heard of it, they hated him profoundly. Those who served the queen in her chambers, and there were more than a hundred of them, discussed it together, saying that they would never love him or speak to him; no lady would look at him and no maiden address him. When Melion heard this, he became very downcast. He no longer wished to seek adventure and had no desire to bear arms. He was grief-stricken and very unhappy, and he lost some of his reputation. (15–42)

The king heard of this and was most upset. So he sent for Melion and spoke to him. 'Melion', said King Arthur, 'what has become of your wisdom, your reputation and your courtly behaviour? Tell me what the matter is, do not conceal it. If you want land or property, or anything else that I might have, you can have it in accordance with your wishes, provided that it is in my royal gift. If I could', said the king, 'I would willingly bring you cheer. I have a castle overlooking the sea and there is no other like it in the whole world. It is embellished with woods and rivers, and with forests that you love so much. I will give it to you to make you happy again. You can enjoy yourself there.' The king granted him the fief and Melion thanked him for it. (43–62)

Melion went off to his castle, taking a hundred knights with him. The land pleased him a great deal, as did the forest that he loved very much. When he had been there for a year, he had a great affection for the land, for there was no pleasure that he could wish for that the forest did not provide. One day he went hunting with his foresters. The huntsmen who were with him loved him truly, for he was their liege lord and every good quality shone forth in him. They soon came upon a large stag and unleashed the hounds, who soon caught it.[4] Melion paused in a clearing,

courtois dans le français du douzième siècle', *Travaux de Linguistique et de Philologie*, 31 (1993), 195–209.

[4] The text here, which states in v. 78 that 'they soon caught and unleashed it',

listening for his pack. He had a squire with him, who was holding two greyhounds. In the clearing, which was green and beautiful, Melion espied a maiden approaching on a beautiful palfrey. Its trappings were most elegant and she was dressed in fine red silk, which was well laced. Around her shoulders was an ermine cloak; no queen ever wore finer. She had a noble bearing, beautiful shoulders, fair hair, and a small well-formed mouth that was the colour of a rose. Her eyes were clear, bright and sparkling, and she was very beautiful in every respect. (63–96)

The maiden approached alone, without any attendants. She was elegant and of noble bearing. Melion went to meet her and greeted her most courteously. 'Fair one', he said, 'I greet you in the glorious name of Jesus the king. Tell me where you are from and what has brought you here.' She replied: 'I will tell you and not say a word that is untrue. I am very high born and descended from a noble lineage. I have come to you from Ireland and can tell you that I am truly your beloved. I have never loved any man but you, nor will I ever do so. I have heard you highly praised and have never wanted to love anyone else apart from you, nor will I ever give my love to another.' When Melion heard that his wishes had been granted, he put his arms around her and kissed her more than thirty times. Then he summoned all his companions and told them of his adventure. They saw the maiden and there was none more beautiful in the kingdom. He took her to his castle and everyone was filled with joy. He married her in great splendour and celebrated greatly for a period of fifteen days. For three years he loved her dearly. He had two sons by her in that time and was very happy and joyful. (97–132)

One day he went into the forest together with his dear wife. He came upon a stag and pursued it as it fled with its head lowered. There was a squire with him, who was carrying his quiver. They entered a clearing and he looked at a bush, where he saw a mighty stag standing. He looked at his wife with a laugh. 'My lady', he said, 'if I wanted, I could show you a mighty stag. Look there in that bush.' 'By my faith, Melion', she said, 'let me tell you that if I do not have some of that stag I will never eat again.' She then fell from her palfrey in a faint and Melion picked her up. When he could not comfort her, she began to weep bitterly. 'My lady', he said, 'in God's mercy, do not weep any more, I beseech you. On my hand I have a ring. See it here on my ring finger. There are two stones in the setting

appears to be faulty. Some reference to the unleashing of the dogs seems to have been omitted.

such as no one has ever seen: one is white and the other red. You can hear a great marvel concerning them. When I have taken off my clothes, touch me with the white one, placing it on my head, and I will turn into a large, strong wolf. For love of you, I will capture the stag and bring you back some of its meat. I beseech you in the name of God, wait for me here and look after my clothes. In your hands I leave my life or death, for there would be no way out for me if I were not touched with the other stone, for I would never again become a man.' (133–72)

He called to his squire and told him to remove his boots. He came up to him and removed them and Melion went into the woods. He took off all his clothes and remained naked, wrapping himself in his cloak. Once she saw him naked and with no clothing, his wife touched him with the ring. He then turned into a large, strong wolf, thus bringing upon himself great torment. The wolf departed, running very swiftly to where he saw the stag lying and soon set off, following its tracks. His suffering will be great before he captures it and gets hold of it, or before he gets any of its meat. The lady said to the squire: 'Let us leave him to have his fill of hunting'. She mounted her horse, delayed no longer and took the squire with her, making straight for her country, Ireland. She came to a harbour, found a ship and spoke straightaway to the sailors, who took her to Dublin, a city on the shore that belonged to her father, the King of Ireland. Now she had what she wanted, and as soon as she came to port she was received with great joy. Let us leave her at this stage and speak of Melion. (173–204)

Melion chased after the stag at great speed, followed it into the forest and brought it down straightaway. He tore a large piece of meat from it and carried it off in his mouth, quickly returning to the place where he had left his wife. But he did not find her there – she had returned to Ireland. He was very upset when he did not find her in that spot and did not know what to do. Nevertheless, even if he was a wolf, he retained the sense and memory of a man. He waited till evening and saw a ship that was being loaded and would sail that night to Ireland. So he made his way towards it and waited till nightfall. Taking a risk, he got on board for he had no concern for his life. He hid under a plough beam, concealing himself thoroughly. The sailors made good speed, for they had a favourable wind. They headed for Ireland and everyone had what they wanted. They hoisted the sails on high, guided by the sky and the stars, and on the morrow at daybreak they saw the country of Ireland. (205–36)

When they came to the port, Melion waited no longer. He emerged from his hiding place and leapt from the ship on to the shore. The sailors bawled at him and chased him with their oars; one struck him with a stick. They almost managed to catch him, so he was happy once he had escaped from them, and he made his way up a mountain. For some time he searched about the country where he knew his enemies were. He was still carrying the lump of meat he had brought from his own land and, being ravenously hungry, he ate it. The sea journey had troubled him greatly. He went into a forest, where he found cows and oxen, and he strangled and slew many of them, starting his attacks there. In his first assault he killed more than a hundred. The folk who lived in the wood saw how their beasts had been savaged and they hastened to the city, telling the king that in the forest there was a wolf who was ravaging the whole land and killing large numbers of their cattle. But the king did not believe them. Melion made his way through the forest, over mountains and through wasteland, and linked up with ten other wolves. He flattered and cajoled them so much that he took them with him and they did everything he wished. They roamed all over the land, harassing men and women. For a whole year they continued to do so, laying the entire country to waste. They killed men and women and destroyed the whole land. They protected themselves very well and the king could not trap them. (237–80)

One night they had roamed far and were weary and tired. They went to rest in a wood close to Dublin, on a hillock by the shore and next to a plain, with open country all around. They were betrayed and trapped, for a peasant saw them and straightaway hurried to the king. 'My lord', he said, 'the eleven wolves have lain down in the round wood.' When he heard this, the king was very pleased and told his men about it. He spoke to them and said: 'Barons, listen to me! Let me tell you truly that this man has seen all eleven wolves in my forest.' They had nets spread around the forest that were used for catching boars. When all the nets had been set up, the king mounted his horse, delaying no longer and telling his daughter to come and witness the hunting of the wolves. They then entered the wood quietly and secretly. They surrounded the wood completely, for there were plenty of people carrying axes and clubs, and some with naked swords. Then a thousand dogs were roused and they soon found the wolves. (281–312)

Melion saw that he was betrayed and knew that he was in difficulty. The dogs harassed the wolves greatly and they rushed towards the nets. They were all cut to pieces and killed. The only one to escape was Melion, and he did so by leaping over the nets. Through cunning, he escaped from them and went off into a large wood. The king and his men returned to the city. He was very happy and rejoiced that he had caught ten of the eleven wolves and thereby taken vengeance on them very successfully; only one of them had escaped. His daughter said: 'That one is the biggest and will continue to inflict misery on people'. When Melion had escaped, he climbed a mountain, very sorrowful and upset about the loss of his wolves. He suffered for some while, but succour would soon be at hand. (313–36)

Arthur was coming to Ireland, wishing to make peace. Quarrels had broken out in the land and he wished to reconcile the enemies. He wanted to conquer the Romans and to take the Irish knights with him in his war. The king came secretly, bringing only twenty knights with him and an entourage that was not large. The weather was fine, with a good wind, and his ship was large and richly decked out. There was a good navigator and the ship was well equipped, with plenty of men and arms. Their shields hung over the side and Melion recognised them. He first identified Gauvain's shield, then spotted Yvain's and then that of King Yder, all of which pleased him and made him happy. He noticed the king's shield, and you can be certain that he rejoiced at this. He was very pleased and joyful, as he thought he could yet find mercy. (337–60)

They sailed towards the land, but the wind blew straight at them and they could not reach the port. This caused them much discomfort. They made for another port, which lay two leagues from the city. Formerly, there was a great castle there, but it had now fallen into ruin. When they arrived, it was night and had grown dark. The king arrived at the port, much wearied and exhausted, as the ship had made him feel very ill. He called to his seneschal and said: 'Go ashore and see where I can rest this night.' The seneschal returned to the ship and summoned the chamberlains. 'Come ashore with me', he said, 'and make ready the king's lodging.' They left the ship and went to the lodging, taking with them two candles, which they promptly lit, together with bedding and mats. They rapidly furnished the place, and the king then disembarked and went straight to his lodging. When he had gone in, he rejoiced that it was so pleasing to him. (361–90)

Melion did not delay, but made straight for the ship, pausing near the castle. He recognised them easily and knew that if he was not rescued by the king he would die in Ireland. But he did not know how to proceed, as he was a wolf and could not speak. Nevertheless, he would go forward and trust to luck. He approached the king's door. He knew all the knights, but he did not stop for a moment. He went straight up to the king, thereby risking death. He lay down at the king's feet and did not want to get up again. You would have seen that they were all astonished. The king said: 'I see something strange here! This wolf has come to me, and let me tell you that he is tame. Woe betide anyone who lays a hand on him or touches him.' When the meal was ready and the barons had washed, the king washed and sat down, with the dishes before them. The king summoned Yder and had him sit beside him. Melion lay at the king's feet; he knew all the barons well. The king glanced at Melion frequently and gave him a piece of bread, which he took and began to eat. The king marvelled at this and said to Yder: 'Look! I can tell you that this wolf is tame'. The king gave him a piece of meat and he ate it gratefully. (391–428)

Then Gauvain said: 'My lords, look, this wolf is completely unnatural'. The barons all said among themselves that no one had ever seen such a courtly wolf. The king called for wine to be put into a basin in front of the wolf. The wolf saw it and drank some of it. I can assure you that he wanted it very much and that he drank a fair amount of it. The king saw this very clearly, and when they had risen from the table and the barons had washed they went outside on to the shore. At once the wolf was with the king and they could not get him away from him, wherever they went. When the king wished to go to sleep, he asked for his bed to be made ready. He retired to bed, as he was very weary, and the wolf went with him. He could not be parted from him and lay at the king's feet. (429–50)

The King of Ireland received news that Arthur had come to see him. He was very pleased and delighted at this, and he arose early and went to the port, taking his barons with him and hurrying straight there. They greeted each other warmly, Arthur showing him great love and honour: when he saw him approaching, he did not want to display pride, so he rose to his feet and embraced him. The horses were made ready, and without delay they mounted and went towards the city. The king got on his palfrey and his wolf was well cared for. He did not wish to leave him behind, and the wolf was constantly at his stirrup. The king was very joyful because of Arthur, and his retinue was large and richly attired. They came to Dublin and dismounted in the large palace, where the king went up into the tower, with the wolf hanging on to his tunic. When King Arthur was seated, the wolf sat at his feet. The king looked at his wolf and called him to come close to the high table. The two kings sat down together. It was a richly attired assembly, with the barons serving their king well. Throughout the household everyone was copiously served. (451–85)

Melion looked around and in the midst of the room he saw the man who had taken away his wife. He knew that he had crossed the sea and gone to Ireland. Melion seized him by the shoulder and he could not withstand his assault. Melion pulled him down in the hall and would have killed him and finished him off, had it not been for the king's men-at-arms, who came in great haste, bringing sticks and cudgels from all sides. They would have slain the wolf, but King Arthur shouted out: 'Woe betide anyone who touches him,' he said. 'By my faith, I am telling you that the wolf is mine.' Yder, the son of Yrien, said: 'My lords, you are not acting wisely. If the wolf had not hated him, he would not have attacked him.' 'Yder, you are right,' said the king. Arthur left the high table. He went up to the wolf and said to the youth: 'You will say why you were attacked or you will die.' Melion looked at the king and gripped the youth, who cried out. He begged for mercy from the king and said he would tell him everything. At once he told the king how the lady had brought him there, how she had touched Melion with the ring and brought him to Ireland. He told him and revealed to him everything that had happened. (486–520)

Arthur said to the king: 'Now I know that he speaks the truth. I am very pleased for my baron. Fetch me the ring and bring your daughter, who took it. She has deceived him grievously.' The king left and went to her chamber, taking King Yder with him. He flattered and cajoled his daughter so that she gave him the ring and he brought it to Arthur. As soon as he saw it, Melion recognised it. He came up to the king and knelt down, kissing both his feet. King Arthur was going to touch him, but Gauvain would not permit it. 'Fair uncle', he said, 'do not do this! Take him to a chamber, just the two of you in private, so that he does not feel shame in front of people.' The king summoned Gauvain, and he took Yder with him and led Melion to a chamber. When he was inside, he closed the door and placed the ring on his head. His face became that of a man, and his whole shape changed. He then turned into a man and spoke. He fell at the king's feet and they covered him with a mantle. When they saw that he had the form of a human, they rejoiced greatly. The king wept out of pity for him. Weeping, he asked how this had come about. They had lost him through an act of wrongdoing. (521–58)

Arthur sent for his chamberlain and had him fetch costly clothing. He dressed and equipped Melion well and took him back into the hall. Everyone in the household was amazed when they saw Melion entering. The king brought in his daughter and gave her to Arthur to do with as he wished, whether to have her burned or mutilated. Melion said: 'Without fail, I will touch her with the stone.' Arthur replied: 'No you will not! For the sake of your fair children, leave her be!' All the barons begged him and Melion gave way.

King Arthur stayed there long enough to settle the war. Then he returned to his own land, taking Melion with him, who was very happy and rejoiced greatly. He left his wife in Ireland, commending her to the Devil. He would never love her again because of the way she had treated him, as you have heard in this tale. He did not ever want to take her back; rather he would have let her be burned or hanged. Melion said: 'It will always be the case that he who believes his wife in all things will, in the end, be ill-served by her. One should not believe all she says.' The lay of Melion is true, all the barons say so. This is the end of *Melion*. (559–92)

2. *Tyolet*

Introduction

Preserved in just one manuscript (S), *Tyolet* is one of five Arthurian lays in this collection, the others being *Cor*, *Mantel*, *Melion* and *Trot*.

Tyolet is a youth who has spent his life in a forest with his mother. A fairy-type figure has taught him to whistle in such a way that he can catch as many beasts as he desires. One day he spots a large, plump stag, but the animal fails to respond to him; instead, it leads him to a dangerous stretch of water. Suddenly a roebuck appears and this time he does catch the animal. Meanwhile, the stag he had been pursuing is transformed into a knight on horseback. Tyolet becomes confused and calls him a 'knight-beast'. He asks him a series of questions and thus learns about knighthood. When he returns home, his mother reluctantly equips him with the armour that had belonged to his dead father and advises him to go to King Arthur's court. Shortly after his arrival there, the daughter of the King of Logres arrives and offers her love to the man who can bring her the white foot of the stag that lives in the forest and is guarded by seven lions; her dog will act as a guide. Several knights attempt the feat, unsuccessfully. A major obstacle is a broad and dangerous river, but Tyolet follows the dog into the river and manages to reach the other side. His whistle attracts the stag and he removes its foot, but the animal's cries attract the lions. Tyolet kills them all, but collapses beside them. An unknown knight arrives, and on being told what has happened he makes his way to Arthur's court with the stag's foot in order to claim the maiden's hand. Sensing that something is not right, Arthur imposes a week's delay. When the maiden's dog returns, Gauvain follows it and discovers the injured Tyolet, who is taken to a doctor. Gauvain returns to court where, after the week's delay, the false claimant demands his prize and denies Gauvain's accusation that he is boasting of another man's achievements. Soon Tyolet himself arrives and he asks the knight who had killed the lions. Unable to answer, the knight confesses. Tyolet pardons him and marries the maiden. They reign together in her country.

During the course of the narrative, Tyolet is initiated with remarkable speed into the world of chivalry, and soon after his arrival at court he is provided with an opportunity to demonstrate his prowess and thereby win the hand of a princess. A prominent factor in his life is his relationship with women. At the outset he lives a fairly humdrum existence with his mother and their ability to feed themselves is greatly enhanced by the gift of whistling, bestowed on him by another female figure, this time a fairy. It is when his mother hands over his father's armour to him that he is ready for the next stage in his life. On arrival at Arthur's court, he is catapulted into a quest for a bride by the daughter of the King of Logres, and in due course he is taken to her domain, where he reigns alongside her. His ability to attract animals with his quasi-magical whistling is an important factor in his quest and thus in his swift social elevation. There is a fourth female personage in the text who comes across Tyolet when he is wounded and takes him to a doctor.

Tyolet is also helped by a series of male personages: his father (whose armour is available to him when he needs it), the knight-beast (who communicates to him the basics of chivalry), King Arthur (whose court is of sufficient prestige to convince the King of Logres and his beautiful daughter that it will provide a suitable husband for her and a ruler for their country), Gauvain and other Arthurian knights (who support him and welcome him to court) and the doctor who heals his wounds. The male universe in the work, however, is also somewhat tainted. When Tyolet sees in the distance 200 knights, they are returning from a mission in which they have, in accordance with their orders, captured a fortress and reduced it to ashes. If such a brutal mission was perhaps not unusual at the time, it does support the knight-beast's unexpected definition of a knight as a much-dreaded beast that captures and devours other beasts. In the early stages of the narrative, Tyolet clearly plays the part of the naïve but gifted youth, thus following in the footsteps of Perceval in Chrétien de Troyes's *Conte du Graal*. When he enters the chivalric world of Arthur's court, Tyolet will discover that knighthood does have its cruel and dangerous side, as he is left for dead by another knight who, despite Gauvain's castigation of his behaviour, comes close to winning the prize of the maiden's hand in marriage.

As with the other lays in this section, the supernatural in *Tyolet* rubs shoulders with the realistic. Like all aristocratic parents of the period, the parents of the beautiful princess are clearly concerned that she should find an appropriate husband and produce an heir. But at the same time, the maiden's condition for the granting of her love, that her suitor must bring her the stag's white foot, clearly suggests that, along with the magic dog she brings with her, she is not part of the real world. Textually, the author's description of the maiden (vv. 696–98) recalls Marie de France's description of the supernatural lady in *Lanval* (vv. 94–96), who also carries off her beloved to her own country at the end of the narrative. The impression we have in both cases is that the hero, in order to achieve a better life with his beloved, is leaving behind an inadequate and unjust world, one that cannot meet the standards demanded by the newly formed couple. We can note, however, that Lanval enters into a passionate relationship with his mistress, whereas in Tyolet's case there is no specific mention of love between the princess and Tyolet. Unlike Lanval, Tyolet has to win the maiden's hand through the performance of a specific, and life-threatening, task. There is certainly an element of wish fulfilment within the story, as young knights in the audience would have delighted in the swift career progression of the hero who advances from obscurity to power and riches in double quick time.

Further Reading

Arthur, Ross G., '*Tyolet* and the Marginalization of the Romance Feminine', *LittéRéalité*, 4 (1992), 65–72.

Braet, Herman, *Deux lais féeriques bretons: Graelent et Tyolet* (Brussels: Aurelia, 1979), esp. pp. 61–70.

Joris, Pierre-Marie, 'L'Étoile sibylline (lecture du lai de *Tyolet*)', *Médiévales*, 11 (1986), 49–65.

Luttrell, Claude, 'The Arthurian Hunt with a White Bratchet', *Arthurian Literature*, 9 (1989), 289–90.

Translation

In times gone by, when Arthur governed Britain, which would later be called England, the country was not, I believe, as populated as it is now. But Arthur, whose fame was great, had with him knights who were very bold and fierce. These days there are still a good many men who are very brave and renowned, but they cannot be compared to those from the past, when the most powerful knights, the finest and the most generous, used to travel a great deal at night, seeking and finding adventures. They also travelled by day, without any squires accompanying them, and travelling all day long they would not find, for perhaps two or three days, a single dwelling or keep. Also on dark nights they encountered great adventures, which they would tell and relate. These adventures were recounted at court, just as they had come across them, and worthy clerics of the time had them all written down. They were put into Latin and transcribed on to parchment so that, when the time came, they would be listened to with pleasure. Now they are told and recounted, and translated from Latin into the vernacular. The Bretons, who, as our ancestors tell us, composed a number of lays, composed one that I will relate to you, according to the tale with which I am familiar, of the handsome and clever youth, bold, fierce and courageous, whose name was Tyolet. He was very skilled at catching by whistling all the beasts he desired. A fairy had bestowed this gift on him and taught him to whistle. God never made any beast that he could not catch by whistling. (1–48)

His mother was a lady who at that time lived in a wood. She had been married to a knight who had lived there day and night. He had lived all alone in the forest, with no other house within ten leagues and had died a good fifteen years ago. Tyolet had become tall and handsome, but never in all his life had he seen an armed knight. He had scarcely ever seen anyone else at all. He lived in the wood with his mother, not leaving it for a single day. He had remained in the forest, for his mother loved him very much. Having no other occupation, he roamed around the wood at will. When the beasts heard him whistle, they came to him at once. He would kill those he wanted and take them to his mother. He and his mother lived off this prey. He had no brother or sister. The lady was very worthy and behaved with perfect loyalty. One day she asked her son tenderly, for she loved him dearly, to go into the wood and catch a stag, so he did her bidding. He went into the wood at once, as his mother had asked. He remained in the wood until terce,[1] without finding any beast or stag. He was very angry with himself for not finding any beast. (49–84)

He had decided to go straight home when beneath a tree he saw standing there a stag that was large and plump. Straightaway, he whistled and the stag heard him and looked at him. But it paid no attention to him; instead it moved away. Slowly it left the wood and Tyolet followed it

[1] Terce (or tierce) was the third hour of the day (about 9 am, but it could vary according to the season).

until it led him straight to a river and crossed over it. The river was large and swift-flowing, broad, long and dangerous. The stag crossed over the river and Tyolet cast a glance behind him. At once he saw coming towards him a plump, tall and large roebuck. He came to a halt, whistled and the roebuck came towards him. He stretched out his hand and killed it on the spot, taking out his knife and thrusting it into its body. While he was flaying it, the stag that had crossed to the other side of the river changed shape. [It soon took on human form][2] and assumed the appearance of a knight. Fully armed at the water's edge, he was mounted on a horse with a flowing mane and seated like an armed knight. The youth observed him and had never seen his like. He looked upon him in amazement and gazed at him for a long time. He wondered at such a thing, for he had never before seen anything like it. He stared at him intently, and the knight addressed him and spoke to him first, very pleasantly and amiably. He asked him who he was, what he was seeking and what his name was. Tyolet, who was very worthy and bold, replied that he was the son of the widow who lived in the great forest. 'I am called Tyolet by those who wish to use my name. Now tell me, if you know, who you are and what your name is.' (85–132)

The man who was standing on the bank replied at once, saying that he was called a knight. Tyolet asked him what kind of beast a knight was, where it lived and where it came from. 'In faith', he said, 'I will tell you without a word of a lie. It is a beast that is much dreaded; it captures and eats other beasts. For much of the time it dwells in the woods as well as on open land.' 'In faith', [Tyolet] replied, 'I am hearing wonders. For never since I learnt to walk and began to move about the woods have I been able to find such a beast. I am acquainted with bears, lions and all other forms of game. There is not a beast in the wood that I do not know and cannot capture without undue effort, apart from you, whom I do not know. You are the very image of an audacious beast. Tell me now, knight-beast, what is that on your head? And what is hanging around your neck? It is red and very shiny.' 'In faith', he replied, 'I will tell you, without a word of a lie. It is a coif that is called a helmet, and it is made entirely of steel, and this cloak I am dressed in is a shield with strips of gold.' 'And what are you wearing that is full of little holes?' 'That is a coat fashioned from iron; it is called a hauberk.' 'And what is it that you have on your feet? Be kind enough to tell me.' 'They are called greaves and are made of iron;

[2] There is a line missing here, so the insertion in square brackets is conjectural.

they are well made and well fashioned.' 'And what is around your waist? Tell me if you will.' 'It is called a sword and is very beautiful; its blade is sharp and tough.' 'And the long piece of wood you are carrying? Tell me, do not conceal it from me.' 'Do you wish to know?' 'Yes indeed.' 'It is a lance, which I carry with me. Now I have told you the truth concerning everything you have asked about.' (133–82)

'My lord', said [Tyolet], 'thank you. Would to God, who never lies, that I might have such equipment as you have, so fine and handsome, and that I had such a coat and such a cloak as you have, and the same head piece. Tell me, knight-beast, through God and his holy festival, if there are any other beasts like you, or any as beautiful as you are.' 'Yes', he said, 'in truth. I will soon show you more than a hundred.' It was only a short while later, as the tale recounts, that two hundred armed knights were making their way across a meadow. They came from the king's court and had been carrying out his orders. They had captured a fortress, set fire to it and reduced it to ashes, and they were going home, fully armed and in three squadrons in close array. The knight-beast then spoke to Tyolet and told him to go onwards a little and look across the river. He did as he was told, looked across immediately and saw the knights riding, fully armed, on their warhorses. 'In faith', he said, 'now I can see the beasts who all have coifs on their heads. I have never seen such beasts as these, nor such coifs as I see here. Would to God and his holy festival that I were a knight-beast.' The man who was armed on the bank spoke to him once more: 'Would you be brave and bold?' 'Yes, indeed, I swear to you.' And the other said to him: 'Go now, and when you see your mother again and she speaks to you she will say: "Fair son, tell me what is on your mind and what is troubling you." You should tell her promptly that you have much to think about, that you would like to resemble the knight-beast you saw and that this is why you were deep in thought. She will say to you at once that she is very upset that you have seen such a beast, which deceives and kills others. And you should tell her on your oath that she will know sorrow because of you if you cannot be such a beast and wear such a coif on your head. As soon as she hears this, she will quickly bring you the very same equipment, coat and cloak, coif and belt, and greaves and a long, smooth piece of wood, just as you have seen here.' (183–246)

Then Tyolet departed, for he was very anxious to get back home. He gave his mother the roebuck he had brought and told her about his adventure, just as he had found it. His mother replied to him at once that she was very upset 'that you have seen such a beast that captures and devours many another'. 'In faith', he said, 'this is the way things are. If I cannot be a beast such as I saw, I know full well and see that you will know sorrow because of me.' But when his mother heard this, she responded swiftly. All the arms she had that had belonged to her husband she quickly brought to him. She armed her son with them splendidly, and when he had mounted his horse he looked just like a knight-beast. 'Do you know, fair son, what you will do now? You will go straight to King Arthur, and I will tell you all that you need to know: do not associate with any other man, or pay court to any woman of ill repute.' (247–74)

Thereupon, he left her and she kissed and embraced him. He journeyed day after day over hills, plains and valleys until he came to the court of the king, who was courtly and valiant. The king was sitting at dinner and being richly served. Tyolet made his entrance just as he had come, fully armed. On horseback, he came before the high table, where Arthur the king was sitting. He did not utter a single word or address him in any way. 'Friend', said the king, 'dismount and come and eat with us. Tell me what you are searching for, who you are and what your name is.' 'In faith', he said, 'I will tell you, because I will not eat before doing so. King, my name is knight-beast. I have cut off many heads and people call me Tyolet. I am very good at catching game. I am the son, fair lord, if you please, of the widow of the forest. She sends me to you with confidence to learn all about good breeding. I want to learn wisdom and courtliness, and I want to know about knighthood, how to tourney and how to joust, and how to dispense gifts and how to be generous. For there has never been a king's court, and there never will be one, I believe, where there is so much wealth or breeding, courtliness or learning as in yours. Now that I have told you what I am searching for, tell me, king, what you think.' The king replied: 'Lord knight, I retain you. Come and eat.' 'My lord', he said, 'thank you'. Then Tyolet dismounted. He took off his armour, put on and donned a tunic and a light cloak. He washed his hands and went to eat. (275–320)

Lo, a maiden suddenly appeared, a haughty damsel. I do not wish to describe her beauty [because one could not find anyone more beautiful].[3] Never did Dido, I believe, or Helen, have such a fair countenance. She was the daughter of the King of Logres and was seated on a white palfrey. Behind her she carried a white brachet.[4] There was a golden bell hanging

[3] A line is missing here, so this insertion in square brackets is conjectural.

[4] A *brachet* is a female hunting hound that hunts by scent.

around the neck of the white brachet and its coat was very fine-textured and pure. She came before the king on horseback and greeted him: 'King Arthur, my lord, may God protect you, the all-powerful who lives above on high.' 'Fair friend, may he who protects those who are good take care of you.' 'My lord, I am a maiden, daughter of a king and queen, and my father is King of Logres. He and my mother have no more children and they ask you out of friendship, as befits a king of such great worth, that, if any of your knights were bold and fierce enough to cut off the stag's white foot, fair lord, and were to give it to me, I would take him as my husband and would care for no one else. Never will any man have my love unless he gives me the white foot of the stag, which is large and handsome and has hair so shiny that it almost seems golden. It is well guarded by seven lions.' 'In faith', said the king, 'I promise you that such is the agreement: that he who gives you the stag's foot will have you as his wife.' 'And I, my lord king, promise that such is the agreement.' (321–62)

They confirmed this agreement and established it between the two of them. In the hall there was no knight who had ever performed a deed worthy of esteem, who did not say that he would go in search of the stag, if he knew where it was. 'This brachet', she said, 'will take you to where the stag lives and roams.' Lodoer had a great desire for it. He was the first to set off in search of the stag's foot. He asked King Arthur for the opportunity and he did not refuse him. Lodoer took the brachet, mounted his horse and departed in search of the stag's foot. The brachet, which went with him, led him straight to a river that was very large, broad and black, menacing and swollen. It was eight hundred fathoms wide and a good two hundred deep. The brachet plunged into the river. Its instinct led it to expect that Lodoer would follow it in, but he did nothing of the kind. He said he would not go in, for he had no wish to die. After a while he said to himself: 'He who does not have his life has nothing. He keeps a good castle, I believe, who keeps himself from being harmed.' Then the brachet came back out and returned to Lodoer, and he departed, carrying the brachet behind him. He headed straight for the court, where a great many barons were assembled. He gave the brachet back to the maiden, who was very courtly and beautiful. Then the king asked him if he had brought the foot and Lodoer replied to him that others would yet be shamed by it. Then throughout the hall they mocked him, and he shook his head at them, telling them to go and look for the foot and bring it back. Many of them went in search of the stag and asked for the maiden's hand. (363–410)

Not a single one of them who went there failed to sing the same song that Lodoer, who was a valiant knight, had sung, except for just one knight. He was very brave and agile and was called knight-beast; his name was Tyolet.[5] He went straight to the king and quickly asked that the maiden should be kept safe for him, because he would go in search of the white foot. Never, he said, would he return before he had cut off the stag's white right foot. The king gave him leave to do so and Tyolet put on his equipment, dressing himself in full armour. Then he went to the maiden and asked her for her white brachet. She gave it to him gladly and he took leave of her. They rode and journeyed until they both arrived at the ford, and at the great, swift-flowing river that was very deep and menacing. The brachet plunged into the river and swam quickly across it. Tyolet went in after him. He followed the white brachet on his horse, on which he sat, until he emerged on to dry land. Then the brachet brought him to the point where it could show him the stag. Seven lions guarded the stag and they loved it very dearly. Tyolet looked and saw it in the middle of a meadow, where it was grazing; none of the seven lions was in sight. (411–49)

Tyolet spurred his horse and rode up to the stag. He then began to whistle, and at once the stag came towards him in very docile fashion. Tyolet whistled seven times and then the stag stopped in its tracks. He drew his sword immediately and took hold of the stag's white right foot, cutting it off right through the joint. Then he thrust it into his hose. The stag cried out loudly and the lions came rushing up at once and caught sight of Tyolet. One of the lions wounded the horse on which he was sitting, armed, so badly that it tore off its right shoulder at the front, both hide and flesh. When Tyolet saw this, he struck one of the lions with the sword he was carrying so hard that he cut through the sinews of its breast; he had no further trouble from that lion. His horse collapsed beneath him, so Tyolet abandoned it and the lions attacked him. They did so from all sides, breaking his good hauberk. The flesh on his arms and sides was so badly wounded in many places that the lions very nearly devoured him. They tore all his flesh, but he killed every one of them. He escaped from them with difficulty, collapsing beside the lions, which had injured him so badly and done him so much harm. He could never have got up on his own. (450–89)

[5] The way in which Tyolet is presented here, as if he had not been part of the story up to this point, has led some commentators to question the unity of this lay. Have two originally unconnected stories been brought together here?

Lo, a knight suddenly arrived, seated on an iron-grey horse. He stopped and looked, lamenting and grieving greatly for Tyolet. Tyolet opened his eyes, for he had fallen asleep through weariness. Tyolet told him his story, recounting it from start to finish. He drew the foot out of his hose and gave it to the knight, who thanked him for it warmly, as he was delighted to have the foot. He took leave of him and departed. On his way he realised that, if the knight who had given him the foot remained alive, and if he himself had no wish to flee, he could suffer misfortune because of this. He turned back at once, having made up his mind that he would kill the knight, so that he would never challenge him. He gave him a good blow to his body – he would recover fully from this wound – and was convinced that he had killed him. Then he set off on his way. He kept going straight until he came to the king's court. He asked the king for the maiden, showing him the foot of the white stag. But he did not have the white brachet, which had led Tyolet to the stag. Tyolet kept it with him morning and night, but the knight had not been bothered by this. Regardless of who had removed it from the stag, in accordance with the agreement the knight who had brought the foot, wanted as his wife the maiden who was so noble and beautiful. But because Tyolet had not arrived, the king, who was so wise, asked for a week's delay. Then he would assemble his court. At that time he had only his retinue, which was very noble and well bred. So the knight accepted the delay and remained at court for that period. (490–534)

But Gauvain, who was so courtly and well versed in every matter, set out in search of Tyolet, for the brachet had returned and he took it with him. The brachet soon led him to the place where he found Tyolet in a faint, in the meadow beside the lions. When Gauvain saw the knight, and the slaughter he had accomplished, he lamented over the valiant knight greatly. At once he dismounted and spoke to him very tenderly. Tyolet replied in a feeble voice, but nevertheless, with regard to what had happened, he told him the whole truth. Lo, a maiden suddenly arrived on a fine and handsome mule. She greeted Gauvain graciously and he returned her greeting. Then he summoned her to him and embraced her tightly, begging her very tenderly and very gently to take this knight, who was so worthy of esteem, to a doctor in the Black Mountain. She did what he asked, taking the knight and entrusting him to the doctor. In Gauvain's name she entrusted him to the doctor and he received him gladly. He removed his armour, laid him on a table and cleansed his wounds, which were caked in blood. When he had tended to him thoroughly and removed all the congealed blood, he saw that he would recover. In a month's time he would be perfectly well. (535–74)

Meanwhile, Gauvain had returned to court and dismounted in the hall. There he found the knight who had brought the white foot. He had remained at court until the week was up. Then the knight came to the king and greeted him. He asked him to honour the agreement that the maiden had established, and he himself had guaranteed, that she would take as her husband the man who gave her the white foot. The king said: 'That is true.' When Gauvain had heard all this, he immediately stepped forward and said to the king: 'This is not so. Even though I ought not to be so bold, here before you, who are king, as to ever contradict a knight, a man-at-arms, a groom or a squire, I would say that he is acting wrongly. He never took the stag's foot in the manner he stated. It is a matter of great shame for a knight, who is willing to boast of another's deed, to don another's cloak, to draw another's crossbow, to boast of another's achievement, to use another's hand with which to joust and to draw out of the bushes the serpent that is so dreaded. Now this will never happen here. What you say is worthless. Go and make your assault elsewhere. Go and seek your fortune elsewhere. You will not be taking the maiden away.' 'In faith', he said, 'my lord Gauvain, 'you are treating me like a peasant in saying to me that I dare not carry my lance into combat in order to joust, that I am capable of drawing another's bow and using another's hand to draw the serpent from the bushes, as you have mentioned. As far as I believe and am aware, there is no one who, if he wanted to prove this in combat against me, would fail to find me on the battlefield.' (575–620)

While this dispute was going on, they looked across the hall and saw Tyolet, who had arrived and dismounted at the block outside. The king rose to greet him, threw his arms around his neck and then kissed him as a sign of great love. Tyolet bowed to him as befits a lord. Gauvain embraced him, and Urien, Kay and Yvain, son of Morgan,[6] and Lodoer went to embrace him, as did all the other knights. When the knight who wanted to have the maiden by virtue of the foot he had brought, which Tyolet had given to him, saw this, he went and spoke to the king again and made his request once more. But when Tyolet heard that he was

[6] This seems to be the earliest reference to Morgan the Fée as Yvain's mother. Morgan is traditionally presented as Arthur's sister, with whom he had an incestuous relationship in his youth, the resulting child being Mordred, who is responsible in the *Mort le roi Artu* for the destruction of the kingdom.

asking for the maiden, he spoke to him very gently, asking him in friendly fashion: 'My lord knight, tell me, while you are before the king, on what grounds you wish to have the maiden. I would like to know.' 'In faith', he said, 'I will tell you. It is because I have brought her the white foot of the swift-moving stag. The king and the maiden herself have agreed to this.' 'Did you cut off the stag's foot? If this is true, let it not be denied.' 'Yes', he said, 'I cut it off and brought it here with me.' 'And the seven lions, who killed them?' The knight looked at him and said nothing; rather he became red and flushed. Tyolet addressed him again: 'My lord knight, who was it who was struck by the sword, and who was it who struck him with it? Tell me this, I beg you. I believe it was you.' The knight bowed his head and was much ashamed. 'When you committed such a misdeed, it was like getting a broken neck after performing a good deed.[7] In good faith I had given you the foot that I cut off the stag and you rewarded me in this way, by almost killing me. In truth, I ought to have died. I gave it to you and now I regret it. Your sword, which you carried, you plunged right into my body. You certainly thought you had killed me. If you wish to deny this and prove yourself in front of these barons, I tender my pledge to King Arthur.' (621–78)

The knight recognised that he was telling the truth and immediately begged him for mercy. Fearing death more than shame, he did not contradict his account in any way. He surrendered to him in front of the king, ready to do his bidding. Tyolet pardoned him as a result of the advice he received from the king and all his barons, and the knight fell to his knees. He was about to kiss Tyolet's foot when Tyolet raised him up and kissed him with great affection. I have since heard no more of him. The knight gave him back the foot and Tyolet took it and gave it to the maiden. In beauty she surpassed a lily or a new rose when it first blooms in the summertime. Tyolet then asked for her hand. King Arthur gave her to him and the maiden consented. Then she took him to her land, where he was king and she was queen. Here ends the lay of *Tyolet*. (679–704)

[7] The Old French text reads: 'Mes ce fu de bien fet col fret / Quant vos feïstes tel forfet'. For other interpretations of these lines, see Burgess and Brook, *Eleven Old French Narrative Lays*, p. 140.

3. *Graelent*

Introduction

Graelent is preserved in two manuscripts: (i) S and (ii) Paris, BNF, fr. 2168 (Tobin's MS A). Our translation is based on S.

Graelent is a knight in the service of the King of Brittany. His reputation for generous entertaining and the distribution of largesse inspires the queen to fall in love with him. But when she summons him he rebuffs her advances, and eventually her love turns to hatred. She poisons the king's mind against him so that his pay is withheld and he gradually sinks into poverty. One day, he goes hunting with borrowed equipment and follows a white hind that leads him to a naked maiden bathing in a fountain. She is clearly a supernatural figure. Graelent forms a liaison with her and she bestows on him money and garments, enabling him to regain his status at court. Then one day the king has the queen stand on a table so that everyone can pay tribute to her unique beauty. Graelent, however, declares that he knows a more beautiful woman. This public announcement strips him of all the wealth given by the fairy, and it results in the threat of imprisonment if, within a year, he cannot produce the latter in order to substantiate his boast. When his trial begins, the fairy eventually turns up to vindicate him, and as she leaves he follows her. He comes upon a river, but undeterred plunges into it and has to be rescued from drowning by her handmaidens. He then disappears to her land, leaving his distressed horse behind.

Graelent has clear affinities with Marie de France's *Lanval* and shares themes with *Guingamor*. The queen's propositioning has links to the tale of Potiphar's wife from Genesis, but it is expanded here to include a lecture from the hero on the nature of love.[1] Although the queen does

[1] Having been sold into slavery by his brothers, Joseph is taken into Potiphar's house as a slave and soon put in charge of the entire household. Potiphar's wife tries

not subsequently denounce Graelent to her husband, she ensures that he suffers. The episode with the fairy has echoes in *Lanval* and *Guingamor*, although in *Lanval* the fairy offers her love from the outset while in *Graelent* he forces himself upon her before obtaining her love. The trial scene in *Graelent* is also not unlike the trial scene in *Lanval*, but where in Marie's lay the hero rides off immediately afterwards to the fairy's lands, in *Graelent* there is a sort of coda as Graelent chases after her and risks the perils of the river, while his horse continues to fret at his disappearance. The crossing of the river, a traditional Celtic motif of delineation between the real and the fairy world, is also to be found in *Guingamor*.

None of the main characters in *Graelent* could be considered totally admirable. The king listens to his wife's slanders without seemingly giving Graelent a chance to defend himself. He merely cuts off his pay and is not above exhibiting his wife as a trophy object, presumably in order to satisfy his own vanity. The queen is vindictive and she tells lies to the king in order to get her own back on Graelent for turning her down and to avenge her hurt pride. Graelent, although described as generous, cannot be said to treat women with much respect, as he angers and frightens his future beloved and seemingly forces himself upon her,[2] and he is not above lecturing the queen and trying to impose on her his concept of love. His boasting of his mistress's superior beauty has to be considered unwise. But his motive in so doing may, of course, have been to take revenge on the queen who had caused him so much trouble.

to seduce him, but is rejected. She then falsely accuses him of attempted rape and he is thrown into prison by Potiphar (Genesis, chapter 39). See Frederick E. Faverty, 'The Story of Potiphar's Wife in Mediaeval Literature', *Harvard Studies and Notes in Philology and Literature*, 13 (1931), 81–127. In our collection the theme of Potiphar's wife appears again in the *Chastelaine de Vergi*.

[2] In the MS A version, edited by Tobin, it is clear that Graelent rapes the maiden. In our version, from MS S, which has two extra lines (vv. 293–94), it is not clear whether he forces himself on her because he cannot persuade her to love him or whether, after his entreaties, she eventually relents and allows him to have his way with her. See Burgess and Brook, 2007, pp. 365–66 and the note to vv. 293–94 (p. 411).

Further Reading

Cross, Tom P., 'The Celtic Elements in the Lays of *Lanval* and *Graelent*', *Modern Philology*, 12 (1914–15), 585–644.

Illingworth, Richard N., 'The Composition of *Graelent* and *Guingamor*', *Medium Aevum*, 44 (1985), 31–50.

Segre, Cesare, '*Lanval, Graelent, Guingamor*', in *Studi in onore di Angelo Monteverdi*, 2 vols (Modena: Società Tipografica Editrice Modenese, 1959), II, pp. 756–70.

Vincensini, Paul, 'Viol de la fée, violence du féerique: remarques sur la vocation anthropologique de la littérature médiévale', in *La Violence dans le monde médiéval* (Aix-en-Provence: Publications du CUERMA, 1994), pp. 545–50.

Translation

I will tell you the story of Graelent, as I understand it. The lay is good to listen to and the melody good to retain. Graelent was of Breton birth, from a good and noble family. Handsome of body and noble of heart, he was called Graelent Muer.[3] He did not possess extensive domains, but he was courtly and wise, and a good knight with a great reputation. There was no lady in the land so powerful that, if he were to seek her love, she would not have been obliged to pay heed to him. (1–14)

The King of Brittany was waging a great war with his neighbours and he summoned knights to his service. In this way Graelent came to him, and because he was a good knight the king retained him willingly, cherishing and honouring him greatly. He made great efforts to tourney and to joust, and also to inflict harm on the king's enemies. He often entertained in his lodging and gave very generous gifts. The queen heard praise of him and accounts of his excellent deeds, and of his great valour, prowess, beauty and generosity. She fell in love with him in her heart and summoned one of her chamberlains, saying: 'Tell me, do not keep anything from me, have you heard much talk of the good knight Graelent?

[3] Graelant Muer is Graelent's full name, and it is used by the author as the title of the lay in the last line of the text. On other forms of the name Graelent, regularly abbreviated in MS S to 'Gra.', see Burgess and Brook, *French Arthurian Literature IV*, p. 410. The second element in the name seems to derive from Breton *mor*/*muer*, 'great'.

Is he praised by many people?' 'My lady', he said, 'he is very valiant and very much loved by all.' The queen then replied to him: 'I want to make him my beloved. I am in great turmoil because of him, so go and tell him to come to me. I will grant him my love completely.' 'You would be giving him a very fine gift', he said, 'and it will be astonishing if he is not filled with joy. There is not a single good monk from here to Troy who, if he looked upon your face, would not very soon undergo a change of heart.' (15–48)

When he had said this, he left the lady and went to Graelent's lodging. He greeted him in an appropriate manner and gave him his message: that he should go and speak with the queen and be sure not to delay. The knight replied: 'Go on ahead, my fair, dear friend.' The chamberlain departed and Graelent set off. He mounted an iron-grey horse and took a knight with him. They both came to the castle and dismounted before the hall, passing by the king and making for the queen's chambers. When the queen saw them, she called to them, greeting them warmly and honouring them. She put her arms around Graelent and held him in a tight embrace. Then she made him sit down beside her on a cushion, next to her bed. She looked very tenderly at the beauty of his body and his face and spoke to him in friendly fashion. He made a courtly reply, but said nothing that pleased her. She remained thoughtful for some time, astonished that he had not begged her to love him with true passion, and as he had not done so she asked him if he had a beloved or if he were in thrall to love, since he fully deserved to be loved by someone. (49–82)

'My lady', he said, 'that is not what I desire. Love is no laughing matter. A man must be of great worth to undertake to become a lover. Five hundred men may speak of love who do not know the slightest thing about it, or what loyal passion is, so mad and foolish are they. Their idleness, lies and deceit do harm to love in many ways. Love demands chastity in thought, word and deed. If one lover is loyal and the other fickle and false, then the love will be corrupted and it cannot last for long. Love is not worthy if it lacks a companion, and love is not true unless it concerns two people and is between two bodies and two hearts. Otherwise it is quite worthless. Cicero, who spoke of friendship, said very clearly in his work that a beloved should want what the other lover wants.[4] In that way the companionship will be true. If she refuses

[4] The reference here is to Marcus Tullius Cicero (106–43 BC) and his book *De amicitia*.

love, he should not offer it, for their passion would not be right. Once one contradicts the other, there is only a minimal amount of love. One can easily find love, but to keep it properly requires sense, tenderness, openness and prudence. Love does not care for any wrongdoing, but it requires loyalty to be promised and upheld. For this reason, I dare not get involved with it.' (83–116)

The queen listened to Graelent, who spoke in such a courtly fashion that even if she had had no desire for love he would have troubled her. She knew well, and perceived without any doubt, that he was an intelligent and courtly man. So she spoke to him more freely, revealing her heart to him completely. 'Graelent, friend', she said, 'I love you fervently. I have never loved anyone except my lord, but I love you with such passion that I grant you all my love. Be my beloved and I will be yours.' 'My lady', he said, 'my thanks to you, but it cannot be thus, for I am in the king's pay, and when I took my oath to him the other day I promised him loyalty and faith in respect of both his life and his honour. He will never know shame on account of me.' He then took his leave and departed. (117–38)

The queen saw him go and began to sigh, feeling very distressed and unsure of what she should do. However, she did not want to let it rest at that. She repeatedly sought Graelent's love and sent her messengers to him with costly gifts, but he refused them all. When she saw that her efforts had failed completely, she hated him and caused trouble for him with his lord, deliberately slandering him because of it. While the king conducted the war, Graelent remained in his land. He had spent so much money there that he had nothing left, for the king was holding back his pay and making him wait. It was at the queen's instigation that he had not given him any of it, as she had advised him not to give him anything because, if he left, he would seek to do him harm. For this reason the king kept him with him, so that he could not serve anyone else. What would Graelent do now? It was no wonder he was distressed, for he had nothing left to mortgage, except for a hack that was scarcely worth anything and a servant whom he had brought up. His men had deserted him and he could not leave town, as he had no mount to ride and did not expect help from anywhere. (139–71)

It was in the month of May, when the days are long, that his host rose early and went to the town with his wife to dine with one of his neighbours. He left the knight all alone, for he had with him in the house no squire, servant or groom, just the daughter of the hostess, who was very noble and courtly. When the time came to dine, she went to speak to the knight, begging him earnestly to be of good cheer and to come and eat with her. He did not want to agree to this and instead called to his squire, telling him to bring him his hunting horse and to put on its saddle and bridle. 'I will go out to amuse myself, for I have no desire to eat.' The squire replied that he had no saddle. 'My friend', said the maiden, 'I will lend you one and give you a good bridle.' The squire brought out the horse and saddled it in the house, and Graelent mounted it and rode through the town, having donned an old skin cloak that he had worn for a very long time. The men and women who looked at him jeered and mocked him, but he paid no heed to this. (172–203)

Outside the town there was a clearing, part of a large, dense forest through which ran a stream. Graelent went in that direction, distraught, sad and grief-stricken. He had only just entered the forest when in a dense thicket he saw a pure white hind, whiter than snow when it lies on a branch. The hind sprang out in front of him, so he hallooed and spurred towards it. But he would never catch up with it. Nevertheless, he followed it closely until it led him on to a heath, towards the source of a spring, the water of which was clear and beautiful. A maiden was bathing in it, with two maidens serving her. They were on the edge of the spring and the clothing she had taken off was lying in some bushes. Graelent saw the maiden who was naked in the fountain, and rode quickly over to her. Because the maiden was so beautiful and so slender he took no further interest in the hind. She was fair-skinned, rosy and fresh-complexioned, with laughing eyes and a beautiful brow. There was no more beautiful woman in the whole world. Nothing on earth pleased him so much and he completely forgot his misery. (204–34)

Not wishing to touch her in the water, he left her to bathe at her leisure. He went and seized her clothing, thinking that in this way he could keep her there. The handmaidens noticed the knight and were dismayed by what he had done. Their mistress addressed him, calling to him angrily: 'Graelent, leave my clothes alone! You would scarcely improve your reputation if you took them away with you and so left me naked. That would be a most wretched and greedy act. At least give me back my chemise. The cloak can remain yours, and you can get some money for it, as it is a fine one.' Graelent replied with a laugh: 'I am not the son of a merchant or a burgess, who would sell cloaks. Even if it were now worth three castles, I would not take it away. Come out of the water, my friend, take your clothes and get dressed. I beg you to speak with me.' 'I do not wish to come out,' she said, 'so that you can grab hold of me. I have no desire to speak with you and am not as ill-mannered as you.' He replied to her: 'I will just wait and will keep your clothes until you come out from there. Fair one, you have a very beautiful body.' (235–66)

When she saw that he intended to wait and would not return her clothing to her, she asked him to promise her that he would do her no harm. Graelent assured her of this and handed back her chemise. She dressed herself immediately. He placed her mantle in front of her and then put it on her, thus giving it back to her. He took her by the left hand and drew her towards him. He asked and entreated her for her love and for her to make him her beloved. She replied to him: 'Graelent, what you seek is a great outrage. I do not think you are being wise, and I can only marvel greatly that you dare to speak to me in this way. Do not be so bold, for you would soon be in a sorry plight. It is not fitting for someone of your lineage to love a woman of my rank.' Graelent found her very arrogant and realised that she would not do anything he desired through entreaties, but he did not want to leave her. He begged and entreated her in an attempt to find favour with her, until he did with her what he pleased in the thick of the forest. When he had had his way with her, he begged her most tenderly not to be too angry with him, but instead to be both noble and well bred. She should now grant him her love and he would make her his beloved. He would love her most loyally and never leave her. (267–304)

The maiden heard and understood Graelent's entreaty and saw that he was courtly and wise, a handsome knight, brave and generous, and that if he left her she would never have such a good lover. She duly granted him his request and he kissed her tenderly. She spoke to him in these words: 'Graelent, you took me by surprise and I love you most sincerely. But I forbid you one thing: that you should say anything openly through which our love could be discovered. In great abundance I will give you money and clothing, gold and silver. The love between us will be very good. Night and day I will be near you and you will be able to laugh and sport with me. You will see me beside you, but none of your companions will see me, or ever know who I am. Graelent, you are loyal, brave, courtly and very handsome. For you I came to the spring. I will suffer great pain for you, but I was well aware of what would happen. Now show great restraint. Mind you do not boast or say anything through which you could lose me. Beloved, you should remain in this land, close by. But after that, dear beloved, let this be the place to which you return, for I love this region.

Leave now, it is past nones.[5] I will send you my messenger and let you know my wishes.' (305–42)

Graelent took leave of her and she kissed and embraced him. He came to his lodging and dismounted from his horse. He went into his chamber alone and leant on the windowsill, thinking deeply about what had happened. He turned his head towards the town and saw a servant coming swiftly on an iron-grey hunting horse. The youth was leading a pure white steed in his hand, holding it by the bridle. It had a large bag on its back and passed through the main street, making for Graelent's lodging. The youth got down off his mount and greeted the knight, who had come to meet him. Graelent asked him where he had come from, what his name was and who he was. 'My lord', he said, 'have no fear, for I am a messenger from your beloved. Through me she sends you this steed, and she wants me to remain with you. I will discharge your debts and take care of your lodging.' When Graelent heard this news, which seemed to him very good and fine, he kissed the servant warmly. He then received the present of the warhorse; there was none so fine on earth, nor so sturdy or so swift. He himself placed it in the stable along with the servant's hunting horse. The servant took down his trunk and brought out from it a large coverlet, made of costly brocade, with precious silk on the other side. He placed it on Graelent's bed and then brought out gold, silver and fine clothes for his lord to wear. He summoned Graelent's host, gave him a large amount of money and told and commanded him that his lord should be free of debt and his lodging well provided for. He was to make sure that he was well fed, and that if there was any knight in the town who wanted food and lodging he should bring him back with him. (343–92)

The host was a worthy and courtly man and a very valiant and excellent burgess. He prepared costly dishes and asked throughout the town for any needy knights, prisoners or crusaders. He brought them to Graelent's lodging and took great pains to honour them. That night there was a great deal of joy, with both instruments and entertainment. Graelent was joyful and richly attired. He gave generous gifts to the harpists, the prisoners and the minstrels. There was no burgess in the city who had lent him money to whom he did not give gifts and do honour, so much so that they regarded him as their lord. From that time onwards, Graelent was at his ease. He no longer saw anything that displeased him. He saw his beloved at his side

[5] Nones is the ninth hour of the day and varied between noon and mid-afternoon, according to the season.

and could laugh and joke with her a great deal. At night he felt her next to him. How could he have any anxiety? He travelled very frequently. In the land there was no tournament at which he was not the first,[6] and he was greatly loved by other knights. Now Graelent lived a good life and had very great joy with his beloved. If this could have lasted for a long time, he would never have had to ask for anything more. (393–424)

Thus it was for a full year, until the king was to hold a festival. At Pentecost each year he summoned his barons by proclamation, and all those who held lands from him were with him on that occasion and served him with great honour. When they had eaten that day, the king would make the queen climb up on to a high bench and remove her cloak. He would then ask everyone gathered there: 'Lord barons, what do you think of her? Is there on earth a more beautiful queen, courtly lady or maiden?' Everyone was obliged to praise her and to say and affirm to the king that they knew of no woman so beautiful, be it a young girl, a lady or a maiden. That year there was a great assembly and the court was proclaimed for a week. A remarkably large number of people were present and the king summoned Graelent. After the meal the king made his wife climb up on to a large table, and he begged and commanded his barons and asked them, in accordance with their friendship, to let him know the truth, whether they knew of a woman as beautiful as her. There was no one who did not praise her and value her beauty greatly, except for Graelent. He kept silent, smiling to himself and thinking in his heart of his beloved. He thought the others were foolish for shouting out on all sides and praising the queen in this way. (425–60)

He covered his head and lowered his gaze, and the queen looked at him. She pointed him out to the king, her lord: 'My lord, see what dishonour this is! There is no one here who has not praised me, except for Graelent, who has mocked me. I know that he has hated me for a long time. I think he is envious of me.' The king called to Graelent and asked him, in front of his people and by the faith that he owed him as his natural vassal, not to conceal it, but to tell him why he had lowered his head and smiled. Graelent replied to the king. 'My lord', he said, 'listen to me. Never has a man of your rank done such a thing or acted so outrageously.

[6] It not clear from the text whether this indicates that Graelent was so keen to attend tournaments that he was always first to arrive, or whether, at the end of each day's performances, he was regarded as the most successful of the knights present. A similar issue arises in the lay of *Doon*, v. 209.

You are making a spectacle of your wife and do not have a single man here whom you are not forcing to praise her. They say that they do not know her equal. I can tell you one thing in truth: one can easily find somebody more beautiful than she is. Yes', he added, 'one worth thirty of yours.' The queen was very distressed and she begged her husband, for mercy's sake, to make the knight bring forth the woman he had heard him mention and about whom he had made such a boast. He should let the two of them be put on display and, if the other is more beautiful, let him be acquitted, or, if not, let him be given his rightful punishment for the slander and the insult. (461–97)

The king ordered him to be seized, and he said that never again would he have love or peace from him, nor would he ever be let out of prison, unless the woman was produced whose beauty he had praised so much. Graelent was taken and held. He would have been better off remaining silent. He asked the king for a delay, realising that he had spoken slanderously and thinking that he had lost his beloved. He was perspiring from distress and anger and deserved to be in this sorry plight. But many people at court pitied him and there was a great throng around him that day. The king let the matter drop until the following year, when he would again be holding his festivities. He would summon all his allies once more, his barons and all his closest advisers. Graelent should then be brought there and he should bring the lady he had praised so much before the king. If she is as beautiful and worthy as he has said, let this be his proof. Let him then be discharged and he will lose nothing. If she does not come, he will be judged and at the king's mercy. Everyone knew that this was appropriate. (498–524)

Graelent left the court, angry, sad and distressed. He mounted his good warhorse and returned to his lodging. He asked for his chamberlain, but could not find the one whom his beloved had sent to him. Now Graelent was in a bad way and would rather be dead than alive. He entered a chamber alone and begged his beloved to have mercy on him and be willing to speak to him. But it was to no avail, as she would not speak to him and he would not see her again for a year. Graelent was greatly distressed and had no rest day or night. As he could not have his beloved, he lost all interest in life. Before the year had passed, he was so grief-stricken that he had neither strength nor power. Those who saw him said that it was astonishing that he had lasted so long. (525–47)

On the day the king had fixed to hold his festival, he assembled a large number of people. The guarantors brought Graelent to the king and into his presence. He asked him where his beloved was. 'My lord', Graelent replied, 'she is not here. I cannot make contact with her, so do with me what you will.' The king was the first to respond: 'You spoke very churlishly and did wrong by the queen, contradicting all my barons. You will never again speak ill of anyone when you leave me.' The king then spoke in a raised voice: 'My lords', he said, 'I beg you not to be sparing in your judgment, in accordance with the words you heard Graelent speak and the way he shamed me in my court. Any man who brings dishonour upon my wife does not love me truly. Do not expect anyone who takes pleasure in beating your dog to have any love for you.' The members of the court went out and gathered together to reach a judgment. They remained silent for a long time, with no dispute or commotion. They felt great distress for the knight whom it was their duty to judge. (548–78)

Before any of them could utter a word or record their testimony, a servant arrived. He told them to wait for a short while, as two maidens were coming to the court who were more beautiful than any in the kingdom. They would help the knight greatly, and if it pleased God they would free him. The members of the court were happy to wait, and before they had made a move the maidens arrived, very beautiful and well dressed. They were both tightly laced in silk tunics and were very comely and slender. They dismounted from their palfreys and had them held by two servants. They came to the king in the hall and one of them said: 'My lord, listen to me. My lady commands you, and through the two of us begs and informs you, that you should delay this trial for a while and not let a judgment be made. She is coming here to speak to you in order to free the knight.' (579–602)

As the maiden was speaking, the queen felt a great deal of shame. Not long afterwards two much more beautiful girls, with rosy and white complexions, arrived before the king in his palace. They told the king to wait until their lady had come. Everyone fixed their gaze on them and their beauty was praised by many. Women did indeed exist who were more beautiful than the queen. When the lady came, all eyes at court were on her. She was truly beautiful, with a gentle appearance and a gentle expression, and with beautiful eyes, countenance and features. There was no blemish in her and everyone looked at her with wonder. She was dressed in dark red silken material, which was richly embroidered with gold and fitted her closely. Her cloak was as valuable as a castle. She had a fine, handsome palfrey whose bridle, saddle and harness were worth a thousand pounds in Chartres coin. Everyone went out to see her, praising her face and her body, her appearance and her features. She arrived at a gallop and rode up to the king; no one could find fault with her. She dismounted away from the throng, leaving her palfrey to roam. She addressed the king in courtly fashion: 'My lord', she said, 'listen to me, and all of you, my lord barons, listen to what I have to say to you. You know all about Graelent and what he said to the king in front of his men on the occasion of the great assembly, when the queen was put on display. He said that he had seen a more beautiful woman and everyone is aware of this remark. It is true that it was an insult, insofar as it made the king angry, but in this he spoke the truth, for no woman has such great beauty that no other is as beautiful. Now look and say what is right. If through appearing here I can acquit him, then the king should declare him innocent.' (603–54)

There was no one, great or small, who did not say publicly that even one of the handmaidens who were with her was the queen's equal in beauty. The king himself made the judgment before his court and granted that Graelent should be acquitted, for it was right that he be declared innocent. While the trial proceeded, Graelent did not forget what he should do. He had his horse brought forth, intending to leave with his beloved. When she had done what she aimed to do and had heard what the court said, she asked for and took leave of the king. Then she mounted her palfrey and left the hall, together with her maidens. Graelent got on to his horse and went after her, riding swiftly through the town. He kept on shouting for her to take pity on him, but she did not reply to him in any way. They maintained a straight course until they reached the forest. They kept to their path through the woods and travelled as far as the river that had its source in the middle of the heath and ran through the centre of the forest. The water in it was very clear and beautiful and the maiden entered it. Graelent tried to go in after her, but she began to cry out to him: 'Flee, Graelent, do not enter! If you come in, you will drown.' (655–88)

He took no notice of this, but followed her in, so great was his desire. The water closed over his head and he came to the surface with great difficulty. She took hold of his reins and dragged him back to land, then said to him: 'You cannot cross, however much you may strive to do so'. She ordered him to go back and then entered the river once again, but he could not bear to see her leave him and went into the water still on horseback. The current carried him downstream, separating him from his horse. He was close to drowning when the maidens who were with the lady cried out: 'Lady, in God's name, have mercy! Take pity on your beloved. Look, he is dying in great pain. God, it was a bad day for him when you first spoke to him and granted him your love. My lady, look, the current is carrying him away. In God's name, release him from his suffering. It is a grievous thing if he has to perish. How can your heart bear this? Lady, your beloved is drowning. Let him have some help from you. You are being very cruel and harsh. If you do not make an effort to help him, you will be committing a great sin against him.' (689–721)

The maiden took pity on him when she heard them thus lamenting so much. She could no longer ignore him or fail to act, so she turned back quickly and went downstream. She seized her beloved by the waist and pulled him along with her. When they had reached the other side, she removed his wet clothes and wrapped him in her mantle. Then she took him off to her land. People in the region say that Graelent is still there and alive. His horse, which had become separated from him, went back into the forest, very distressed over the loss of its master and was not at peace night or day. Afterwards, for a long time, it neighed in that region and was heard throughout the land. People tried to capture it and retain it, but no one ever managed to get hold of it. It refused to let anyone near it and no one could ensnare or capture it. A long time afterwards, for many a year, in the season in which its master had left it, people heard the noise, the neighing and the cries that the good horse made because of its lord whom it had lost. The marvel of the good horse, the adventure of the knight and the way he had departed with his beloved were heard throughout all Brittany. The Bretons composed a lay about it and it was called *Graalent Muer*. (722–56)

4. *Guingamor*

Introduction

Guingamor is preserved in only one manuscript (S). This lay has been attributed to Marie de France and an edition by Peter Kusel is included in the third edition of Karl Warnke's influential *Die Lais der Marie de France* (Halle: Niemeyer, 1925, pp. 233–55). Marie's authorship was definitively disproved by Russell Weingartner in 1969 (see Further Reading below). Over the years there has also been considerable discussion of the order of composition of the lays *Graelent*, *Guingamor* and *Lanval*. We accept the order established in 1957 by Cesare Segre: *Lanval*, *Graelent*, *Guingamor*, with the latter two drawing extensively on *Lanval*. Richard N. Illingworth adds that *Guingamor* drew material from *Graelent* (see the Further Reading section for *Graelent* above).

In response to a dare issued by the queen to all the knights present at court, Guingamor, the nephew of the King of Brittany, sets off to hunt a magic white boar. The queen's unstated aim is to be rid of Guingamor, as she had unsuccessfully propositioned him and is afraid he might denounce her to the king. Fortunately for her, Guingamor tacitly understands her intention and volunteers to go on a mission from which no previous knight has ever returned. Once the boar is located, Guingamor leaves behind all his companions and chases after it alone. After a while, he comes upon a magnificent deserted palace, but continues the hunt and encounters a naked fairy bathing in a fountain. Intrigued by her, he hides her clothes, but she demands them imperiously, calling him by name and promising him the boar if he will stay with her for three days. He accepts and is taken to the palace he had previously come across. He discovers there ten knights who had set out on the quest for the boar and never returned. On the third of the three days agreed upon, he asks permission to leave, only to discover that he has in fact spent 300 years with the fairy. She allows him to depart with the boar's head, but warns him not to eat when he is back in his own world. He disobeys and, as a result, promptly ages rapidly. He is, however, rescued by the fairy's handmaidens and brought back to her domain, never to be seen again in his own country.

There are several themes in *Guingamor* that are common to other texts. At the beginning there is a version of the Potiphar's wife episode in Genesis, when the queen propositions Guingamor only to be turned down (see p. 37n1). This scene also features in Marie de France's *Lanval*, with the difference that in *Guingamor* the queen does not denounce him to the king, but nevertheless manages to get him out of the court. There is also a similar episode in *Graelent*, but again the queen does not denounce him, instead she lies about him to the king in order to cause him harm. A large part of the narrative of *Guingamor* is taken up by a detailed account of the hunt, and this may well reflect the author's interest in, and knowledge of, this sport, while at the same time creating a sense of the passage of time, as Guingamor endeavours persistently, but unsuccessfully, to catch up with his prey. Only the fairy, as a superior being with superior knowledge, can help him. As the narrative draws to its conclusion, Guingamor cannot resist the urge to return to his original land to show his uncle, the king, that he has triumphed in his quest. But the king is now long dead, and the state of the decayed woodland graphically underlines the psychological and temporal distance between the old world and that of the fairy.

Further Reading

Badel, Pierre-Yves, 'Masculin, féminin dans le lai de *Guingamor*', *Cahiers de Civilisation Médiévale*, 35 (1995), 103–14.

Brook, Leslie C., 'The Notion of Adventure in *Guingamor*', *Reading Medieval Studies*, 14 (1988), 3–16.

Maraud, André, 'La Tradition fantastique ou le héros conteur: le lai de *Guingamor*', in *Frontières du conte*, ed. François Marotin (Paris: Éditions du CNRS, 1982), pp. 25–31.

Sturm, Sara, '*The Lay of Guingamor: A Study* (Chapel Hill, NC: University of North Carolina Press, 1968).

Weingartner, Russell, 'Stylistic Analysis of an Anonymous Work: The Old French *lai Guingamor*', *Modern Philology*, 69 (1971–72), 1–9.

See also the items by Illingworth and Segre and in the Further Reading section for *Graelent*.

Translation

I will relate the story of a lay. Do not think it was invented, for what I will tell you is the truth. The lay is called *Guingamor*. In Brittany there once lived a king who ruled the land and the country. He was a most noble baron, whose name I truly do not know. He had a nephew called Guingamor, who was very wise and courtly and a brave and sensible knight. Because he was so brave and handsome, the king held him in great affection and intended to make him his heir, for he could not have any children himself. Guingamor was very much liked because he made fair promises and gave generously, greatly honouring knights, men-at-arms and squires. He was esteemed throughout the land, for he was very noble and well bred. (1–22)

One day the king went hunting in the forest for relaxation. His nephew had been bled that day and was somewhat indisposed. So, unable to go into the woods, he went to rest in his lodging, retaining several of the king's companions with him. He arose at daybreak and went to amuse himself in the castle. He met the seneschal and threw his arms around his neck, chatting for a while before going to a gaming table to play. The queen left her quarters and came to the door of the room, intending to go to the chapel. She was very tall, noble and fair, and she paused for some while to look at the knight, whom she saw playing at the table, neither continuing on her way nor moving. He seemed to her to be remarkably handsome in body, face and person. He was sitting by a window and a ray of sunlight fell upon his face, lighting it up and giving him a fine colouring. The queen gazed at him for such a long time that she was overcome by emotion. On account of his handsome features and noble air she became smitten with love for him. She retraced her steps and summoned a handmaiden, saying: 'Go to the knight who is sitting in there at the chessboard and tell him to come to me.' (23–60)

The handmaiden came to the knight, greeted him in her mistress's name and asked him to come and speak with the queen. Guingamor left the game and went with her. The queen called to him and had him sit down beside her, but he did not realise why she was being so welcoming. The queen spoke first: 'Guingamor, you are very brave, worthy, courtly and charming. Good fortune awaits you, for you can find love at a very high level. You have someone who loves you and is courtly and fair. I know of no other lady or maiden in the kingdom equal to her. She loves you with a profound love, so take her as your mistress.' The knight replied to her: 'My lady, I do not know how I might love a lady passionately, unless I had first seen her, made her acquaintance and got to know her. I have never heard speak of her, nor do I wish at this time to labour for love.' The queen replied: 'Friend, do not be so evasive. It is I whom you should truly love. I am not to be refused, for I love you with all my heart and will do so for the rest of my life.' The knight thought about it and replied prudently: 'My lady, I know well that I must love you, for you are the wife of my lord the king and so I must bear you honour, as to the wife of my overlord.' The queen replied: 'I do not mean love of that kind. I want to love you passionately and be your beloved. You are handsome and I am attractive. If you set your mind to loving me, we can both be very happy.' She drew him towards her and kissed him. Guingamor heard what she said and the kind of love she wanted. He felt great shame and blushed deeply. He pulled away angrily and attempted to leave the room, but the lady tried to hold him back, seizing his cloak and breaking the fastenings. He went off without his cloak, returning to the gaming table he had left and sitting down again, most upset. He was so angry that he forgot about his cloak and continued his game without it. (61–120)

The queen was in great turmoil and very distressed on account of the king. Having spoken to Guingamor in the way she had done, and revealed so much of her feelings, she was afraid he might denounce her and ruin her in his uncle's eyes. She called to a handmaiden to whom she was very close, gave her the cloak and sent it back to Guingamor. The handmaiden put it around him, but he was so upset and engrossed in his thoughts that he did not notice her give it to him. She then retraced her steps. The queen remained in great fear until that evening, when the king came back from hunting and sat down to his meal. He had had a very successful day and his companions were all merry. After the meal they jested and laughed, telling each other of their exploits, each speaking of how he had done, whether he had missed or shot well. Guingamor had not been with them, a fact that weighed heavily upon him, so he remained silent and spoke not a word. The queen looked at him, and with the intention of upsetting and angering him, she uttered these words, which each may judge for himself. Turning to the knights, she said: 'I hear you boasting greatly and relating your adventures. But there is no one present, among all those whom I see here, who would be so bold as to dare to hunt, or to blow his horn for the white boar who dwells in the forest outside here, even for a thousand pounds in gold. Whoever could capture the boar would achieve wondrous acclaim.' (121–62)

Not wishing to attempt this challenge, all the knights fell silent. But Guingamor well understood that she had proposed this for him. Everyone in the hall was deep in thought and there was no dispute or argument. The king was the first to respond to her: 'My lady, you have often heard about the adventure of the forest. Know that it displeases me greatly whenever I hear speak of it. No man has ever gone there to hunt the boar and returned. The heath there is dangerous and the river perilous. I have suffered great harm in it, having lost ten of the very best knights in this land, who went to hunt the boar.' (163–82)

The discussion ended at that and the company broke up. They went to their lodgings to rest and the king went to bed. But Guingamor did not forget the speech he had heard. He went into the king's bedchamber and knelt before him: 'My lord', he said, 'I am asking you for something I need, which I beg you to grant me. Do not refuse to give it to me.' The king said to him: 'I grant it to you, fair nephew. Tell me what you wish and ask me with confidence. There is nothing that you could want that I would not grant you.' The knight thanked him and then told him what he was asking for and what boon he had granted him. 'I will go hunting in the forest', he said. He asked for the king's bloodhound, his brachet and his hunting horse, and for the loan of his pack of dogs for the day. (183–206)

The king heard what his nephew said and the request he was making. He was very unhappy and did not know what to do. He wanted to retract his promise and told Guingamor that he should drop the matter and not ask such a thing. He would not permit him to go there and hunt the white boar, even for his own weight in gold, for he would never return. If he were to lend him his good brachet and give him his hunting horse – he possessed nothing he loved so much and would not give them away for any living thing – they would never be seen again and he would lose them straightaway. He said that if he lost them, he would be sad forever. Guingamor replied to the king: 'My lord, by the loyalty I owe to you, I would not refrain from hunting the boar tomorrow for anything, even for the whole world. If you are unwilling to lend me the brachet you hold so dear, the horse and the bloodhound, and the pack of the other dogs, I will take my own, such as they are.' The queen suddenly appeared, having heard the speech and what Guingamor was asking for. You may be sure that she was very pleased. She begged the king to do what the knight requested, as she thought she would then be rid of him and never see him again in her lifetime. She begged the king until he granted Guingamor the request. (207–44)

Guingamor sought leave to depart and returned joyfully to his lodging. He could not sleep that night, and when he saw that dawn was breaking he quickly ordered preparations for his departure. He sent for his companions and all the king's retinue. They were apprehensive on his account and would have hindered and prevented him very readily, if they could. He sent for the king's hunting horse, which the king had lent him the previous night, together with the brachet and his good horn, which he would not have given him for his weight in gold. Guingamor arranged to take with him two packs of the king's good dogs and did not forget his bloodhound. The king went out to escort him, and the inhabitants of the city, the burgesses, the peasants and the courtiers also came along with him, displaying great sorrow and weeping profusely. Even the ladies went along, all showing wondrous grief on Guingamor's account. The huntsmen went ahead to the thicket closest to the city, taking the bloodhound with them. They looked for the boar's tracks, as that was where it usually dwelt. They found the tracks and recognised them, having seen them several times. They tracked the creature until they found it under a bush with thick branches. Then they led the bloodhound forward and let it bark, forcibly driving the boar from the thicket. Guingamor blew the horn and ordered one of the packs to be unleashed, then he had the other one led forward. They were to wait for him close to the forest, but not to enter it. (245–86)

Guingamor began the pursuit, and the boar, having left the thicket very much against its will, started turning this way and that. The dogs followed it, barking furiously, and they drove it close to the forest. But they were all tired out and could not work effectively, so the huntsmen had the other pack unleashed. Guingamor continued to blow his horn and the dogs kept yelping, following the boar on all sides, close on its heels. It would never return to the thicket again, but plunged into the forest, and Guingamor went after it, carrying behind him the brachet he had borrowed from the king. Those who were accompanying him, the king and all his knights, and the others from the city, came to a halt outside the forest, as the king would not let anyone proceed further. They remained there as long as they could hear the sound of the horn and the dogs barking. Then they all turned back and commended Guingamor to God in heaven. The boar went off into the distance, tiring out most of the dogs, so Guingamor took the brachet, removed its leash and sent it after the boar, which it pursued eagerly. The knight made a great effort to blow the horn loudly and to chase after his uncle's brachet, to help it. Its soft yelping pleased him greatly, but in next to no time he lost both the brachet and the boar, hearing neither barking nor snorting. Very upset and displeased, he made his way through a dense part of the forest, thinking he had lost the brachet. He had never felt so unhappy because his uncle loved it dearly. (287–329)

He went on through the forest and paused on a high mound, feeling very sad and bewildered. The weather was clear and the day beautiful. He heard the birds all around, but paid no heed to them. He did not stop there long, as he heard the brachet barking in the far distance, so he began blowing his horn, feeling full of anguish until he could see it. Then he saw both the brachet and the boar approaching in an open beech grove and crossing his path towards the heath. He thought he could catch up with the boar quickly, so he spurred on and rode hard, not wishing to delay. He rejoiced in his heart, telling himself that if he could capture it and return safely, he would be talked about for evermore and would win great fame thereby. Filled with great joy, he put the horn to his mouth and blew it. It gave forth a wondrous sound. The boar passed in front of him with the brachet in close pursuit. Guingamor spurred on with great speed through the dangerous heath and across the perilous river, straight through the meadow with its lush grass and flowers. He had almost caught up with it, when he looked ahead and saw the walls of a mighty palace, which was skilfully built with no mortar. It was enclosed in green marble, and over the entrance was a tower that, to look at, appeared to be of silver; it gave off marvellous brightness. The doors were made of fine ivory and inlaid with gold trefoils, with no bar or lock. (330–71)

Guingamor approached at great speed, and seeing that the door was wide open and the entrance completely free he decided to enter it and to find some worthy knight who was responsible for guarding this enclosure. He hoped to enquire and discover who was the lord of this palace, as he had never seen one so splendid and took great pleasure in looking at it. He thought he would be able to catch up with the boar before it had gone far, because it was very weary. He went inside, still on horseback, and paused in the middle of the palace, looking all around him. He found nothing at all there, however, but discovered that everything was of pure gold. Even the rooms all around were made of stones of paradise. But what seemed the worst thing to him was that he found there neither man nor woman. On the other hand, he rejoiced at having come upon such an adventure, which he could relate in his own land. He returned at great speed, through the meadows alongside the river, but he could not see any trace of his boar. He had lost both it and the dog. (372–400)

Now Guingamor was distraught. 'By my faith', he said, 'I am betrayed. I can well consider myself a fool, for in order to gaze at a dwelling I think I have wasted my efforts. If I do not have my dog and lose the boar, I will never again feel joy or happiness, nor will I return to my country.' Deep in thought, Guingamor made for the highest part of the forest. He began to listen to see if he could hear the brachet barking, and he heard it away to his right. He listened hard, with great concentration, until he heard it afar off, and the boar too. He began blowing his horn again and set off to catch them up. The boar crossed his path ahead and Guingamor chased after it, urging on and hallooing the brachet. He reached the edge of the heath and came upon a spring there, beneath a leafy olive tree, green and flowering and with thick branches. The spring was limpid and beautiful, with gold and silver shingle. A maiden was bathing in it while another was combing her hair and a handmaiden was washing her feet and hands. She had beautiful limbs, long and smooth. There was nothing in the world as beautiful as this maiden, who was naked, neither the lily nor the rose in bloom. As soon as Guingamor saw her, he was struck by her beauty. He reined in his horse, and seeing her clothes on a large tree, he went over without delay and put them in the hollow of an oak tree. After capturing the boar, he intended to come back and speak to the maiden, whom he knew well would not go away naked. But she caught sight of the knight and called to him, addressing him imperiously: 'Guingamor, leave my clothes alone! May it never please God, nor may he wish that it should be related among knights how you committed such a great wrong as to steal a maiden's clothes in the depths of the forest. Come forward, do not be afraid, and lodge with me henceforth. You have wearied yourself all day and hardly had any success.' (401–56)

Guingamor made his way towards her, carrying her clothes and proffering them to her. He thanked her for her offer, but said he would not stay with her, as he had lost track of his boar and the brachet that had been following it. The maiden replied: 'My friend, no one in the world would ever be able to find it again, however hard he tried, except with help from me. Give up your foolish venture and come with me on the following promise. I swear to you faithfully that I will deliver to you the captured boar and give you the brachet to take back to your land after three days. I give you my word.' 'Fair one', replied the knight, 'I will stay with you willingly on the condition you have stated.' He dismounted and stopped there while the maiden quickly dressed, and the handmaiden who was with her brought her a mule, well decked with fine equipment, and a palfrey for her own use. No count or king had a better one. Guingamor followed the maiden, lifted her into her saddle, then mounted and took hold of his reins. He glanced at her repeatedly with a joyful heart and saw that she was very tall, noble and fair. He readily set his heart on having her love him as a mistress, and he looked at her lovingly, begging that she grant him her love. Never before had his heart been troubled by any woman he had seen, nor had he ever been concerned about love. She was wise and well bred and replied to him that she would gladly love him, which gave him great joy, and once her love was granted he embraced and kissed her. (457–502)

The handmaiden rode on ahead, spurring on until she came to the palace where Guingamor had been. She decked it out sumptuously and had the knights mount their horses and ride to meet their mistress on account of her beloved, whom she was bringing. There were some three hundred or more of them, all clothed in silk tunics with gold thread, and each one accompanied by his beloved. The company made a fine spectacle. Here were young men carrying sparrowhawks, and beautiful goshawks, moulted and unmoulted. There were as many again in the palace, playing backgammon or chess. When Guingamor had dismounted, he saw the ten knights who had been lost from his land when they had gone out to hunt the boar. They all rose to their feet to meet him, greeting him with great joy, and Guingamor embraced them. He was magnificently lodged that night, with good food in abundance and with excellent amusements and great splendour. There was music from harps and viols,[1] and songs from youths and maidens. (503–30)

He marvelled at the noble company, at the beauty and the richness. He thought he would stay there for only two days, intending to return home on the third. He would have his dog and his boar, and he would tell his uncle about the adventure he had witnessed, then return to his beloved. But it turned out quite differently for him, for he had been there for three hundred years [when he left]. The king and his retinue were dead, as were all those of his lineage, while the cities he knew were destroyed and had fallen into ruin. Guingamor requested leave to depart in order to

[1] A viol (Old French *viele* or *viole*) was a stringed instrument used by minstrels to accompany their songs.

return to his country, and he asked his beloved to give him back the boar and his brachet. 'My dear', she said, 'you will have them, but you will leave to no avail. Three hundred years have passed while you have been here. Your uncle and his courtiers are dead and you have no friend or relative there. One thing I will tell you: there is no man old enough who could tell you anything about them, however much you were to ask him.' 'My lady', he replied, 'I cannot believe that what you say is true. But if it is as you have said, I will come back straightaway and return here, I promise you.' She said to him: 'I warn you, when you have crossed over the river to return to your own country, do not eat or drink, however hungry you may feel, until you have returned here, for you will quickly come to grief.' She had his horse fetched and the great boar carried in, and she returned his dog to him on its lead. (531–74)

He took the head of the boar, for he could carry no more, mounted his horse and rode away. His beloved accompanied him to the river, which he crossed over in the boat. She commended him to God and left him. The knight set off and continued that day until noon, without ever leaving the forest. It was so unpleasant and overgrown that he did not recognise it at all. In the distance, to his left, he heard a woodsman chopping with his axe and making his fire and charcoal. Guingamor spurred on towards him and greeted the poor man, asking him where his uncle the king was and in what castle he was staying. The charcoal burner replied briefly: 'By my faith, my lord, I know nothing of that. The king you are enquiring about died more than three hundred years ago, to my knowledge, together with all his men and retinue, and the castles you mentioned have all been destroyed long since. There are some old folk who often tell of that king and his nephew, that he was extremely brave and how he went hunting in this forest, but never returned afterwards.' Guingamor heard what he said and was filled with great sorrow for the king he had lost in this way. He replied to the charcoal burner: 'Listen to me and to what I say. I will tell you my adventure, for I am the one who went hunting, intending to return with the great boar.' Then he began telling him of the palace he had come across and what it was like inside, of the maiden he had found and how she had lodged him for two whole days. 'Then I departed,' he said. 'She gave me my boar and my dog.' (575–624)

Guingamor handed him the head of the boar and instructed him to keep it until he got back to his house and to tell the people in the land what he had told him. The poor man thanked him and Guingamor took his leave of him, setting off back. It was already well past nones and the day was approaching evening. The knight felt such great hunger that he thought he would go raving mad. Beside the path he was following he came upon a wild apple tree, laden with large apples. He went up to it, picked three of them and ate them. In so doing, he acted foolishly, for he forgot what his beloved had stipulated. As soon as he tasted them, he became disfigured and decrepit, and so enfeebled in his body that he could not help falling from his horse. He lost the use of his hands and feet, but when he was able to speak he began to lament feebly. The charcoal burner had followed him and saw clearly what had happened to him. He did not think that there was any hope of him surviving until evening. As he started to go towards him, he saw two maidens arrive on horseback, beautifully dressed in rich attire. They dismounted beside Guingamor and rebuked him strongly, reproaching him for not adhering to the advice which he had heeded badly. Carefully and gently they lifted him up and set him on a horse. They took him to the river and crossed over in a boat, with his brachet and his hunting horse. The peasant turned back and that night went to his dwelling, carrying the boar's head. He related the adventure wherever he went. He affirmed it and swore it on oath, presenting the head to his king, who had it displayed at many a festival. So that the story could continue to be told, the king had a lay composed about it. It retained the name of *Guingamor* and that is what the Bretons call it. (625–78)

5. *Desiré*

Introduction

Desiré is preserved in two manuscripts: (i) S and (ii) MS Cologny-Genève, Bibliotheca Bodmeriana, Codex Bodmer 82 (MS P in Prudence Tobin's edition). Our translation is based on S, a slightly longer version of the story.

The tale begins in Scotland with the hero's parents, who are childless until they visit St Giles in Provence. The wife soon becomes pregnant and they name their son Desiré (the Desired One'). When he grows up, he enters the service of a king and, having been made a knight, wins fame. Summoned by his father, he returns home. While there, he goes riding in the forest and decides to visit a hermit he had known in his youth. On the way he encounters a beautiful maiden whom he attempts to woo, but she persuades him to let her take him to her mistress. She turns out to be a fairy and Desiré falls in love with her. They become lovers, and when he leaves her she gives him a ring, telling him he will lose it if he transgresses in any way. Thereafter, they meet regularly and she bears him two children. Having been away fighting a war for his king, Desiré returns home and one day visits the hermit to whom he confesses his love for the fairy. The hermit imposes a penance and the ring immediately disappears. He cannot find his beloved at the usual meeting place. In despair at losing her, he becomes ill, and it is only after a year, when he is close to death, that the fairy appears to him. She reprimands him, but after this their relationship starts up again.

Several years later, while out hunting, Desiré and the king both shoot at a stag, but they miss their target and then cannot find their arrows. A youth appears, carrying the arrows and declaring that he is Desiré's son. He is taken to court to be with his father, but after a couple of months he suddenly leaves in order to return to his mother. A distraught Desiré rides after him and comes upon a dwarf who is cooking meat over a fire. The dwarf offers to take Desiré to a castle where his beloved is to be found. He shows her to him through a window, but in jumping in to get to her, Desiré injures himself. He is rescued and returned to the dwarf. The following Pentecost, when the king summons all his barons, a lady arrives with a boy and a girl. They are Desiré's children and she asks the king to dub the boy a knight and marry off the girl, while she herself will marry Desiré. These requests are granted. The king marries the girl himself and Desiré is taken to his bride's land, never to return.

Desiré shares with *Lanval*, *Graelen*t and *Guingamor* the theme of a knight falling in love with a fairy. As in *Lanval* and *Graelent*, the hero loses his beloved through a transgression, but he is eventually forgiven and disappears with her to her land, never to be seen again. The hero in *Desiré* is a well-rounded courtly knight who, before becoming involved in a love relationship, first establishes a reputation for himself in tournaments. Significantly, the fairy seems to have chosen him as her lover specifically because of his reputation for valour and his achievements as a distinguished knight, for when she grants him her love she lectures him on the knight's duty not to abandon chivalry but to maintain his reputation. Desiré subsequently distinguishes himself in war (there is a much longer description of the war in the version in S than in the equivalent passage in P). But when the fairy's love is withdrawn, Desiré sinks into lethargy, thereby revealing the level of inspiration that love can bestow on chivalric achievement. *Desiré* also manages to blend the supernatural world discreetly into the real feudal and courtly world. The supernatural world is represented by the fairy, the dwarf, who is clearly associated with her, and the mysterious loss and retrieval of the arrows. But the blending of the two worlds is achieved largely through the light touch of Christian spirituality that runs throughout the narrative. This begins with the parents' trust in St Giles to perform a miracle for them, which he does, and continues with Desiré's visits to the chapel and the hermit, his confession and the fairy's surprising offer to accompany Desiré to church and, visible to him but not to others, partake of the communion alongside him. This serves to soften the image of the fairy as an otherworldly creature and to dispel any hint of evil in her. There is also eventually a Christian marriage between her and Desiré. But in the end, Desiré finds the fairy's world more enticing than his own.

Further Reading

Gosman, Martin, 'Le Lai de *Desiré*: une lecture', *Rapports – Het Franse Boek*, 52 (1982), 97–110.

Sturm-Maddox, Sara, 'Configuring Alterity: Rewriting the Fairy Other', in *The Medieval 'Opus': Imitation, Rewriting, and Transmission in the French Tradition. Proceedings of the Symposium Held at the Institute for Research in Humanities October 5–7 1995, The University of Wisconsin-Madison*, ed. Douglas Kelly (Amsterdam and Atlanta, GA: Rodopi, 1996), pp. 125–38.

Subrenat, Jean, 'L'Aveu du secret d'amour dans le lai de *Desiré*', in *Mélanges de langue et de littérature françaises du Moyen Age et de la Renaissance offerts à Charles Foulon, II, Marche Romane*, 30 (1980), pp. 277–86.

Verhuyck, Paul, 'Le Lai de *Desiré*: narrèmes hagiographiques', *Les Lettres Romanes*, 40 (1986), 3–17.

Translation

I have devoted my care and attention to relating an adventure, from which those who were alive at the time composed a lay, so that it would be remembered. It is the lay of Desiré, who was so brave and wise.[1] (1–6)

In Scotland there is a region lying beyond the broad expanse of ocean called Calder, near the Blanche Lande. There lies the Black Chapel, which is very beautiful and of which tales are told. There once was a vavasour living there, who was highly regarded in his country.[2] All the land he possessed he held in chief from the King of Scotland. He had a wife in keeping with his rank, and he loved her greatly for she was very wise. But misfortune afflicted them in that they had no children. This distressed them terribly and they prayed very frequently to God that in his compassion he would comfort them and give them a son or a daughter.

[1] In the manuscript we are translating (S), the hero's name appears within the text as Desirré or Desirrez. In v. 5, and also at the end of the text (v. 822), the title of the lay is given as *Desirré*. In the manuscript edited by Tobin (P), the name of the hero is Desiré or Desirez and the title of the text is *Dessiré* (v. 5) and *Desiré* (v. 764). In modern usage, to which we adhere, both the hero and the text are usually referred to as Desiré.

[2] A vavasour, literally a vassal of vassals, was a minor nobleman who held his fief from a king or great lord. He would have his own vassals and is a not uncommon, and often very positive, character in courtly literature.

One night, as they lay in bed, the lady said to her husband: 'My lord, I have heard it said that in Provence, beyond the sea, there is a most blessed holy relic, and ladies go there with their husbands. No one ever makes a request at such a time of need without receiving help in some way, and without the request being answered. By God's grace, Giles has received the specific gift of granting the birth of children. I have seen some of them, but I do not know how many. My lord, let us make preparations, cross the sea and go there.' (7–38)

The lord fully agreed to this and they prepared their journey. They crossed the sea without delay and went to pray at the shrine of St Giles, presenting to him on his altar a solid silver statue weighing, I think, seven marks. They asked him for a son or daughter, and when they had finished their prayer they went back to their own country. Before she reached home, the lady became pregnant with a son. Her husband was filled with joy and had never been so happy, as was all his family. When their son was born, they named him Desiré, as such a long time had passed without their having a child. Now St Giles had performed a miracle. They brought up their son and looked after him as someone they cherished. He was handsome in body and face, and when he reached the age at which he could be parted from them, they sent him to serve a king. The king taught him about hunting and hawking by the river, and gladly took charge of him. The king loved and cherished him greatly, and he dubbed him a knight. (39–68)

When Desiré had become a knight, he promptly crossed the sea. He spent time in Normandy and attended tournaments in Brittany. He was highly esteemed by the French and loved by everyone else, as chivalry was then greatly valued. If a knight from another land left his homeland to seek his fortune, either in tournaments or in war, he was never attacked on all sides or ransomed by his companions. Desiré was there for seven years without ever returning home. He distinguished himself and jousted a great deal, until he was summoned by the king. He returned to his own land and was very well looked after by the king who, because of his prowess, cherished him greatly and showed him very great honour. Desiré was brave and very handsome, and everyone praised him. He would never leave the king except to go to Calder. (69–92)

His father summoned him to go and visit his mother. This was at the beginning of summer, and on the fourth day of his visit he arose early, dressed and made himself ready. He was suitably attired in the finest quality fabric, in breeches, shirt and fine linen which were whiter than an April flower, and he wore a mantle of miniver. He asked for his spurs, intending to go out riding for pleasure. He requested his good horse, which was large and handsome, and he himself was noble and fair in body, face and bearing, with no blemish on him. He mounted his horse and was a very fine knight, with fine legs and feet. Sitting squarely in his stirrups, he spurred his horse and rode down through the town. He departed unaccompanied, making his way towards the Blanche Lande. He saw the trees, white and in flower, and heard the cries of the birds. His blood stirred and started and his heart leapt, for the birdsong delighted him greatly. He made his way into the forest, and in the clearing within the wood a holy man had his hermitage. Desiré used to go and visit him, and in his youth he would often partake of his fruit when he travelled around and went riding with his father. He decided to visit him and, if he found him, to speak with him. (93–132)

As he made his way towards the chapel, he looked and saw a maiden dressed in dark purple and wearing a very fine chemise. Her complexion was fair and rosy, and her body was shapely and noble. She was bareheaded, with no wimple, and she had bare feet because of the dew. She was making her way to a spring that gushed forth beneath a great tree, and in her hand she held two golden basins. The knight was not uncourtly, rather he dismounted and greeted her, intending to make her his beloved. He laid her down upon the fresh grass, and I think he would have had his way with her, but she cried out to him for mercy: 'Knight, away with you! You will not gain much if you cause me dishonour. Do not do anything reprehensible. Let me be, I beg you. I belong to a maiden and there is none more beautiful in the whole world. I will let you see her shortly and, if you are able, make sure that she does not escape you, whatever I tell you. If you are well loved by her, you will not go astray for any reason. You will have an abundance of gold and silver entirely at your disposal. Do not think I am lying to you, and if she is not to your liking you cannot fail with me, for I will do whatever you wish. Trust me completely, for I give you my word. I will help you whenever you need, in whatever way I can.' (133–72)

When Desiré heard what she said, he let her go and the maiden took him straight to where her mistress was, in a bower. The bed was ready. Its coverlet had a checker board pattern with two pieces of silk brocade, very fine and costly. It was surrounded by fresh flowers and in front of the lady a young girl was sitting. The maiden who had brought Desiré stopped some distance away and called to him: 'Vassal', she said, 'pay heed now.

In that bower over there, take what I promised you. Have you ever seen such a beautiful countenance, such beautiful hands or arms, or such an attractive and tightly laced body, more beautiful or finer textured hair, any more comely or better plaited? Never was such a beautiful maiden born. I have acquitted myself well with you. Go on in, fear nothing, for you are a good and valiant man. Venus, the goddess of love, did not have such beauty, or such love as the maiden has whom you can now see. Do not be afraid.' (173–200)

Desiré heard her and made his way over to the maiden, leaving his horse to roam. When the maiden saw him, she waited no longer, but left the bower and entered the thickest part of the wood. Desiré went after her, saw her and followed her closely. He moved quickly and was not faint-hearted, so he very soon caught up with her. He seized her by the right hand and spoke pleasantly to her: 'Fair one', he said, 'speak to me. Why are you fleeing so fearfully? I am a knight from this land and I will be your vassal and your beloved. I will serve you as best I can in order to gain your love.' The maiden thanked him for this, bowed low to him and said she was not fleeing from him, or rejecting his offer. She granted him her love and he did with her as he would with his beloved. He spent a long time with her and left her very unwillingly. But she gave him leave and told and instructed him about where he could speak to her and how he could find her. 'Beloved Desiré', she said, 'you will go to Calder and I will give you a ring made of gold. One thing I will tell you. Mind that you do not transgress, if you are striving to love sincerely. If you do transgress in any way, you will lose the ring at once, and if it should come about that you lose the ring you will have lost me forever, with no chance of getting me back or seeing me again. Mind that you act correctly and do not let me become a hindrance to you. I have no regard for a knight who does not attend tournaments frequently. A knight who has a beloved must certainly perform deeds of valour, spend very lavishly, and continually maintain a good house. Before you had my love, you were a man of great valour. It is not right that a knight's standing should suffer because of love. (201–54)

She placed the ring on his finger and he kissed her and drew her towards him before mounting his horse and returning to his lodging. He spent lavishly and distributed many gifts. He was not slow to do good deeds and gave away more in a single month than the king did in half a year. Because of his beloved, whom he adored, he returned to that region. They spoke to each other frequently until, I understand, he had a son and daughter by her. She did not tell him this and he knew nothing about it. (255–68)

On one occasion the king had summoned him and taken him out of the land, to act as his companion in a time of crisis and to wage war a long way away.[3] The war went very well for him and he defeated his enemy. He besieged him in one of his castles, but before long his enemy emerged from the castle together with many knights, fully armed, I can inform you, in order to engage in combat with the king and his men. On that occasion he jousted with Desiré before the castle gate. They struck blows against each other's shields and their coats of mail felt the force of their swords. The owner of the castle was felled, and Desiré immediately pulled up his horse, which was swift, took hold of his sword and struck him with it. He urged him to surrender, which he did most unwillingly, but when he saw that he could not hold out against Desiré, he gave him his sword by the blade. Desiré handed the knight over to the king, and the knight begged him for mercy so much that the king made peace with him, while safeguarding himself as his lord. The knight agreed to this peace and swore before the king on holy relics. (269–98)

When they had returned home, Desiré took leave of the king and went back to his own land in Calder, where he was born. Having arrived there, he stayed overnight and then rose early next morning. He mounted his horse and for relaxation made his way directly towards the Blanche Lande, where he was accustomed to find his beloved. All alone, I can tell you, he came upon the hermitage where lived the saintly hermit who knew the knight. He decided to go and speak with this holy man and make his confession to him, not knowing when he would come there again. He opened the door, went inside and found him in the chapel. 'My lord', he said, 'I have come to make confession and be absolved.' The hermit agreed to this, and Desiré sat down and bowed. He revealed to him those of his sins of which he was sure and certain. He confessed to him about his beloved and about how she first came to him. The hermit gave him advice and imposed a penance on him. (299–328)

When he had been absolved and blessed, he returned to his horse, used the stirrup to mount and grasped the reins. He looked at his fingers and then at his hand, but could not see his ring. I can tell you that he was not

[3] In Tobin's base manuscript the passage from this point to the end of our paragraph is missing. Thus, from this point on, Tobin's line references are very different from our own.

pleased by this, for he knew full well that he had lost it. He had never felt so sorrowful, and he left, remaining there no longer. He quickly made for the place where he expected to find his beloved, for he wanted to speak to her. He stayed there all day without seeing her or speaking to her. Since he could not speak to her, he considered himself to be very unfortunate. 'Fair love', said Desiré, 'where are you, since you do not come? Are you angry with me? I must die if I do not see you. You have taken your ring from me. I know well that I have lost it through you. I will never again feel joy or pleasure. Alas, unhappy me, what have I done wrong? I love you more than anything else and you are certainly not behaving properly. The hermit gave me confession, but he never spoke ill of you. I asked for pardon from him for my sins. If I have acted unreasonably, fair one, do not get angry. Impose my penance on me. I will abandon what the hermit told me to do and the fasting he imposed on me when you wish it and do your bidding.' (329–64)

He was unable to beg for mercy sufficiently for her to be willing to speak to him. His heart was filled with sorrow and he roundly cursed the hermitage, and likewise the hermit himself, whom he cursed repeatedly, also the horse that carried him there and himself for ever having spoken to him. He cursed himself a great deal in a short time, saying more than a hundred times that he should not remain there. He lamented profoundly, praying more than a hundred times that the whole place should be shamed and consumed by hellfire, along with the hermit who lived there and the mouth with which he had spoken, and all those who had confessed to him or who would ever speak to him. (365–82)

When he saw that all this was to no avail, he was forced to return home. Extremely upset, he went back to Calder. His grief caused him to become lethargic, and shortly afterwards he fell ill. His great joy turned to sadness and his song to tears. He languished for a year or more, and everyone thought he was finished. They all said he was dying, and he himself said so too. He lay in bed for a year, but hear what happened at the end of it. One day his squires and servants left him sleeping and went off to amuse themselves, not daring to wake him. When he had slept for a long time, he woke up and regained his wits. He began to realise that he was alone and this distressed him greatly. (382–404)

As he lay in such anguish, his beloved came to speak to him. He looked at her and recognised her, and with the joy that this gave him he raised himself up on his elbow in the bed. She spoke to him, saying: 'Fair lord, you are in a sorry state, quite out of your mind and lost. Why are you letting yourself die? Make some effort. This is of no use. I have hated you for some while, and indeed you deserved it thoroughly. You spoke of me in your confession and you will never get me back. Was I such a burden to you? It was not such a great sin, for I have never been married, or engaged or promised in marriage, and you do not have a wife. I think you will regret this. When you sought confession, I knew well that you would lose me. What is the use of confessing a sin if one cannot abandon it? You have often feared that I had bewitched you. Do not be concerned about this, for I am not of evil origin. When you go to church to hear mass and pray to God, you will see me standing beside you and partaking of the blessed bread. You have wronged me greatly, but because I have loved you so much I am willing to give you another chance. You can see me every day, laughing and sporting with you, so abandon your grief. But you will certainly not have anything more, nor will you ever again seek confession.' (405–44)

The knight replied to her: 'Fair lady, I thank you. The comfort you give me has cured me and restored me to health. Nothing has ever given me such pleasure.' He kissed her. Then she departed and he remained there, happy and joyful. He was completely cured and filled with happiness, and because of the joy he anticipate he recovered from his great torment. When he went to the church to pray, he saw his beloved standing next to him, eating the bread that was blessed, making the sign of the cross and blessing him. He spoke to her repeatedly and, having recovered, he felt no pain. He travelled about and spent money, just as he had done before he had incurred his beloved's hatred. (445–62)

The king had a great love for him and never left him day or night. On one occasion they went hunting in the forest for relaxation. Their bows and arrows were brought along with them, as they intended to hunt in the castle's enclosure. The king and Desiré came to a stop near a large tree, where both of them shot at a huge stag, but both missed it. The arrows fell close to them on the grass, where they could see them. They were disappointed at having missed, and throwing down their bows and loosening the strings they went to fetch their arrows, where they had seen them fall. But they could not find them or see them. The king said to Desiré: 'We have been completely bewitched. Our arrows fell here, before my eyes. I saw them. Now we cannot find either of them. That has to be seen as very curious.' (463–86)

As they were speaking in this way, they saw a youth in front of them. He was handsome, fair and grown up, and he wore a tight-fitting coat of red silk material. He was remarkably handsome and fair. His hair was blond and curly, and his face well proportioned and highly coloured. He held the arrows in his hand and was not uncourtly in his speech. He first of all greeted the king and gave him back his arrow, then he gave Desiré his and spoke to him very politely: 'My lord', he said, 'you are my father and my mother has sent me here. She wants me to be with you, so that I can see and get to know my family. When you first spoke to her, in the woodland where you fathered me, she gave you a little ring made of gold. Then you lost it and this distressed you greatly. I have brought it here with me. Put it on your finger, my lord.' (487–510)

Desiré clearly recognised the ring. He took hold of the young boy and embraced him gently. He kissed him time and time again, on his eyes, his face and his chin. Immediately the king and all his companions kissed him, making a great fuss of the boy. Desiré told the king where the boy had been fathered. They took him away with them and cherished him greatly. Desiré loved him and held him so dear that he could not part with him day or night. When the boy had been with him for two months and come to know his family, he rose early one morning, got dressed and made himself ready. He mounted his horse and went to meet his father as he was returning from church. Desiré was just about to get on his horse when the boy said: 'My lord, listen to me. I wish to take leave of you. I must go to my lady, for I cannot remain here any longer.' 'Come now, fair son', said Desiré, 'by God's saints, do not kill me! I would certainly rather be dead than see you leave me.' 'My lord', he said, 'I must do this.' He spurred his horse and set off, departing at a gallop. (511–43)

Desiré mounted his horse, keen to catch up with his son but fearing he had lost him. He spurred after him, repeatedly calling him by name and begging him to stop and speak with him for a while. But the boy did not listen to him and carried on along the straight path until he entered the forest. Desiré followed him all day long till nightfall, but the youth rode hard, and Desiré made as much haste as he could until his horse stumbled. He collided with a large tree and fell backwards on to the ground. He got back on his feet and led his horse. That day Desiré suffered anguish and pain. He lost his son, not knowing which way he had gone. But he had not gone far in the wood when he glanced over to the right and caught sight of a fire beneath an oak tree that was broad and leafy. Do you know what Desiré thought when he saw and came across this fire? That some nobleman was sleeping there who was going hunting the next day, or who had been out hunting that day and was spending the night in that place. He made his way very quickly towards the light from the fire he could see, but found there a dwarf, all on his own and tightly clad in embroidered silk. He was grinding pepper in a mortar and roasting on the brazier pieces of meat from a huge, fully grown boar. (544–81)

Desiré approached and greeted the dwarf quietly, but the latter made no reply. He greeted him once again, more loudly, for he thought the dwarf was deaf or dumb. The dwarf went into the foliage, leaving the pepper and the mortar, and ran to get Desiré's horse. He took it to one side, removed the bridle and loosened the saddle. Then he gave the horse fresh grass. He returned to the knight, and from grasses, reeds and heather prepared a bed for him, throwing on to it and placing over it a large, embroidered coverlet. He made the knight sit down on it, but refused to speak to him and returned to the grinding of his pepper. When the pepper was well mixed into a sauce and the meal ready, he took two basins of gold in his hands and hung a towel around his neck. He gave the water to the knight and the towel to dry his hands. Desiré recognised the basins as soon as he saw them.The maiden whom he had first encountered on the heath had carried them, but he did not want to give any sign of this to the dwarf. The dwarf placed a cloth before him and the salt cellar and knives, and then two simnel cakes. He gave the knight wine in a large goblet of pure gold, and in a silver bowl he put in front of him the pieces of roast meat. The knight took a knife, cut off a large piece of meat and, dipping it into the pepper, offered it to the dwarf, who ate it. He removed the cover from the goblet and offered him a drink of wine first. Desiré never ate a morsel without offering one just as good to the dwarf. (582–628)

The dwarf saw that he was so well mannered, so noble, so handsome and so well educated that he could no longer maintain his unwillingness to speak to him. 'My lord knight', said the dwarf, 'you are not foolish or uncourtly, and you are welcome here. Even if I am to be beaten for it, if you please, I will speak to you and not keep up the prohibition. Nevertheless, I have been sent to meet you, in order to give you lodging and serve you, so rejoice. I was fully aware of your coming.' The knight replied to him: 'My friend, many thanks. May good fortune favour the person who sent you here and who has given me joy in this respect.' The dwarf replied: 'It is your beloved, who loves you more than her life.' 'My beloved! O God', said Desiré, 'now I have all I could desire.' 'In faith, my lord, you are right, for I will do my very best to enable you to speak with her. If you are willing to go with me, I will take you close to her chamber, so that I can show you her bed.' 'My friend', said the knight, 'I will go with you most willingly.' (629–58)

When they arose from their meal, the dwarf took Desiré to the castle where his beloved was. They approached the chamber, finding no door or window, except for one window at the far end up on the right. Inside they could see burning candles that gave off a great light. In the chamber there was a bed, well equipped and well prepared; two maidens were lying in it and I believe that they were asleep. The dwarf called to Desiré and showed him how things were. 'My lord', he said, 'look over there! That is your beloved who is lying there, and that is her sister on the other side. Go on in, do not be concerned. You will find a maiden there whom I think you will recognise. The girl is sewing by candlelight a tunic that belongs to my lady.' (659–80)

Desiré prepared himself and jumped through the window with his feet together, but he lost his footing and fell in front of the bed, wounding himself severely in the side. The whole chamber resounded and his beloved's sister awoke. She was very much afraid and cried out, which made the knights get up quickly and arm themselves. The maiden, who was awake and sewing the tunic, took the knight by the hand and led him outside, saying to him: 'My lord, I am giving you the reward I promised you. If you were captured in this room, you would, I assure you, be put to death. In the name of your honour, make sure that my service is not wasted if you ever come upon an opportunity to reciprocate.' 'Gladly, fair friend, by my faith, you can depend on me. If I were ever to find an opportunity, I would repay this service.' 'My lord, do not forget me.' 'I will not, my friend', he replied. (681–708)

The maiden led him away until they found the dwarf. She punched him in the chest, and said: 'Evil dwarf, fool! Why did you betray this noble man? Away with you, flee from here!' They departed at great speed and went straight back to their fire. Desiré felt that he was wounded. He reclined on the bed and considered himself to be greatly shamed. When he saw daylight, he grasped his saddle and mounted, then returned to his own land. His side was badly wounded, so he stayed there for a long time, until the king was due to hold court in his residence in Calder. At Pentecost he summoned all his barons and neighbours and many people went there, as they loved their lord. Desiré, who was on very good terms with the king, attended the festival. (709–32)

After leaving the church, where they had heard the service, the king was just about to eat, and was already seated at a high table, when a noble maiden came riding through the hall on an ambling mule, together with a young girl. They were richly dressed and their garments were worth a hundred silver marks. They rode on two white mules and carried two handsome sparrowhawks. They were gazed at in wonder by the king and by those who were with him. They were extremely beautiful in body, face and bearing. With them was a youth; there was none so handsome in the whole world. They came to a stop before the high table and the older of the maidens greeted the king. 'My lord', she said, 'listen to me. I have come here to you and wish to entrust this boy to you, for he is very noble and valiant. Give arms to this youth and marry off this maiden. The truth is that I am their mother and Desiré here is their father. You should be pleased to take care of the offspring of such a fine knight, and of a lady such as myself. I am doing you a very great honour today in setting out from my land and coming here to your court. Now tell me what you propose to do.' The king, in the hearing of all, granted her request and asked her to dismount. 'I should like you to stay with me, for before I leave the court I will have the young man dubbed and the maiden married.' 'King', she said, 'that cannot be. First my request will be carried out, then marry me to my beloved, because I want to take him away with me. We will then be together legitimately. He will spend all his days with me and never again seek confession, penance or pardon.' (733–82)

The king had arms brought with the intention of dubbing the young man the following day. He himself girded on his sword and then gave him the accolade. There were two [other] kings at the festival, one from Moray and one from Lothian. They fixed on his spurs in courtly fashion, on their knees. When he had been richly dubbed, the king, in the hearing of all his barons, told them that he would take the maiden and make her his queen. He would keep her for himself, for he had never seen anyone so beautiful. Desiré was nearby and very anxious to be married to his lady, and for her to be given to him there. They went together to the church, and there they were both wed. When they had returned, the maiden took her leave for she wanted to return to her own land. 'Desiré, fair beloved, mount your horse,' she said, 'and let us depart. Let us thank the King of Scotland, for your son has now been dubbed, you will leave him in this land, and your daughter is married. It has been a splendid day for us. Know in truth that they will come back to see us when they can.' Desiré mounted and left with his beloved, who took him away. He remained with her in such a way that he never came back. He no longer had any wish to return. Those who knew this adventure composed a lay about it, which is called *Desiré*. (783–822)

6. *Doon*

Introduction

Preserved in only one manuscript (S), *Doon* is set in both Britain (mainly Scotland) and France. At 286 lines, this lay is one of the shortest in the collection.

A beautiful maiden lives surrounded by female companions in the Chastel des Puceles (Castle of Maidens) in Daneborc (Edinburgh). Seeing marriage as a form of servitude, she refuses to marry and comes up with a plan to keep any suitors at bay. Thinking it to be an impossible task, she states that if she were to take a husband it would only be a man who could ride from Southampton to Edinburgh in one day. Surprisingly, some of her suitors succeed in this challenge, but no marriage takes place for she kills them during the night as they lie exhausted in the bed she has prepared for them. The challenge comes to the attention of a knight from Brittany, and thanks to his horse, Baiart, and his own wits, he not only completes the ride but also survives the attempt to kill him while he sleeps. He also overcomes a second, unexpected challenge: to ride in one day as far as a swan can fly. The maiden has no option but to marry him. However, after three days, he announces that he is returning to his own land and that she is pregnant with a son. He leaves a gold ring for the boy, telling his wife to send him, when he is fully grown, to the King of France to be raised and educated by him. The boy becomes the most valiant knight in France and eventually jousts with his father at a tournament, inflicting on him his first ever defeat. Doon recognises his son through the ring on his finger and they return to Britain, where husband and wife live happily ever after.

We are not told why Doon takes deserts his wife, but he may have felt that she had wronged him by the imposition of a second test of his suitability as a husband. Once more, there are numerous realistic elements in the story, but other aspects suggest the world of the supernatural. The marriage and the tournament that leads to the restoration of harmony between the couple are perfectly in line with feudal and chivalric ideals. But at the same time, both the wife, who murders her successful suitors, and Doon, who takes flight to his own land after his marriage and thereby inflicts a lengthy, and perhaps excessive, punishment on his wife, represent the cruelty typical of the fairy figure. The clearest non-realistic factor present in the narrative is Doon's ability to inform his new bride that she is pregnant by him with a son, and he is also able to tell her that in due course the son will be able to find his father. The instruction to his wife that she should send the boy to the court of the King of France to receive an education is perfectly normal practice, as an heir would not normally have been brought up in the household in which he was born.

There is a supernatural feel to Doon's ability to avoid dying in the lady's bed, especially when one considers his awareness that at daybreak he will no longer be at risk. His horse, Baiart, also seems to have magical properties. Together, Doon and Baiart give the impression of being able to handle whatever obstacles they might encounter. The maiden from Daneborc displays no obvious supernatural characteristics, but a number of factors, when taken together, suggest that she is not an entirely realistic figure: her status as mistress of the Castle of Maidens, her determination not to enslave herself through marriage when all those around her clearly expected her to take a husband, her imposition of an ordeal on her suitors and her capacity (but only during the hours of darkness) to put her successful suitors to death in a specially prepared bed without the knowledge of the members of her household.

The fact that the maiden of Daneborc has inherited her land and wealth, and that she is concerned about the loss of her independence if she marries, is perhaps unusual rather than unrealistic. When she marries, she has no love for her husband at first, but his extraordinary powers and ability to provide her with a son and heir explain why she waits for him and welcomes his return. Like his father, Doon's son clearly has the high level of chivalric prowess that contemporary society demanded in a suitable heir. Also realistic are the location of the tournament, at Mont-Saint-Michel in Brittany (Doon is a Breton knight), and Doon's crossing from Brittany to Southampton on his way to Edinburgh is perfectly normal.

As in *Melion*, there is in *Doon* an effective and harmonious balance between realism and the supernatural. If there is a clash within this story, it is not between the real world and the non-real world, but between the aspirations and fantasies of males and females. In this lay a supremely powerful and independent woman does her utmost to maintain her position in a world in which men strive to exert dominance over her through marriage. Both before and after her marriage, she controls the vassals (here called 'barons', v. 156) who hold lands from her, and she clearly wards off any external threats to her lands. She is thus a role model for the female members of the audience. The narrative also focuses on a knight who, in a fashion that would inspire male admiration, uses his prowess and special powers to tame this formidable lady and to take possession of her lands (when she does become Doon's wife, she makes him 'lord of her country', v. 160). Moreover, the couple produce a male heir who will secure the future and safety of their lands and who even succeeds in uniting his parents and ensuring that they can spend their later years together in peace and harmony.

Further Reading

Arthur, Ross G., 'The Ideology of the *Lai de Doon*', *Romance Quarterly*, 38 (1991), 3–13.

Curry, John, 'The Speed of a Horse and the Flight of a Swan', *AUMLA*, 90 (1998), 85–90.

Frizza, Katherine, 'Le Lai de *Doon*, ou le fonctionnement de la brièveté', *Médiévales*, 9 (1985), 55–63.

Translation

Doon is a lay that many people know. There is scarcely a good harpist who does not know how to play the melody, but I wish to tell and relate to you the adventure that made the Bretons call this lay *Doon*. It seems to me, if I recall correctly, that near Edinburgh, which is in the north, there once lived a maiden who was exceedingly courtly and beautiful. She held the land as her inheritance with no other lordship over it. She dwelt in Edinburgh and loved the place very much, and because of her and her damsels it was called the Castle of Maidens. The maiden I am telling you about became haughty on account of her wealth and she scorned all the men in the land. There was not one who was so renowned that she was prepared to love him, to wed him or to encourage him to woo her; she had no wish to enslave herself by reason of marriage. All the most valiant men in the land tried frequently to win her hand. They wanted her to take a husband, but she rejected them all outright. She would never take a husband, she said, unless he succeeded for the love of her in journeying in a single day from Southampton by the sea as far as the place where she dwelt. Such a man, she told them, she would wed. In this way she thought she would be rid of them, and they did leave her alone (1–36).

But things could not remain this way. When the men in the land heard of this – I will tell you the truth about it – many of them made the attempt, following the paths they were to take. Without delay they mounted great horses, which were strong and able to run well, for they had no wish to tarry. But many of them could not last the pace or complete the journey There were those who were successful, but they were weary and worn out. When they had dismounted and made their way up to the castle, the maiden came to greet them. She honoured them greatly and then had them taken all alone into one of her bedchambers to rest. In order to kill and trick them she had beds prepared for them with fine coverlets and fine sheets. The men who were exhausted and weary lay down and went to sleep. They died as they slept in the soft bed. The chamberlains found them dead and reported the news to their lady. This made her very happy because she had taken revenge on them. (37–64)

The news about the haughty maiden was carried far and wide. In Brittany beyond the sea it came to the ears of a knight, who was very brave, valiant, wise, courtly and daring. Doon was the man's name. He had a good horse, whose name was Baiart, and it was very swift. Not for two castles would he have given it away. He had such trust in his horse that he decided to take up the challenge for the maiden and the land, and to see whether he could win her. As soon as he could, he crossed the sea and arrived at Southampton. He sent word to the maiden and informed her through his messenger that he had arrived in the land. She should send trusted servants to him who would let him know the day she had told them he should depart. When she saw his messengers, she gladly sent her men to him. She appointed and set the day on which he should come to her land. It was one Saturday morning that Doon set out on the road. He rode so well that by the evening he had completed his journey and arrived in Edinburgh, where he was received with great joy. (65–96)

Not one of the knights and servants, great or small, did not honour him, serve him and make him very welcome. When he had spoken to the maiden, he was taken to a bedchamber to rest as soon as he wished. The knight ordered them to find him some dry firewood and bring it to him in the chamber. Then they should let him rest, for he was worn out from his travel. They did as he requested and he closed the door and locked it, not wanting anyone to spy on him. With a flint he made a fire, came close to the flames and warmed himself. At no time that night did he lie down in the bed that had been prepared for him. If this man, who was very weary and worn out, had wanted to lie down in this fine bed, misfortune would soon have befallen him. He who has the harder bed suffers less and recovers more quickly. In the morning, at daybreak, he came to the door and unlocked it. He lay down in the bed, covered himself up and slept in comfort. Those whose task it was to guard the chamber expected to find him dead, but they found him in good health. They were all happy and joyful. (97–128)

Doon rose early, dressed and made himself ready. He went to speak to the maiden and to ask her for what she had promised. The maiden replied to him: 'Friend, it cannot be so. You will have to make your body and your horse undergo further trials. In a single day you must travel as swiftly as a swan can fly. Then I will marry you without further ado.' He asked for a delay in this, until Baiart had been cared for and he himself had rested. The departure was fixed for the fourth day. Doon set off on his journey. Baiart sped along and the swan flew on. It was a wonder that the horse was not killed, but the swan could not fly as swiftly as Baiart could gallop. That night they reached a place where there was a splendid castle, where he was well received and his horse well rested. He remained there for as long as he wished. When he felt ready, he departed and went to Edinburgh. He asked for what had been promised. She could not delay the issue any longer, so she summoned all her barons and on their advice married Doon, making him lord of her land. (129–60)

When he had married the maiden, the celebrations lasted for three days. On the fourth day he rose early. His horse was brought to him and he commended his wife to God, because he intended to return to his own region. The lady wept and was grief-stricken at her beloved's departure. Tenderly she begged him for mercy, but it was to no avail. She beseeched him to stay and told him that he was betraying her. He refused to listen to her at all, for he was anxious to depart. 'My lady', he said, 'I am leaving. I do not know whether I will see you again. You are pregnant by me and you will, I know, have a son. You should keep my gold ring for him. When he is fully grown, you should give it to him, telling him to keep hold of it. Through the ring he will be able to find me. Send him to the king in France and let him be brought up and educated there.' He gave her the ring and she took it. Then he left, delaying no longer. He departed and remained there no more. She was very distressed and lamented greatly. She was pregnant, that is the truth. (161–89)

When her son was born, her household rejoiced. She looked after and cherished the child until he could ride a horse and go hunting and hawking by the river. She gave him his father's ring and told him to keep hold of it. The young man was made ready and sent to the King of France. He took with him a large amount of gold and silver and spent very generously. At court he was greatly loved, for he gave generous gifts, having been very well brought up. He remained in France until the king dubbed him a knight and he went in search of tournaments, seeking fame far and wide. He did not hear of any conflict without wishing to get there first. He was greatly loved by knights and very well thought of. There was no man of such valour in the land, and with him he had a great company of knights. (190–213)

The young man went to a tournament at Mont-Saint-Michel in Brittany; he wanted to encounter the Bretons. No one there jousted as much as he did, or won so much by his own hand. His father was on the opposing side and he was very keen to joust with the young man. Lance raised, he entered the ranks. He was envious of the other man's reputation. They spurred towards each other at full tilt and struck each other great blows. The son unhorsed the father. If he had known it was his father, he would have been very upset that he had done this. But he did not know who he was, and Doon did not recognise him; he had wounded him severely in the arm. When the tournament came to a close, Doon summoned the young man to come and speak with him and he spurred towards him. Doon addressed him: 'Who are you, fair friend, you who have knocked me down off my horse?' The young man replied: 'My lord, I do not know how it happened; those who were there know.' Doon heard what he said and replied, saying: 'Show me your hands at once.' The young man was not ill-bred. He took off his gauntlets straightaway and showed and proffered both his hands. (214–46)

When he saw the young man's hands, he recognised on his finger the ring he had given to his wife and was very happy and joyful. From the ring he had seen he recognised that this was his son and that he had fathered him. In everyone's hearing, he spoke to him, saying: 'Young man, I realised when you jousted with me today that you were of my lineage. You are very courageous. Never has a blow from a knight caused me to fall from my horse, and no one will ever unhorse me, however great a blow he may give me. Come and kiss me. I am your father. Your mother is a very proud woman. I won her with great effort. When I had married her, I departed and have never set eyes on her since. I entrusted this gold ring to her and told her to give it to you when she sent you to France.' 'My lord', said the son, 'that is the truth.' They kissed and embraced. Displaying great joy, they went back together to a lodging house. Then they made their way to England. The son took the father to his mother, who loved him dearly and desired him greatly. She received him as her lord, and afterwards they lived together in great honour. About Doon and his fine horse, and his son whom he loved dearly, and the journeys he made for the lady he loved, the Bretons composed the melody for the lay that is called *Doon*. (247–86)

7. *Espine*

Introduction

Espine (*Hawthorn*) is preserved in two manuscripts: (i) S and (ii) B: MS Paris, BNF, fr. 1553. They relate a broadly similar version of the tale, but our translation is taken from the version in S (Tobin's edition is based on B).

At the outset of the story, the hero and heroine are young children at court, the boy being the son of the king and a concubine and the girl the daughter of the queen by a previous marriage. From the start there is a close affection between them, which, as they grow up, develops into adolescent love. One day the queen finds them lying on the boy's bed together, kissing, and thereafter they are separated and watched closely. The youth is dubbed a knight, and when a maiden comes to court and states that on the eve of the feast of St John (June 24) more adventures occur at the Hawthorn Ford than anywhere else, the king's son, not having found any suitable adventures since being dubbed a knight, is determined to take up the implied challenge in order to test himself. On the appropriate evening he leaves, despite his father's efforts to stop him, and his beloved goes and sits under a fruit tree to pray for his safekeeping. She is then magically transported to the ford, and when he recognises her, the youth joyfully embraces her. A knight arrives on a white horse with red ears. He and the youth joust and the youth wins the horse, which he presents to his beloved. Two other knights appear and the youth defeats one of them. The other knight tells him that the horse he has won does not need feeding as long as its bridle is left on. He also jousts with the youth to enhance his renown, but the beloved steps in and all three knights disappear. Back at court the couple are married. One day the wife removes the bridle and the horse promptly disappears.

The portrayal of love in this lay is unusual in its scope, in that it starts with innocent childhood affection, develops into adult love and is tested first by enforced separation, then reinforced by chivalric deeds, before eventually ending in marriage. At the same time there is the commonplace blend of love and chivalry. When the young couple are separated, the youth asks to be made a knight. His unstated reason for this may well be that he wants to enhance his reputation and thereby make himself worthy of his beloved. Initially, his father had restricted him to engaging in contests near home, so he seizes the opportunity to keep vigil at the Hawthorn Ford. Fortunately for him, his beloved magically finds herself with him at the ford, so she is able to witness his prowess when confronted by a trio of adversaries. On their return to court, the adventures are publicly related and the news is joyfully received. The marriage then takes place.

The lay is also notable for its supernatural and folklore elements. The idea that strange things can happen on the eve of St John's feast belongs to folklore, while the ford is a traditional Celtic motif marking the separation between the real and supernatural worlds. It is from the far side of the ford that the three adversaries appear. The hawthorn bush is also a frontier symbol, while the fruit tree, under which the boy's beloved goes to rest and falls asleep, is associated with love. The maiden's magical transportation in her sleep is engineered by benign forces from the Other World, in response to her express wish to be reunited with her beloved. A further magical element is the horse won by the hero. It represents a gift from the Other World, and comes with the warning that it must be treated as stipulated: in this case the bridle should never be removed. For a while the hero is able to cherish his horse and to use it in many conflicts, until his wife, out of curiosity, or perhaps jealousy at the amount of attention it receives, removes the bridle and the horse disappears.

Although this lay has not always found favour with critics, it has the undoubted merit of portraying a love that grows and matures. It makes free use of a number of supernatural elements that propel the story towards a successful outcome for the couple. The author clearly regarded the hawthorn bush as the central defining element and so named the lay after it, thereby foregrounding the role of the supernatural within the tale.

Further Reading

Löfstedt, Leena, 'Une nouvelle lecture du *Lai de l'Espine*', *Neuphilologische Mitteilungen*, 101 (2000), 253–59.

Wais, Kurt, '*Lai de l'Espine*: Schionatulander und Iron der Brandenburger', in *Festschrift Wilhelm Giese: Beiträge zur Romanistik und Allgemeinen Sprachwissenschaft* (Hamburg: Helmut Buske, 1972), pp. 457–97.
Walter, Philippe, 'L'Épine ou l'arbre-fée', *PRIS-MA*, 5 (1989), 95–108.

Translation

Whoever may regard lays as fanciful, be assured that I do not regard them as lies. The adventures I have found, which are recounted in different ways, I have not told without proof. I am making known the stories that are still to be found in Caerleon, in the church of Saint Aaron, and they are known in Brittany and have been witnessed in many places. (1–10)

Because I have found it in writing, I wish to bring to your attention an adventure concerning two children, which has remained hidden for a long time. In Brittany there lived a youth, wise, courtly, brave and handsome. The son of a king and a concubine, he lived with his father and stepmother. The king cherished him, as he had no other children, and the queen loved him dearly. For her part, the queen had a daughter by another husband, a maiden who was wise and courtly. The daughter of a king, she was noble and beautiful. The children were both of the same lineage, but they were not the same age. The elder of the two, the boy, was only seven years old, and the two children loved each other dearly. Because they got on well, they readily played together, and in this way they fell in love, with the result that neither of them ever discovered anything without sharing it with the other. As far as I am aware, these children were brought up together. The girl would accompany the boy, and the man who had the task of guarding them allowed them everything, not forbidding them anything, neither food nor drink, except sharing the same bed. But this they had no wish to do. (11–43)

As soon as they were of an age when Nature could permit it, they turned their thoughts towards loving each other. Together they had formed a certain kind of love, which they had already maintained for many a day, but now there became lodged within them a love with which they were endowed by Nature. Neither of them was unaware of this, and Nature made them turn their attention to enjoying their love, by kissing and embracing each other. Eventually, she brought them to the point where she united them in this love, and all their earlier feelings were completely transformed. The more each of them experienced it, the more this love grew between them. Now they loved each other more loyally, and if they had shown as much good sense in concealing their new love as carefully as they had their former love, they would not have been caught out so easily. But they were soon discovered. (44–66)

It so happened that one day the youth, who was very courtly and handsome, returned from hawking by the river and his head ached because of the heat. As there was noise and clamour, he secretly went into a bedchamber to lie down quietly, in order to ease his pain a little. His beloved was in her chamber in front of her mother, the queen, who was giving her very good instruction. As soon as she heard that he had returned, she did not wait for any friend or companion, but without a word to anyone went straight into the chamber where her beloved was lying alone. He received her delightedly, for he had not seen her that day. Without the slightest concern, she lay down next to him and he kissed her passionately a hundred times. They certainly acted with great foolishness, for the queen discovered them. She went straight to the bedchamber, making her way there very quietly. There was no lock to keep her out, and finding the chamber unlocked she went in at once. She entered and found them lying together in a tight embrace. She clearly recognised the signs of the love that bound them together. (67–98)

The queen was very distressed. She seized the girl by the wrist, dragging her from the bed with some difficulty. She took her back to her bedchamber, scolding her all the while, and afterwards kept her in close confinement and punished her very severely. The girl suffered much anguish, and for his part the young man was grief-stricken when he heard of the beatings, the punishment and the chastisement her mother inflicted on her. He did not know what to do or what to say, for he realised that she had been shamed, that he too had been betrayed and that she was completely lost to him. He was distressed about his beloved, and so grief-stricken at what had happened that he did not dare leave his bedchamber. He gave himself up to grief. 'Alas!' he said. 'What shall I do? I will never be able to live without her. O God, what misfortune and what a catastrophe! How heedlessly I acted. Certainly, if I do not get my beloved back again, I know that because of her I will lose my life.' (99–124)

While he was lamenting in this way, the queen went to the king, giving him a full account of how the children had been behaving. The king replied to the queen that she should henceforth watch over the maiden and that he would do the same for the boy, making him remain at court. In this way they would be kept apart. 'Make sure that this affair remains a secret!'

Then they finished speaking, but the youth, who was bent on displaying his grief, did not delay for any reason, coming at once to his father and addressing him nobly. 'My lord', he said, 'I request a favour from you. If you wish to help me in some way, you should make me a knight, for I wish to go to another land to achieve fame as a mercenary. I have clung to the fireside for too long and I am a skilled swordsman.' The king did not refuse him, but did just as he was asked. Then he told him to remain in his court for a year, attending tournaments in the meantime and guarding passes and defiles, where many adventures occurred in that land for anyone who wished to seek them. The young man agreed to this for he dared not refuse. He remained with his father at court and the maiden remained in her mother's bedchamber. But they were both so closely guarded that they could not speak to one another and had no opportunity for anything, either to speak to, or to hear, each other, through messengers or in person. Their love thus tormented them all the more. (125–64)

A week before the Feast of St John, in the very same year as the youth was dubbed a knight, the king returned from hunting, having captured a large amount of fowl and game. For relaxation that night, he sat down after supper on a carpet in front of the high table, along with many courtly knights. His son was with him. They were listening to the lay of Alis, which was being played by an Irishman on his rote.[1] He sang and played it very sweetly. After this, he began another lay and there was no noise or disturbance from anyone. He played for them the lay of Orpheus, and when he had finished the knights immediately began to converse. They told of the adventures they had often witnessed, which had occurred in Brittany. Among them was a maiden, who said: 'At the Hawthorn Ford, on the night of the Feast of St John, more adventures occur than at any other time of the year, but no cowardly knight would ever go and keep vigil there on that night.' The youth, who was possessed of great daring, heard and listened to this, for sincethe time he had girded on his sword he had never encountered any adventure in which he could show under duress whether he was cowardly of brave. (165–98)

When the maiden's tale was over, the youth addressed the king and his barons. 'My lords', he said, 'I boast to you, in the hearing of everyone, great and small, that on the night spoken of by the maiden I will keep vigil at the Hawthorn Ford and confront my adventure there, whatever it might be, either pleasant or harsh.' When the king heard him, he was

[1] The rote was a five-stringed harp, somewhat like a zither.

grief-stricken and thought that these words were childish folly. 'Fair son', he said, 'abandon your stupidity.' He replied: 'I will not,' adding that he would still go. When the king heard that he would not give up his plan, he did not wish to oppose him any longer. 'Go then, in God's name,' he said, 'and be brave and confident. May God give you good fortune.' (199–216)

That night they all went to bed, but the knight waited impatiently until the seventh day arrived. His beloved was filled with dread, for she had heard the news that on that night he was to go and keep vigil, as best he could, at the adventurous ford. When the day drew towards evening, the knight was filled with hope. He armed himself with good armour, mounted a good horse and went straight to the Hawthorn Ford. What did the maiden do? She went alone into a garden, for she wanted to pray for her beloved, that God would bring him back safe and sound. She let out a sigh, lamented and then sat down beneath a fruit tree, grieving to herself: 'O God', she said, 'Heavenly Father, if it were ever possible, or could be, that a prayer, or an adventure, came to pass for anyone, so that they knew joy once more, fair Lord God, now I beseech you to let my beloved be with me, and I with him, if this could be. O God, how relieved I would be! No one knows what a hard life I lead, and no one could know it, apart from the person who loved someone he could not have at any price. But such a person knows this by heart.' (217–50)

Thus spoke the maiden, seated beneath the newly grafted tree. For some time she was sought and looked for, but could not be found, for not a living soul knew she was there. She was so absorbed in her love, and in crying and lamenting, that the day came to an end and night returned. Then she became a little weary and reclined beneath the fruit tree. Her heart started a little, and because of the heat she dozed for a while. She had not been asleep for long, and I do not know how this happened, but she was taken from beneath the tree and placed at the Hawthorn Ford, where her beloved was keeping vigil. He did not remain unaware of this for long, for he came back to the hawthorn bush and found the maiden sleeping there. She awoke in fright and was astonished, as she did not know where she was. She covered her head and was very afraid, but the knight reassured her: 'Come now', he said, 'you have no reason to fear. If you have the power of speech, speak to me with confidence, for I can see that you are a woman. If you are God's creature, be assured, but tell me your tale, and in what way and how you came here so suddenly.' (251–82)

The maiden took heart. Her wits returned to her and she realised she was not in the garden. Then she addressed the knight: 'Where am I then?'

said the maiden. 'Maiden, at the Hawthorn Ford, where many adventures take place, some good, some bad.' 'Ah, God', she said, 'how relieved I am. My lord, I am your beloved, and God has heard my prayer.' That was the first adventure that happened to the knight. His beloved ran to embrace him and he dismounted at once. He took the maiden tenderly in his arms and kissed her a hundred times. Then he sat down beneath the hawthorn bush. She explained everything to him, telling him how she had fallen asleep in the garden and what had happened to her before he had found her sleeping. (283–304)

When he had heard everything, he looked across the ford and saw coming towards him a knight with his lance raised for combat. His armour was completely red, as were his horse's ears, while the rest of its body was white and tightly bound around the flanks. The knight did not cross the ford, but came to a stop on the other side. The youth told his beloved that he intended to perform a feat of arms and that she should watch from there and not move. He had found his joust, so he jumped on to his horse. His first thought was to do battle with the knight on the other side. As fast as their horses could go, they approached each other in order to exchange great blows on top of their red shields so that they were completely shattered and split. Their lances were smashed to pieces but, without being harmed or injured, they both tumbled down on to the shingle. There was no friend or companion to help them to remount, so now let each of them strive to get back up. The shingle was smooth and level, and when they were back on their horses they placed their shields against their breasts, lowering their lances of ash. The youth was ashamed that his beloved had seen him on the ground in this first joust. In the end he struck his opponent so hard that his shield bore signs of the blows. But his opponent struck him back at once. Chunks of wood flew from their lances and one or other of them had to take a fall. It was the knight in red armour who abandoned the straps on his shield and the saddle on his swift horse. In full view of the maiden, her beloved forced him down on to the shingle. He seized his horse by the reins, entered the ford, crossed it and left his opponent lying on the other side. (305–50)

He came to his beloved at the hawthorn bush and handed the good horse over to her. The other knight did not lie there for long, for he very soon received help. Two knights came towards him and helped him on to a horse. Then these two crossed the ford. The youth was alarmed by this, because they were not on an equal footing. But he did not need to be afraid. Neither knight would be helped by the other if he intended to perform a feat of arms. He would fight in courtly fashion, each man on his own. When all three were on horseback, in courtly fashion and without haste, the last knight to come crossed the ford. When they were safely across, they did not say a word to him, but indicated that they would joust. One of them came to a standstill and stopped and the other prepared his arms, waiting in fine and courtly fashion to joust with the youth. When the latter saw how things were, he was quickly reassured and remembered full well that he had come to the shingle at the ford in order to win renown and seek adventure. He made to attack his opponent and, with his lance raised and shield in hand, clashed with him on the shingle. They both spurred their horses, charged at each other and exchanged blows with the metal of their lances, so that the wooden lances splintered, without either of them losing their saddles. The knights were so strong that their horses collapsed and each man tumbled to the ground. (351–89)

Then they attacked each other with their fine swords. The fight had just begun, and one of them would have been wounded when the other knight, coming from a distance and away to one side, separated them. He broke up the fight between the two of them and their swords struck no more blows. Then the knight spoke to the youth, saying to him in a courtly and polite manner: 'My friend', he said, 'get back on your horse and joust with me once more. Then you can duly depart, for there is no need for you to remain here any longer. You would not tolerate the suffering caused by this crossing place until daybreak, even for the whole city of Tyre. If you were harmed here, or killed by mischance, you would have lost your renown and never be spoken of. No one would know of your adventure, for it would remain hidden for all time. The maiden would be taken away along with the fine Castilian horse that you have conquered through your prowess. You have never seen anything so precious for, as long as you leave the bridle on it, you would be wrong to feed it, and it will always be plump and handsome. You have never seen one so swift, nor one with finer qualities, nor one more suited to a jouster. But do not be surprised at this, because you are brave and bold. Once the bridle has fallen from it, it will promptly be lost.' (390–426)

The youth heard and understood that he spoke with reason and what he predicted was true. He wanted to go to the maiden, but first he wanted to joust with the knight, so that he could then leave him more worthily. He seized a lance of ash and joined his reins up with his shield straps. He moved well away from the knight and they charged towards each other on the shingle. They spurred their horses for battle, with their lances grasped and extended. They struck each other such fierce blows on their silver shields that they were completely broken and split, but they did not let go of their stirrups. Then, when he had steadied himself, the youth struck the knight so hard that he would have come tumbling down if he had not clung on to his horse's neck. The youth passed beyond him, shattering his lance on his shield, then turned around and came back towards him. The knight pulled himself up and on his return found him perfectly ready. Each of them covered himself with his shield and they drew their swords. They gave each other huge blows, so that sparks flew from their shields. But they held on to their saddles, because they did not want to abandon their stirrups in order to deal and strike blows. The maiden, who was watching the combat, was terrified, for she feared greatly for her beloved and begged for mercy the knight who had been the first to joust with him, asking him to separate them at once. He was courtly and well bred and came rushing over and put himself between them. The knights separated, crossed the water and went away. (427–68)

The youth delayed no longer, but came at once to his beloved, who was filled with dread beneath the hawthorn bush. He raised the maiden up in front of him and led the good horse on his right. Now his troubles were over. He journeyed night and day until he came to his lord's court. The king saw him and was filled with joy, but he marvelled, wondering where he had found the maiden. Then he summoned the queen, and that day, as I have heard tell, the king summoned his men, his barons and other people in order to bring about reconciliation between two barons who were quarrelling. They reached agreement before the king. In the hearing of all those assembled the tale was recounted of what happened to the knight at the ford where he went to keep vigil, beginning with the maiden, how he found her beneath the hawthorn bush, then the jousts and the horse he had won from his adversary. (469–94)

The knight then took his horse to many conflicts far and near and had care lavished upon it. He took the maiden as his wife and cared for and retained the horse until the lady, in order to verify the truth about the horse her husband had cared for so much, removed the bridle from its head. So the horse was lost. As a result of this adventure I have related, the Bretons composed a lay. Because of what happened at the ford, the Bretons were determined to give the lay no other name than that of *The Hawthorn* [*l'Espine*]. They did not call it after the youngsters, rather they named it after the hawthorn, and so it is called the *Lay of the Hawthorn*, which begins and ends well. (495–514)

8. *Tydorel*

Introduction

Preserved in just one manuscript, S, *Tydorel* is set in Brittany. After ten years of marriage, the King of Brittany and his wife remain childless. One summer's day, while they are residing in Nantes, the king leaves his wife and goes hunting. Taking her companions to a garden for some relaxation, she falls asleep, but wakes to find that she is all alone. She sees a knight approaching and he offers her his love, saying that she will never know joy if she refuses him. She accepts his love with the proviso that he tells her who he is and where he comes from. He takes her to the edge of a magical lake and, leaving her, enters the water on horseback. After some time, he reappears on the opposite bank, then returns to her, forbidding her to ask further questions. He predicts that she will have a son by him. She will call him Tydorel and he will never sleep. It will be necessary for him to be entertained each night with stories and songs. She will also have a daughter, who will be the ancestor of the Breton counts Alan and Conan. He takes her back to the garden, where they become lovers. The predictions are fulfilled and she and the king, who was delighted by her pregnancy, bring up Tydorel lovingly. He is entertained throughout the night, until a few years later a wounded and impoverished knight, seeking an audience with the queen, sees the lovers together. He soon dies as a result of what he has seen, and the knight never returns. Shortly afterwards, the king dies and Tydorel reigns with great success for ten years. But when the king's messengers go to fetch a young goldsmith's apprentice, whose turn it is to keep the king entertained, he claims he does not know any stories. His widowed mother has told him to say to the king that he who does not sleep is not born of a mortal. Hearing this, Tydorel goes to his mother and demands an explanation. She tells him the whole story and he puts on his armour, rides to the lake and plunges into its deepest part, never to be seen again.

From start to finish, *Tydorel* is a supernatural lay: the lady wakes up to discover that her companions have disappeared; the knight-lover demonstrates his ability to survive in the deepest part of a lake (the lake itself is magical in that the wishes of all those who succeed in crossing it will be granted); the knight can predict the birth of his son and daughter; he knows that his son will never be able to sleep and will require nocturnal storytellers to entertain him, and that his daughter will have two sons who will be part of the lineage that will go on to produce the Breton counts Alan and Conan;[1] the knight who sees the lovers in bed dies in pain within a few hours; the son inherits his father's ability to live under water. All this contrasts with, and also complements, the real world in which the lay is set. Like any kingdom, Brittany requires a male heir, ideally one who is handsome, brave and generous and who is also a skilled and fearsome leader. Tydorel is all this and more, and with him at the helm the land had never been better protected. The link between these two strands within the narrative is three unpretentious personages: a badly injured knight, who is seeking to obtain money from the queen (such a request would presumably have been a run-of-the-mill occurrence at court); an old and sick widow (but one endowed with a special level of perspicacity that is required to move the story forward); the widow's son, who is a skilled goldsmith (i.e. a member of the thriving artisan class) but is so badly cut off from reality that he has no stories to tell. This rather motley collection of society's unfortunates (the widow and her son are terrified of the king's messengers) represents, ironically, the end of the line not for their fellow sufferers but for those at the peak of society's power structure. The first to be affected is Tydorel's mother, who loses her lover, and then Tydorel himself, the misfit king who returns to his true home and is never seen again. While ruling the kingdom, he has been in the real world, but not of it.

Grafted on to the intertwined supernatural and realistic dimensions of the story (symbolised, on the one hand, by the fate of Tydorel and, on the other, by that of his sister) is a wish fulfilment tale of a high-born lady who is fortunate, at the outset, to enjoy a loving marriage with a king. The one stumbling block is her crucial failure to produce an heir,

[1] The knight also knows that members of the daughter's family will sleep far more soundly than other people (vv. 144–46). Identification of Count Alan and Count Conan, his son, is not easy. Both Alan II and Alan III had sons named Conan. If Conan is Conan II (duke 1040–66), then Alan must be Alan III (1008–40). For a full discussion, see Burgess and Brook, 2007, pp. 308–09.

but this is remedied by the arrival of a knight who is said to be the most handsome man in the world. Falling passionately in love with this knight, who becomes her faithful lover, the lady manages for a number of years not only to juggle her two relationships but also, thanks to this knight, to provide her husband with a son and heir. At the close of the narrative, Tydorel's mother has already outlived her husband by ten years. She has lost her son, but she still has her memories and also her daughter who, she knows, will ensure continuity and found a powerful dynasty. Her long-hidden secret also appears safe. So, all in all, this is an attractive package for the lay's female readers/listeners, whether they are ambitious maidens or unhappily married or childless women. And all this can be achieved while remaining within courtly society.

Further Reading

Frappier, Jean, 'A propos du lai de *Tydorel* et de ses éléments mythiques', in *Mélanges de linguistique française et de philologie médiévales offerts à Monsieur Paul Imbs* (Strasbourg: Centre de Philologie et de Littératures Romanes, 1973), pp. 561–87; repr. in Jean Frappier, *Histoire, mythes et symboles: études de littérature française* (Geneva: Droz, 1976), pp. 219–44.

Ipotési, Monique, 'L'Interdit sexuel dans le lai de *Tydorel*', *Lectures*, 7–8 (1981), 91–100.

Sobczyk, Agata, 'Le Lai de *Tydorel* ou la magie de silence', in *Magie et illusion au Moyen Age*, Senefiance 42 (Aix-en-Provence: Centre Universitaire d'Études et de Recherches Médiévales d'Aix, 1999), pp. 509–18.

Translation

I will relate to you as it happened the story of a new lay, which is called *Tydorel*. The lord who ruled Brittany and was its king through inheritance, following many members of his lineage, in his youth took a wife, the daughter of a duke, whose hand he sought. Because of her beauty and nobility, the lord of the Bretons took her. He cherished and honoured her greatly and she loved him deeply. He was never jealous of her and she was never unworthy of him. (1–14)

They were together for a good ten years without being able to have any children. In midsummer, I believe, as they recount in this land, the king spent time in Nantes because of the forest, which he loved. One day he had gone hunting and the queen was relaxing. She had gone into a garden after the midday meal, taking ladies and maidens with her and remaining with them. They enjoyed themselves greatly and many of them ate fruit. Beneath a fruit tree she had spotted, the queen became weary. She lay down on the grass, reclining on one of the maidens. If the queen was weary, this maiden was four times more so. She fell asleep with her head down. The queen awakened and wanted to join the others, but she was unable to find a single one of them; this she found astonishing. She looked down the garden and saw a knight approaching at a slow and leisurely pace. Of all those alive in that day he was the most handsome man in the world. He was dressed in material from Ratisbon and was noble, tall and well formed. When she saw him coming towards her, she was filled with great shame and fear. She stopped in her tracks, deep in thought. Do you know what the lady thought? That it was some powerful lord who had come to speak to the king and was coming to her since he was unable to find him. So she should greet him. (15–54)

The knight took her by the left hand in courtly fashion and thanked her for her greetings. 'My lady', he said, 'I have come here for you, whom I love and desire greatly. Tell me your pleasure, whether you know and believe that you could love me with the sort of love I seek from you. Do not make me entreat you for long. I will love you loyally, and if it cannot be otherwise I will leave this place and you will remain behind. But be aware of this: you will never again know joy.' The lady looked at him intently, at both his appearance and his beauty, and she fell passionately in love with him. She agreed to love him, on the understanding that she knew who he was, his name and where he came from. 'In faith', he said, 'I will tell you, without a word of a lie. Come with me and you will see, for otherwise you will not know.' He took her with him and they both left the garden. He found his horse, which he had tethered to a tree by the reins. The horse was white like a flower, and there was none more handsome or better on earth. He found his sword and his arms and swiftly armed himself there. (55–86)

Then he mounted his horse, took the lady and placed her in front of him on his horse. In this way he set off with her. They had scarcely travelled very far on a slope beside the forest when, beneath a broad and high mound, he got her down off the horse at the edge of a lake. This was where many people had attempted a challenge: anyone who could swim across the lake was always granted whatever he conceived in his heart, and whatever he desired to know he would know. He made her sit down on the bank and entered the lake on horseback. The water closed over his head and he plunged into the deepest part. He remained there long enough to cover four leagues. The lady never stirred. He emerged on the other side and then returned to the lady. 'My lady', he said, 'in this wood I come and go along this path. Do not ask me anything more.' (87–109)

He raised her up on to the horse. 'We will love each other for a long time, until we are discovered. You will have by me a very handsome son and you will call him Tydorel. He will be very valiant and very brave. In beauty he will surpass all the knights in this land and no one will ever wage war against him. He will overcome all his neighbours, for he will possess great prowess. He will be Lord of Brittany, but he will never close his eyes in sleep. When he is old enough to understand, have someone stay awake with him constantly, wherever he might be residing. From each surrounding house have a man summoned, in turn, who can sing and make merry, and let him tell him some story, something he knows, good or bad. Anyone who failed to do this risked being put to death. Then you will have a beautiful daughter. When the maiden has grown up, she will be given to a count of this very region. She will have two brave and valiant sons, courageois, bold and skilled in combat, worthy, courtly and strong. They will be very fine knights and remarkably handsome. Nature will do her very best for them, for they will be very brave and valiant, and they will have many children. But because of their lineage they will sleep far more soundly than other people do. From them will come Count Alan, and then later his son Conan.' (110–48)

When he had told her everything he wished, he came to the garden and got her down from the horse. Returning her to the spot from which he had taken her, he did with her what he pleased. He departed and took his leave. When he had left the garden, the maidens who had earlier wandered off returned and the queen departed, keeping quiet about her adventure. She often spoke to her beloved, for he came back to her frequently. Her stomach grew and got bigger. The king learned of this and was filled with joy that the queen was pregnant. But he did not know the true state of affairs. The peasant says to his neighbour, in a spiteful saying in his own language: 'A man thinks he is bringing up his own child when it does not belong to him at all.' This is what happened to the king in this case; the child was not his, but someone else's. He was absolutely delighted at the queen's pregnancy, and so were all his vassals and his allies, who did not know how things were. The time came and the son was born. He was well brought up and well looked after. They had him named and called Tydorel in rightful baptism. He never closed his eyes and slept. He never went to sleep: he was always awake. All the king's men, who saw this, considered it a great marvel. (149–82)

When he had reached the right age and grown and become bigger, they had people take it in turns to stay up with him each night. They told him stories and fables, just as his mother had told them to do. The sister, who was born after him, was married to a count. The knight who fathered them came back to the queen repeatedly, for he loved her greatly and she him – she could not have loved him more – until they were discovered by a man who saw them. A knight was lying injured in the town, badly wounded. He was in great need of help; all his money was gone. He made a great effort, got up and went to the queen in order to ask and beg her to give him some of her money, for she was accustomed to give a great deal to those who needed it. She often gave the needy clothing and horses, gold and silver. Finding open the door to the chamber where she lay, he went in, and beside the queen he saw the man who would become a cause of pain and suffering for him: in his arms he held the lady. Then he left and never returned. Because of his pain the knight became ill that day and deteriorated. The next day he died at the hour at which he had seen and looked at the lovers. (183–218)

After this deed I am telling you about, the King of Brittany died and the Bretons made Tydorel their lord. They had never had a better one, one so brave, so courtly, so valiant, so generous or so liberal, nor one who protected the land better. No one dared wage war against him. He was much loved by maidens and greatly desired by ladies. His men loved and served him, and foreigners feared him. For ten years he was a powerful king, as those in the land say. When those ten years had passed, during which he had been in power, he went to spend time in Nantes. He loved this region greatly, because his mother lived there and because he received all his advice there. As long as he stayed there, throughout the houses in the city, each day, as their turn came, men were taken who were to stay up with the king at night and tell and relate stories to him. One Saturday, I heard tell, as evening was approaching, the messengers came to a house to fetch the man summoned to the king. There had been some delay and they had gone inside. (219–50)

A widow lived there, who was old, feeble and sick. With her she had a son whom she had raised for a very long time. He refused to be separated from her, or to leave the city. She had entrusted him to a goldsmith, who had taught and instructed him; he was very knowledgeable about his craft. From what he could earn, the son fed his mother each day and provided for her most honourably. They ordered him to get ready to go with them for the vigil that night in the king's chamber; he should make sure he knew how to please him. He replied to them: 'Get out! I have never known anything of this sort. I know no stories or songs, nor how to tell a tale.' The messengers were angry and they threatened the youth. If he refused to go willingly, they would take him by force, and he would be put in a place such that things would be worse for him for evermore. His mother was terrified of them. 'Fair son', she said, 'go with them.' He replied: 'Let me be. If I am unable to sing, he will throw me into his prison and put out one of my eyes.' 'Fair son', she said, 'listen to me. You will go and stay up with the king. When he asks you to tell a story, or recount some tale, or sing a song, reply that you do not know any. If he becomes very angry, say this to him: "he is not born of a mortal who does not sleep, or cannot close his eyes". In this way you will make him think, so that he will let you be. Go on, fair son, in full of confidence, may God grant you good fortune with him.' (251–94)

When he heard this advice, he quickly went to court and entered the king's chamber. The messengers went to their lodgings, leaving him with the king, who summoned him to sit beside him. When evening came and night fell, the chamberlains went to bed. The king was seated on a raised bed. He called him and said to him: 'My friend, tell me something to hold my attention and you will be acting well'. 'My lord', he said, 'I have never told a story, so help me God, or ever sung a song. My father died fifteen years ago and my mother is a poor woman; she has brought me up with great difficulty. I have never left her. I have seen and heard little, and retained even less.' The king said to him: 'This is astonishing! There is no one as ignorant as you, or so you say. You must be a complete fool. But you are not going to make fun of me like this. When you leave me, you will have no desire to mock or to make a fool of anyone else.' He started to threaten him severely because he refused to tell him a story. 'My lord', the youth replied, 'just as I say, I have seen and heard little, except that I have heard it said and related by many people in truth that he is not born of a mortal who does not become drowsy and close his eyes.' (295–330)

The king fell silent and bowed his head. He thought very deeply about the fact that he never slept. He knew full well that the youth had heard that he was not born of a mortal. He was sad and grief-stricken that everyone rested while he remained awake night and day. He rose swiftly, took his sword from the bedside and went into his mother's chamber. He came to her bed and woke her up. When she saw him, she sat up, reclining on her elbow. 'Son', she said, 'have mercy, in God's name! What is this? What do you want here?' 'By God!' he said, 'you will die. You will never escape my clutches unless you tell me the truth about whose son I am. I want to know. The person who was to stay up with me told me this just now by way of reproach. "It seems to me that, if I recall correctly, he is not born of a mortal who does not sleep." Everyone sleeps and I stay awake. Now I have heard this and am amazed.' (331–56)

She replied: 'What I know of this I will tell you gladly, fair son. You are my son and I am your mother. The king was not your father. We were together for ten years and could not have children. The king very often took up residence in this town with his men. One day he went out hunting, and because of the heat I went to take my ease in a garden, on the fresh grass and among the flowers. I took some of my maidens with me and disported myself with them. We enjoyed ourselves greatly and many of them ate some fruit. I sat down beneath a beautiful fruit tree with one of my maidens. I felt very heavy with slumber, and the maiden also fell asleep; I could not awaken her. I woke up and was afraid. Terrified, I left her and, since I must tell you the truth, a knight came to me there; he was extremely handsome. Nature had fashioned him with the greatest care and brought together in him everything she knew of beauty. He was very well dressed, tall, broad-shouldered and well formed. He begged me for my love, threatening me and saying that if I did not love him passionately I would never again know happiness. He would leave and I would remain behind, never knowing any joy or happiness. (357–94)

'I was very frightened. He sought my love insistently, and seeing that he was so handsome and comely, so courtly and eloquent, I loved him very deeply, and he loved me passionately. I asked him who he was and he told me he would show me. He took me out of the garden to the place where his horse was tethered. He found all his arms there that he had brought with him. He armed himself with them most nobly and his equipment was very fine. He put on his armour and then he mounted his horse. He took me by the right arm and placed me in front of him on the horse. In this way I set off with him. Know that I am telling you no lies. Into that wood he took me, to that large lake where men attempt the challenge, and got me down off the horse. There I sat and waited. Know this to be the whole truth. He swiftly left me and on horseback went into the lake, to the very deepest part, fully armed. He remained there long enough to travel four leagues, then he came back and spoke to me again, telling me that he left his land when he wished to do so. He came and went that way, just as he pleased, and he had no wish to take anyone with him, neither coming nor going. He carried his arms himself, came alone and went all alone, having no desire for any company. Never, as long as I was his beloved, did I see any groom or squire who had to ride with him. (395–436)

'He returned to me in this very fashion and many a time forbade me – for my life's sake I should be mindful of this – from asking him anything more about his situation. I never asked him again, for I did as he commanded. I kept his command well, for I never asked him anything else. He said he would love me for a long time, until he was discovered. He knew full well, and repeatedly told me, that he would be discovered, found out and recognised, saying: "And you will have a son by me who will be very brave and noble, and also handsome, fair and comely, generous, courtly and lavish, and brave on foot and on horse." You would become a noble vassal, and be small, scarcely very tall, but you would be very brave and valiant, and you would never sleep: "He will never sleep night or day." When he was old enough to understand, he said, I was to command people to take it in turns to sit up with him each night, to sing songs and tell stories. When he had said and revealed all this to me, he took me to the garden. Fair son, this is the truth. That day you were conceived. He returned to me for a long time, for more than twenty years, I believe, until he was discovered by a knight, who died a painful death as a result. He departed, never to return, and I do not know which paths he took.' When Tydorel heard this, he left his mother. He returned to his chamber, woke his chamberlains and gave orders for his arms to be brought and his good horse to be fetched. They did as he commanded and he armed himself at once. As soon as he was armed, he mounted his horse. Spurring it, he came to the lake and plunged straight into the deepest part. There he remained in this fashion and never came back. This tale is held to be true by the Bretons who composed the lay. (437–90)

9. *Trot*

Introduction

The lay of *Trot* is preserved in only one manuscript: Paris, Arsenal 3516. At 303 lines, it is one of the shorter lays in this collection. It is also one of five Arthurian lays, the others being *Cor*, *Mantel*, *Melion* and *Tyolet*.

A knight at Arthur's court named Lorois decides one day to go and hear the song of the nightingale. As he draws near the forest, a group of eighty happy maidens emerges, all elegantly dressed. This group is followed by a second group of similar size, and this time the maidens are accompanied by their lovers. Next comes a further group of one hundred maidens, who are lamenting and riding emaciated horses trotting uncomfortably. Then a group of a hundred men emerges, suffering in the same way as the previous group of ladies. Finally, a maiden approaches on horseback. Her animal is also trotting and causing her such distress that she can scarcely speak from the pain. But she manages to tell Lorois that the maidens in the first groups have been faithful servants of love, whereas all those who are suffering have treated love with disdain. She warns that this will be the lot of any living woman who does not love. Lorois returns to court to warn the ladies and relate his adventure.

The lay of *Trot* is commonly compared with a passage in the *De Amore* of Andreas Capellanus (Book I, Chapter 6, Section E), which bears some similarities to the events described in the lay.[1] Although this is only a short lay, consisting basically of one extended episode, it nevertheless manages to incorporate a well-integrated mixture of elements. Lorois's link with the essential theme of the lay (i.e. the need to engage in love) is discreetly signalled by his urge to go out and search for and to hear the song of the nightingale, a symbol of love. There is a significant emphasis

[1] See the edition of *Trot* in Burgess and Brook, 2007, pp. 484–85 and P. G. Walsh, ed. and trans., *Andreas Capellanus on Love* (London: Duckworth, 1982), pp. 104–11.

on clothing: Lorois is elegantly attired, as are the women and men in the happy groups, while those in the other groups are more unkempt. In this way clothing reflects contrasting states of mind – happy, contented and fulfilled as against unhappy and physically uncomfortable. A further clear distinction is made between the manner in which the respective groups ride. Those among the happy have a smooth ride on ambling horses; those who are unhappy are on trotting horses, which means that they are constantly jolted. Lorois's encounter with the various groups takes place in a dream-like vision, with an easy association of the real and supernatural worlds. This eschatological vision illustrating rewards and punishments is really a pagan appropriation of the medieval Christian concept of the afterlife in which the judge is not God, but the god of Love.

Further Reading

Burgess, Glyn S., 'The Lay of *Trot*: A Tale of Two Sittings', *French Studies Bulletin*, 66 (1998), 1–4.

Karnein, Alfred, 'The Mythological Origin of the *Lai du Trot* and its Arthurian Superstructure', *Bibliographical Bulletin of the International Arthurian Society*, 24 (1972), 199–200.

Lecco, Margherita, 'Composizione e cronologia relativa nel *Lai du Trot*', in Lecco, *Saggi sul romanzo del XIII secolo* (Alessandria: Edizioni dell'Orso, 2003), pp. 115–22.

Translation

I want to recount to you an adventure, very well rhymed, with nothing left out. I will relate it to you as it happened and never tell you a word of a lie. The adventure was very remarkable, and it happened once upon a time in Brittany to a very wealthy knight, who was bold, courageous and fierce. He was from the Round Table which belonged to King Arthur, who knew very well how to honour a fine knight and how to make frequent and lavish gifts. The knight's name was Lorois. He was from the Castle of Morois and had five hundred librates of land;[2] you could not find any land better situated. He had a very fine dwelling surrounded by a high wall and with very deep ditches that had been dug out very recently. Below the

[2] A librate (Old French *livrée*) is an area of land that brings in one pound of rent.

castle, close by, were rivers and forests where the knight liked to go and take exercise frequently. (1–24)

Then one April came, that glorious and splendid season, when Lorois rose one morning and dressed himself elegantly. He had put on his linen shirt, soft and delicate, and girded on a belt – I have seen many worse. He looked nothing like a fool, for he had put on a tunic of splendid blood-red cloth, trimmed with an ermine hem. He was very well shod, as he had on laced-up shoes and wore hose with slashes, very suitably arranged. When he was dressed and shod, he had no wish to delay any longer, so he ordered his squire to bring him his horse. He wanted to go into the forest to listen to the nightingale. Without further bidding, the servant did what his lord wished. He put the saddle on his horse and then laced up its breastpiece. When he had put on the bridle, the horse was not dying of hunger. It had a very fine coat and was well cared for, and without further ado the servant brought it before his lord. The knight mounted the horse and on his feet his squire fixed a pair of golden spurs. Then he girded on his sword with its gilded handle. (25–60)

When he had done this, Lorois left his dwelling without any companion. He galloped off straight towards the forest, along the river and by the meadow, where there was an abundance of flowers, white, red and blue. Without stopping, the knight rode at a good pace, affirming and swearing that he would not go back until he had heard the nightingale, which he had not heard for a whole year. And when Lorois drew near the forest, he looked ahead of him and saw emerging from the forest, in fine and leisurely fashion, as many as eighty maidens, who were courtly, beautiful and very elegant. None of them wore cloaks, nor did they wear hats. But, in order to smell as sweet as possible, they had chaplets of roses and of eglantine set on their heads. They were wearing tunics and nothing over them for the weather was hot. A number of them had a belt around their waist, and there were many who, because of the heat, were ungirdled. To give themselves more freedom, they had let their tresses fall free from their hair, which fell over their ears, brushing their rosy cheeks. (61–96)

There was a very fine company of them, and each lady had ribbons in her hair. They all had white palfreys that carried them so serenely that in truth there was no one who, if he were seated on one of these palfreys and did not see it move, would have failed to believe that the horse was not in motion. Yet they were riding faster than one would have galloped on the tallest Spanish horse. I can assure you that from there to Germany no rich duke or castellan had the means to buy the bridle that the poorest maiden there had placed on her palfrey. On a horse beside her, each maiden had her lover, elegant, noble and becoming, merry and singing gaily. I assure you in truth that they were very elegantly attired, for each man had dressed carefully in a tunic and mantle of costly silk lined with ermine and high tails, with spurs of gold fixed on their feet. The horses on which they were sitting were ambling speedily and very steadily. I assure you that one such harness is beyond the means of a wealthy king. Between them there was no envy, for each man there had his own beloved, and each made merry without impediment, this maiden with this man and that one with that man. Some of them were kissing, others embracing, and there were those who were talking of love and chivalry. (97–133)

Their life was one of great delight, and Lorois, who was watching them, crossed himself at this wonder and said that it was truly a marvel; never would he see its equal. And while he was marvelling at it, he saw coming out of the forest eighty ladies who were just like the others. Each one had her lover and all the ladies were elegant, just like those I have already described. They rode along with a great display of joy and were following the others. But a short while afterwards there was a great noise of moaning and groaning in the forest and he saw as many as a hundred maidens coming out of this forest who were in a very sorry plight, on black jades, emaciated and weary. The maidens advanced at more than a walking pace, and they were alone because they had no men with them; they were suffering the greatest torment. But you can be absolutely certain that they had deserved this, as you will hear me relate, if you are willing to listen to me. They were in very grievous torment and were trotting in such pain that there is no wise man or fool on earth who could have endured such a painful trot for even a single league, even if he were given fifteen thousand marks of silver. (134–66)

The reins of their bridles were made from lime bark and were very ill-fitting, and their saddles were broken and patched up in more than a hundred places. Their saddle cushions, in similar fashion, were stuffed with straw so that, without a doubt, one could have tracked them for ten leagues by the straw that was falling from their cushions. Each of them rode without stirrups, and they had no shoes or hose; in fact, their legs were completely uncovered. Their feet were in a bad state, for they were covered in cracks. They were dressed in black tunics and had bare legs, right up to their knees and, most inelegantly, their arms were left completely uncovered up to the elbows. They were suffering most grievous torment. It was thundering and snowing over them and there was such a mighty storm that no one could have endured it, beyond merely watching the great pain and sorrow they were suffering night and day. (167–92)

Lorois, who was watching at them, came close to fainting. When he had seen all this, he scarcely had to wait before he saw as many as a hundred men whose torment was similar to that of the maidens whose innards were being shaken up. When he had seen all this, scarcely had any time passed when he saw a lady advancing who was sitting on a chestnut-coloured jade and trotting so painfully that, I assure you, her teeth were chattering in such a manner that they were almost breaking into pieces. The knight, who was watching her, made up his mind that he would go and talk to the lady in order to enquire and ask what this marvel could be that had taken place before him. Lorois spurred his horse vigorously and galloped towards the lady. He came up to her and greeted her, and the lady looked at him. I can tell you that, a little later and very slowly, she returned his greeting, for she could hardly speak because of the trotting movement of her horse. And even if she had stopped, this would not have prevented her from shaking, for her horse was prancing about so much. (193–225)

Any knight, young or old, if he had sat on that horse, would have been unable to cling on in that position to the saddle or the mane, which was going up and down, to avoid falling off the horse. But the lady could not fall off, and for this reason she uttered many a sigh. Then the knight addressed her: 'My lady', he said, 'very gladly, if you please, I would like to know who these people are who have passed here.' She replied: 'I will tell you as best as I am able, but I can scarcely speak properly. So I have to say this to you quickly. Those women who are riding out in front are displaying such great joy among themselves for each of them in her opinion has the man she loved the most in all the world. She is able, just as she wishes, to kiss, embrace and caress him. These are the women who in their life have served Love loyally and who loved their men passionately. They obeyed Love's commands fully. Now they are being rewarded by Love, so that they have nothing but joy. They are certainly fully at their ease and have nothing to displease them. Neither winter nor storm can spoil the eternal summer they enjoy, and they can lie down, rest and sleep whenever they wish. (226–58)

'Those women who ride behind them, lamenting and sighing constantly, and who trot so painfully and are in such grievous torment, with faces pale and wan, ride at all times without men. They are those, I assure you, who never did anything for Love, nor did they ever deign to love. Now Love is making them pay dearly for their great pride and their arrogance. Woe is me! I have paid a high price for it. It grieves me that I have not loved, for never in winter or in summer will we have any repose or comfort and not be constantly in anguish. We were born at a very inauspicious hour when we were not made privy to love. But if any lady heard tell of us, and our plight was related to her, if she did not love during her lifetime, I assure you that most certainly she would come with us and repent too late. For the peasant is accustomed to tell us: anyone who begins too late to shut his stable door has lost his horse and is then in distress. Our hearts work similarly. We have repented too slowly.' (259–88)

The lady finished her speech, and the knight listened to her intently and understood what she said. Then she continued on her way. Lorois delayed no longer. He returned to the Castle of Morois and recounted the adventure, what the lady had related to him, the harnesses, and he told maidens, ladies and young girls that they should guard against trotting, for it is much better to amble … behind someone who was trotting so painfully.[3] The Bretons made a lay of this. It is called the *Lay of the Trot*. Here ends the *Lay of the Trot*. (289–304)

[3] The line between 'amble' in v. 300 and 'behind' in v. 302 is impossible to read because of a hole in the manuscript.

Fun and Games

10. *Mantel*

Introduction

Mantel (*Mantle*) is preserved in five manuscripts: (i) S; (ii) A: Paris, BNF, fr. 1593; (iii) B: Berne, Bibliothèque de Berne 354; (iv) C: Paris, BNF, fr. 353; (v) T: Paris, BNF, fr. 837. Our translation is based on S.[1] The length of the text varies considerably. S is the longest version at 913 lines; the shortest, at 727 lines, is BNF, fr. 353. The title accorded to this lay has varied over the years. A popular early title was *Le Mantel Mautaillié* ['The Ill-Fitting Mantle'], but it has also been called *Le Lai du Cort Mantel* ['The Lay of the Short Mantle'], or just *Le Cort Mantel* ['The Short Mantle']. The only term that is common to all titles, medieval or modern, is 'Mantel', so we have retained this as our title. *Mantel* is one of five Arthurian lays in the present collection, the others being *Cor*, *Melion*, *Trot* and *Tyolet*.

King Arthur holds court at Pentecost and many knights and ladies are present. When the time comes for the main meal, Arthur states that it would not be appropriate to eat before some new adventure has come to the court. A handsome youth then arrives, saying that he has been sent by a maiden from afar, who requests a boon from King Arthur.[2] Having been granted the boon, the youth then draws from his pouch a superbly crafted mantle. It has been made by a fairy and is designed to detect any disloyalty in women: if any lady or maiden has betrayed her husband or lover, the mantle will be either too long or too short. The lady whom the mantle

[1] For a French prose translation of T, see Nathalie Koble, *Le Lai du cor et Le Manteau mal taillé: les dessous de la table ronde* (Paris: Éditions Rue d'Ulm, 2005), pp. 55–87.

[2] A boon is a favour asked of his overlord by a knight. The favour is unspecified, so the lord must grant it whatever its nature to prevent his generosity being compromised. Once it has been granted, the recipient then indicates the precise nature of the gift, and it is normal for the lord to wish that the request had not been made. See also *Guingamor*, vv. 183–206.

fits perfectly will be able to keep it. The youth wants the king to have the ladies of the court try on the garment without being told of its properties. The queen, who wants the mantle for herself, does so, but it turns out to be too short for her. There follows a lengthy section in which a variety of ladies try on the mantle with different results; sometimes it is too short, sometimes too long. Their failures are accompanied by reactions from the menfolk and there is a good deal of sarcasm and ribald comment. The ladies curse the youth and express their reluctance to try on the garment, but the king orders them to do so. As they fail the test one by one, they are led away by the seneschal Kay, who creates, as it were, a new kind of community based on shared transgression. As this community grows, Kay suggests that the knights should refrain from mockery, since each man has his own burden to bear. Instead of being scorned, the wives and lovers, he says, should be loved and cherished. Finally, the youth asks Arthur to have his court scoured for any woman who has not yet appeared, as it would reflect badly on his famous court if the mantle were returned. A search begins and a maiden who has been 'indisposed', the beloved of a knight named Caradoc, is discovered. Caradoc does not want her to try the mantle on, but the maiden is happy to do so with his permission, and it turns out to fit her perfectly. This is the first time, says the youth, that he has found a woman without any villainy in her. The youth then departs and the king sits down to eat. After the meal, Caradoc leaves with his beloved. The mantle had been placed in an abbey in Wales, where it has now been discovered. The author jokes that the ladies in his audience would not thank him for making them try it on. He concludes by saying that only those with a very just cause should say anything bad about women.

Mantel is a tale of disappointment and humiliation. At the outset King Arthur and his knights have the utmost confidence in the fidelity of their wives or beloveds. But this confidence is quickly shaken when the ladies try on the mantle, which, as it changes size, reveals a variety of sexual misdemeanours. The issue of fidelity or loyalty in medieval society could not be more serious, as it is fundamental to the social and military bonds that link men together within the feudal system, and is equally fundamental to marriage or love relationships. But as the procession of failures gathers pace it is comedy that frequently rears its head, starting with the queen's disgrace. So the disloyalty begins at the top. This vein of comedy continues as failure follows failure, betraying the beloveds of the members of a court that is highly praised and celebrated throughout the world. As one woman after another fails to demonstrate her loyalty to the man who loves her, the tale could have descended into banality. But the audience will soon have realised that each failure can be divided into four segments: the preliminaries, the donning of the mantle, the way in which the mantle reacts to each of the ladies and the responses of the wearers and/or the onlookers. The preliminaries include the choice of the lady to try on the garment, the optimism of her beloved (Arthur chooses two ladies and is wrong about both of them) and the ladies' growing anxiety about the whole process. In the case of Caradoc's beloved, we learn of his misgivings about the test itself. He would prefer to live in a state of ignorance than to discover that she was guilty of some misdeed.

Amid the distress and humiliation undergone by those who fail the test, there is a further comic element: on some occasions the mantle reveals more of their bodies than the ladies would have liked. In the case of Gauvain's beloved, her right knee is revealed, and a similar thing happens to Yvain's lover. Things are even worse for Yder's mistress, as her entire rump is exposed. This unexpectedly visible flesh quickly elicits bawdy comments from the knights. An interesting aspect of the manuscript is that some of these remarks were seemingly too sexually explicit for the scribe of MS S, and he decided to tone them down.[3] In general, in *Mantel* there is an air of irony or sarcasm when the garment does not fit, with remarks sometimes directed at the wearer, sometimes at the knights. In Arthurian romance Kay has a reputation for dishing out sarcasm, so when his own beloved fails the test, Bruns sanz Pitié gleefully points out that he must be very happy and joyful that she has proven to be so loyal. In the case of Yvain's beloved, Guivret proffers a misogynistic comment that a man who trusts a woman is very foolish.

It is not clear whether, in humiliating and ridiculing such august Arthurian personages, the author is merely using them as a source of comedy or whether the intention was to expose the self-delusion, backbiting and pretensions of either the court of King Arthur, a dominant force in contemporary entertainment, or of the actual courts of his own day. He comments that when Carodoc's beloved received the mantle from King Arthur, the other members of the court were all very envious. They would have loved to have spoken out against it, but did not dare reveal what they were thinking. There is a clear dig here at the two-faced nature

[3] For a full account of the modifications made to sexually explicit passages, see the Burgess and Brook edition, pp. 15–18.

of court society, so it is no surprise that Caradoc, whose beloved is also victorious in the lay of *Cor*, makes a swift exit from court, taking with him the only maiden who has no villainy is her. The Arthurian court is no place for her.

Further Reading

Baumgartner, Emmanuèle, 'A propos du *Mantel Mautaillié*', *Romania*, 96 (1975), 315–32.

Bennett, Philip E., '*Le Lai du Cort Mantel* et la critique de la courtoisie', *Les Lettres Romanes*, 32 (1978), 103–21.

Kelly, Kathleen Coyne, *Performing Virginity and Testing Chastity in the Middle Ages* (London: Routledge, 2000).

See also the Further Reading section for the lay of *Cor*.

Translation

I wish to tell you the truth concerning an adventure that took place in the court of the good king who ruled Brittany and England free of homage, because it has not been told properly. At Pentecost in the summer King Arthur held plenary court. Never has a king ever held such a splendid court. From numerous far-off lands came many kings, many dukes and many counts, as the story relates. King Arthur had proclaimed that every valiant youth should come at once, and included in the summons was the command that those who had a beautiful maiden should bring her along with them. What more should I tell you? There were so many maidens there that I cannot give you the figure. It would have been very difficult to choose the most beautiful and the most courtly. The queen, who was not troubled that they were all gathered together, took them to her chambers. The queen was very courtly and she amused and disported herself with them. To give them pleasure, she shared out among them robes of many kinds, even the least valuable of which was very fine and made of silk cloth, variegated or grey. Anyone who wished to describe to you the pattern and the workmanship of the cloth would have to spend a very long time doing so to give a full account of it. But I must direct my attention elsewhere. The queen acted in a very praiseworthy fashion, for she then had belts, clasps and rings brought out for them. No one had ever seen such an abundance of jewels, nor so much honour as was in evidence when the queen at that time had them brought out for her maidens. Then she gave to each one as much as they wanted to take. (1–47)

I wish to pay heed to another matter and to speak of the good King Arthur, who had very splendid and excellent robes given to the knights, and an abundance of new armour and magnificent horses from Spain, Lombardy and Germany. No knight there was so lowly that he did not receive both a robe and a warhorse, and arms if he wished to take any. Never before had such wealth been distributed at a festival. The king should be praised for this, and he did not do it grudgingly; rather did he make it appear at all times that none of this disturbed or troubled him. This great court was assembled on the Saturday of Pentecost. There was great merrymaking in that place and everyone was very joyful and happy. When they saw that night was about to fall, they went to their lodgings to sleep. The squires made up the beds and each one put his lord to bed. In the morning, when it was broad daylight, they gathered once more at court and all went together to the principal church with the king. The queen went with her maidens to attend the service. I do not wish to delay any further at this stage or to provide a lengthy account for no purpose. As the tale tells us, when the service was over, they all returned to their lodgings and the queen went to her curtained chambers, taking all the maidens with her. The servants were fully prepared to serve food to the king. On the tables were tablecloths, salt cellars and knives. (48–90)

But, as this was a high festival, it was not fitting that King Arthur should eat or drink anything, or that anyone should be seated, until some new adventure had come to court. Gauvain summoned the seneschal and asked him why it was that the king was refusing to eat, because it was very close to nones. Kay spoke to the king about this: 'My lord', he said, 'why is it that you are not eating straightaway? Your food has been ready for a while.' The king laughed at this and looked at him. 'Tell me, seneschal', he said, 'when did you see an annual festival at which I sat down to eat before I had witnessed some new adventure at my court?' Lo, riding hard, a youth came along a street. His horse was sweating from the strain, for he was approaching at a very great pace. Gauvain was the first to see him and he called out to the knights: 'If it pleases God, we will soon be eating! For I can see a youth on a large grey nag coming through a gate at speed, bringing some news.' Lo, the youth arrived and dismounted before the hall. There were plenty of servants to take his horse. The youth did nothing wrong, as he was wise and well spoken. He removed his cloak and threw it at once on to the neck of the grey horse. When he had taken off his cloak, he was exceedingly handsome. His neck was white and his face handsome, his eyes large and his nose well placed, his shoulders broad and his arms fair. I can tell you in just a single word that Nature has never made anyone more handsome. He had a gracious body, broad hips and feet that were long with a high instep. The youth possessed wise words and fair speech in abundance. (91–139)

When he had entered the hall, he spoke in a courtly and elegant fashion: 'May the God who made and created everything save and protect this company.' 'And may God bless you, my friend,' said Kay the seneschal to him. Your horse is bathed in sweat, tell me where you are heading.' 'My lord', he said, 'first point out to me which one is Arthur the good king for, by the faith I owe you, I will give him news that will not be pleasing to everyone, but someone will experience joy because of it.' Everyone was keen to hear what it was that the youth wanted. 'Upon my word', said Kay, 'my fair friend, there he is on that throne.' The knights drew back and let the young man move forward. Having no wish to delay, he came before the king and gave him a fine greeting: 'May the God who created the whole world and everyone in it, and does as he wishes in every way, protect the finest crowned king there has ever been, or ever will be. My lord', he said, 'it is now right that I tell you what I am seeking. A maiden has sent me to you from a very distant land. She seeks a boon from you forthwith, and you must give it to her, for if she does not receive it on this occasion she will never ask for it again. You will not hear any mention again either of the boon or of the maiden, who is so comely and beautiful, until I know for certain whether I will have the boon from you. But I can tell you one thing clearly, and I want everyone to be fully aware of it, that I will not be seeking any outrage against you in which you would suffer any shame or loss.' (140–84)

Gauvain spoke first: 'This boon cannot be refused,' he said, 'since there is no villainy in it'. The king granted it to him cordially and promised him willingly and cheerfully that, whatever it might be, he would have it immediately. The youth took a pouch and from it drew out a mantle. No one has ever seen one so fine, for a fairy had made it. No one could describe it or account for the workmanship of the cloth. Let us now forget the workmanship and I will tell you a marvel that has no equal: the fairy had incorporated into the cloth a device that reveals unfaithful ladies. If the lady who puts it on has done wrong in any way to her good husband, if she has one, the mantle will not fit her properly. And the same for the maidens: any one of them who has erred in any respect towards her beloved will find that it will never fit her truly, without being too long or too short. In the hearing of the whole court, the youth explained and related everything about how the mantle was fashioned. Then he said to the king straightaway: 'My lord', he said, 'I ask that, without any further delay and without giving them this information, you have the mantle put on by the ladies and maidens, of whom there is a large gathering here. I learnt of this from a long distance away and have come from a foreign land just to request this boon.' (185–224)

Everyone looked at the mantle and Gauvain said: 'This boon is a fine one and it was right to ask for it. Have the queen summoned immediately.' 'Gauvain', said the king, 'go to her straightaway, along with Yvain and Kay, and tell her to come to me, and that there is no lady or maiden who should not also come without delay, for I wish to honour properly the boon I have granted to the youth.' The three men he had chosen went to her at once. They found the queen, who was getting ready to eat and washing her hands, for she was very upset that she had been without food for so long. Gauvain was the first to speak to her: 'My lady', he said, 'the king summons you, and commands you forthwith to come without delay and join the ladies out there. And bring these maidens, for he wants to see how beautiful and comely they are. One of them will have a great reward, for a youth has now come to the king and brought him a mantle. No one has ever seen one so splendid; the cloth is of costly silk. The king promised him that it would be given at once to the one whom it fits best.' (225–59)

Then the queen made her way there, very graciously and without delay. She took with her a very elegant company of ladies and maidens. No one had ever seen so many beautiful women at any gathering, for each of them had taken pains to adorn herself elegantly. When they came out of the chamber, they were gazed upon ardently by all the barons of the court because they were so comely. All the knights came running up to see what was going on. The king took the mantle and showed it to the queen. Then he told her and promised her that the woman whom it fitted best and most perfectly would have it immediately. But he never told them anything more. If they had known the rest, they would have preferred that it had been burned, even if it had cost a thousand marks. The queen was first to take it and at once she hung it around her shoulders, for she would have very much liked it to be hers. But if she had known the full story, how the mantle was sewn, it would never have been placed around her shoulders. It scarcely came down to her shoes. From the shame she felt at this, her whole face became dark and discoloured. Yvain was standing next to her and he saw her face change completely. 'My lady', he said, 'it appears to me that it is not too long for you! Know that, if anyone removed the width of a reed, or even less, it would still not fit you. That maiden over there, standing beside you to the right, is just about your size, no taller or shorter, and she is the beloved of Tor, the son of Arés. Give her the mantle next, so that from her you can see more easily if it could fit you properly.' 'Very willingly', said the queen. The maiden removed her own mantle and put it on very gladly. The mantle became shorter than it had on the queen. 'Now it has soon shrunk,' said Kay, 'and it has not been worn much!' The queen asked all the barons around her: 'Is it longer on me then?' she said. 'My lady', said Kay the seneschal, 'you are a little bit more faithful than she is, but it is only by a very small amount. I have expressed myself badly, for you are not more faithful. There is just less villainy in you.' (260–322)

The queen enquired of him: 'Tell me about this faithfulness at once, how it works and what part of it relates to the mantle.' Kay told her the whole truth about it, from start to finish, just as the youth had related it. About the mantle and the fairy, and the use she had made of it, he told her the whole truth, without skipping over a single word. The queen came to the conclusion that if she showed any sign of anger her shame would be all the greater, so she turned it into an amusing game. 'Let everyone put it on then,' she said. 'Why are these ladies delaying, when I have already done so?' 'Ladies, ladies', said the king, 'today you should demonstrate the good faith you bring to your lords, and the loyalty of the love shown by the maidens for whom the knights strive and put themselves in great danger.' Today, if anyone had been courting them, they would have claimed to be absolutely pure. There would not be a single one who would not swear, if anyone were willing to believe it, that she had never done anything wrong! When the ladies heard how the mantle had been sewn, and about the use the fairy made of it, there was not a single one who did not wish to be back in her own region, where she was honoured, for there was no lady bold enough, nor any maiden, to dare to take it. 'We can return it,' said the king, 'to the youth who brought it here, as it will not be retained in this place for any of the maidens who are here.' The youth said: 'That is not right. I will never take it back until I have seen that all the women have put it on, for what a king has promised must by right be maintained.'

The king replied to him: 'Fair friend, what you say is right. There will be no more excuses to avoid putting it on.' (323–73)

Then you would have seen them bow their heads, blanch, turn pale and quiver with anger and spite. There was not a single one who did not want her companion to take it, and not one of them would be filled with envy! Kay summoned his beloved. 'Fair one', he said, 'come forward. In the presence of these knights I boast that you can easily put it on. You have no companion or peer to equal your loyalty and worth. Today you will vanquish all those who are present here, without question.' The maiden replied: 'My lord', she said, 'if it please you, I would prefer it if someone else put it on first, for I can see here more than a hundred, each one of whom has such great beauty. I do not wish to impugn their loyalty, yet none of them dares to take possession of it. I would not wish to go before them, lest it were held against me.' 'You would be wrong to fear any ill will,' he said, 'for they have no such intention.' The maiden took it. In the presence of the barons she put it on and the mantle became shorter, around the thighs, with nothing below. The two flaps at the front could not cover her knees. 'Truly you have no peer!' Bruns sanz Pitié said to her. 'Master Kay the seneschal must be very joyful and happy, for you have been proved to be loyal!' When Kay saw that it fitted her so badly, he would not have wanted this for all the money the king could pledge, for he could not disguise his shame, which had been witnessed by so many people. (374–415)

Then Yder, the son of Nut, said: 'He who is himself accustomed to making use of it every day must get his share of ridicule! Seneschal, what have you got to say? Why then does the mantle not fit Androete the joyful?' The maiden was distressed, because she did not see any way out of this. At length, Kay said: 'My lords, you are too hasty. We will now see without delay how many of yours it will fit. Let them all come forward straightaway and we will see how it fits them.' Androete took off the mantle and threw it on to a seat. Filled with shame, she went and sat down. When the ladies heard that things had gone so badly for her, they cursed the youth roundly, for they were well aware that excuses would be of no avail. It would be no use objecting that they did not need to put it on. The good knight Lodoer addressed the king on this matter: 'My lord', he said, 'it seems to me that we are all very uncouth. My lord Gauvain's beloved, who is so beautiful and comely, ought to have put it on first: Venelas, the worthy and the courtly.' This upset my lord Gauvain, for in this matter he had scarcely protected his honour. 'Let her be called,' said the king. Lodoer called her at once, and the maiden rose, for she did not dare to refuse. The king had the mantle brought to her and she took it. She hung it around her shoulders straightaway, for she did not dare seek a delay. Behind her it fell down to the ground, so that there was a full foot trailing her, and the right flap rose up so that it revealed the knee, while the left knee remained covered up. The mantle wrapped itself all around it. (416–63)

Kay the seneschal was pleased when he saw the flap so short, for he had thought that in the court there was no maiden so loyal. 'Upon my word', said the seneschal, 'from today, thanks be to the Lord God, I will not be the only one to be mocked. For that flap I can see there has some sort of meaning for us! I will give my opinion about it: the fair-faced maiden perhaps fell asleep, and if anyone, such as a sorcerer, had visited her one morning and sought her favours he could have done to her a deed the like of which should not be recorded in circumstances such as I am relating to you.' My lord Gauvain was so upset that he never said a word. Kay said he would take her to sit down with his beloved and bring them some companions. The king took by the right hand the beloved of my lord Yvain, who was the son of King Urien, the good and noble knight, who loved hounds and hawks so much. 'Fair one', he said, 'this mantle should be yours by right, for I know of no reason within you why you should not truly have it.' 'One cannot know everything,' Guivret le Petit said to him. 'Do not speak too confidently before we know how things have turned out.' She put it on straightaway and the mantle extended to the right, so that it trailed her by a good foot; the left flap rose up a little above the knee. 'My lord, my lord', said Guivret, 'the man who trusts any woman is very foolish, when each one deceives her beloved. Just now you told us that this maiden would certainly have it, so proven was her loyalty. Now things have turned out in such a way that you can easily see whether she should have it by right! I will tell you something about the cloak. There is no woman who fails to know that the mantle will show that she has done wrong. The fastenings fit very poorly. Now I will tell you what I think about this: the mantle that hangs to the right shows us that she falls of her own free will. She readily does whatever she pleases, and the other flap that rises so high shows us that she is very little troubled by this. I do not know whether I speak frivolously, but of one thing I am in no doubt: an honourable man certainly never transgresses.' (464–527)

The maiden was so distressed that she did not know what she should say. Instead, she took the mantle by the silk fastener and threw it down.

She cursed wholeheartedly the youth who had brought it. Kay the seneschal said: 'Fair one, do not be angry. You should go and sit with the maiden Venelas, and with my own beloved, for as yet they do not have much company.' Straightaway, the king summoned the beloved of the Welsh youth called Perceval. 'Fair one', said the king, 'come forward. You will undoubtedly have this mantle. Your heart is so pure that I know full well you will be keeping it.' Girflet hastened to speak: 'My lord', he said, 'in God's mercy, do not make such predictions until you have seen how things turn out in this matter.' The maiden, who knew and saw assuredly that she could not do otherwise, took [the mantle], but when she was to put it on the clasps broke and fell down to the ground, along with the entire mantle. Her heart trembled with anguish so that she did not know where to turn, for she saw many good knights there, many squires and many youths. She roundly cursed the mantle and the one who had brought it there, for it would never rightfully fit any lady or maiden. No matter how courtly or beautiful she might be, it would not make it fit her any better. Tears came into her eyes; no one was too lowly to see them. At once Kay led her over to his beloved and Gauvain's, saying to her: 'I am giving you some company, do not distress yourself.' But none of them thanked him and he came back laughing. (528–75)

The youth immediately picked up the mantle, which was lying on the floor. 'Now you must look for the clasps on it, my fair friend,' the king said to him. He fastened them on at once because he had them in his pouch, as he did not want the matter to be impeded in any way, nor for the women to find any excuse to avoid putting it on immediately. The king picked it up straightaway, then spoke very angrily: 'We have been without food for too long!' he said. 'Why are these women so reluctant, since they will never sit down to eat until they have put it on? It might be troublesome to them, yet they will put it on in turn.' Girflet, who was treacherous and cruel, replied to him: 'My lord, do not say this. You could free them all from this, if it were to please you. Do you want to humiliate them any further? Since they see the mantle here, let them swear and grant, in the hearing of their lords and their beloveds, that they have done wrong and erred. Do you wish to hound them?' The king would have freed them at that time, in accordance with Girflet's advice, when the youth darted forward. 'My lord', he said, 'I demand that you keep the agreement with me just as you promised.' The knights were very worried and not one of them knew what to say. Yder angrily summoned his beloved, who was sitting next to him, for that morning he had thought in truth that there was no one so loyal at court. 'Fair one', he said, 'the seneschal told me today that I was too hasty because I mocked him with regard to his beloved, be it ever so little. But I trusted in you so much that I spoke harshly. Be aware that I am now sorry, because I can now see you hesitating. Go and put on the mantle and let there be no delay.' Why would she quibble when she had no alternative but to try it on? (576–627)

The king had the mantle brought to her. She took it and immediately hung it around her shoulders, for she did not dare seek a delay. The flaps fell down to the ground, so that they trailed behind her by a full twelve inches. Most of the knights had thought that there was nothing but good in her, until they saw her rear, which was completely uncovered. Girflet, who was first to see this, cried out at once: 'Maiden, this hangs out too much! It is not appropriately tailored. It will never be sufficiently shrunken in front as to make it fit all round!' Kay, who could not help himself because Yder had taunted him, paid him back at once for his kindness: 'Yder, what do you think of this? Has your beloved done nothing wrong? Now you have the chance to mock! One could not even find two maidens whose faithfulness is proven. The world is so fashioned that each man thinks he has one. Today you thought you knew that she was loyal. The woman whose rear is visible covers herself badly! Now I will tell you how things are: her beloved must cherish her, just as the mantle shows us!' Yder had no idea what he should do or say, so he took the mantle very angrily and threw it down at the king's feet. Then Kay took the maiden by the hand and led her over to be with the others. 'Upon my word', he said, 'this gathering will, if it pleases God, soon be large and fine! Today there will not be any maiden or lady left here in this company, for it would be very uncouth if one of them were to mock another.' (628–71)

What more should I tell you? One after the other, the maidens put on the mantle and their lovers watched them. It never fitted any of them properly, and each time he saw what had happened Kay took them and led them to sit down in the row. In the court there was no knight who had a lover or a wife whose heart was not filled with grief. If only one could have seen their demeanour, how each glared at the other! But they were somewhat consoled by the fact that no one could insult anyone else without sharing the insult himself. Kay the seneschal said to them: 'My lords, do not get angry. Our jokes are very evenly distributed, since each man has his own burden to bear. They must henceforth be cherished and loved by us, for today they have been well tested, and we must take comfort from the fact that we cannot mock each other.' My lord Gauvain replied: 'This is an awkward dilemma for me. I do not know how to choose the best, but we have had the worst of it, for it would be tiresome and wrong if our shame were alleviated. I must feel distress because of my own shame, but we must not mock each other.' Kay said to him: 'This is not necessary. I have long heard it said in a proverb that grief over a trifle can pierce the wretched to the heart. But a curse on anyone who believes this, or ever approves of it, that a good knight is shamed if his beloved has made another man her lover. Rather must he find a good reason for it. Why should he be any the worse for it, if her wickedness has been proven? If he had married her nine times, or twenty-nine times, or thirty-seven, let the blame fall on him who is responsible!' (672–718)

Tor, the son of Arés, replied: 'This is rather bad counsel! But the seneschal is telling the truth about this matter and providing some relief for us, because many a good knight shares this agony, and not just in this court.' The youth darted forward. 'My lord', he said, 'what is going to happen? I think it will be necessary for me to take the mantle back. Have the chambers here checked to see if any maiden is in hiding. Your court has been truly praised and celebrated throughout the world. I have heard it said in my region that never did any adventure occur, early or late, in whatever place, that turned out in this fashion. Your court is so full of high-born people, it seems to me, with so many worthy knights, rich ladies and maidens. There have never been so many women as beautiful as there are now, I can tell you. Since there are so many high-born people, and your court is so populated, it will be shameful if the mantle goes back. Be aware that the court will be reviled for the news, which travels so fast, will now go to many a region, and be aware that in your court there will be fewer adventures.' 'Upon my word', said my lord Gauvain, 'the youth is right about this. Have the chambers here searched to see if there is any maiden, great or small, who should come forward at once.' (719–56)

The king gave the order to go and look, and Girflet darted off as soon as the king had commanded it. He found a maiden. She had not been hiding, rather she was somewhat indisposed and was sitting on a bed. Girflet said to her straightaway: 'Get up at once, maiden, for a new adventure has come to this hall. Never has one like it been seen and you must come and see it. You must play your part in it, since all the others have done so.' The maiden replied to him: 'My lord, willingly, at once, but let me get dressed properly.' The maiden rose, dressed herself and got ready as best and as well as she could, in the finest gown she possessed. Then she entered the hall and, when her beloved saw her, be aware that he was very upset. Hitherto, he had been happy and joyful because she had not been there, for if he had had his way [she would not have put on the mantle at any time, for he loved her so passionately][4] that he did not ever want to hear of the matter if she had committed any wrong, because it would destroy his solace. His name was Caradoc Briebraz. Then the youth came forward and brought her the mantle, telling her and describing to her how cleverly it was crafted and why he had brought it there. Caradoc, who was very upset by this, said in everyone's hearing: 'My sweet beloved, in God's name, do not put it on if you have any doubts at all, for I love you so sincerely that I would not wish to know your wrongdoing, even for a fortune. I would prefer to remain in doubt. Not for all the money in France would I want to be certain, for he who loses his beloved has lost a great deal, it seems to me. I would rather be dead than alive to see you sitting on the row in which Gauvain's beloved has been placed.' (757–810)

Then Kay the seneschal, who was very evil and disloyal, said to him: 'Should such a lover not be very happy then? You are going to be filled with grief if you love her so much. Look at more than a hundred sitting there, who were thought this morning to be more perfect than pure gold. Now you can see them all sitting in the row because of their misdeeds.' The maiden, who was not abashed, replied to him very demurely: 'My lord', she said, 'it is absolutely true that many worthy men have suffered this hurt, but I must not boast that I might exceed all these maidens in loyalty and worth. Yet if it does not displease my lord I will put on the precious mantle.' 'Upon my word', said the knights, 'you cannot avoid this.' She was still unwilling to put it on until she had permission to do so from her beloved, who was angry. But against his will he gave it to her and she took the mantle and put it on at once in the sight of all the barons. It was neither too long for her nor too short; it reached down to the ground evenly. 'It was right to seek out this maiden, it seems to me,' said the youth. 'Maiden, your beloved should be happy and joyful. Know one thing for certain, that I have taken it to many places and more than a thousand women have put it on. I have never in my life seen any woman in whom there was not some villainy, not one, except for you alone. I bestow on you the garment that is worth a full tower of money, because you should indeed have it.' (811–52)

[4] The lines in square brackets are omitted from MS S, the base manuscript for the translation. They are found in other manuscripts and are incorporated here as they are needed for the sense.

The maiden thanked him for it. The king himself granted it and said it was hers by right. There was no knight, baron or maiden who opposed it, and they were all very envious that she had won it before their eyes. Neverthless, no one dared give any sign of this, for the only thing they could think of to say was in her favour. Then my lord Gauvain said: 'Maiden, I assume that you do not owe your reward to anything other than your loyalty. Let those who see your loyalty approve of it and grant you your reward. They would gladly have spoken against this if in any respect they had seen a reason why you should not have it. One thing you can know, that many of them are distressed by this.' The youth took his leave, for he had no wish to remain there any longer. He did not even wish to wait for the dinner, for he wanted to give his lady his message straightaway. The king and all his people immediately sat down to dine. Know that many a good knight sat there was filled with anger and resentment. I do not wish to say anything more about the meal, except that they were very well served. (853–85)

When the meal was over, Caradoc took his leave and, happy and joyful, he went back to his own land with his beloved. Squires placed the mantle in an abbey in Wales and it has now been rediscovered. I know very well who has it, and he is going to bring it everywhere for ladies and maidens! My lords, give them this news: that I will take it everywhere and they will have to put it on. In truth, I know well that they will not take advantage of this! It would be a waste of my effort if I were to give them this present. They would hate me forever, and I could be scorned if I admonished them in any way. For this reason I must be careful – for my own sake, not for theirs. Yet, whatever happened in the past, they now have nothing but honour. But people are still reproaching them for the wickedness that existed in those days. May God never protect anyone who says anything other than good things about them, unless he knows a very just cause. (886–914)

11. *Cor*

Introduction

Cor (*Horn*) is preserved in only one manuscript: Oxford, Bodleian Library, Digby 86. The lay is attributed to Robert Biket ('Ceo dist Robert Bikez', v. 589), about whom nothing is known. *Cor* is one of five Arthurian lays in this collection, the others being *Mantel*, *Melion*, *Trot* and *Tyolet*.

In order to celebrate Pentecost, King Arthur holds a feast at Caerleon attended by a large number of knights and maidens. A handsome youth arrives bearing a magic ivory horn, which is sumptuously decorated and has golden bells attached to it. When shaken, these bells compel all those who hear them to cease what they are doing and to listen, enthralled. After making the assembled court pause and listen, the youth then addresses the king. He tells him that the horn is a gift from the King of Moray and the king gratefully accepts it. The youth refuses to eat with them, rather he departs, promising to return for his reward. The horn is admired by all and at the king's request the chaplain interprets the inscription on it. He reads it out to the whole assembly: the horn was fashioned by a spiteful fairy who has arranged a spell on it whereby no man can drink from it without spilling its contents down himself if he has been cuckolded or jealous, or has a wife who has ever had lewd thoughts about any man other than her husband. The assembled ladies are disconcerted, but Arthur confidently insists on having the horn filled with wine in order to test it out. When the wine spills all over him, he has to be restrained from stabbing the queen. The queen excuses herself by saying that the strict truth revealed by the horn can be explained by the fact that she had given a golden ring to a youth as a token of love, to thank him for having slain a giant who had wrongfully made an accusation against Gauvain. Yvain proposes that all the men should try it and the king insists that the other kings present do so. Predictably, they all fail. Seeing that the humiliation and mockery are shared by all the kings, Arthur laughs and forgives the queen. She in turn invites all the knights present to try out the horn, and one named Caradoc confidently takes it and is encouraged to drink from it by his beautiful wife. He succeeds in drinking from the horn and the king gives it to him to keep, along with the fiefdom of Cirencester, which until then he had held only temporarily. The author confirms the presence of the horn in that town.

As in the case of *Mantel*, this comic lay revolves around a chastity test in which, once again, the fidelity of the women at court is tested.[1] But the principal difference here is that it is the men who have to perform the test, unlike in *Mantel*, where the women have to don the magic mantle. The comic aspect of the lay is first illustrated by the reaction of the chaplain, who laughs when he is shown the inscription on the horn. This is followed by the somewhat laddish humour of the spilling of wine over the men's clothes. The king's anger with his queen is quickly dispelled by Yvain's intervention, preventing the poem from becoming too serious. The intention of the King of Moray in sending the messenger with the special horn may only be guessed at. Arthur makes it clear that he has a peace agreement with this king, and perhaps the latter could not resist indulging in a piece of mischief to embarrass Arthur. In any event, it allows Arthur to show kingly qualities in not seeking to get his own back and in readily forgiving his wife. Once Arthur laughs, the tension of the situation evaporates and, as in *Mantel*, it is Caradoc and his lady who win the day. Caradoc's prompt departure could be explained by a wish to take up immediately the fiefdom that has now been granted to him permanently and to look after his prize horn. Perhaps, too, he wanted to avoid any jealousy or hostility from the other members of the court. In any event, an initial situation that could have turned out very badly for everyone becomes one of intense relief in the shared embarrassment that the horn engenders. So the upshot of the horn test is, ironically, to reinforce the cohesiveness of the court. Moreover, the general air of forgiveness and happiness at the end could be seen to stand as a secular illustration of the Christian belief in the sinning nature of man and the common need for forgiveness.

[1] See the section 'The Horn and Mantle Tests', in the edition of *Cor* by C. T. Erickson (pp. 4–11).

Further Reading

Bennett, Philip E., 'Some Reflexions on the Style of Robert Biket's *Lai du Cor*', *Zeitschrift für romanische Philologie*, 94 (1978), 321–41.

Bloch, R. Howard, 'The Arthurian fabliau and the Poetics of Virginity', in *Continuations: Essays on Medieval French Literature and Language in Honor of John L. Grigsby*, ed. Norris J. Lacy and Gloria Torrini-Roblin (Birmingham, AL: Summa Publications, 1989), pp. 231–49.

Rider, Jeff, 'Courtly Marriage in Robert Bicket's *Lai du Cor*', *Romania*, 106 (1985), 173–97.

See also the Further Reading section for the lay of *Mantel*.

Translation

This is about an adventure that took place at the court of the good king who ruled the whole of Brittany and England free of homage, just as one finds it written down.[2] On the day of Pentecost good King Arthur held in Caerleon, as we were told, a feast that was very costly. It was very splendid, as the account of it relates, for twenty thousand knights were seated at dinner with twenty thousand young women, ladies and maidens; it was an extraordinary gathering. Each man had a companion. Those who had no wife ate with a female partner, their sister or their beloved, and it was a very courtly occasion. The king had summoned his knights from every region, from Esparlot in Brittany as far as Germany, and from the city of Bodloan as far down as Ireland.[3] He had summoned them in a spirit of fellowship, so that on the day of general absolution they would be in Caerleon. (1–30)

Everyone came that day, the great and the small, but before they had eaten, they would all become angry. For, lo, a youth, very comely and

[2] It is not clear whether the distinction in v. 3 between 'Bretaine' and 'Engleterre' is between Brittany and England, or between Britain as a whole and Anglo-Saxon and Norman England.

[3] Esparlot has not been identified. For the place name we have rendered as Bodloan, the manuscript has Boillaunde, which could be Bodloan, the home of Iaginvius in Geoffrey of Monmouth's *Historia Regum Brittaniae* (ed. Neil Wright (Cambridge: D. S. Brewer, 1985), I, viii, X, x), which could in turn be Ballon in Maine (see Bennett, ed., p. 64). In Wace's *Roman de Brut* Bodloan is the home of Jaguz (ed. Ivor Arnold (Paris: SATF, 1938–40), vv. 12795–96).

handsome and on a swift-moving horse, came speedily up to the palace. In his hand he held a horn with four bands of gold around it. The horn was of ivory, carved in low relief, with stones in it that had been set into the gold: beryls, sardonyx and splendid chalcedonies. It had been fashioned from an elephant's horn. I have never seen one so large, so sturdy or so handsome. On it was a ring, inlaid with silver, and there were a hundred tiny bells made of pure gold. In Constantine's time, a fairy who was skilled and wise created them, and the horn had had a spell placed on it, as you will soon hear. If anyone tapped the horn lightly with his finger, its hundred little bells rang out so sweetly that neither a harp nor a viol, a maiden's merriment or one of the Sirens at sea, would have been as pleasing to the ear. A man could travel a whole league on foot before the bells became inaudible, and anyone who heard them would forget everything else. (31–70)

The messenger entered the palace with the horn he was carrying. He saw the large company of knights all brimming with courage. He took hold of the horn, which was hanging around his neck. Dressed in a long-sleeved tunic, he raised it on high, struck it and the palace resounded. The bells rang out, and so harmonious were they that because of them all the knights stopped eating. Not one of the maidens who were in charge of the plates, nor any of the skilled cupbearers who were serving the drinks, bearing wooden bowls or great goblets of pure gold filled with distilled or flavoured wine, or with wine spiced with honey or herbs, could continue their work. They spilt whatever they were holding. Nor could any seneschal, however strong, worthy or brave, have failed to fall or totter while carrying dishes. The man cutting the bread also cut his hand! They were enthralled by the horn and everything else was forgotten. They all ceased talking to listen to the horn. Arthur, the powerful king, was rendered so dumbstruck by it, and the counts and kings fell so silent because of it, that not a soul spoke. (71–109)

The messenger went quickly to the king with the horn in his hand. He recognised ten other kings from their very splendid garments. Around King Arthur everyone was dumbstruck because of the horn. The messenger addressed him and greeted him warmly, and the comely youth said to him with a smile: 'May the God who lives on high protect you, King Arthur, and all your knights whom I see gathered here.' Arthur replied to him: 'May he also give you joy.' 'My lord', the messenger said to him, 'now listen to me for a moment. The King of Moray, who is brave and courtly, sends you this horn, which he has taken from his treasury, with a certain condition. Listen to his wishes, without either being indebted to him or bearing him any ill will.' 'My friend', said the king, 'your lord is courtly, and I will accept the horn with its four bands of gold, without being indebted to him or bearing him any ill will.' King Arthur took it, for the youth handed it to him. Arthur had wine given to him in his goblet of pure gold and then he addressed him: 'Take this plate, sit before me, and eat and drink. When I have eaten, I will make you a knight and in the morning I will give you one hundred pounds of pure gold.' The messenger replied with a laugh: 'It would not be fitting for squires to eat at a table for knights. I will go to the inn and take some rest. When I am equipped, clothed and attired, I will return to you and claim my promised reward.' (110–64)

Then the messenger left him and departed. Fearing that he may be followed, he went out of the town. The king remained in the palace. He had never been so disturbed. His knights were gathered all around him. He held the horn by the ring, and never having seen one so fine he showed it to Gauvain, Girflet and Yvain. His eighty vassals looked at the horn, as did all the barons who were all milling around. The king took back the horn and in the gold saw an inscription engraved in silver. He said to his chamberlain: 'Hold this horn in your hand and show it to my chaplain. He will read the inscription for me. I want to know what it says.' The chamberlain took it and passed it to the chaplain, who read the inscription. When he saw it, he began to laugh and called to the king: 'My lord, listen to me. Straightaway I will whisper in your ear and reveal to you such a marvel that never in England, or in any other land, has one so great been heard of. But this is not the place for me to speak of it.' (165–200)

The king did not delay, rather he declared and swore that he should relate it in everybody's hearing, so that his knights would hear it, as well as the ladies and maidens, and the noble girls who were gathered there from foreign lands. 'Something so greatly desired', said the king, 'will not be concealed.' Everyone there rejoiced when they heard the king say that they would all hear what the inscription said. But there were those who rejoiced and later repented, and some who were very happy about it later became angry. The chaplain, who was neither foolish nor ill-bred, said: 'If I had been heeded, what has been written here would not be read out today, nor what the inscription states. But since you wish it, you will hear it openly. Mangoun the fair-haired of Moray tells you this: the horn was made by a fairy, who is taunting and spiteful, and the horn has had a spell laid on it. No one, however wise or foolish, will manage to drink from it if he is cuckolded or jealous, or if he has a wife who has had lewd thoughts about someone other than himself. The horn will never permit such a man to drink; rather the contents will pour over him, whatever it may contain. He could never be of such high status, or have such great confidence, that it would fail to pour over him and his clothes, even if they were worth a thousand marks. Whoever drinks from this horn has a wife who has never thought, out of disloyalty, for financial gain or for any more handsome man on earth, that she wanted to have a better man than her own lord. If his wife is sufficiently virtuous, then he will be able to drink, but I do not think there is any knight from here to Montpellier who has taken a wife, who will ever be able to drink a single drop from it, if what the man who wrote this inscription has said is true.' (201–62)

God, many a happy lady would be distressed that day! None of them was loyal enough that she did not lower her gaze. Even the queen hung her head and all the barons in the assembly who had wives knew how things stood. The maidens joked and jested among themselves. They looked at their beloveds and indulged in gentle mockery, saying: 'This very day you will see the jealous ones put to the test! Today you will see those who are jealous ones, those who are cuckolds and those who turn a blind eye.' Arthur was furious, but he let it appear that he was happy. He spoke to Kay: 'Fill this splendid horn for me, for I will endeavour to find out if I can drink from it.' Kay the seneschal did so quickly. He filled it with spiced wine and handed it to the emperor. King Arthur took hold of it and raised it to his mouth, expecting to be able to drink, but he spilt it on himself, right down over his feet. This made the king angry and he said: 'This is the worst thing that could happen.' He grabbed a knife and intended to stab the queen in the heart below the breast when Gauvain, Kadoain and Yvain took it from him. The three of them along with Girflet took the knife off him. They pulled it from his hand, reprimanding him severely. 'My lord', said Yvain, 'do not be so wicked, for there is no woman born, even if she is married, who has not had some lewd thoughts. So I am not surprised if the horn spilled over. Everyone here will try it, those who have wives, in order to find out whether they are able to drink from it. Then you can reprimand the queen with the fair countenance. You are a very honourable man and my lady is loyal. I have never at any time heard anyone speak ill of her.' (263–322)

'Yvain', said the queen, 'now let my lord light a fire of thorns and cast me on it. If a single strand of my hair is burnt, or any of my clothes, let him have me dragged along and torn asunder by a warhorse, for I never loved any man, and never will love one, but him alone. This horn tells the whole truth, and for a very minor cause it has caught me out utterly. The other year I gave a ring to a youth, a young boy who had killed a giant, a base criminal who in an act of great treachery in this very place made an accusation against Gauvain, his own first cousin. The youth defended him and fought with the giant, and with the blade of his sword he cut off his head. As soon as the giant was killed, the youth took his leave of this place. I offered him my love and gave him a ring, for I thought I could retain him for the benefit of the court. But even if he had remained here, he would have had no more love from me,' said the queen. Certainly since I was a girl and was given to you, I have been blessed. Not once have I committed any other indiscretion at any time in my life. On earth there is no man so rich, not even the King of Rome, that I would love him for all the gold in Pavia, nor any emir or count. The person who sent this horn has brought great shame on me. He has never had any love for a woman! I will never again be happy until I am avenged.' (323–72)

King Arthur then said: 'Say no more about this. No neighbour have I, however powerful, no relative or cousin whom I would love in my heart if he made war on Mangoun. I made an agreement with him before all my people, that as long as I live, I would not wish him harm. It is not right for me to go back on my word; that would be villainy. A king who does this is not at all to my liking.' 'My lord', said the queen, 'since I was a maiden and was given to you, I have been blessed. A lady of high birth would be committing an outrage, when she has a good husband, if she took another man as her beloved. He who seeks a better wine than that made from grapes, or deliberately seeks bread that is better than that made from wheat, should be hanged and his ashes tossed into the wind. Except for God, I have the best of the three men who ever became king.[4] So why would I go searching for one more handsome or more valiant? This I tell you sincerely, my lord, that you are wrong to be angry with me. Never should this horn be passed into the hands of a noble knight in order to shame his wife.' The king said: 'They will do this. Everyone will try it, kings, dukes and counts, and I will not be the only one to be shamed!' (373–414)

King Arthur gave the horn to the King of Snowdon and, as soon as he had taken hold of it, it spilt over him. Then King Nut took it and it

[4] The three kings were originally David, Alexander and Arthur; Charlemagne later replaced David (see Erickson, ed., p. 57).

did the same to him. Aguisant of Scotland tried to drink from it by force, but he spilt it all over himself, which made him very angry. The King of Cornwall tried to drink from it without fail. It poured all over him and this made him very cross, and then the horn spilt over King Gohor. Over King Glovien it spilt copiously, and as soon as he held it in his hands, Kadoain spilt it. Then King Lot took it and considered himself a real fool, and Caraton poured it over his moustache. Neither of the two kings from Ireland failed to spill it and it spilt on the thirty counts, who were very much ashamed by this. Not a single man assembled there who tried the horn managed to taste anything from it. It poured over each king and each one became angry. Those who passed it on were very upset because of it. They declared that the horn should be assigned to the Devil, along with the man who brought it and the one who sent it. For anyone who put his trust in this horn would bring shame on his wife. When King Arthur saw that it had spilt over everyone, he had no more grief or anger, rather did he begin to laugh, and he showed great joy because of it. He addressed his barons: 'My lords, now listen to me, I am not alone in being mocked. The man who presented me with this horn gave me a great gift. By the faith I owe to all those whom I see here, I would not give it away for all the gold in Pavia, and no man will have the horn who cannot drink from it.' (415–72)

The queen reddened because of this great marvel about which she dared not speak. She was more beautiful than a rose. The king looked at her and she seemed very beautiful to him. He drew her towards him and kissed her three times. 'My Lady, I set aside my anger against you fully.' She replied: 'My lord, my thanks to you'. 'So take up the horn, all of you, great and small.'[5] A knight took it and smiled at his wife. Of all the members of the court he had the greatest joy and was the least scornful and the most courtly, and when he was wearing his armour he was the one most feared for in Arthur's court there was no better warrior, nor anyone more skilled with his hands, except for my lord Gauvain. He had blond hair and a reddish moustache, fine, sparkling and laughing eyes, and his body was comely, his feet arched and straight. He was a true knight and his name was Caradoc. He was a man of great renown, with a very loyal wife who was sister to King Galahal and born in Cirencester. She sat on his left, very beautiful and comely, and looking very much like a fairy.

[5] Erickson attributes these words to King Arthur, but they could be an intervention by the poet or a continuation of the queen's reply to him (see Bennett, ed., p. 63).

Her figure was well fashioned and she had long auburn hair. No woman present was as beautiful as she, apart from the queen. (473–516)

She looked at Caradoc and did not blanch, rather she spoke to him, saying: 'My fair friend, you would be wrong to fear that you will not drink from the horn at this high feast. So keep your head high and you will do me honour. I would not take as my husband any man, however powerful, even if he were an emir, if it meant leaving you, my beloved. I would refuse to take him as a husband and would rather become a nun and dress in a nun's habit. For every woman ought to take after the turtle dove: from the time she takes a mate she will never take another. This is the way a woman should behave if she is of good birth.' Caradoc was very happy and he jumped to his feet. He was handsome and comely, and a true knight. He placed the horn to his mouth; I have told you what is involved. When it had been filled, it contained a measure and a half;[6] it was full of red wine. He said to the king: 'Wassail!' He was tall and strong and he drained it. Filled with joy, he leapt over the table. He ran over quickly to King Arthur and, as he did so, said to him, but not in a low voice: 'My lord, I have drunk it all, may you be certain of this.' 'Caradoc', said the king, 'you are brave and courtly. You have indeed drunk it. More than a hundred people have witnessed this. Keep hold of Cirencester. Two years have now passed since I put you in possession of it and I will never take it away from you. Have it for the rest of your life and for the life of your son. And for your wife, whose deeds are worthy of great praise, I will present you with this horn, which is worth one hundred pounds of gold.' Caradoc replied: 'My lord, thank you'. He sat at dinner beside his wife of fair countenance. When they had eaten, each one took his leave. They went back home to their lands, from where they had come. They took their wives back and loved them all the more. (517–82)

My lords, Caradoc, who accomplished this deed, composed this lay. Anyone who was in Cirencester at a high feast could in truth see this horn there. Robert Biket says this, who knows a great many good yarns. Based on what an abbot had told him, he composed this tale about how the horn came to be in Caerleon. (583–94)

[6] The term 'measure' here translates the Old French *lout* (or *lot*). A measure and a half would be about six pints.

12. *Aristote*

Introduction

Aristote (*Aristotle*) is preserved in six manuscripts: (i) S; (ii) A: Paris, BNF, fr. 837; (iii) B: Paris, BNF, fr. 1593; (iv) D: Paris, BNF, 19152; (v) E: Paris, BNF, Bibliothèque de l'Arsenal 351; (vi) F: Saint-Omer, Bibliothèque Municipale 68. Our translation is based on S. MSS S and E fail to provide us with the name of an author, but the other four manuscripts give the author's name as Henris (v. 543 in the edition by Maurice Delbouille and v. 545 in that by Alain Corbellari). This Henri was long thought to be Henri d'Andeli, a native of Andelys in Normandy and the author of several other works that are usually described as *dits* (the *Bataille des vins*, the *Dit du chancelier Philippe* and the *Bataille des sept arts*). However, more recent research, especially that of Corbellari and François Zufferey, has led to the suggestion that the author concerned is Henri de Valenciennes, a cleric or professional writer who was attached to the court of Count Baldwin IX of Flanders and VI of Hainaut. This Henri wrote the *Vie de saint Jean l'Évangéliste* and the *Jugement de Nostre Seigneur*. A comparative analysis of the language, style and rhymes of the three *dits* plus the lay of *Aristote* and the known works of Henri de Valenciennes strongly suggests that the lay was not composed by Henri d'Andeli.[1]

The tale tells of the fate of the famous philosopher Aristotle, who tries to interfere in the love life of his equally famous master, King Alexander the

[1] For further details, see the Burgess and Brook edition of *Aristote*, pp. 10–14; the joint article by Alain Corbellari and François Zufferey, 'Un problème de paternité: le cas d'Henri d'Anderli. I: arguments littéraires; II: arguments linguistiques', *Revue de Linguistique Romane*, 68 (2004), 47–78; and Zufferey's article 'Henri de Valenciennes, auteur du *Lai d'Aristote* et de la *Vie de saint Jean l'Évangéliste*', *Revue de Linguistique Romane*, 68 (2004), 335–57. Delbouille dates the poem to 'before 1230 and perhaps before 1225' (p. 30) and Zufferey to around 1215.

Great. The king has conquered Greater India, but instead of relaxing in the company of his men, and preparing for future military endeavours, he is in thrall to a maiden with whom he has become infatuated. His men begin to grumble about this behind his back and their complaints come to the ears of his tutor Aristotle. Thinking he should intervene, Aristotle argues that it is wrong to forsake one's companions in favour of a single woman, and a foreigner at that. Alexander responds by praising the notion of commitment to one woman and by claiming that those who reprimand him lack love within themselves. Aristotle's retort is that Alexander has gone blind and lost his wits. He is acting like an animal and should be put out to pasture. Aristotle's tirade is initially successful, and for a time Alexander stays away from his mistress. But this separation merely fuels his desire, and he cannot stay away from her for long. Faced with his beloved's surprise that a true lover could absent himself in that way, Alexander blames Aristotle and the maiden decides to turn the tables on him. Alexander is to get up early next morning and to watch what happens from his tower window. Scantily clad, the maiden frolics around the garden, singing songs and making a garland of flowers for her hair. Aristotle is so captivated by her that, when she comes close to him, he grabs her by the tunic. She pretends to be surprised that it is Aristotle who has done this. In order to improve his chances of gaining her favours, he promises to put things right for her with Alexander if she allows him to satisfy his desire with her. First, she replies, he must allow her to put a saddle on him and he must carry her around the garden on his back. As he does so, she sings a triumphal song. All this has been witnessed by Alexander, so Aristotle's credibility has now been completely undermined. Aristotle does, however, counter by saying that if he at his age has succumbed to love, there can be no surprise that Alexander would do so (nevertheless, he cannot escape the consequences of his passion). The author tells us at the end that Aristotle has extricated himself cleverly from his predicament, but that for her part the maiden has been successful in her aims.

The lay revolves around the humiliation of the famous philosopher Aristotle and his abortive attempt to restore the love-sick Alexander to his military lifestyle. The incongruity of Aristotle's behaviour relates to his great reputation for learning and to his apparent unsuitability as a lover. The maiden describes him as grey-haired and pale-faced and Aristotle himself goes further, describing himself as old, grey, ugly, wan, swarthy and thin. He is certainly not the ideal 'fins amanz' ('perfect lover') to which Alexander's beloved refers in v. 156 (see also v. 77) when he returns to her after a short absence. There is also a second example of incongruity, one that is a catalyst for the entire story. King Alexander himself, 'the most powerful man in the world' (v. 84), King of Greece and Egypt and now conqueror of Greater India, has, in Aristotle's words, abandoned all the men in his realm for one foreign woman. What has brought this about is the personified figure of Love, who creates the story as we have it by holding him, and later Aristotle, in bondage. Among the numerous comments about love in this lay are the ideas that it seizes and ensnares everything, takes away any regrets one may have for what one is doing, makes its victims oblivious of themselves and exerts power over both the poorest and the most powerful man on earth.

A curious but effective aspect of the maiden's seduction of Aristotle is the singing of songs. The insertion of songs into Old French narratives was not unusual in the late twelfth or early thirteenth century, but the lay of *Aristote* is one of the earliest examples. That Aristotle is vulnerable to the words and music of popular songs is an extra comic dimension to his susceptibility to the maiden's physical charms. She sings four songs (in MS S there is a fifth song, sung by Alexander), manipulating the lyrics for her own ends and using them as weapons to facilitate her victory over Aristotle. The combination of the first song and the maiden's manoeuvres brings about a realisation in Aristotle that he could become prey to irrational behaviour and uncontrollable desire. But a further comic element in this lay is that such awareness, even in a famous philosopher and logician, is powerless to prevent him from succumbing to a maiden's play-acting and deception. When he grabs the maiden, it is effectively she who tightens her grip on him. There is now no way out. He has to agree to sort things out for her with Alexander and to let her use him as a packhorse, thereby providing Alexander with a visual spectacle of his humiliation.

Surrounded by highly trained knights, Aristotle's contribution to the world of horses and saddles is to walk around the garden with a beautiful maiden on his back. The traditional association between horse riding and sexual intercourse will not have escaped contemporary readers/listeners, but in this case no intercourse takes place. Instead, there is a descent into farce that provides the lay with its memorable image, one that is well attested outside of the lay itself: not only, unsurprisingly, in marginal illustrations in manuscripts but also, unexpectedly, in mural decorations on town halls, on tapestries and caskets, and even on cathedral façades (see the article by Pietro Marsilli in Further Reading and the cover image for the present volume). These images were often used as a symbol of the power of women over men and of men's inability to control their bestial urges. Perhaps also involved in the lay is a sadomasochistic element that draws on and mocks the practice in which a dominant rider mounts and rides another person for their mutual erotic pleasure. In *Aristote* it is Aristotle, as he carries the maiden around the garden, who is being taken for a ride, all in the name of the restoration of normal relations between the maiden and Alexander. On a higher level, Aristotle's degradation will have been seen as timely by those in contemporary academic circles who were opposed to his influential philosophical views. When, at the close of the narrative, he is confronted by Alexander, all that remains for him is a damage limitation exercise. But, as we have seen in the plot summary above, Aristotle copes well with this personal crisis (he is even commended by the author, vv. 405–06), and he can now remind Alexander from personal experience that his infatuation with his maiden will not be devoid of consequences.[2]

Further Reading

Ladd, Anne, 'Attitude towards Lyric in the *Lai d'Aristote* and some Later Fictional Narratives', *Romania*, 96 (1975), 194–208.

Marsilli, Pietro, 'Réception et diffusion iconographique du conte de *Aristote et Phillis* en Europe depuis le Moyen Age', in *Amour, mariage et transgressions au Moyen Age: actes du colloque des 24, 25, 26 et 27 mars 1983, Université de Picardie, Centre d'Études Médiévales*, ed. Danielle Buschinger and André Crépin, Göppinger Arbeiten zur Germanistik 420 (Göppingen: Kummerle, 1984), pp. 239–69.

Nolan, Barbara, 'Promiscuous Fictions: Medieval Bawdy Tales and their Textual Liaisons', in *The Body and the Soul in Medieval Literature: The J. A. W. Bennett Memorial Lectures, Tenth Series, Perugia, 1988*, ed. Piero Boitani and Anna Torti (Cambridge: D. S. Brewer, 1999), pp. 79–105.

[2] The epilogue or conclusion to MS S, from which our translation is taken, consists of only ten lines, but in the versions printed by Delbouille and Corbellari they are considerably longer, over seventy lines. These lines largely consist of a lengthy diatribe on the nature of love, but they do include a pardon laughingly issued to Aristotle by Alexander for his admonishing attitude, and here Aristotle leaves Alexander to act as he wishes. See the Burgess and Brook edition, pp. 19–20.

Translation

No one should refrain from recounting and narrating fine words. Rather one should gladly listen to them, for from them, as one listens to them, one can learn sense and courtliness. Good men should rejoice over fine things, for that is right and fitting. The wicked scowl as soon as they hear them uttered, for just as good people praise fine things, and go around saying fine things, slanderers despise them when they cannot do them any worse harm. For the nature of envy is such that it always dwells deep in the hearts of those who have been reduced to such a state that they cannot hear a word of praise for anyone without wishing to contradict it. I am amazed at why this matters to them. Wicked and uncourtly people, why do you burden others with your slander and your torment? Any excuse for this is very poor, and you are committing mortal sin on two counts: the first is to indulge in slander and the second is to pin your wickedness on others. This is indeed cruel and villainous behaviour, [but envy never ceases to run. I should not care to pause or to delay at this point, as I do not think it would do me any good][3] to rebuke the cruel wretches, whom one can call Ganelon, and who could not refrain from slander until they died, so committed and accustomed to it have they become.[4] (1–33)

Now I will return to my tale of an occurrence I have undertaken to relate, for I thought highly of the subject matter when I heard an account of it. It should definitely be made known, told and recounted in rhyme, without coarseness and without incurring reproach. For a work with coarseness running through it should not be recounted at court. As long as I live, in no work of mine will I ever seek to use coarse words. I have never done such a thing, nor will I ever do so, in any work or story that I may compose, since coarseness is destructive and everything is affected by its flavour. I will never become the writer of anything I hear in my lifetime that contains any coarse words. Instead I will relate, as a truly moral tale, something that is pleasing and of value and will replace fruit and spices.[5] (34–54)

[3] These lines are borrowed from MS D.

[4] Ganelon is the traitor in the *Chanson de Roland*, and his name is used in several later texts to designate treachery.

[5] Fruits and spices were apparently eaten at dessert to sweeten the mouth.

The tale concerns Alexander, King of Greece, an illustrious figure. He demonstrated his anger to so many princes in order to bring them down and subdue them, and to further enhance his own status. This he accomplished through his mother Largesse, which appears harsh to all who are avaricious but kindly to all who are generous. For just as the avaricious love money, those who are generous hate holding on to it, because no good can come of it. The good King of Greece and Egypt had recently trampled on Greater India and taken up residence there. And if you were to ask me why he remained in that land so willingly, and took his ease there, I can readily tell you why. Love, which lays hold of and embraces so many people, seizing and ensnaring everything, held him in such bondage that he became a true lover, for which he had no regrets, since he had found a beloved as beautiful as any he could wish for. He had no desire to woo anyone else and wanted merely to remain and be with her. Love is truly strong and powerful when it can make the most powerful man in the world so humble and obedient that he pays no heed to himself, but is oblivious of himself because of another. This is right, because love is so precious, and when it has taken hold of a man he should not attempt any rebellion against it, for it is a fact that love has just as much true power over a king as it does over the very poorest person in either Champagne or France, so absolute is its lordship. (55–95)

The king dwelt with his beloved, and many men and women talked about the fact that he was so smitten, and that he led such a foolish life that he never left her side, like someone who could not help himself. Many of his people did not dare speak of this, but behind his back they chided him about it so much that his tutor Aristotle heard of it, and it is understandable that he should wish to dissuade him from it. He began to advise him politely, saying: 'You are wrong to abandon all the men in your realm for one foreign woman.' Alexander replied, making no other excuse: 'How many women should I love, then? In my view those who would wish to call me foolish have never loved, for a man can love only one woman, and by rights only one woman should please me. If anyone who bears a grudge against me for this woman maintains this view, urged by his heart, he will find little love within himself.' (96–119)

Aristotle, who knew everything that pertained to true learning, replied to the king and told him that it was regarded as very shameful that he was behaving in such a way, spending the entire week in the company of his beloved, and not relaxing and enjoying himself with all his knights. 'I think you have become blind, O king,' said his tutor Aristotle. 'You could now be put out to pasture, just like any beast in the meadow. Your wits have become very deranged if, for a foreign maiden, your heart is transformed so radically that one can find no sense in it. I should like to entreat and beg you to abandon such behaviour, for you are paying too high a price for your dalliance.' (120–39)

And so Alexander stayed where he was and held out for many hours and days, without going to, or approaching, his beloved, because of the words and the reprimand he had repeatedly heard from his tutor. But his desire for her did not diminish, even though he did not go to her as was his wont. He nevertheless loved her more and wanted her more than he had ever done at any time. Shame, calumny and alarm restrained him, until he returned to the woman who pleased him greatly. The fair maiden, who had been very disconsolate at the king's absence, leapt to her feet and said: 'My lord, I have been fully aware of your great distress, but how can a true lover refrain from seeing what pleases him so much?' Thereupon, she wept and remained silent. The king replied to her: 'Beloved, do not be surprised at this, for there was a reason for my absence. My knights and barons blamed me very harshly because I was sporting with them only too rarely. My tutor also said it was wrong and he reprimanded me for it severely. Indeed, I know very well that I have behaved badly, but I was afraid of scorn and shame.' 'My lord, I know well what this is about,' said the lady, 'so help me God. But if ingenuity and sense do not fail me, I should like to take revenge on him for this, so that you will be able to reprimand your grey-haired, pale-faced tutor all the more and reproach him for a worse affair, if I can live until tomorrow afternoon and Love, whose strength will never wane, gives me its force. Nor will his dialectic and learning ever prevail against me, unless he is very good at parrying. This you will witness tomorrow. Lord king, rise early [and position yourself] at the windows of this tower, and I will make my arrangements.' (140–87)[6]

Alexander was filled with joy at what he heard her say and he began to play a tune and sing this song:

> Fair Erembour rose early:
> 'You are very worthy, my fair sweetheart;
> I have no wish to pay heed to anyone else.

6 The text in square brackets is conjectural.

May God give me a poor reception.
My love is exactly as I desire it,
So that I lay no claim to any other woman.'

Then he left his beloved and departed, while she remained behind. In the morning, when it was the right time and hour, she arose without waking anyone else, and getting up did not bother her. Clad in just her chemise, she entered the garden beneath the tower in a blue spotted tunic, for the summer morning was fragrant with a gentle breeze. Nature had decked her fair countenance with lilies and roses. In her whole body there was nothing that did not rightfully belong there. Do not imagine that she had either a wimple or a headband tied on, for her long, thick blonde tresses made her look beautiful and suited her well. The lady, who had such a beautiful head of hair, would not have deserved to have it cut. (188–217)

She frolicked around the garden, raising her tunic as she moved and singing in a low voice, not loudly:

Now I see her, I see her, my beloved,
The fair blonde, I give myself to her;
The spring emerges there serenely,
Now I see her, I see her, my beloved,
There is a lovely lady there
Amid the irises, beneath the alder grove.
Now I see her, I see her, I see her,
The fair blonde, I give myself to her.

This little song was heard by the king, who was straining his heart and ears at the window in order to hear it. His beloved made him rejoice greatly at her words and at her singing. Before the day was out, his tutor Aristotle of Athens would be sure to proclaim that Love, if it is good, loyal and constant, longs to be embraced. He will not go around reprimanding the king any more, or causing him grief, for he will find such strong feelings within himself that he will be intoxicated with longing. (218–41)

Aristotle rose and sat at his books. He saw the fair one coming and going. This stimulated thoughts in his heart such that they made him close his books and say: 'O God, should this paragon now come closer to me here, I would abandon myself to her mercy. What? Would I do that then? I would not. There has never been a time when I, who know so much and can do so much, have found so much folly in my heart that a mere glance would steal my heart away. Love wants me to make it my guest, but honour considers such thoughts and such outrage to be shameful. Nonsense! What has become of my heart? I am old and grey, ugly and wan, swarthy and thin, and sharper in philosophy than anyone known or imagined. I have made very poor use of my studies, I who have never ceased to learn. Now Love, which has captured so many worthy men, strips me of my learning, all the better to grab hold of me. Through learning I have become ignorant, ignorant have I become through learning, since Love is seizing hold of me, so that I cannot gainsay it nor oppose its will.' (242–70)

In this way the tutor lamented. The lady made a garland of many flowers with a little sprig of mint. As she did so, she thought of love, and sang while picking the blooms:

> These loves have taken hold of me.
> Sweet one, I love you very much.
> These loves have taken hold of me,
> Just where I hold forth my hand.

Thus she sang, thus she disported herself, but Aristotle was very upset that she did not come any closer to him. She knew very well what was necessary to inflame and attract him. She intended to shoot an expertly feathered arrow at him. So hard did she work and strive that she drew him to her, just as she had planned. In fine and leisurely fashion, she placed her garland on her lovely head, giving no sign at all that she had seen or noticed anything. In order to deceive him all the better, and enchant him the more successfully, she approached the window singing a verse from a weaving song, for she did not want him to remain hidden any longer, as she had put so much effort into the matter:

> In a garden, by a spring,
> Whose water is clear and its shingle white,
> Sits a king's daughter, her hand on her cheek.
> Sighing, she calls upon her dear beloved:
> O, fair Count Gui,
> Your love deprives me of laughter and solace. (271–304)

Having uttered these words, she passed so close to the wide, low window that Aristotle grabbed her by the tunic. He thought he had suffered a great deal, so profoundly had he desired her. At this blow the old cat's candle fell right down on to the ground and he was irredeemably captured.[7] The maiden shouted out: 'Who is this?' she said. 'God, help me! Come now, who has grasped hold of me here?' 'My lady, welcome', said he who was completely in the clutches of the folly that was mastering him. 'Tutor', said the lady, 'come now! Is it you that I see here?' 'Yes', he replied, 'my fair one. For your sake I will put at risk body and soul, life and honour. Love and Nature have done so much to me that I cannot be separated from you.' (305–25)

'O tutor', she said, 'since it comes about that you love me so much, you will never be blamed for it by me. But things have been going very badly. I do not know who has made me quarrel with the king and blamed him for taking his pleasure so much with me.' 'My lady', he said, 'enough now, for through me will be settled the ill will and the rumours, and the blame and the strife. But in God's name come inside and let me satisfy my desire with your smooth and noble body.' 'Tutor, before I play the wanton with you', said the fair one, 'you must do a very unusual thing for me, if you are so infatuated with me. I have felt a very great urge to ride on your back a while, on the grass in this fine garden. I would like', said the maiden, 'to have a saddle put on you, so that I will ride with greater dignity.' (326–49)

The tutor replied joyfully that, as someone entirely devoted to her, he would gladly do this. Nature had certainly disturbed him when the maiden made him carry a palfrey's saddle on his shoulders. If Nature urges him on, Love makes a fool of a wise man when the very finest scholar in the world has himself saddled like a packhorse and is then made to go on all fours, crawling over the grass. Pay heed to the proverb, which I will relate at the appropriate time. He had the maiden climb on to his back and then he carried her. The young maiden took delight and pleasure from riding him; she led him around the garden and sang loud and clear:

> This is the way he goes who is led by Love;
> Master Fool is carrying me.
> This is the way he goes who is led by Love,
> And this is the way for those who support them. (350–71)

Alexander was in the tower and had clearly seen the whole performance. 'Tutor', said the king, 'what is this? I can plainly see that someone is riding

[7] The old cat's candle is a reference to the tale of Salomon and Marcoul, in which Marcoul sends some mice to Salomon, who abandons the candle he was looking after in order to chase them. The tale was intended to show the superiority of nature over nurture.

you. What? Have you gone out of your mind, to be reduced to this state? The other day you forbade me so firmly from seeing her and now she has brought you to such a state that there is no reason in you. Instead, you are behaving like an animal.' Aristotle raised his head and the maiden dismounted. Then he replied shamefacedly: 'I was right if I feared for you, who are all ablaze with youthful ardour and burn with the true spirit of young manhood, since I, who am well on in years, could not stand up to Love and prevent it from bringing me to the sorry situation in which you have seen me. No matter what I have learned and read, Nature, which seizes and devours everything, has deprived me of it in a single hour. And know full well that, since I have clearly been forced to perform such an obvious act of folly, you cannot escape it without loss or without being blamed by your people.' (372–402)

Aristotle had extricated himself from his misdeed in a very fine and elegant fashion, and the lady had succeeded in everything she had undertaken. It is better to be without companionship than to have a female companion. Through this lay I say to you finally: there are those who think their heart is very noble and unquestionably very knowledgeable, but who in a crisis find it very impoverished. (403–12)

13. *Lecheor*

Introduction

Preserved in one manuscript, S, *Lecheor* is certainly a comic and perhaps a parodic work. It is a lay about a lay, one that is composed by a group of ladies on the occasion of the annual festival of St Pantelion in Brittany. At this festival, knights and ladies traditionally exchanged stories about love and chivalry and the adventure judged to be the finest was turned into a lay. In the year in which the lay is set, the content is different, even shocking. After outlining a whole range of chivalric activities, one of the ladies concludes that they are all accomplished for the sake of just one part of a woman's body: her cunt. She adds that a woman without a cunt would never find a lover. This surprising choice of subject matter is nevertheless supported by the knights present and the lay is preserved and cherished like all the other compositions generated by the festival. The author provides for the work the commonly used title of *The Lay of the Lecher* (*Le Lai du Lecheor*, v. 118),[1] hinting that if he (or she?) used the lay's 'true name' ('droit non', v. 119) he would be rebuked. The true name, *Le Lai du Con* (*The Lay of the Cunt*), would of course give the game away from the outset of the narrative and lessen the impact of the poem's content.

Lecheor is unusual in that it does not have a hero or a heroine. The target of the ladies' observations is knights as a whole, but it is interesting to note that the knights actually present at the festival do not react negatively to the damning conclusion that whatever acts they perform, including deeds of bravery and attendance at tournaments, they have only one thing on their minds: their lady's *con*. No matter what they may have achieved personally in the last year, they all have no qualms about backing

[1] The Old French term *lecheor* is not restricted to the sense 'lecher'. It can also be translated as 'glutton, debauchee, scoundrel, paramour', etc.

the ladies' lay and they even contribute towards the composition of the final version. However, the earthy subject matter of the lay is surprising in that the ladies present at the festival appear to be the epitome of courtliness: they are noble, beautiful, well educated, wise and beautifully attired for the occasion. The ladies in the group that initially creates the chosen lay are said to be the 'flower of Brittany' (v. 57). They all agree that knights have a one-track mind where women are concerned but, again perhaps surprisingly, they do not hold this against them.

When the lady poses a series of questions, to which she will finally give her answer, there is no sense that she is targeting inadequate knights. Her concern is with good knights ('bon chevalier', v. 69) and in particular with what makes them good, a crucial issue in a world dominated by military and courtly values and the desire for fame. She asks for whom knights are 'franc' and 'debonere' (v. 75), terms which are difficult to define but which embrace the concepts of nobility, worthiness, goodness and generosity of spirit. She does not see an obsession with women's genitalia as a hindrance to social values and good behaviour. This probably explains why the knights themselves are happy to promote her subject for the annual lay. But at some stage members of the audience must have realised that by standing conventional wisdom on his head, by saying that knights do what they do not from motives such as honour and fame but purely for sexual reasons, the lady has effected a shift in the balance of power from men to women. Good knights are beneficial to society because they have low, not high, ideals. All good deeds are performed for the cunt (v. 95).

Further Reading

Brook. Leslie C., 'The Creative Process in the *Lai du Lecheor*', *French Studies Bulletin*, 36 (1990), 3–5.

Brusegan, Rosanna, 'Le *Lai du Lecheor* et la tradition du lai plaisant', in *Miscellanea mediaevalia: mélanges offerts à Philippe Ménard*, ed. J. Claude Faucon, Alain Labbé and Danielle Quéruel, 2 vols (Paris: Champion, 1998), I, pp. 249–65.

Eley, Penny, 'Intertextuality in Action: The *Lai du Lecheor*', *French Studies Bulletin*, 69 (1999), 8–10.

Méla, Charles, 'Un paradoxe littéraire: le *Lai du Lecheor*', *Colloquium Helveticum*, 5 (1987), 59–71.

Translation

In days gone by, so the Bretons tell us, many people used to assemble on St Pantelion's day to honour the festival of the saint, the noblest and most beautiful women in the land, ladies and maidens, who were in the region at that time. There was no lady in the land who was not present that day and they were all very richly attired. Each one made a great effort to be well dressed and well attired. Trials were conductd there, and deeds were recounted concerning love and passion, and noble acts of prowess. Whatever had happened in that year was listened to carefully and retained. They related their adventures and the others listened to them. They retained the best of them, repeating and recounting it. It was often told and recounted until it was praised by everyone. Between them they composed a lay about it, such was their custom, and the knight whose adventure it was would put his own name to it. The lay was named after him. This, you must know, is the truth. Then the lay was preserved until it was known everywhere. For those who were skilled musicians on viol, harp and rote, carried it forth from that region to the countries to which they journeyed. (1–36)

At the festival of which I am speaking, to which the Bretons came in this way, the assembly took place on a high mountain so that everyone could hear more easily. There were many clerics and knights there, and many people from other professions. There were noble and beautiful ladies there, and young girls and maidens. When they had left the church, they all assembled together in the place where they had arranged to meet. Each one recounted his deeds and each one related his adventure; they came forward one by one. Then they set about preparing the tale they would put forward. The ladies sat to one side and gave their opinion. They were wise and well bred, noble, courtly and esteemed; they were the flower of Brittany, its finest and most worthy women. One of them was first to speak, saying with great conviction: 'Ladies, let me have your advice on a matter that is a great marvel to me. I hear these knights talking a great deal of tournaments and jousts, of adventures and love, and of entreaties addressed to their beloveds. They never mention the reason why all these great deeds are performed. (37–68)

How is it that these knights are brave? For what reason do they enjoy tourneying? For whom do these young men dress so well? For whom do they put on new clothes? For whom do they send gifts of their rings, their ribbons and their jewels? For whom are they courtly and noble? For what reason do they refrain from doing harm? For what reason do they enjoy dalliance and kissing and embracing? Do you know of any explanation, apart from one single thing? None of them will ever have dallied so much, or uttered enough fine words or entreaties, that before he can take his leave he does not wish to come back to this. From this derive the great benefits for which all honourable deeds are performed. Many men have been greatly improved by it, and increased their fame and reputation, who would not have been worth a button if it were not for their thoughts of the cunt. I pledge you my faith, no woman has such a beautiful face that, if she had lost her cunt, she would ever have a friend or lover. Since all good deeds are performed for it, let us not attribute them to something else. Let us compose a new lay about the cunt, and those it will truly please will hear it. However well the best composers perform, you will soon see them all turn towards us. (69–100)

The seven ladies were in agreement with her. They said that she had spoken very well. Then they began the lay. Each one put music and song to it, and sweet notes with a high pitch. They made the lay a fine and courtly one. All those who were at the festival abandoned the lay they were composing. They turned towards the ladies and lavished praise on their work. When they heard the excellent subject, they composed the lay along with them, and it was preserved and cherished by clerics and knights. It was much loved and much enjoyed, and it is still not hated. Many people say of this lay that it is the *Lay of the Lecher*. I do not wish to utter the true name in case I am rebuked for it. According to the tale I have heard, I have thus brought the lay to an end for you. (101–22)

14. *Ignaure*

Introduction

Preserved in only one manuscript (Paris, BNF, fr. 1553), *Ignaure* has a named author, Renaut (v. 621). This Renaut has been identified as the 'Renals de Biauju' who composed the romance *Le Bel Inconnu* (v. 6249). He has long been seen as a member of the Beaujeu family from the Mâconnais, but it is now thought more likely that he was from the rival Bâgé family. Despite some intriguing parallels, it remains uncertain whether the author of *Le Bel Inconnu* also wrote the lay of *Ignaure*, and there is a further complication in that there was more than one Renaut in the Bâgé family.[1]

As in the lay of *Lecheor* (see above) and Marie de France's *Chaitivel* (vv. 233–37), the question of the poem's title is raised by the author in the concluding lines. We are not expecting the title, which the author tells us was bestowed on the text by the French, the Bretons and, unusually, the Poitevins: the *Lay del Prison* (*Lay of the Prisoner* or *Lay of the Capture*, v. 660). Our surprise derives largely from the fact that neither prisons nor captivity had loomed large within the tale. We are told that Ignaure is handed over to the custody of his captor's loyal servants (vv. 511–13) and that the ladies seek to find out if he has been released from 'prison' (v. 563). The author states that he himself is being held in his beloved's 'sweet prison' ('douce prison', v. 655), but the final section of Renaut's version of the story would not have been part of traditional versions, whose title the author purports to offer us. Perhaps we are supposed to infer that Ignaure is a prisoner of his own sexual inclinations. However, the scribe's *explicit* to the text, 'Chi define li lays d'Ygnaure' ('Here ends the lay of Ignaure'), provides us with a title that seems closer to the mark.

[1] See G. Perrie Williams, ed., *Le Bel Inconnu* (Paris: Champion, 1929), pp. vii–viii; R. Lejeune, ed. of *Ignaure*, pp. 39–43. For further details, see the Burgess and Brook edition of *Ignaure*, pp. 8, 44–45.

The lay tells of a fun-loving and renowned knight of modest means and background, whose attractiveness to women is such that he wins the love of the wives of twelve peers who reside at the castle of Riol (perhaps the castle of Rieux in the *arrondissement* of Vannes in Brittany). His prodigious ability to maintain a sexual relationship with all twelve ladies for over a year eventually comes to grief when he is captured, castrated and killed by the cuckolded husbands. The catalyst for his grisly end is a meeting of the twelve wives where they attempt to find the noblest of what they thought to be twelve different lovers. They elect one of their number to act as 'priest' and be the recipient of the name of each lady's lover. Hearing that only one name, Ignaure, has emerged from the eleven confessions, and that he is also the lover of the priest herself, the ladies decide at once to seek revenge on hm. When he next arranges an assignation with one of them, they plan to corner him and stab him to death. However, this plan comes to nought when Ignaure sweet talks the ladies and convinces them that he is committed to all of them as a true lover. It is agreed that he be allowed to keep one lover and he chooses the priest. But making far more frequent visits to just one lady than he would have done to twelve exposes him to danger and he is betrayed by an informer. Caught in bed with his remaining mistress by the husband, his fate is decided by the twelve cuckolded husbands. They resolve to feed his 'lowest member down below' ('daerrain membre aval', v. 542) to the ladies, along with his heart. Although hampered at first by the ladies' refusal to eat, the husbands are in due course able to inform their wives that they have just ingested that part of their lover's body that had given them the most pleasure. When all the ladies are aware of what they have eaten, they vow never to eat again and they spend their remaining days in praising and lamenting their lover's attributes.

Despite the fact that by the end of the narrative there are thirteen dead bodies (the twelve wives and their dismembered lover) and twelve widowed husbands, there are undoubted comic elements in this lay. At the outset, the twelve wealthy and powerful knights in the castle of Riol are all being cuckolded, not by twelve lovers but by just one, a man who caters for the emotional and sexual needs of all twelve wives. Philandering seems merely to be an extension of the love of fun that characterises Ignaure's view of the world, which is summed up at the outset by his departure one spring morn to seek the May blossom, in the company of minstrels with their little flutes and pipes. As far as Ignaure's love life is concerned, it seems to be a question of the more the merrier, and the knock-on effect is that his lovemaking helps him to further his chivalric career. For, much to the surprise of his fellow tournament competitors, he turns up with a substantial entourage of knights, all paid for by donations from his mistresses. There is certainly a degree of parody of the total commitment of two lovers to each other within the courtly world of the 'fine amor' ('pure love') that was so lauded by many contemporary writers.[2] But there is also religious parody, with twelve female 'disciples' in thrall to one charismatic male and the election of a mock female priest to hear confession, not of sins but of the delights and charms of their illicit sexual partner. The act of beating the breast during confession is even replaced by a suggestion that it is the bum that should be beaten, since this part of the woman's anatomy is the seat of the sins that affect these particular penitents (see also the analogy between claps of thunder and sexual thrusts in vv. 160–99).

Once the confessions have been made, the revelation that the anticipated twelve lovers are nothing of the sort, being merely the irrepressible Ignaure, is one of the delightful comic moments of the lay. The scene relating the ladies' failure to carry out their plan to avenge themselves by stabbing Ignaure to death degenerates into farce when he not only escapes unharmed but ends up with a consolation prize of the lady of his choice. When he is faced with a life containing only one mistress and throws caution to the wind by visiting her with dangerous frequency, the author draws humour from this situation by pointing out, on two occasions, that a mouse with only one hole cannot survive long and is easily trapped (vv. 373, 481–82; the 'hole' being no doubt a reference to the lady's vagina). When, as the husbands dine together, and Ignaure is about to be betrayed to them by a smirking traitor, culinary humour takes over. The traitor's intervention is referred to as an 'unwelcome dish' (v. 393), and when Ignaure is captured he is said to be facing a very meagre dinner. The theme of food then takes on a new dimension when it is suggested that the ladies should be served a dish containing some

[2] We are told at the beginning that Ignaure is aroused and inflamed by 'fine amors' (v. 36). There is also a link between 'fine amors' and the nickname Nightingale, given to Ignaure by the ladies (v. 37). Nightingales were a common feature of courtly narrative. They were associated with the month of May and have frequently been seen as symbolic of sexuality, intense passion and violent death. A connection between the nightingale and the courtly poet-lover (see the final part of the narrative, vv. 627–56) has also been made. In vv. 164–65 a real nightingale puts in an appearance in a fruit tree.

of their lover's body parts. The end of the narrative is dominated by the ladies' refusal to eat, then by the breaking of their fast, followed by its fatal restoration.

Although tales of a penis or genitals being fed to an errant wife are not unknown in literature and folklore (see the Burgess and Brook edition of *Ignaure*, pp. 36–37), far more common and undoubtedly well known to the audience would have been eaten-heart tales in which a husband kills his wife's lover and serves up his heart to her. After discovering what she has eaten, it is customary for the wife to die.[3] In such cases the hearts of the two lovers act as the seat of their involvement with and commitment to each other, so in these tales the lady is in a sense consuming her own emotional life. But by prioritising the consumption of Ignaure's sexual organs, and stressing that this is the part of his body that has yielded the greatest pleasure for all twelve ladies (they crave it gluttonously, says one of the husbands, v. 573), the author provides a humorous twist to the traditional eaten-heart tale, perhaps parodying the courtly theme of devoted lovers with their quasi-spiritual commitment to one another. But other aspects of the traditional story are maintained. Those who eat the gruesome meal find it very much to their liking (*Ignaure*, vv. 559, 586), and on behalf of their lover they take their revenge against the husbands by vowing never to taste food again.

As the other poems in this section confirm, comic lays often share some characteristics with the genre of the *fabliau*, in which sexual appetites, trickery and revenge are standard features. But the author of *Ignaure* certainly calls his composition a lay (v. 657) and twice gives the title of the work as the *Lay del Prison* (vv. 660–61). The scribe agrees that it is a lay, even if he does not accept the author's title: 'Here ends the lay of Ignaure'. There is no lack of courtly elements in the narrative: the castle setting with its wealthy knights and sumptuously dressed ladies, the reference to 'fine amors', the search for May blossom, Ignaure's nickname Nightingale, the garden scene with its sophisticated dialogue, etc. The

[3] For a survey of 'eaten-heart' tales, see the Burgess and Brook edition of *Ignaure*, pp. 19–35. There are many variations on the story. For example, in the *Roman du Castelain de Couci et de la Dame de Fayel* by Jakemes (ed. John E. Matzke and Maurice Delbouille, Paris: Société des Anciens Textes Français, 1936) the lady's lover dies in the Holy Land and his heart is removed by his squire, who has been instructed to take it back to the lady. The husband intercepts the heart and has it served up to his wife. When she knows what she has eaten, the lady falls under the table and faints, dying shortly afterwards of grief.

amalgamation of these themes within a tale such as this illustrates the flexibility and subtlety of the genre.

Further Reading

Bloch, R. Howard, 'The Lay and the Law: Sexual/Textual Transgression in *La Chastelaine de Vergi*, the *Lai d'Ignauré*, and the *Lais* of Marie de France', *Stanford French Review*, 14 (1990), 181–210.

Di Febo, Martina, '*Ignauré*: la parodie "dialectique" ou le détournement du symbolisme courtois', *Cahiers de Recherches Médiévales (XIIe–XVe siècles)*, 5 (1998), 167–201.

Le Toury, Marie-Noëlle, 'La *fine amour* en question: *Ipomedon* et *Ignauré*', in *'Contez me tout': mélanges de langue et de littératures médiévales offerts à Herman Braet*, ed. Catherine Bel, Pascale Dumont and Frank Willaert (Louvain, Paris and Dudley, MA: Peeters, 2003), pp. 91–97.

Translation

Anyone who is in love should not conceal the fact, rather should he express it in fine words, from which others can learn and extract some fine lesson. I am able to get benefit and honour from this, but I will never become rich. Sense and wisdom, gold and silver, it is for these that people make the greatest effort. The giving of gifts has been taken away and is no more, and no longer will anyone be rewarded. Talent is wasted if it is kept hidden, but that which is displayed and revealed can flourish somewhere. For this reason, I wish to begin a tale, a very strange adventure that once befell a very powerful knight in Brittany, who fully deserves to be remembered. The knight's name was Ignaure and he was widely acclaimed. He was born in Hoël's land, at the noble castle of Riol. He was not of high nobility, but he achieved so much by his prowess that in the entire country there was no knight of such great fame. No one will ever be in better spirits. As soon as May began, he arose at daybreak and took with him five minstrels who played little flutes and pipes. The youth went off into the woods and with great rejoicing brought back the May blossom. He loved to enjoy himself and did so every day of the week. True love aroused and inflamed him, and women called him Lousignol [Nightingale]. (1–37)

In the castle at Riol lived twelve peers. They were brave and wise knights, rich from their lands and their income. Each of them had a wife, fair and noble, of high lineage and from a powerful family. Ignaure, a man of noble heart, courted all twelve wives and each of them granted him her love in accordance with his desire, promising that if he should want anything from her he would be served like a count. Each lady thought he was hers and they were adorned attractively and elegantly. Ignaure was on such good terms with them all and with each one of them when he came to her, that he was not thinking of any of the others, nor did he show any sign of desire for them. He enjoyed a very courtly life! When tournaments were arranged, he made his way to them to seek his fame, with twenty knights or even thirty; yet he had very little income. Everyone was astonished, but the ladies, who loved to make merry, would give him a great many gifts. Ignaure was quite the young nobleman! He loved them all for more than a year, until it came to the feast of St John, which gladdens every living creature, and the noble ladies, as it happened, went into a garden to enjoy some relaxation, all twelve of them. No one was there besides these twelve. (38–71)

There was one lady who was very keen to say what was on her mind. Woe betide anyone who would ever stop her from saying whatever she wanted! 'In truth, say what you will, I know that when you hear my proposal you will gladly agree to it.' 'So tell us what is on your mind, for we are all in agreement.' 'We are ladies, all of us cheerful, elegant, noble and esteemed, wives of the peers of this castle. We all love to make merry. Not a single one of us fails to love passionately, and this day is one for enjoyment. Let us make one of us a priest, and let her go and sit in the middle of this garden, beside that fruit tree, which is in bloom. Let each of us go and tell her, in confession, whom she loves and to whom she has given the gift of love. Thus we will know for certain which one of us has the noblest lover.' They all replied: 'She has spoken well. We agree to this without further ado. You yourself shall be the priest and hear the confessions. Go and sit down next to the fruit tree.' 'I agree to this,' said the noble lady. One of them stood up, dressed in a sumptuous tunic with a cloak of grey fur. She came to the priest and giggled. 'What do you desire?' said the master. 'I have come to confess, lord priest.' 'Be seated then and tell me, and mind you do not lie to me. What is your lover's name?' 'He is the man who has the highest renown and he is a knight of this domain. You know the one I mean, the most handsome man you know. Ignaure, the brave, the learned, is the one to whom I am given.' The priest flushed when she heard the name of her own lover. It was she herself who loved him the most and she controlled herself with the greatest difficulty. 'My lady, now let the next one come. I have heard your declaration.' (72–121)

Another lady came at once, beating her breast with her right hand. 'Sweet sister, beat your bum, which is the source of the sins with which your body is tainted.' 'My lord, I come to make amends.' 'I order you, by way of penance, to name your lover, fair friend.' 'Certainly, I will not lie. I can name for you the most courtly man between here and the Vermandois, the most handsome and the most cultured.' 'You value him very highly. I do not know whether you have proof of this.' 'Upon my word, you misjudge him! His name is Ignaure, the noble one.' The priest's blood froze when she heard her mention the man she thought was pledged only to her. 'My lady', she said, 'go now and sit down over there.' Then there came a very worthy woman, one who was very beautiful and very elegant. 'Sit down, my lady of great learning', she said. She had her sit down and then ordered her to name her lover, insisting that she tell her the truth. 'It is he', she replied, 'who has the most goodness, courtliness and courage. It is not his habit to act recklessly. If you knew the name of the man to whom I have given myself completely, he deserves to be a king or a count. I can name him. He is the noblest of men. His name is Ignaure, flower of Brittany.' When the priest heard this, she crossed herself. Her face went quite pale. 'My lady', she said, 'now go back and sit down. Your lover is very elegant and noble.' (122–59)

Dressed in silk brocade from Constantinople and looking regal, there came another lady with a courtly bearing. On her finger she had a little ring, and when she heard the song of the bird, which was singing like a nightingale in the fruit tree, she both kissed and caressed the ring. 'My lady', said the priest, 'be seated. I believe that you do not hate the man to whom that ring belonged.' She who had just been spoken to replied to her: 'He deserves to be a count.' 'Name him then, as he is so noble.' 'He is Ignaure, flower of chivalry.' When she heard this, she almost went out of her mind and her face flushed immediately. 'My lady, now go back to your seat.' Then a lovely lady came forward. She was beautiful and very gracious. 'Tell me, my lady, what is the name of the man who has the gift of your heart?' 'It is the man with whose name this land resounds. We should invoke his name when it thunders, then the lightning bolts would not strike us.' 'You are mistaken,' said the priest. 'You have called his name often enough, but that did not prevent a bolt from striking you. His name would never have protected you and the bolt was not destroyed.' 'May God bring such bolts back to me, and may I not complain that there are too many of them!' 'My lady, stop talking about this now and just name him, sweet sister.' 'Ignaure the noble-hearted one is his name and he makes the whole of Brittany tremble.' The priest smiled bitterly at the remarkable prowess of this man, whom each of the ladies had named. They never mentioned anyone else. (160–99)

When they had all confessed, they gathered around the priest. 'My lady, now tell us what you think. Which one has the worthiest lover?' 'In truth, each one of you has given me the name of just one knight. He has brought great shame on us. I too am in love with him, and all of you as well. In God's name, woe betide him for this! It is Ignaure who is responsible for all of this. He will pay for it without delay.' 'How can we best avenge ourselves?' 'We will agree among ourselves that the next one of us to whom he comes will arrange a meeting with him in this garden, and with all of us as well, without fail. We will be informed of the day and will all be there without delay. Let everyone bring a sharp knife. On this sumptuous and brazen rogue, who has wronged us all, let cruel vengeance be taken.' (200–22)

They all agreed to this plan, then left the garden and departed, each with sorrow in her heart. Ignaure, who was unaware of this plot, went to one of them. He embraced and kissed her a great deal, but was unable to go any further. 'My lady, how can it be that you are so aloof with me?' 'My lord, I am not aloof. On this occasion, bear with me, but I want you to pledge to me that you will come and speak with me on Sunday in my lady Clemence's garden. There you can accomplish your desires.' 'My lady', he said, 'at your pleasure. I will do your bidding.' He took his leave of her at once. There and then was the noble knight sentenced to death, unless he realised what was in store for him, or good fortune kept him away. She sent word to the others, and that Sunday, without quibble, they hid in the garden, well equipped with sharp knives that they kept under their cloaks. The lady who had planned this deception entered the garden in stately fashion, in such a way that Ignaure could see his lover. He arrived by another path, and with him he had a servant who acted as his messenger, collecting rents due to him. The lady, who was on the look-out for him, had left the gate ajar and the knight came in quite openly. Before he departed, he was in for a bad time! (223–59)

The lady came to meet him and he sent his messenger back to his lodging, having no desire for a witness. He locked the gate, and happily and calmly they went and sat down beneath a fruit tree. The lady embraced the young man and he kissed her very tenderly. But she would not grant him any further pleasure, for she had other things on her mind. The ladies came dashing out from all sides, inflamed with anger and rage, they who had been loved by the knight, who was very high-spirited and charming. 'My lady', he said, 'is this a trick? You have led me into a trap.' The ladies came up to where he was sitting and made a circle around him. Ignaure spoke to them. 'Welcome', he said at once. 'But', they replied, 'it is ill come for you.' 'It is right that your presumption should be exposed. Before you leave this spot, you will have the reward due to a faithless man, one who is treacherous and disloyal.' The priestess spoke first. 'Wait a moment, I beg you, allow me to have my say, then let each one of you state whatever she wishes. Ignaure, now do not lie to me. I have been your lover for many a day and I had given my heart to you.' 'My lady, I am your lover, your vassal and your knight, with a true heart, pure and sincere.' One of the ladies rose, filled with contempt, and she spoke to him haughtily: 'Ignaure, you are a good-for-nothing. What? Are you not my lover then?' 'Yes, my lady, so help me God, neither my heart nor my love has failed you. I will never fail you as long as I live.' Another lady was overcome with jealousy and she glared at him cruelly: 'Ah!' she said. 'Wretched traitor, this excuse will not suffice for me! Do you love someone other than me? You gave me your word that you were all mine.' 'My lady, I love you truly and will love you without fail.' 'What?' said another. 'What did you say? Do you not love me faithfully?' 'Yes, with all my power, and you and all the others I love truly, all of them, unreservedly, both their solace and their delight.' (260–315)

Then you could have heard a great commotion, women yelling and quarrelling and threatening the good vassal. They drew out the knives they had hidden. 'Ignaure, you have committed such a great crime that you are going to die forthwith. No one, other than God, can protect you.' 'Ladies, you would never be so cruel that you could commit such a great sin. If I now had my helmet laced upon my head and were riding my warhorse from Aquilée,[4] with my shield around my neck and my lance in my hand, I would get off my horse here and commit myself to your mercy. If I were to die at such fair hands, I should be a martyr among the saints. I well know that I was born at an auspicious hour.' When they heard these words, each of them wept. The knight's fine speech softened

[4] The place of origin of Ignaure's horse is not certain. The text has Equilanche, which some editors have emended to Equitanche. Aquilanche, the area around the province of Aquileia (the modern province of Udine in Italy), has been suggested.

their hearts greatly. The one who had heard the confessions said: 'Ladies, let us all come to an agreement, in truth, that you do my will, and may it not distress you'. 'We grant it, since it is agreeable to you.' 'Ignaure, you have deceived us thoroughly, this has now become abundantly clear to us. We will never love you again in the same way. But let us bear in mind and acknowledge that the one of us who pleases you best will be yours and will remain so; each of us wants to have her own lover.' 'I would not do this on any account; rather will I still love all of you, just as I have done until now.' 'Do as I say,' said the priest, 'or, by my head, you will die. Choose whichever one of us you want.' 'My lady', he said, 'you are the one. I am very upset over the loss of the others, because they are all most worthy, but your love fills me with desire.' 'I am very grateful to you,' said the noble lady. The others were very upset, yet they all swore that they would never love him and would leave him to her, freely and in peace. (316–62)

When they had come to their agreement, each one returned home and Ignaure went back to the town. Now you can imagine that it was necessary for him to go to his lover very frequently. If all the ladies had been his, he would not have done so, but now he had only a single path. He went often, not caring if he were seen. Because of these frequent visits, he was betrayed, tricked and found out. A mouse with just one hole cannot last long. By some chance or other, the words uttered by the foolish women in their confessions came to be known. What they said had been overheard in the garden. In the castle there was a traitor, very treacherous and very cruel. He often went to the lodging of the lady, who carelessly failed to keep things hidden, until he discovered the whole affair. Once he knew it, it was not hidden for long. (363–83)

One day the twelve peers all went to eat together. The rogue also went, I believe. Before he left the dwelling, he would tell them such a tale as would anger the shrewdest man there. The rogue began to speak and he laughed and crossed himself. 'What are you laughing at now, rogue? This is an unwelcome dish! I know what your intentions are. You are preparing some slander for us.' 'In faith', he said, 'I have seen something remarkable, which I am having great difficulty in relating to you. I cannot stop laughing at it.' 'May God help you, is it about us?' 'Yes, by God, about all of you.' 'Tell us the truth then, we are ready.' 'I will do so, if there is something in it for me.' 'There will be, never fear.' 'If I had some assurance from you, I would tell you, by Saint Germain.' One of them said: 'I will take this matter in hand if we cannot avenge ourselves'. 'My lords, if I tell you the truth about something, and I am quite certain of it, will you do me any harm or injury?' 'Not at all, you could never say anything of that sort.' 'You are all being cuckolded by a single man, just as I see you in this place, but one woman is lord and master.' (384–414)

When they heard what he said, each man was beside himself with anger, for this was a dreadful insult. 'Is he a burgess or a knight? Give us his name; that is the wisest thing to do.' 'The name of the vassal whose actions are so contrary to justice is Ignaure.' He told them the whole story, all about the garden and the confessions, and how the angry ladies had intended to kill him with their knives. 'The youth was terrified, for he was very close to death. Then they told him to choose the one he liked best; she alone would remain his. The others would withdraw and never again have any love for him. Like it or not, he did so. He chose one of your wives, the most beautiful and the wisest. I know which one of you is her lord.' 'Which one is it? Do you know?' He said to one of them: 'It is you.' The man replied in a fury: 'Praise God: if I am her lord, I am worth a lot more than the rest of you!' When the meal was over, he made them pledge that they would never reveal to anyone the course of this whole affair. They paid the man forthwith. He took his leave and the others remained, lamenting their shame. 'They will have control over the castle if we cannot avenge ourselves. That would make us true cowards.' One of them said: 'I agree with you. If you accept my plan, we will avenge ourselves properly for this. There is no point in using spies, since he has abandoned all of the women, except for the one he visits frequently. If her husband made a promise to us to watch him wherever he goes, he would easily catch him.' 'You have spoken well,' they all said with one voice, and the husband, beside himself with anger, replied that he would certainly watch out for him. 'My lord, let us know when you have caught him. Then we will go and avenge our shame.' (415–66)

They agreed to this plan and returned to their lodgings, anxious to bring down the man who took no care to conceal his actions. Ignaure, who loved to make merry, enjoyed himself in the castle, in front of his mortal enemies. The man whose wife was his beloved watched him day and night, in order to capture him. If he could catch him with his wife, he would keep his promise to all the others. Ignaure went very frequently to his loved one, to take his pleasure. The mouse that has just one hole is very soon captured and trapped. He was caught one morning with the lady with whom he had lain. The husband who was master of the house had found out about it from his spy. He knew the ins and outs of his dwelling, and he entered the stone-walled bedchamber through a subterranean chamber, with his helmet laced upon him and his sword drawn. He found Ignaure, who was in bed with his wife and suspected nothing. 'Ha!' he said at once, 'you have no business being here!' 'My lord', he said, 'in God's name, have mercy on me. You can see what a grim situation this is for us. I have sorely wronged you. It is no use me denying or concealing this.' (467–97)

With him the lord had two youths who were his nephews. They wanted to cut Ignaure to pieces, but the lord forbade them from doing this. They would take sweeter revenge. 'You will not kill him, upon my soul!' The lord addressed his wife: 'My lady, your lover needs to be bathed, and then I will have him bled. Make sure your lord has clean sheets!' The lady, who was dreadfully upset, tore at her hair. The lord took the vassal away. In a paved chamber he had him secretly guarded by men he trusted greatly. He promised Ignaure shame and suffering. His dinner would be very meagre! Then he informed the other peers about everything he had done and achieved. The lady, who was gravely tormented, let the other ladies know the whole truth about her predicament and about how Ignaure had been caught. 'I do not know whether he is alive or dead, and each of us has had from him all she desired. Now help me in my hour of grief. Just as each of us has had pleasure from him, let the grief be shared.' They all promised the messenger that they would never eat again, until they had found out for certain whether Ignaure was alive or dead. Then they began to fast. The lord had all his companions assemble in secret and they discussed what sentence they could mete out to the man who had caused them shame and suffering. One of them said: 'These filthy sluts have all sworn to fast until the time comes when they find out whether he will be put to death or released. In four days' time let us remove from the vassal his lowest member down below, the delights of which used to please them, and have it made into a meal, with the heart put into it as well. We will make twelve bowls out of all this and trick them into eating it, for we could not take any better revenge on them.' (498–548)

They accepted this plan and dismembered the good knight. As they had earlier agreed, they divided the food and served it up to the twelve ladies, who were fasting. Each one already had what her heart desired, so much so that they rejected the sweet aroma that was good and fine. But their lords praised the dish so much that they drank and also ate, and they did not despise the dish. When their spirits were revived, each lady begged her lord, for the love of God, to tell her truthfully whether Ignaure was out of prison. The one who had caught him in his house replied: 'My lady priestess, you used to be his mistress. You have eaten the object of your great desire, which gave you so much pleasure, for you had no wish for anything else. In the end it has been served up to you. I have killed and destroyed your lover. You can all share in the pleasure that comes from what women crave like gluttons. Is there enough of it for the twelve of you? We are now well avenged for your misdeed.' The lady fainted straightaway. When she came to, she sighed and wept. She hated death, which was taking so long, and had no interest in anything she could see. She sent word to her companions, to let them know what they had eaten. The messenger explained to them clearly what they had just enjoyed eating. They all made a vow to God that they would never eat again and would never again have a meal of such quality. (549–86)

They carried out their promise, just as they had made it. While they still lived, they composed a lament for him. One of them mourned his beauty and his limbs, which were so fair and shapely that the very finest were ugly in comparison. This is what they said about the youth. Another mourned his great valour, his noble body and his largesse, and a fourth his eyes and his flanks.[5] His eyes were so sparkling and merry. Another mourned his tender heart; there would never be one of its kind again. Alas, how we have changed you! The jealous ones have avenged themselves very cruelly, but we will not eat again. In this way we will take our revenge.' Another mourned his fine feet that sat so well in his stirrups. He was more accomplished than anyone else at hunting with dogs and birds, and more charming. They all mourned the pleasure he gave. Who could be more perfect than he was? All those who heard these lamentations wept on account of their grief. Neither their friends nor their relatives could persuade the noble ladies to eat. They did not forget their lover and quickly began to waste away. They wrung their hands, sighed and uttered lamentations continuously. (587–617)

Everyone grieved over their death. The lay, which should be remembered by everyone, has twelve full stanzas, for the subject matter is entirely true. As Renaut testifies, Ignaure, the good vassal, died, and those who were his lovers died for love of him. May God have pity on their souls, on those of both the knight and the ladies, and may there be a blessing on the lady who has had this lay written, which must be pleasing

[5] The text in this passage appears to be faulty. There is mention here of a fourth lady, but she is only the third to be mentioned. See the note to vv. 595–96 in the Burgess and Brook edition (p. 112).

to lovers. She has bound me so firmly that I cannot be untied. She has a long neck, white and plump, and she is not wrinkled or skinny. She is charming, very polite and whiter than newly fallen snow. You will not hear any further details; the rest of her is covered up. That is the finest link in the chain. But I do not think I am the man who can describe it from experience, except that, from the outside, I can see her breasts pushing out her tunic, so that they raise it up a little, for they seem to be very firm. I can see her beautiful shoulders, slender hands, delicate fingers and beautiful arms in her sleeves, and although she is a little broad in the hips she has a very attractive waist and her bearing is very elegant. She is neither too small nor too tall, and she is remarkably comely and very refined in her manners. She is the chain of love in all its perfection. Be aware that through this chain the lady leads me wherever she wishes me to go. I am in a very sweet prison and have no desire to escape from it through ransom. That is the subject matter of this lay. I will bring it to an end for you. The French, the Poitevins and the Bretons call it the *Lay of the Prisoner*. Here ends the *Lay of the Prisoner*. I know absolutely nothing more about it. It was composed for Ignaure, who was dismembered for love. Here ends the *Lay of Ignaure*. (618–65)

15. *Oiselet*

Introduction

Oiselet (*Little Bird*) is preserved in five manuscripts: (i) S; (ii) A: Paris, BNF, fr. 837; (iii) D: BNF, fr. 24432; (iv) C: BNF, fr. 25545; (v) E, BNF, fr. 1593. These manuscripts are usually divided into two groups: SAD and CE. Our translation is based on the version in S.

A rich peasant has purchased owns a beautiful manor and a magic garden from the impoverished son of a knight. The garden is the focus of interest throughout the tale and it is described at some length. It is visited twice daily by a little bird that perches in a pine tree that shades a fountain. The bird sings a magic song that has the power to make any listener feel happy and to inspire thoughts of love. The garden is destined to last only as long as the bird comes to sing. The peasant sits beneath the tree each day to listen to the song, but one morning the bird sings of the importance of loving God, as God loves lovers, and of being generous and courtly. This message is meant for an aristocratic listener, but when the bird espies the peasant it changes its song abruptly, showing contempt for him and calling on the garden to wither and the manor to collapse. It accuses him of being interested only in money. The peasant then traps the bird, intending either to sell it or to get it to sing exclusively for him. The bird refuses, and when the peasant threatens to eat it, it manages to persuade him to let it go free, in return for learning three secret truths that no one else has ever known. The truths are revealed one by one, and after each one the peasant has an angry outburst, claiming that what the bird has told him is common knowledge. The bird then tells him that he should have heeded the final truth and not let it go free, as its body contains a precious stone weighing three ounces that has the power to grant anyone's wishes. The peasant is beside himself with rage, whereupon the bird tells him that he should have realised that his statement about the weight was a lie, as the bird itself did not weigh more than half an ounce. After adding that he should not have dismissed the truths so readily, the bird flies away, never to be seen again. The garden subsequently falls into ruin and the tale concludes with a moral regarding covetousness.

In most of the lays in this collection the setting and narrative revolve to a great extent around the world of the court and courtly values. In *Oiselet* the normal courtly world is more peripheral, as a result of the sale of the property, hitherto in aristocratic hands, to a rich peasant. This transfer of ownership would seem to reflect the difficulties experienced in the thirteenth century by formerly landed gentry, who have been forced to sell their lands to peasants and burgesses enriched by the money to be made from the ever-growing urban markets. The garden had been created by a knight, and clearly the bird did not realise for some time that there had been a change of ownership, as it continued to sing of love as though the property still belonged to an inhabitant of the courtly world. Its refusal to continue to sing in the same way indicates that the aristocratic, courtly world considered true love to be its exclusive domain. The bird thus becomes the mouthpiece for this world in its contempt for that of the peasant, who is portrayed as ignorant, mercenary and gullible.

The three pieces of wisdom imparted by the bird are: 'Do not weep for what you never had', 'Do not believe all you hear' and 'Do not throw down at your feet what you hold in your hands'. This is the order in which they occur in three of the five manuscripts (SAD), while in the other two (CE) the order of the first two truths is reversed.[1] Clearly the two groups of manuscripts derive from different traditions, so that at one point different preferences were recorded. In any event, the outcome of the encounter is nihilistic, as both of the two worlds, the courtly world and the peasant's, are symbolically destroyed: 'No one came there again, or lived there' (v. 406). We have included this work in our 'Fun and Games' section as, although aristocratic readers/listeners would have mourned the loss of the idyllic, even magic features of the garden, throughout the lay they would have revelled in the way the bird (and the author) toys with the upstart, ill-educated peasant. Even in a first experience of the work they would have known that the garden's new owner was in for a shock and that his attempt to establish himself in an unfamiliar world would be doomed to failure.

[1] For an edition and translation of the section in MS C that presents the three *sens* in a different order from that in S, see our edition of *Oiselet*, pp. 160–65.

Further Reading

Brook, Leslie C., 'The Bird's Three Truths in the *Lai de Oiselet*', *Reading Medieval Studies*, 19 (1993), 15–25.

Lee, Charmaine, 'Il giardino rinsecchito: per una rilettura del *Lai de l'Oiselet*', *Medioevo Romanzo*, 5 (1978), 66–84.

Le Saux, Françoise, '"Dieus et Amors sont d'un acort": The Theology of Love in the *Lai de l'Oiselet*', in *The Court Reconvenes: Courtly Literature across the Disciplines. Selected Papers from the Ninth Triennial Congress of the International Courtly Literature Society, University of British Columbia, 25–31 July 1998*, ed. Barbara K. Altmann and Carleton W. Carroll (Cambridge: D. S. Brewer, 2003), pp. 91–97.

Translation

It happened in former times, well over a hundred years ago, that there was a rich peasant. I am not sure of his name, but he was an extremely wealthy man, with woods, meadows and rivers, and all that befits a man of status. If I tried to tell you the sum of all he owned, you would think the account fictitious. He had such a beautiful abode that there was none such in the whole world, neither so fair nor so charming. I will now tell you what it looked like. I do not think that one could ever create such a tower or magnificent keep. A river ran all round it, enclosing the entire estate, and there was a garden of great worth, surrounded by water and open to the air. The person who built it was no fool, rather he was a noble knight. After the father, the son owned it and he sold it to this peasant, and so it passed from hand to hand. You know well that through bad inheritance, estates and manors fall into ruin. (1–26)

The garden was wondrously beautiful. Herbs of many kinds that I cannot name were there, but to tell the truth there were roses and flowers, giving off very strong scents, and spices such that anyone who was ill and infirm, and lying on his sick bed, would go away healthy and strong, if he lay in the garden for one whole night. It was garnished with good herbs and the lawn was so even that there were no mounds or dips. The various trees rose to a great height at the top and there was no such beautiful garden on earth. Whatever fruit you asked for could be found there throughout every season. The man who created it was very clever. It was made by enchantment and there was much proof of this within it.

The garden was fair and spacious, and perfectly circular. In the middle was a fountain, beautiful, limpid and wholesome, flowing with such vigour that it appeared to be bubbling madly, yet it was as cold as marble. It was shaded by a beautiful tree, whose branches were spread wide and artfully arranged with a thick covering of leaves. Around the time of the finest summer's day, when it came to the month of May, you could not see the rays of the sun, so thick were the branches. It should be highly prized, and such was its nature that its leaves always remained on the tree. However much a storm or tempest raged, no leaf or bark was torn off. (27–70)

The pine tree was delightful and lovely and a bird came there to sing, twice daily and no more. Let me tell you for a fact that it came there in the morning and then again in the evening. The bird was beautiful and pretty, but it would delay the narrative if one were to describe it to you. It was smaller than a finch, but slightly larger than a wren, and it sang so well and so beautifully that no nightingale, blackbird, thrush or starling, it seems to me, or skylark or lark, is as pleasing to hear as its song, let me assure you. The bird was so skilled in singing lays and new songs, rotrouenges[2] and other ditties that a fiddle, harp or viol would be superfluous. There was a wondrous thing about its song. You never heard its equal, for the song had such power that no man was ever so sorrowful that, when he heard the bird sing, he would not cheer up at once and forget his great sorrow. If he had no thoughts of love, he would immediately be smitten and think himself as worthy as an emperor or king, whether he were uncouth or courtly. If he were over a hundred years old, and not dead to this world, and he heard the bird's song, he would not fail to think immediately that he was a young man and consider himself so handsome that he would be loved by young girls, damsels and maidens. There was another wondrous thing, too. The garden could not survive unless the little bird came there to sing its sweet songs, for from the song came forth the essence that sustained the strength of the flowers. If the bird departed, the garden's great beauty would fade. It would immediately wither and the fountain would dry up, as both flourished because of the bird. (71–123)

The peasant who owned the garden was in the habit of coming daily to hear the sweet singing by the fountain beneath the pine tree. One morning he came there and washed his face in the water, and from the pine tree the bird in full voice sang a song that was full of delight.

[2] The rotrouenge is a form of lyric poetry that modern scholars have found hard to define, as only four examples survive, three with a refrain and one with music.

A lesson could be learned from it. The lay was very delightful to listen to and one would be all the better as a result. The bird sang in its own tongue: 'Hearken', it said, 'to my lay, be you knight, cleric or layman, who concern yourselves with love and feel its pains. I address myself to you, maidens, who are attractive and fair and wish for earthly joy. I say to you, and swear as a truth, that above all you should love God, uphold the law and his commandments, go readily to church and hear his service. For by listening to God's service no one can suffer harm, and as a truth I state that God and lovers are in accord and he does not hate true love that is conducted without villainy. God heeds sincere prayer and does not ignore almsgiving. God delights in all generosity, for there is no blemish in it. God also loves honour and goodness, and he loves love and loyalty. The miserly are the envious ones, the avaricious the covetous ones, the villainous the wicked ones and the evildoers the foul ones. Only courtesy, honour and loyalty sustain love. If you abide by this, you will win both God and his love.' (124–68)

This is what the bird sang in its song, and when it saw the peasant seated beneath the pine tree, gazing at it, wicked and envious, it sang differently for him: 'Cease flowing, river! Tower, perish! Dwelling, collapse! Fade, flowers! Herbs, wither! Trees, stop bearing fruit! Here were wont to listen to me noble ladies and knights, who valued the fountain. They lived longer and loved more passionately because of it, and upheld chivalry. Now this envious peasant hears me and loves wealth far more than he does wooing. Once my singing ceased for him, he fell prey to covetousness. The others used to listen to me in order to make merry and rejoice, and the better to refresh themselves. Yet he comes here to eat better!' When it had said this, it flew off, and the peasant, who remained there, reflected that, if he could catch it, he could very quickly sell it for a high price. If he could not sell it, he would put it in a cage and keep it there all day long. (169–99)

He took his snare and set it, then watched, sought and searched until he perceived the branches where the bird most frequently perched. He made a trap and set it, adjusting it very skilfully. When the morning arrived and the bird came to the garden, it perched straightaway on the pine tree and the unfortunate, hapless and wretched one was immediately caught in the trap. The peasant climbed up and seized the bird. 'This is the reward for serving a peasant,' said the bird. 'You have captured me, but you have acted unwisely, it seems to me, for you will get a poor ransom for me.' 'On the contrary, I will get plenty of songs! Now you will sing for me more often. You have served me in your way, now you will serve me as I wish and do my bidding.' 'I have come off the worse. I used to have for my pleasure woods, rivers and meadows, and now I am shut in a cage. I will have no more delight or joy. I used to live off prey. Now I will be given food, as one does to a prisoner. Let me go free, dear friend, for you may be assured and certain that I will never sing in prison.' 'By my faith, then I will eat you! You are not going to play any other tricks!' 'You will get a poor meal in me, for I am feeble and tiny. Your reputation will not improve if you kill such a thing. Let me live and you will do well. It would be wrong to kill me.' 'Indeed, it is no use you pleading, for the more I am beseeched, the less I will do, I assure you.' (200–42)

'Indeed', replied the bird, 'it is true, for custom tells us this: all reasoning angers a peasant – I have long since heard it said. But I will show you something else, for necessity makes one do many things. My strength cannot protect me in this, but if you let me go I will teach you three truths that no one of your lineage ever knew, and they could prove very useful to you.' 'If I may be sure of it', said the peasant, 'I would do so at once.' 'Such faithfulness as I have', said the bird, 'I pledge to you.' The peasant thereupon let it go free. The bird flew off to the pine tree, having escaped by its words. It looked unkempt and ruffled, for it had been badly mistreated and roughly handled. It smoothed down its plumage with its beak and settled itself as best it could. The peasant, who had to know the three truths, ordered it to tell him.[3] (243–67)

The bird was full of cunning and said: 'If you heed this carefully, you will learn a very fine truth: *Do not weep for what you never had*.' The peasant was very angry and replied aggressively: 'You have broken your pledge to me. Three truths you were due to teach me, so you gave me to understand, that no one of my lineage ever knew. But everyone knows this, and no one is so stupid, nor ever was, as to weep for what he has not got. You have lied to me so grossly.' The bird replied to him: 'Would you like me to repeat it, so that you do not forget it? You are so busy arguing that I fear you may forget it. I do not think you will retain it.' 'I know it far better than you do,' said the peasant, 'and have done for a long time. A curse on anyone who is grateful to you for teaching him what he already knows! Nor am I as uncouth, upon my soul, as you take me for. However, since you have escaped me, and I no longer have power over you, I will overlook it, but do not mock me. I know this one, now continue.' (268–98)

[3] It is at this point that the order of the three truths differs depending on the manuscript used. See p. 161n1.

'Listen to me,' said the bird, 'the other one is good and fair: *Do not believe all you hear.*' The peasant wrinkled his nose in anger and said: 'I knew that well!' 'Then retain it, my friend. Mind you do not forget it!' 'Now I am very well instructed,' said the peasant, 'in learning truths. You are making me listen to nonsense, asking me to retain this. I wish I still had my hands on you! But if you were to keep the agreement with me, you would tell me the third truth. Tell me what it is and I will listen.' (299–313)

'Listen carefully and I will tell you. The third is such that whoever knows it would never become a poor man.' When the peasant heard this, he greatly rejoiced and said: 'This I must know, for I am always on the look-out for wealth'. You should have heard the bird goading him! 'It is time to eat,' said the peasant, 'teach it to me at once.' When the bird heard him, it said: 'I warn you, peasant, that *what you hold in your hands, you should not throw down at your feet.*' Then the peasant became furious, and after remaining silent for a while said: 'Was there not anything else? These are mere childish words that I know perfectly well. Every poor person in the world knows this as well as you do. You have lied to me and fooled me. Everything you have taught me I knew already.' (314–37)

The bird then replied: 'By my faith, if you knew these truths, you would not have let me go when you had me in your hands.' 'You have spoken truly,' said the peasant. The bird, who was wily, said to him: 'This one is worth the other two, and more than a hundred others.' The peasant replied: 'How so?' 'How so? I will tell you, wretch, you do not know what happened to you, for if you had killed me, as you considered doing, there would never have been a day, I swear to you, when you would not have been much better off.' 'Ah, for Heaven's sake, what could you do then?' 'Listen, you vile, perverse peasant, there is in my body a stone that is very precious and valuable, weighing a good three ounces. Its power is so great that whoever owned it would never ask for anything that would not immediately be provided.' (338–61)

When the *vilain* heard this, he wrung his hands and tore his clothes, and declared that he was a miserable wretch. He tore at his face with his nails, and the bird rejoiced greatly, watching him from the pine tree. It waited until it saw that he had ripped all his clothes and wounded himself in many places, then it said to him: 'Wretched peasant, when you held me in your hands I was lighter than a sparrow, a tomtit or a finch. I did not weigh even half an ounce.' Grumbling angrily, he said to the bird: 'Indeed, that is true.' 'Peasant, now you can clearly see that I lied to you about the stone.' 'Now I know it for sure,' he said. 'But indeed, I believed it before.' 'Peasant, I will straightaway prove that you did not know the three things, and that even when you said, "No one is so stupid, nor ever was, to weep for what he has not got," immediately, I believe, you wept for what you never had, nor ever will have. You are confused about the three truths. Retain them, fair friend. It is good to heed good advice. It is said that he does not heed who hears, and that one man may speak good sense who is little given to reflection. Another may speak of courtly acts who would not know how to perform them and another may consider himself well educated who is schooled in folly.' (362–98)

Having said this, the bird flew away and never entered the garden again. It went off, and it happened at that time that the garden faded and withered. The bird never came there again. The leaves fell from the pine tree and the fountain dried up. No one came there again, or lived there, and the peasant lost his delight. Now may all men and ladies know, the proverb says clearly: whoever covets everything loses everything. (399–410)

16. *Espervier*

Introduction

Espervier (*Sparrowhawk*) is preserved in just one manuscript: S. At 232 lines, it is one of the shortest lays in this volume.

At the outset two knights are on very good terms with each other and share many aspects of their lives. Things change, however, when one of them takes a wife on the advice of his companion, whose name is Ventilas (the author claims he does not know the other knight's name). Despite her fun-loving nature and her many fine qualities, the author hints that spotting evil in such a woman is harder than in one who is silent (this is one of several remarks in this lay that concern human behaviour in general). The lady gets on very well with her husband's companion Ventilas, but out of jealousy the husband begins to suspect, with no justification, that there is something untoward going on between them. This leads to the break-up of the friendship, but it also stimulates a relationship between the wife and Ventilas that would not have happened if it had not been forbidden. The lovers meet whenever they can and one day, when the husband is out, Ventilas sends his squire to the lady to ask if it is safe for him to visit her. While she is hurriedly getting ready, she asks the squire to hold her mirror so that she can check to see if she is well turned out. As he kneels down before her, he is overcome with passion and tries to embrace her. His advances are rejected, so he begins to force himself upon her. Just then his lord arrives and the lady tells the squire to go and hide. She and her lover then take their pleasure with each other. Things get even worse when the lady's husband unexpectedly arrives. Ventilas panics, but as a diversion the lady creates a scenario in which, sword in hand, he is to dash around the house shouting that if he can get his hands on 'him' he will kill him and then leave. The husband thinks that he is the one being threatened, but the wife calms the situation by inventing the story that Ventilas was angry because the squire had lost his sparrowhawk. To escape his master, the squire had come running to their house. The squire was then told to come out from his hiding place behind the bed and the husband is now convinced that his wife has not been unfaithful to him. He even gives the squire his own sparrowhawk to take to his master as a replacement.

Although the author bestows on his work the title *Li lays de l'Espervier* (*The Lay of the Sparrowhawk*, v. 228), there can be no doubt that this poem, perhaps more so than any other lay in this collection, presents features that are frequently associated with the genre of the *fabliau*: (i) misunderstandings (at first, the husband was wrong about the lovers' affair, then he was right but still loses out in the end); (ii) a quick-thinking wife rescues her lover when her husband returns home unexpectedly (in this case, the lady has to rescue not one but two frightened occupants of the house); (iii) the author's principal aim was to provoke laughter. However, the reference to the work as an *aventure* that is worthy of being remembered (vv. 1–8, 225–29) suggests that we are dealing with a lay, and the information that it is performed on the harp and the rote would seem to allude to a Breton-style composition, which the author may have known about but never actually heard himself.[1] The symbolic use of the sparrowhawk, as a symbol of victory in love, would suggest a lay rather than a *fabliau*. Ironically, the husband passes a real bird over to his rival in place of a fictitious bird.

Whether scholars have viewed this work as primarily a lay or a *fabliau*, or both, there seems to be consensus that it is a high-quality tale. It is clear from other lays included in this section that characters who are at home in the courtly and aristocratic world can easily be catapulted into a universe in which they are humiliated or endangered. The catalyst for the change in their circumstances is usually love or lust, and the predicament in which the characters find themselves is usually created by a desire for revenge. In *Espervier* the lady's ploy to save her two visitors, and herself, from retribution for adultery and attempted rape is, brilliantly, to make the squire afraid of his master and the husband afraid of her lover. She diffuses the overall situation by downgrading the crisis, which could have ended in death or injury, to one involving a missing bird. Part of the humour of this story is that if the squire had not been

[1] Marie de France concludes the lay of *Guigemar* by saying that the lay was performed on harp and rote (vv. 884–85). See also the beginning and the ending of the lay of *Doon* above.

present in the house (a feature that gives this particular tale its twist), the lady would have had to come up with a different solution in order to hoodwink her cuckolded husband. But we know that she would have been quite capable of doing so!

Further Reading

Burgess, Glyn S., 'The Lay of *Espervier*', in *The Medieval Imagination: Mirabile Dictu. Essays in Honour of Yolande de Pontfarcy Sexton* (Dublin: Four Courts Press, 2012), pp. 17–31.

Noomen, Willem, 'Le *Lai de 'Espervier*: une mise au point', in *Mélanges de linguistique, de littérature et de philologie médiévales, offerts à J. R. Smeets*, ed. Q. I. M. Mok, I. Spiele and P. E. R. Verhuyck (Leiden, 1982), pp. 205–25.

Paris, Gaston, '*Le Lai de l'Épervier*', *Romania*, 7 (1878), 9–21.

Translation

A very brief tale, which has not often been told, have I heard tell in truth, and I want to bring it to your attention. One cannot tell every tale, nor treat them all in the vernacular or write them all down. One hears many related that are very worthy to be recalled, for anyone who wished to pay heed to them could learn some good lessons. There were once two knights who loved each other very much. There was never the slightest jealousy between them and they led very fine lives, upholding chivalry and riding together every day. Without the other, each of them would have had nothing. Everywhere, in good times and bad, they shared with one another all they had. They partook of each other's troubles and whatever they had belonged to them both. (1–21)

It came about that, on the advice of his companion, called Ventilas (I never heard the name of the other man), one of them married a very worthy woman, noble, courtly and of great intelligence. Just as I heard the story I will relate it to you very briefly. The lady was of very good breeding and esteemed for her beauty. She was good humoured, noble and cheerful, and no one perceived any fault in her playful and cheerful manner. For I can tell and relate to you very truly that one can detect wickedness more easily in a woman who remains silent than in one who is high-spirited, talkative and fun-loving. The lady was very well bred and her husband loved her very deeply for her beauty and her virtue. Ventilas honoured her greatly and spent a good deal of time with her. He treated her in a very friendly manner and loved her very much. But there was nothing untoward about this love, for she was his companion's wife. The husband watched his comings and goings, and the way he spoke to her, and feared that between the two of them there was something that should not be. Her husband then became suspicious. In truth one can say that out of jealousy one can speak ill of a woman who is not intent on folly. But evil gossips are everywhere and, in order to increase her reputation and honour, a woman can act in a friendly manner who has no intention of behaving foolishly. The husband did not consider this a laughing matter. (22–61)

It happened one day that Ventilas was with the wife and was speaking with her just as he normally did. Then the husband became very angry. 'Ventilas', he said, 'I'll have you know that what's going on does not please me. What you are doing to me, I can well see, is offering me Tassel's company.'[2] 'Come now, fair lord, you are quite wrong to say this, for I would rather die!' 'Keep quiet. I wouldn't believe you if you took an oath or swore this.' 'I can well see that the friendship between us could go on for too long.[3] I wish to put an end to it now.' So saying, he departed. (62–77)

Afterwards, he thought many a time of the lady, and she of him, until they became united in love. They lived a league apart from each other, and through these circumstances they loved each other. If it had not been forbidden them, there would perhaps not have been any love between them, for this happens to many people: he who admonishes them thereby inflames them, and it is quite right that there are many people who do what they are forbidden to do. If anyone were to beg them to do something, they would always do the opposite. The two of them loved each other greatly. He loved her and she loved him, and she spoke to him very often. It happened one day that the husband had gone out for some relaxation. I do not know whether he was hunting or hawking. The knight did not delay. He immediately sent word to the lady, in order to find out

[2] Tassel's company is when one's companion is disloyal or treacherous. See Burgess, ed. of *Espervier*, p. 45. The name Tassel may refer to Tassilo III (742–94), Duke of Bavaria, who, having sworn an oath, betrayed his uncle Pepin le Bref and later Charlemagne. It could also be a variant of the term *taissel* 'badger'.

[3] It is not always easy to apportion direct speech in this text. The words in this sentence could be attributed to the husband, but it must be Ventilas who speaks the line 'I wish to put an end to it now.' See Burgess, ed. of *Espervier*, p. 45.

if he could speak to her. The messenger mounted and hastened on his way, coming to where the lady lived. He dismounted and went straight to the chamber where she was accustomed to be, and told her that his lord would come to her as soon as he could. The lady jumped out of bed. Once she was bathed, she dressed herself sumptuously and made herself ready; she was attractive and elegant. (78–109)

Then she wanted to fasten on her wimple. 'Fair lord', she said, 'come closer. Take this mirror and hold it in front of me, so that I can see it and make sure that my dress looks good.' He took it and knelt down. He saw that she was beautiful and looked at her, and the more he looked at her the more he was smitten. Her beauty overwhelmed him and he came nearer to her, taking hold of the lady and embracing her. 'Get away, you fool,' she said. 'Get away from here! Are you mad?' – 'My lady, have pity! Wait a moment!' Listen to this scoundrel. The more he is forbidden, the more he is inflamed![4] For this type of ache, it is commonly said, is worse than toothache. Just as he was holding the lady and struggling with her so violently, the knight, who was the squire's lord, suddenly arrived. 'Get out of here, you fool,' she said. 'Get out, wretch! Do you hear your lord?' 'Alas, sinner that I am! What devils are bringing him at this time? If I had my way, he would not come yet!' 'Get away quickly,' said the lady, 'and go and hide immediately.' He hid, but this upset him greatly. The lady got up quickly. Then her beloved suddenly arrived. Not noticing anything untoward, he took the lady and embraced her, joking, laughing and conversing with her. As he was wont to do, he took his pleasure with her. (110–43)

Just as he was making love to her, her husband suddenly arrived. The knight jumped up: 'My lady', he said, 'what can we do? I don't know how we can escape from this. I don't see any way out for us. I'm not worried for myself, just for you.' 'Don't have any fears for me,' she said. 'You will soon see that you have no cause. If it pleases God, I will escape. But do what I tell you. Draw your sword at once, and then just say: "By the body of God, if I got hold of him, he wouldn't escape. I'd kill him." Then get going quickly. Leave me to my fate. Say what I am asking of you, anything else would be wrong.' The knight made for the door, drawing his sword and going around swearing: 'By the body of God, if I found him, nothing in the entire world would allow him to escape from having his head cut

[4] This sentence seems to be an intervention by the author, but it is possible to consider it as a continuance of the lady's direct speech. See the preceding note.

off!' The husband heard him and stopped. He pulled back and did not move. He thought he was the one being threatened and had no wish to go near him. When he saw that he had left, he went straight to his wife, with his sword drawn and filled with anger. 'By the body of God, you are now going to die!' 'God, Holy Cross, in Our Lady's name, what's the matter, my lord?' said the lady. 'What's the matter? Don't you know? Ah! You will certainly regret betraying me.' 'Betray, my lord? By the Virgin Mary! Come now, in God's name, don't say that!' 'Am I not saying what I have seen? Your fancy man, who was here, was doing his worst to me, saying that if he got hold of me he'd kill me.' (144–84)

'Fair lord, so God help me, you're wrong to vent your anger against me. But, because you are angry, you'll say whatever you wish. Yet, if you let me speak, you'd hear the truth about it.' 'The truth? You're going to need it! Tell me.' 'Willingly, my lord. The knight who has just left here had gone hawking a short time ago. He'd given his sparrowhawk to his squire, he told me, and the squire, when he'd given it to him, let it loose without his leave. He's not seen or heard it since. When the knight found out …[5] I don't know how, being afraid of him, his squire came straight here and hid behind that bed there. Fair friend', she said, 'come out, you're quite safe now.' The squire, who had heard everything, jumped up and was rightly filled with joy. 'Certainly, my lady, you're telling the truth. May you be honoured by God, for I've now got my life back because of you, my fair, sweet lady. My lord is certainly very angry. He wanted to kill me thus because of his bird that I had lost. He'd have profited little if he'd killed or maimed me.' 'Enough, come on now!' said the husband. 'A curse on his anger! Then there would then have been no way out. Fair brother, take my sparrowhawk and give it to him from me.' The squire thanked him and departed, and he told his lord how things had turned out. (185–224)

This tale was true. It should be retained in people's minds. It all happened this way, they say. Its name is the *Lay of the Sparrowhawk* [*Li lays de l'Espervier*], which is worthy to be remembered. I have heard the story told, but I have never heard the tune, played on the harp or the rote. (225–32)

[5] There is a gap of at least two lines here. Presumably they would have described the knight's angry reaction to the loss of his sparrowhawk and the squire's subsequent flight.

17. *Nabaret*

Introduction

Nabaret is preserved in just one manuscript: P (Cologny-Genève, Bibliotheca Bodmeriana, Codex Bodmer 82). At forty-eight lines, it is the shortest lay in the present collection.

The lay concerns a power struggle between husband and wife. A knight has a wife of high lineage who, in his view, spends too much time and money on her appearance. He accuses her of dressing to please another man, but his exhortations fall on deaf ears. He turns to her family for help, but instead of providing a solution to his problems this only makes matters worse. For she tells her parents that if he does not like her dressing fashionably, there is only one form of revenge that a jealous man can adopt: 'He should let his beard grow long and have his whiskers braided' (vv. 38–39). The parents, and all those who later hear it, find the riposte highly amusing.

The problem for the modern reader is that it is not easy to determine precisely why the wife's remark stimulates such hilarity. Is she saying that her husband should change his appearance in such a way that he will become her rival in looks, and she will be jealous of him rather than he of her? Or does she mean that by taking her advice he would make himself look as odd as she would if she did what he wanted her to do. Or perhaps what the wife wishes to convey is that, although he is no doubt still a relatively young man, his view of her behaviour is redolent of an old man, or a patriarchal figure, who, at a time when young men were clean shaven, would have been more likely to sport a moustache or a braided beard. The implication would then seemingly be that if he wants to behave like an old man she for her part has no intention of looking any older that she actually is. Whatever she means, the notion of revenge is clearly important to the lady, as she mentions it twice (vv. 36, 40). But why would a brave and courtly knight want to take revenge on his wife by looking like a much older, authoritarian figure? This could only have had the effect of making it more likely that his wife would turn to another man for affection and admiration.

When summoned to assist the husband to exert control over their daughter, the wife's relatives would no doubt have expected her to provide a defence of her behaviour and ultimately to agree to mend her ways and moderate her expensive tastes.[1] Her decision not to attempt to defend herself but to mount an attack on her husband and recommend that he should be the one to take action comes as a surprise. If the lady is of superior birth to her husband (she is said to be of 'very high lineage', v. 6), it is possible that her recommendation that he should alter his facial appearance is tinged with scorn for his social, perhaps even sexual, inadequacy. Whatever the truth of the matter, we are clearly dealing with a clever woman who is able to think up a means of revenge that would backfire on its perpetrator if it were carried out. One thing we do know is that at the end of the narrative the balance of power between the spouses has shifted in the wife's favour. The husband has been outmanoeuvred, and her excessive pride (v. 11) has not been dented.

The notion of a woman wriggling out of a sticky situation with a clever quip, or turning the tables on a husband who thinks he is in control, could tempt one to classify this work as a *fabliau*. It certainly contains no supernatural or magic element, no *aventure* and no amorous passion (this could well have been an arranged marriage). But the author uses the term 'lay' four times (vv. 1, 46, 47, 48), even presenting his poem as a 'Breton' lay (v. 1). Moreover, Nabaret and his wife are described in a way that is perfectly normal in courtly literature. He is a brave, courtly, bold and fierce knight and she is a noble, courtly, beautiful and comely lady. But the contradiction between the characters as they are described and their actions within the narrative could justify calling this poem, as does Mortimer Donovan, an 'elevated fabliau' (*The Breton Lay: A Guide to Varieties*, p. 99).

[1] Line 26 ('De ses parenz plusurs manda') could be interpreted as 'he summoned a number of HIS relatives' (see Rosanna Brusegan, 'La Plaisanterie dans *Le Lai de Nabaret*'), but it is not likely that the husband's family would have laughed at the wife's defiant riposte or recounted their son Nabaret's humiliation 'in many places'.

Further Reading

Brusegan, Rosanna, 'La Plaisanterie dans le *Lai de Nabaret*', in *Risus mediaevalis: Laughter in Medieval Literature and Art*, ed. Herman Braet, Guido Latré and Werner Verbeke (Leuven: Leuven University Press, 2003), pp. 129–41.

Schoepperle, Gertrude, 'The Old French *Lai de Nabaret*', *Romanic Review*, 18 (1922), 285–91.

Skårup, Povl, 'Le Lai de *Nabaret*', *Revue Romane*, 8 (1973), 262–71.

Translation

The lay we call *Nabaret* was composed in Brittany. Nabaret was a knight, brave and courtly, bold and fierce, and he had a great deal of land as his inheritance. He took a wife of very high lineage, noble, courtly, beautiful and comely. She devoted a great deal of effort to her dress and appearance and to the choice of laces and wimples, and she was excessively proud. Nabaret would not have been concerned by this, for her appearance would have pleased him greatly had it not been for her display of vanity. He often became very angry and repeatedly chastised her. He often showed his anger, in her presence and in private, saying that she was not doing it for him, but thinking of someone else. Her beauty was pleasing to him and it suited him well. As she was unwilling to abandon, because of him, her wimples and laces and the great pride she displayed, he summoned several of her relatives. He made his complaint to them and had them speak to his wife. He told the relatives what displeased him and how it annoyed him greatly that she behaved in this way. Hear how she replied: 'My lords, if you please', she said. 'If he is upset that I dress in this way and am attired in a noble fashion, I do not know of any other revenge. Tell him that I give him word that he should let his beard grow long and have his whiskers braided. That is the way for a jealous man to avenge himself.' Those who heard this reply took their leave of the lady. They laughed and joked a good deal over it, and because of the amusement her words afforded them they recounted it in many places. Those who were trained to compose lays sang a lay about Nabaret and named the lay after him. (1–48)

Passion and Tears

18. *Piramus and Thisbe*

Introduction

Piramus and Thisbe is preserved in a large number of manuscripts, twenty-two in all, only three of which are independent: (i) Paris, BNF, fr. 837; (ii) Paris, BNF, fr. 19152; (iii) Berlin, Staatsbibliotek, Preußischer Kulturbesitz, Hamilton 257. The other nineteen are manuscripts of the fourteenth-century *Ovide moralisé,* including Rouen, Bibliothèque Municipale 1044 (0.4). This manuscript, in the edition by Penny Eley, serves as the basis for our translation. Along with *Narcisus and Dané, Piramus and Thisbe* is often classified as a 'classical' lay.

In the city of Babylon, two noble families live in adjacent palaces. Their children, Piramus and Thisbe, are both superior in beauty. They play together constantly and before the age of seven are smitten by Love's arrow. A servant notices how close they are and reports this to Thisbe's mother, who is afraid of what this might lead to. So, in order to prevent her from seeing Piramus, she confines Thisbe to their palace. A dispute then arises between the two families, dashing any hopes of an eventual marriage between the two children, who are unable to contact one another. As they reach adolescence, they endure the torments of frustrated love, until one day Thisbe notices a crack in the partition wall separating the two houses. To alert Piramus to this, she pushes a belt through the crack, and once he sees it they are able to talk to each other and reaffirm their undying love. Thisbe informs Piramus that she has had a dream in which the gods have told her that they should each leave the city under cover of darkness and meet under a mulberry tree. Thisbe escapes from the palace first, but when she reaches the tree she is frightened by a lion that has just eaten a flock of sheep and come to drink at the nearby stream. Afraid, she runs away to hide in a bush, dropping her wimple as she goes. The lion tramples on it, leaves blood on it and disappears. When Piramus arrives and sees the bloodied wimple and the lion's tracks, he assumes that Thisbe has been killed and eaten by it. In despair, he stabs himself with his sword and his blood spatters over the tree, turning the white fruit black. Thisbe then returns, only to find her lover dying. She takes Piramus's sword and stabs herself, praying that they may be reunited in death in the same tomb.

The main source for the story of Piramus and Thisbe is Book IV of Ovid's *Metamorphoses*, and the author of the lay acknowledges his awareness of Ovid when he states that the names of the children were supplied by the Latin poet (vv. 10–12). In general outline, the lay follows Ovid faithfully, but there are differences of detail and tone. In Ovid the children keep their love secret, but they are never deliberately separated, nor is there a quarrel between the two families. When they discover the crack in the wall, they manage to speak to one another repeatedly over some time, and it is only when they grow weary of this limited means of communication that they decide to escape and agree to meet, as in the lay. It is a lioness in Ovid, not a lion, that comes to drink, and it tears the veil to shreds while Thisbe hides in a cave, not a bush. At the end, the common burial of the pair is confirmed.

In adapting the tale for twelfth-century readers/listeners, the French poet begins with a prologue in which the power and effects of the wound of Love are described. He dramatises the initial idyllic situation of the children, who are happy in their innocent but already strong bond, by the addition or inclusion of the quarrel between the two families, which brings about their enforced separation. This adds an extra degree of frustration and torment to their relationship as they grow older, and there are lengthy monologues in which they each lament their situation and express their frustrations. Eventually they decide to throw off the suffocating constraints of society and endeavour to be free to love as they wish outside the world they have inhabited till now, symbolised perhaps by the fact that Babylon is a walled city. The separation of young, innocent love by knowing grown-ups also occurs in the lay of *Espine* (see above), but in that case things turn out happily and not tragically, as the lovers are eventually able to marry.[1]

[1] In the manuscript we have translated, Thisbe prays that the two lovers will be placed together in a single tomb (v. 875). There is no confirmation at the end of the narrative that this is actually done, but we are told that 'this is the way the two lovers came together' (vv. 907–08). In MS Rouen, Bibliothèque Municipale 1004 (0.44), transcribed by Eley on pp. 87–107 of her online edition, we are told specifically

Further Reading

Cadot, A. M., 'Du récit mythique au roman: étude sur *Piramus et Tisbé*', *Romania*, 97 (1976), 433–61.

Kibler, William W., '*Piramus et Tisbé*: A Medieval Adapter at Work', *Zeitschrift für romanische Philologie*, 91 (1975), 273–91.

Lucken, Christopher, 'Le Suicide des amants et l'*ensaignement* des lettres: *Piramus et Tisbé* ou les métamorphoses de l'amour', *Romania*, 117 (1999), 363–95.

Translation

In the city of Babylon lived two men. They possessed great fame, great valour and great nobility and they were wealthy men of high lineage. These wealthy men had two children, who were similar in beauty and appearance, one a boy and the other a girl. No king or queen had such handsome children. These wealthy men had two children and in his book Ovid names them, saying that one was called Piramus and the other Thisbe. Before they reached the age of seven, Love struck the two children, and in this respect it wounded them more deeply than was suitable for their age. They were equal in age and in disposition, of great beauty and high birth, and equal also in their conversations, laughter and games. Together, the convenience of the location and their opportunity for frequent contact, awakened love in them. (1–22)

O Love, in your gaze there is no escape for young or old. Neither youth nor age can avoid the wound from your arrow. Against your arrow neither a double hauberk nor a double byrnie affords any protection; it cannot miss its mark.[2] No one is safe from it, and without causing any pain it elicits sighs, and without shedding any blood it turns one pale. The head of your arrow carries the flames of love, the shaft in the middle conveys sighs and the feathers bear ruses and entreaties, and the notch at the rear brings the sweetness of love. The arrowhead wounds through the

that the parents buried them in one tomb (vv. 899–900). In Marie de France's *Deus Amanz* the young lovers likewise suffer an early death and are buried together in the same tomb.

[2] The hauberk and the byrnie are long coats of chain mail, leather jackets with metal scales sewn into them. The hauberk usually had sleeves and the byrnie was usually sleeveless.

eyes, the shaft glides into one's thoughts, the feathers cause plans to be hatched and the notch unites lovers' minds. (23–40)

With such an arrow and such a barb did Love wound the boy and the girl while they were still very young, and this wound remained with them until their death. As yet, they had no understanding of Love, but it caused them a great deal of apprehension. Rising in the morning and thinking about one another already brought them pleasure, and they fasted more than they should have done, or was appropriate for their age. In the morning they would each slip away, and they spent the day playing together and enjoying themselves with other children of the same age. In the daytime they were preoccupied with gazing at one another and could not get their fill of this. They would return home late, for parting was painful for them. They delighted in doing many things for which they were greatly threatened and scolded. Just as a jasper is superior to glass, gold to silver and the primrose outdoes the mayweed, so were the two of them superior in their goodness, their worth and their beauty to all those in the city. Nature created them with great reflection, great care and great intelligence. (41–68)

As long as their age was opposed to the demands of love and they were under ten years old, they had great freedom to be together and to converse, amuse themselves and play together. But their tender glances, innocent minds and inappropriate age, together with the certainty that nothing that is good fails to stimulate envy and not a single servant is free from treachery, caused them to be separated and kept under surveillance so that they were unable to be with one another. A servant noticed their behaviour and said: 'Now I have no doubt that these children are deeply in love, and if they were a little older and had such freedom it would be very difficult to keep them apart'. The servant took these tidings to the maiden's mother and she replied to him: 'Now say no more about this, for they shall not be together again.' Then she said to a chambermaid: 'Take care, if you have any regard for me, that Thisbe does not go outside and that she does not see Piramus.' (69–94)

Thereupon, some disagreement arose between the children's fathers, a quarrel and rivalry that lasted all their lives. This situation prevented the children from being together, from being united in marriage and from sending messages to one another. The two children were distraught, as they could not hear or see one another. The separation their parents had imposed upon them seemed very harsh to them, but the fact that they were now watched over more closely, that Thisbe did not dare go outside the house and that Piramus could not set eyes on her, strengthened their love. As their age dictated, they both grew up. They became older and more understanding, their passion grew and their wound got worse, and the fire that nothing can quench increased. Their love increased as they got older and they were soon over fifteen years of age. When they reached adolescence, they became aware of their feelings, having reached the age when it was natural to recognise love. It gave them no respite from long periods of reverie, grievous sighs, great pains and loud laments. Harsh torments settled in their hearts. Day and night they lamented and their whole lives were lived in sorrow. They sobbed and groaned to themselves, not knowing of any remedy for their fate and being unable to find relief through medicine or a physician. The fire burnt deep within their bones and it afforded them no repose. It tormented them day and night and consumed them with deadly flames. This fire and this flame alone tugged at their sinews and ignited their very core. It sapped their strength, altered their looks and put an end to all enjoyment. (95–138)

Piramus was overcome with sadness, with sighs and tears, and with melancholy and cares. Time and again he lamented to himself in this way: 'O unhappy one, you who are sad and sorrowful! Am I going to suffer this torment for long? I grieve all the time and know no joy at all, and the more I grieve the more love inflames me. Indeed, I am lying, rather it is ardour which in this way returns to me day after day. My face and my complexion are drained of colour, just as the frost drains the colour from a leaf. O unhappy one! O Piramus, what are you going to do? In what way are you going to behave? O father who begot me, why do you not take pity on me now? If you do not make different arrangements, either through some stratagem or some reckless act, Thisbe, my fair one, I will find some way to see you. Be mindful that, if I cannot have you through love, I will forcibly abduct you. Death will act as my refuge and my comfort, if this ill, which is so severe, maintains its grip on me much longer, or if this injustice torments me for long. This injustice? O gods, why has there been no accord that would bring peace between our parents? Then we would not have so many guards. Guards? Can I not even manage, through promises or bribery, to find a messenger to send to her? What does it matter? It is of no importance, so help me God. O Father who dwells above, quench the fire that assails me so, the fire that has deprived me of laughter and fun. Nowhere can I find a cure. Beloved, through you my skin has gone pale, my body has been wounded and my flesh grown livid. Fair one, through you I pass my life in tears. May the god of Love allow me to hold her once more, whether by day or by night, in joy or in sorrow! Now I cannot help but faint, I can speak no more. One moment I am cheerful, the next I feel like weeping; one moment I am flushed, the next I feel shivery.' Before he could finish his lamentation, his face began to pale. Weeping and lamenting, he fell to the floor in a faint. Sometime later he rose, and filled with sadness and drained of colour he went to the temple of Venus and prostrated himself on the dark marble. He began to pray that she grant him the opportunity to speak to his beloved Thisbe. (139–206)

Thisbe was confined within the palace and dared not leave it. She often recalled her love, often turned pale and often lamented: 'Alas!' she said. 'At what an inauspicious hour I was born! O God, how wretched is my fate, how harsh the life that has been given me! Never before has any maiden alive been so closely watched over, who could not through deliberation or folly hatch some plan, except for me. But the harder I think about it, the less I see how I could manage, sweet friend, to speak to you. Speak? Thisbe, foolish girl, are you losing your mind? Do you want to disregard your chastity and bring shame on your lineage? Do not do it! Pay heed to reason, which is opposed to you! Do not concern yourself with any feelings that would make you commit such madness. No woman of your lineage has ever been accused of wantonness. Accused? This will not happen to me, in any shape or form. I would rather die a hundred deaths! Thisbe, where did this idea come from? You have soon forgotten Piramus! Alas, why did I mention his name? Friend, I did not mean to do this. Now you can rightly say, I believe, that in a woman's love there is no constancy. Fair, sweet friend, now duly receive this pledge. My lord, because of this outrage I hereby promise you my virginity. Just now I was too overweening. Overweening? I must bow down before you. I would cherish the blame mightily if I heard myself being vilified because of this. (207–54)

'Quite the contrary, as no one, it appears and seems to me, should be able to criticise me or reprimand me in this affair. Crazy woman! Be quiet, foolish, arrogant girl. Why this change of heart? You are now completely out of your mind. I will abandon all my present thoughts. On my father's advice, I will have an equally noble lover, I am well aware. Just as noble? It will cause trouble if Piramus hears me! Yes, I am trembling, I can feel it. It was a disaster for me to have uttered these words. I now repent. O handsome one, tender rose, freshly opened lily, flower of all other youths, have pity on me! Pay no heed to what I am saying. My heart is distraught with fear. I will never have any lover but you. Yet your parents are ill-disposed to us, and mine guard me jealously. What does it matter? It is of no consequence, so help me God. One minute I can feel my heart pounding, the next I am very hot. I am not far from throwing in my lot with you. O unhappy one, what have I said now? Nothing rids me of the sickness that so often troubles me. Hapless one! May the god of Love grant me this, whether I like it or regret it: that at some time soon I may feel Piramus in my arms. This is the end of my tearful lament. I am about to faint; now is the time. This is what I must do each day. This is the least I can do for my beloved.' (255–97)

The maiden fainted three times, and when she revived she stretched forth both her hands towards the heavens and prayed most humbly to the gods to help her find a way to talk to her beloved. The two palaces were adjacent to each other and constructed in such a way that there was a partition and a single wall separating them. In the inner bedchamber, which fewer people frequented and where the maiden was confined, there was a slight crack in the wall. The crack was not very large, and it had remained hidden for many years until Love, from which nothing can be concealed, caused it to be discovered. What is there that Love does not sense? The two lovers first noticed this opening, Thisbe, then Piramus. Thisbe found the crack and took the hanging end of her belt and managed to push its metal part through so that her beloved could see it. Piramus came back from the exercise he had been taking in order to get some comfort from his sorrow. He went into the bedchamber, concealed himself and turned his eyes towards the wall. He looked and noticed the sign that clearly showed him where the crack was. He made his way over to it, took the end of the belt, saw the opening. 'Thisbe', he said, 'fair creature, flower of all other creations, through the sign made by this belt I have come here to offer my apology for not discovering this crack myself. The good fortune of making such a lucky find is yours. If you truly care for me, no lock will keep you from coming here with confidence. Without messengers or concealment, and in a low voice and whispering, we will be able to talk of our plight. Then you will know how Love has set me on fire, without my having committed any offence against him. O God, how harsh life is for anyone who suffers such hardship for long!' (298–348)

On the other side, the maiden was on the look-out and listening intently. She heard these anxious words, drew closer to the wall and put her eye to the crack. She recognised her beloved's face and tried to speak, but could not because of the love that unsettled her so much. At the first sight of him, she shivered, sighed and burned with ardour, quivering, trembling and sweating profusely. Her colour drained away, then came and went. She thought carefully about what she should say to him, and for a time she was lost in thought. Love, which conquers all, oppressed her in so many ways. Eventually, she came to a decision and, pulling herself together, she placed her mouth to the hole and then spoke to him in these words: 'Beloved, I dare call you this – they cannot deny me this – for I cannot hide my feelings from you any longer. I intend to tease you about your valour. It was I who first found a way for us to be together here, for the one who loves more deeply sees more clearly. I heard you lamenting grievously, but you have little idea of what it is to love. It is still a game to you. Leave the grief to me, to whom nothing can bring comfort. I have exchanged joy for tears and for uttering sorrowful laments, mirth for laments, peaceful sleep for sorrowful thoughts, and joy and delight for sighing. Beloved, I cannot remain here any longer. Tears cloud my vision; sighs rob me of speech. Make sure you come back to me tomorrow, then we can speak at greater leisure and comfort one another.' (349–91)

She could no longer speak to him and thus the two of them separated. The day passed and the night came to an end. Next morning, they both returned and came back to their opening. Piramus was the first to speak: 'Beloved, I am filled with great anguish, for I am mortally wounded by you, whom I love. From now on, I will heed the call, like a goshawk when it is hungry. I am hooked more securely than a fish on a hook. I am caught because of you, it seems to me. I do not know what joy or laughter is. If I am held much longer, I will not escape alive. I am dying! The god of Love does not keep faith with us, for his law has left us behind. We are both ensnared in one net. I do not know whom to entreat, you or him. Fair one, with you I take my refuge. If I am to die through you, what an ill-starred life I have led! Beloved, you would be acting very wickedly if I were to lose my life through you, since through you I can get help. Sorrowful one! I who have loved so long am suffering a great deal of grief and torment and cannot satisfy my desire. (392–423)

'Wretch that I am! O fair one, what a sorry plight I am in! How I have been overcome because of my love for you. I am never free from grief day or night. One moment I am deep in thought, the next I am sighing and then weeping. I have lost all my colour, I have had to give up sleeping, drinking and eating, and I cannot speak without sighing. I have certainly learned the meaning of suffering! Delight and all my desires are deserting me. O God, against whose torment I struggle. I will never recover unless I get away. Get away? Love refuses to let me go. Through love I must die. Die? If it pleases God and you, I will not do so. Rather will I entreat you and, I believe, I will not beg you in vain. Thus I will stretch my hand straight out so that you can cure me of this malady and assure me of your love. O wall, you are so thick and hard! But if I felt a little more secure, the crack would be made so wide by my hands that without you being spotted by the guard I would have drawn you through it. Wall, have mercy on these sufferers! Opening, you are so narrow! Stones, if you would just open up enough for us to enjoy a conversation and embrace one another! Beloved, if I were with you, I would have a cure for my great sorrow. But everything is against us. Lodging place, we still ought to cherish you dearly for allowing us to talk through you. Crack, conceal yourself well, so that none of those who threaten us knows about you. I can catch a glimpse of half the face of the one who has taken for herself my heart and my emotions. Wall, you are so cruel and harsh, you who do not open upon my entreaty wide enough for me to be able to kiss the face and mouth of the one whose sweetness touches my heart. O noble wall, do this for me without delay, nothing more. Let us pray henceforth to the heavens above that Lady Venus will help us, so that no one else finds this opening.' (424–89)

The youth lamented and sighed. Then he trembled and could say no more. When his narrative broke off, Thisbe began her lament: 'Beloved, you grieve very deeply, and no wonder, because you love me a great deal. I am well aware that through me you have been mortally wounded – you through me and I through you, by my faith. I do not know how to conduct my life, and I am no less distraught than you are. You are very sad and tearful, and my heart is filled with anguish. Grievously you complain of this torment but, I believe, I grieve even more deeply. Beloved, who say that you are so overcome, my heart has without a doubt been seized by love. It burns more fiercely than a fire in straw. Love is killing and torturing me. Great God, what anger is this, what ill will is it that you have nurtured against me for such a long time? God the Father, who caused me to come into existence, you see my pain, my misery, my suffering. What a wretched life and what misfortune I have known, beloved, since I first made your acquaintance. Henceforth, day or night, I have never been without a wound. No wonder this maiden, who is in such anguish through you, is disturbed because nothing can bring her cheer. (490–528)

'Wrongly have I lost joy and pleasure, and nothing can give me comfort. By day, I am in tears and distraught, in anguish and suffering, in martyrdom and forlorn. By night, I have neither enjoyment nor pleasure. As I lie in my bed, all is quiet and I am in pain and agitated. Then it appears to me that I can see you, but you cannot talk to me, which makes things worse for me than they have been. I shudder, sweating with anguish and torment, then I stretch out my hands, which I give to you. But just as I am about to grasp you, I fail to do so. Beloved, when I go back to sleep, it seems to me that you are there before my eyes, unhappy and downcast. May God allow some good to come to me from this dream! Then it seems to me that some form of voice or lamentation is repeatedly hailing me, telling me this openly: "Thisbe, do you recognise your beloved? Wake up, let us get away from here. Thisbe, the gods have encouraged us to leave the city, and to go straight to the spring near the shingle, beneath the mulberry tree, where we can enjoy ourselves together." Beloved, tell me what you think of this. I want you to trust in my love. In truth, I will steal away in the early part of the night. At midnight I will go and see if I can find you outside. Beloved, your life is my treasure. Mind you do not tarry or arrive late. Get up from your first sleep and look for me at the spring beneath the mulberry tree in the meadows, where Ninus is buried. You will certainly find me there.' (529–82)

Thus the two lovers made their compact and then departed. They said farewell to the opening, which they were never to see again. As they left, each of them kissed the wall. The two lovers were very anxious. The day seemed very long to them and they reproached the sun greatly, repeatedly calling it 'traitor', as it took such a long time to set and held back the night. They said it was doing this on purpose in order to thwart their plans. But the day did pass, night did return and the time did arrive for their enterprise. The watchmen climbed on to the walls and those who felt secure fell asleep. But neither of the two lovers could rest, their thoughts were elsewhere. Each of them was preoccupied with the preparations for their undertaking. Their hearts were now filled with hope, yet they were weighing up in their minds whether they should do this or not. But desire eradicates reason. They were delighted at the sweet thought that they were to be together. They went over their death, their suffering and their loss in their minds. They both experienced joy and pain, but Love conquers at all times. Neither sense nor reason could restrain them from what they had set out to do. Everyone was already fast asleep when Thisbe set off. She rose from the bed where she was lying and left the chamber very quietly; neither door nor lock held her back. She left the chamber confidently, alone in the night and without fear. Such boldness was a gift from Love. When she had left the hall and was going quietly down the steps, she put her left foot forward, she looked to the right, felt the whole palace shudder and saw the moon grow dim. When she had looked all around her, she felt no tinge of fear that she would not succeed in her enterprise, whatever her fate was to be. (583–635)

She had already reached the city walls when a watchman spotted her. But as he saw her at such an hour, he thought she was a goddess. He stepped back and did not challenge her. Thus the maiden continued on her way under this watchman's very eyes. She went down through a gap in the wall and without delay reached the place where they had agreed to meet. She was already sitting on the marble slab by the spring, beneath the tree where they were to meet, and she was beginning to think about the way she would tease the youth for not coming on time, when from the mountain a lion, which had killed a flock of sheep, came across the meadow, still covered in entrails and wool. It came to drink at the spring. The maiden cowered when she saw the ferocious beast approaching, and her blood and colour drained from her. No wonder she was scared. She fled down a path, afraid that the lion would see her. But she was so alarmed and foolish that she dropped her wimple as she went.[3] She quickly ran to hide under the shade of an almond tree. The lion approached with a great roar. It quenched its thirst at the spring, and when it had drunk its fill it went to sport in the meadow. It found the wimple on a path, trampled on it and stained it with blood. (636–73)

When the lion had left the meadows, Piramus arrived. O God, what a great calamity! What a painful discovery! For in the moonlight, as fate would have it, he looked toward the shade of the mulberry tree and saw the gleam of the wimple, and in the dust all around he recognised the lion's tracks and saw the sand dispersed all about and the water in the spring disturbed. He found the trampled wimple covered in fresh blood and assumed it was his beloved's. He looked around and could see no sign of her. Alas! What an unfortunate delay! For Thisbe had not yet returned. She was so afraid of the ferocious beast that she did not dare come back. (674–93)

[3] A wimple is a cloth headdress that covers the head, neck and sides of the face. It was formerly worn by women and is still worn by some nuns.

When Piramus could not see his beloved, he was convinced that she had met her end. He turned greener than an ivy leaf and became as hard as stone. His blood curdled and he was overcome with emotion and ablaze with anger and rage. Then he spoke whatever words anger and grief allowed him to utter: 'Night of sorrow! Night of torment! Mulberry, tree of tears! Meadow, dripping with blood! Spring, why have you not kept safe for me the woman whose blood lies in the sand? How suddenly my efforts, my hopes, my love, my expectations have come to nought! O God, what sorrow this wimple, which I see here stained in blood, represents for me. Beloved, how was it that this beast was bold enough to attack you in that way? What misfortune, what sorrow, what wickedness that you should have perished in such a manner! My dearest, it is a great pity that I go on living, I who assured you that it was safe to come alone to such a place, on a dark night. Alone! Ah, what accursed jaws are satiated by your flesh! Alas! I see blood here and I see clothing. Lion, you who devoured her, I am astonished that you did not leave more of her. Cruel moon, who watched what happened and did not grow dark at that time. (694–730)

'It is wrong that she is dead and I am not. I do not know which grief is the greater for me. Death is my finest consolation. Hapless one, since she is dead and I am still alive! In God's name, earth, swallow me up. Or you, lion who killed her, come back! I am quite ready and with no resistance on my part you can do whatever you like with me. Come back, you who devoured the fair maiden. You drank her blood, so now drink mine! Sorrowful one! My fair beloved! I have been very tardy, because I was not present at your death. Death, come back and take me! O death, why are you delaying? It is very wrong that I am not yet dead. Dear sister, I killed you when I arrived late for my appointed time, and you arrived first. Now I entreat my right hand to strike well. In such a way will I avenge you. Avenge? But first I intend to pray to the gods that in this mulberry tree they provide a sign of death, of hardship and of tears. May they make the tree of such a colour that it is appropriate for sorrow.' Having given vent to such sorrow and made such an entreaty, in a great fury he drew his sword and picked up the wimple with its tip. He kissed the wimple and the blood, then ran himself through, making the sword emerge on the other side of his body. As he lay dying, he kissed the wimple. Such was the love that brought death to this wretched youth! His blood spurted out over the branches, and the fruit, which had been white, turned black. Until that time the mulberry had always been white. Then its colour became black in a testament to sorrow. (731–79)

Then Thisbe returned, so as not to let her lover down. She was very eager to tell him about the danger from which she had escaped. She felt sure she would succeed in accomplishing what she had desired so much. The time was rapidly approaching when their love would enjoy a happy outcome. She was already imagining herself in his company, the two of them embracing each other and speaking of their love, but she was soon going to suffer grief. Quietly she made her way back, and as she drew near to the mulberry tree she thought she had lost her way because of the change of colour she saw, for she had first seen as white the fruit that was now blackened with blood. While she was wondering whether she had taken the right path, she kept going forward and heard the youth sobbing, lamenting, moaning and uttering sighs, and she saw the wimple and how he was pressing it repeatedly to his mouth. When she saw the wound, no wonder she was horrified. And when she saw the sword through his body, her blood drained away and she fainted. (780–807)

She revived, grief-stricken and dejected. She tore at her hair, scratched her face and clawed at her flesh, preferring death to life. She leant over the body, drew out the sword and held it upright. Then she spoke like a grief-stricken woman: 'Sword, of which I have taken hold, you who have caused joy to end in grief, now prove how bold you are. Sword, which has put an end to our love, may you become warm again in my breast, and bloodied by blood from the two of us. Bloodied! O God, what an end, and what hopes we had! How soon our youth has perished! Fair lord, grief was scarcely able to spare you when it was your own hand that wanted to kill you. Unhappy one, how can I speak a word in a place where I can see him gasping his last? I can see that because of me he is in the throes of death. What a miserable form of love I would be showing, beloved, if I did not follow you, and did not kill myself at once. Fair one, what great grief, what hardship! How proud was your heart! (808–40)

'Moon, spring, meadows, mulberry tree, pale night who afforded me such an unhappy omen when I left the hall, hear me. I call upon you as witnesses to my death. O God, how distraught my heart is. Thisbe, hapless one, why do you delay? May you now have the will to die, for neither the time nor the opportunity is lacking. To die? I desire nothing more than to bring my grief to an end. Wrongly do I stay my hand. Wrongly! Love, make my hand strong enough that with a single blow I will be dead, and his soul will gain great comfort if we both die a common death. Beloved, I well know that love has killed you. As we cannot be together in life, death will unite us, it seems to me. Parents, you who planned to keep us locked up, you will soon be grief-stricken. What a terrible misfortune you will see when you find both of us together, dead and in one another's arms! I entreat you to give me this boon: since we were separated in joy and are separated in death, at least let a single tomb contain us and one coffin receive us both.' (841–75)

Then the maiden bent over, kissed him and spoke to him: 'Piramus, see, here is your beloved. Look at her and she will be comforted.' The youth, where he lay dying, half opened his eyes and saw that it was Thisbe, his beloved, who was addressing him distraught. He tried to speak but could not, for death, which held him in its clutches, would not let him do so. But he said this much: 'Thisbe, beloved, in God's name, who has brought you back to life?' Then he fell silent and could say no more. He looked at her and gasped. His heart stopped and he lost his life, leaving her completely distraught. He had died and she had fainted. God, what love has come to an end in this way! The maiden got to her feet and grasped the sword in her two hands. She stabbed herself in the chest, beneath her breast. Blood spurted out on both sides and she fell across Piramus's body. She put her arms around him and held him tight, kissing his eyes, his mouth and his face. She kissed his mouth ardently, and for as long as her consciousness and life endured, she proved herself to be a true lover. Now he has come to his end, and so has she. This is where she died and this is the way the two lovers came together. Say 'Amen', each one of you. May God grant them true pardon, give us redemption and grant us his blessing. (876–912)

19. *Narcisus and Dané*

Introduction

Narcisus is preserved in four manuscripts, three of which are complete: (i) A: Paris, BNF, fr. 837; (ii) B: Paris, BNF, fr. 19152; (iii) C: Paris, BNF, fr. 2168; (iv) D: Berlin, Staatsbibliotek, Preußischer Kulturbesitz, Hamilton 257 (owing to the loss of several folios, this version has only 432 lines). Our translation is based on C, edited by Penny Eley for the Liverpool Online Series. At 1,006 lines in our version, *Narcisus* is, with *Haveloc*, one of only two lays to exceed 1,000 lines.

A mother in Thebes consults a soothsayer who informs her that, if he ever sees himself, her young son Narcisus will die young. The boy grows up and is the most handsome youth ever fashioned by Nature. At the age of fifteen his only interest is hunting; love means nothing to him. Returning from hunting one day, he is observed from a window by Dané, the king's daughter. She immediately falls in love with him and passes a sleepless night in torment, torn between her duty to behave in a responsible manner and her desire for the youth. She looks for him the following morning as he on his way to hunt and her love intensifies. So the next day she resolves to wait for him in a nearby wood and approach him. When she tells him of her feelings, he rejects her scornfully, whereupon she prays that he will experience unrequited love. The gods hear her prayer. Narcisus is hot from the hunt and seeks water to slake his thirst. He comes upon a stream and when he bends to drink, he notices his reflection in the water. He thinks it is a water fairy and promptly falls in love with this beautiful creature. He then spends the remainder of that day and the following night wondering why the creature does not respond to him. Next day, he finally realises that it is his own reflection, but his feelings do not change. In his desperation he now thinks he might be able to love Dané instead, but he suffers a seizure and loses the power of speech. Dané, who is looking for him, then reappears. He dies in her arms and she suffocates herself by holding him tightly.

The ultimate source for the story of Narcisus is Book III of Ovid's *Metamorphoses* but, like other medieval retellings of the story, it has been considerably modified by the Old French author. For a start, Echo has been replaced here by Dané and the ambiance is that of the twelfth century. Dané is not a nymph, as was Echo, but a princess living in a palace, and Narcisus is no longer the son of a river god, but of a nobleman. Also, unlike Echo, who was deprived of the power of speech by Juno and allowed only to echo the words spoken by others, Dané has the full power of speech like any normal human being. It is she, too, who utters the prayer calling for vengeance on Narcisus for his arrogant refusal. In Ovid, it is a rejected male suitor who does so. Narcisus does not turn into the flower that bears his name following his death, as occurs in Ovid, nor does Dané end up, as does Echo, as a disembodied voice.

The lay's prologue warns of the need for moderation in love: it is not wise to get too deeply embroiled and women should avoid pride and haughtiness in their response to any man who is in the grip of love. The story of Narcisus is to serve as an example of the consequences of allowing oneself to be overwhelmed by love. The question of pride and haughtiness, however, applies to Narcisus rather than to Dané, as he disdains love and scornfully rejects her when she confesses her love for him. There is considerable emphasis on the exceptional beauty of Narcisus, who is initially interested only in the common aristocratic pursuit of hunting. When he meets Dané, he notices her beauty, but lectures her on what he considers inappropriate social behaviour on her part, foolishly declaring that he will never allow himself to be ensnared by love. The power of love is shown by their sleeplessness and the intense suffering they endure. Both Narcisus and Dané indulge in lengthy monologues in which they try to understand what has happened to them and decide what they should do about it. The lay ends with an admonition to readers/listeners not to share the couple's tragic end.

Further Reading

Gier, Albert, 'L'Amour, les monologues: le *Lai de Narcisse*', in *Conjunctures: Medieval Studies in Honor of Douglas Kelly*, ed. Keith Busby and Norris J. Lacy (Amsterdam and Atlanta, GA: Rodopi, 1994), pp. 129–37.

Llamas Pombo, Elena, 'Beauté, amour et mort dans les *Ovidiana* français du XIIe siècle', in *Le Beau et le laid au Moyen Age* (Aix-en-Provence: Publications du CUERMA, 2000), pp. 339–50.

Seaman, Gerald, 'The French Myth of Narcissus: Some Medieval Refashionings', *Disputatio*, 3 (1998), 19–33.

Translation

Whoever tries to do everything without advice, it would not surprise me if misfortune befell him. In all things it is indeed right to heed common sense and moderation. Anyone who puts to sea should make sure that the weather is suitable, and when he sees that there is a good wind he can then sail in safety. Likewise, anyone who engages in love and wishes to conduct himself sensibly must watch from the outset that he does not become too deeply involved, for once he has become preoccupied and is somewhat possessed by it, he can no longer do as he pleases; for good or ill, he cannot escape from it. And yet, if it comes about that anyone engaged in foolish love is overwhelmed and oppressed by it, then it is right and proper that his beloved should listen to his pleading and not be too cruel to him, for she might soon suffer loss through her pride and haughtiness. Love that Nature allows, once it has affected both lovers and is completely to their liking, can rightly be pursued. And if it happens that a woman entreats for his love a man who then rejects her, I would wish and say without contradiction that he should be burned or hanged. We have seen misfortune befall many folk because of this. (1–34)

Narcisus, who died through love, should serve as a cautionary tale for us. He cursed love and its power, which then took harsh vengeance on him, making him subservient to a love that in the end brought about his death. There was a soothsayer born in Thebes whose skill was proven. No one could perceive or know from experience that he ever spoke anything but true words. For this reason, he had a great reputation in Thebes. A lady from the city brought her child to him so that she could be told what he thought about him and whether he would have a long life. He told her quite sincerely that he should take good care never to see himself, and that he would soon die if he did so. The mother heard this but did not believe it. She went away mocking him, saying that his words meant nothing. For a long time, people were dubious about this, but in the end he was proved right. (35–58)

Narcisus grew up to be tall, and he was now about fifteen years old. He had a fine body and was quite large in stature; never was such a beautiful person born, or one so noble. Nature had employed all her skill in forming him and devising his appearance, and she had done her utmost to fashion him as she had planned, endowing him with so much beauty that there was nothing she could think up that was not displayed on him. First she made his smiling eyes, gentle and sparkling, clear and shining. But, in order to complete what Nature had created, the god of Love added something of his own, giving him a sweet gaze that set everyone aflame. Nature then made his nose and his face, brighter than crystal or ice. She made his teeth as white as snow, then arranged them in threes. When she had set each of them, she added lips in such a fashion that they were left slightly parted, all done properly and with reason. And his mouth was made, Love implanted a touch of sweetness, so that any woman who once felt his breath would be afire with love for him. Then Nature formed his chin, and all round it she polished it with her own hand, making it soft and smooth. She made his eyebrows clear and well set, and the skin of his forehead soft and gentle, his hair curly and in ringlets, shinier than pure gold. When she had done all this to her liking, she dispersed over his face and over his highly coloured appearance a hue that was not faint and never changed or altered.[4] Come rain or shine, it was never spoilt in any way. It remained the same morning and night, a mix of white and crimson. Love himself was amazed at how well Nature had created him. He looked at it all and found nothing to criticise. Everything he saw seemed to him such that it could not be better arranged for Nature had fashioned him with such resolve, such care and such skill. (59–112)

The youth was now fifteen years of age and he was very handsome and attractive. He loved hunting and hawking, and it was his pleasure and his wish to find a stag or a boar; he could not deflect his heart from this. He had no interest in love and knew nothing of it, disliking and keeping clear of ladies in their chambers. It happened that one day, weary and exhausted, he was returning from the woods. He was all hot from the chase, but this had enhanced his beauty, as his colour had become fresher. It happened that he was passing by a tower in this state, where

[4] This passage (vv. 97–101) has puzzled editors and various interpretations and emendations have been put forward. See, for example, the editions by Pelan and Spence, p. 77, Thiry-Stassin and Tyssens, pp. 124–25, and Eley (whose text we translate), p. 77.

the king of the city's daughter was looking down from the windows. The maiden's name was Dané, and there was none more beautiful than she in all Thebes. She noticed the youth and saw that he was so proud, so noble and so beautiful, with slim hips and broad chest, and well-shaped, nicely rounded arms. His fingers were long and slender, and his legs and feet were straight. She saw that his horse was fiery and made the pathway shake. In everything she saw him doing, nothing could ever displease her. She gazed at him so intently that she did not move for as long as she could see him. She marvelled greatly, and understandably so, at the fact that she was looking at him so readily. While she was hesitating in her heart, and entertaining fleeting thoughts, Love looked in her direction, saw her hesitation and loosed off an arrow. The maiden realised that she had been struck and fell at full stretch on the ground. She quickly uncovered her chest, felt all over it with her hand, expecting to discover an external wound, but it was within her body. (113–54)

Ah, Love, how strong you are! How great is your power! You respect neither king nor count, and you put fear into the wariest. Love is rage and madness that imprisons and binds everyone. Love heats you up, Love sets you ablaze, Love deceives, betrays and lies, Love slays, Love torments, Love darkens and drains the colour from the face, Love entices, Love ensnares, Love prompts men to foolish action, Love sends them in all directions so that they have no further path or way to travel. Love had so inflamed the maiden that she did not know how she might contain herself. She reflected, then sighed, felt first a shiver, then felt hot. She trembled, shook and quivered. In a very short time she was so smitten that her face lost its colour. The night returned, day was over and the maiden was weary from her thoughts. Her bed was made and she went to lie down, turning this way and that, trying to sleep, but she could not. Love would not let her do so. (155–81)

'Alas!' she said. 'Woe is me! I can neither sleep nor rest, and I am forced to toss and turn. I am afflicted and suffering. What is the matter with me? Why do I quiver? My bed feels too hard. May God curse those whose duty it was to make it tonight! They are wicked and vile. Yes! Yes! Now I see! The mattress has not been shaken. I don't think it could have been turned. The feathers are all in a lump, so is it any wonder I am awake? I will have something done about this. I'll get the women up and have my mattress turned.' She then put on a grey fur-lined tunic and went to her nurse's bed. She made her get up and told her to remake her bed completely. The nurse did so at once. She removed the mattress and all the bed clothes and even plumped up the straw. The maiden herself lent a hand. She turned it over and over, pummelling and thumping it. First she wanted it plumped up high, then flat; now she wanted her head to be raised, then her feet. Now the bed head was too low, now too narrow, now too wide, now it hung over at one side. She cursed the nurse, as it was not to her liking. Then she considered that it was all right. Do you know why? Because she had forgotten all about the youth. But after a while she remembered him, and then her torment began again. (182–220)

'Alas!' she said. 'What can this be? I cannot lie comfortably on my left side; now I am on my right. Does it matter? It neither harms me nor does me any good. I can find no trick or ploy to make things any better. Either it's the bed that causes me to suffer or I have become more sensitive than usual, or my body is prey to such a madness that heats my mind. When I try to sleep, I tremble. Now I get up, now I lie down again. Now I want to think again of the youth I saw passing by yesterday. What business do I have with this young man? The thing that torments me most is when I recall his beauty. He is handsome. Who cares whether he is good? He may, perhaps, be wicked and villainous, or jealous and full of anger. What am I saying? What wrong has he done me for me to find fault with him? Why praise him? I must keep quiet about him. I was always so kind-hearted, so where does this wickedness come from? There is no man under heaven who would not say that he is handsome, and exceptionally so! And no man so handsomely built could be bad. I am wrong, I will not think ill of him. In fact, he is both handsome and good. But what is it to you? He will never be yours! How could he ever be mine? It is neither reasonable, proper or right that I should ask for a husband without the king's approval. Approval? Alas, such a long wait! I might never feel joy or delight! Indeed, if I had any sense, I would not wait for his approval. (221–60)

'Where are you getting these words from? You used to be sensible, now you are foolish! Do you want to seek such approval independently? Would it not be better to wait? You are the daughter of a king and queen and they will give you a husband who is appropriate for you. For this reason you must be patient a while. And if he does not please me? What is this, Dané? Are you not ashamed? Do you know what pleasing means? Does this youth please you more? Yes, indeed, but I don't know how to go about it. I cannot see clearly how I can let him know. Do you want him to know? Yes, very much, for he pleases me above all else, as does everything I see him do. O God! Who would not be pleased by him? How handsome and noble he was when I saw him! What feet I saw in silver stirrups! What a face, what a body, what arms, what hands! What a saddle and harness! What eyes, what a mouth to be kissed! How well he sat his horse! O God! Will I ever live to achieve with him what I desire? If I were to be his beloved, I would have been born under a lucky star, it seems to me! It seems to me? Rather is it true, without a doubt! Alas, how I am torn! I do not know what to do, so I am bewildered and in need of advice.' (262–92)

Thus she lamented to herself, and all night she remained agitated. Now she wept, now she reflected, now she lay down, now she sat up, now she felt like getting up again, now she rebuked herself, now she comforted herself, and then she wished she were dead. She remained in great torment and sorrow until daybreak. She was grief-stricken and worn out, but then she enjoyed a little relief from the anguish and pain. Her eyes closed and she slept. Before she could perceive that it was daylight, she awoke and could not sleep. She went and stood at the window, looking to the right and to the left, to discover whether she could see the youth who had so set her afire, for at this hour he should pass by on his way to the woods. Having waited a good while, she leant forward and saw the youth coming in the distance. She had never before seen anyone so handsome or so well built, as it seemed to her, and she lamented, sighed and trembled. She gazed at him and was at peace for as long as she could see him near to her. But when she saw him getting further away, her body gave way, her legs buckled and she fell to the paved floor in a faint. And so her torment began again. (293–324)

At first she thought of sending for him, but then reconsidered, saying she knew no messenger to whom she dared reveal her feelings. 'O God!' she said. 'This ill that afflicts me gives me so much pain! I never knew anything about love and now it makes my countenance change colour. I never knew what love was, and now I have learned of it for the first time, and it makes me shiver without feeling cold. I do not know what to do. If the youth I love so much loved me, or if there were someone who could speak of it and my father were to consent to it, then I could have him rightfully. It is not right that I should ask for him. We are very similar, sharing beauty and age. Even if we are not of the same rank, he is certainly very high born and we are not related. Dané, what are you plotting? This is no use to you at all. Your father has no interest in it. He is too busy with other things. What will become of me, then? I can no longer endure this suffering. (325–52)

'I want to let him know what I am seeking, but there is no messenger to whom I would risk entrusting the message. It would be much better if I spoke to him myself, but I'm afraid he might reject me and, if he did reject me completely, what good could another messenger achieve? No one would handle the issue as well as the person it involves directly, if he dares. Where do you expect to find him? How will you manage to speak to him? I have no worries on that score: I will see him tomorrow morning. I will go out and the women sleeping in the chamber won't know about it. I will wait for him along the path he takes every morning. When he is separated from the others, I will approach, fall at his feet and tell him about everything in my life, how Love has me in his grip. When I have confessed all to him, I will beg him for mercy, for God's sake. What is this, Dané, what are you saying? Have you lost all your senses? Have you abandoned all virtuous behaviour? What madness is prompting you in this way? Are you so mad and so foolish that you would go out wandering about all alone? Are you aware that you are a king's daughter? Indeed, I will take this into account! Love is no respecter of rank, but anyone who does not beg for love does not love. Alas! I have completely lost my mind! What have I just said? When I think of it, I consider myself utterly foolish. I'm not sticking to what I have said. I do not know what I seek, nor do I know which way to go about it. So what? It does not bother me. Love will guide me very well.' (353–92)

When she had said all this and gone over it in her mind, she came to the conclusion that she would go to him. On that she was resolved. The night passed, the day returned. The maiden was in a state of anxiety and did not sleep until daybreak. As soon as it grew light, she quietly slipped out of bed. Love is to be wondered at, which achieves so much, embracing and attracting everything. He makes a wise man shameless, so that any learning he may have is of no use to him. He teaches him to go by night, confidently and with no escort, when the weather is at its worst and most overcast. Love's heart is wicked and ruthless and he takes pity on no one. As soon as Love has captured and ensnared him, his heart trembles and starts to beat fast. Love controls it as best he can, both now and until his death. Love takes no account of right or wrong. (393–414)

Love had taken this Dané, the king's daughter, to himself so much that she did not know where she came from, who her family were. Nor did she restrain her foolish heart. She thought that whatever she did was right. O God, what a foolish decision she had arrived at! She unlocked the door and stole away through a small wicket gate and followed the path as far as it went. She did not tarry until she reached a wood near to the city, for she had noticed from the windows where she used to stand that the youth went there. She squatted in a bush, naked apart from her chemise and a mantle over it. There she awaited the youth and thought about what she would say. 'God!' she said. 'When he comes, let me be bold enough to tell him everything without fear!' With this she finished her entreaty, then looked and saw his companions, and when they came close she hid herself behind a tree, not daring to watch them any longer. They passed by and disappeared. Then Narcisus came along behind, all alone, following a cart track. His companions were already a good bowshot ahead. (415–46)

The maiden made straight for him. He looked at her, saw that she was beautiful and thought she must be a goddess or a fairy, as she was up so early. He dismounted and bowed to her. The maiden drew near him, and before uttering a word she kissed his eyes and embraced him. He was astonished at this and asked her who she was and where she was going. 'My lord', she replied, 'may you not be troubled by a poor maiden who is bereft of all happiness and cares little for her life, except that she has entrusted herself to you. Fair lord, I will tell you this clearly. I desire you above all else, as my heart is completely distraught on your account. It is only right that you should henceforth have pity on me. I did not send word of this to you, instead I am telling you in person. I am begging on my own behalf, not for anyone else. Look at me, know who I am! I who address you thus am the daughter of your lord the king. For love of you I am lost in thought night and day. Love has driven me here safely; Love makes me bold, for I would not have come otherwise. Now have mercy on her who begs for mercy, for upon you my whole life depends. You alone can restore me to health. We are free to love each other. Fair lord, grant me your love, give me back my health and take away my sorrow, for we are of the same age and equally attractive.' (447–82)

Narcisus heard what she said and smiled. He looked at her and said: 'By God, maiden, you are most foolish for ever broaching this subject, and you have taken upon yourself an unwise course by involving yourself with love. It would be better for you to get some sleep! How did you dare to come here all alone? It is an astonishing thing to do and you are too brazen. I consider this to be the height of folly. Is this how a king's daughter should behave? It is not up to either you or me to love, or to know anything whatsoever about it, for we are both still too young. You say that love makes you feel ill. I cannot help you with that, for I know nothing of such suffering, nor will I be undergoing it in the near future. If it is such that it makes you ill, I will take care to avoid it. May it not please God that I experience it, only for it to make me ill! I do not wish to know anything about love and I advise you to go back home, as you are wasting your time with useless begging.' (483–506)

When she heard this, she drew near him, sighing and weeping to no avail, and she cast her mantle behind her; hardly dressed, her body was beautiful. The cold and the path, which was very rough, tormented her so much that the blood ran from her toes, making her whole foot turn red. Tears poured down her face. She held out her hands towards him, bringing them together and intertwining them. He looked at her and noted her fair appearance, but said that this would do her no good. He saw her eyes weeping tenderly, looking at him very lovingly; her hands that were whiter than snow, bare, without gloves or adornment; and her white flesh above her chemise. But he felt no pity for her. God, what a hard, cruel heart! Beneath heaven there was no powerful baron, prince, count or king, however noble, nor any emperor or emir who would hold out for long without weeping in sympathy. Nothing she said to him moved him. He was wrong and gave her no assurance. She still had a lot more to say when Narcisus went on his way. (507–34)

She remained where she was and fainted from grief, and when she came to she cursed her life. 'Alas!' she said. 'My life is finished, for nothing comforts me. I am dead and in a sorry plight, now that my hopes have been dashed so that nothing I might say is of any help. All happiness flees from me. All ills afflict me. Dané, I warned you and you refused to believe anything I said. What? That he would dare treat me in this way? By God, he has made you founder. I know this well, and yet I complain about it. And now I am treated with great disdain. He has refused me. Me! Am I not the king's daughter and he the son of one of the king's men? O God, what a sorry situation! Such a grievous weight to bear! What is going to become of me? God, what a misfortune that I saw his fair eyes, so full of great pride! If he were ugly, it would worry me less, but it troubles me that he is so handsome. He spoke to me in an uncouth manner. What displeased him? I have no idea, by my faith! What could he have disliked about me? How wicked and how vile he is. I am a woman of noble stock and I am a maiden. I am most attractive and beautiful. I have lovely feet and lovely hands. There is nothing more to say about it. He is base and wicked and very badly brought up. Alas! Did he not notice my feet, bleeding and covered in thorns on his account? He did not show any restraint in what he said. (535–70)

'What am I saying now? I still love him greatly, and evermore, indeed, by God, and I want to love him; I cannot forget him. My love for him still overwhelms me, for his beauty, which summons me when I want to break loose from him, draws me back. I do not care what he has done, as long as he repents and comes to me to make amends. But he has no interest in putting things right, for he has an evil nature. I cannot let him go, I cannot abandon him. I cannot stop loving him. I do not know why, and I wonder at it. Now I must adopt a different strategy. I will send a messenger to him. If I return to him frequently, his heart will not be so hard that I cannot win him over by wearing him down. I do not like what I'm saying, for I myself failed in this, so why send someone else to him? I do not know what I am doing or where I am. Who am I then? Who is my father? He is the king. And my mother? Do you not know? The queen. That is not true. I am an orphan and I have no friend or relative, and no good people to advise me. By God, yes you have. You are Dané! Have I gone out of my mind, then? I used to be wiser. Have I become a wild creature? What am I doing in the wood? What have I sought here? I am behaving in a shameful manner. That is Love's doing. What is love? Alas, I do not know! I would be more accurate if I called it madness. It is making me lead a very wretched life: at one moment I'm at peace and the next in conflict. You, gods of heaven and earth, and of the air and the sea, and all of you who know anything about love and are in its power, and you, Venus, who have betrayed me, together with the god of Love, your son: rescue me from this peril and take vengeance on him for whom I am dying without hope! Make him learn what love is, so that he can have no succour!' The gods did not fail to hear her, and whatever she prayed for would be carried out. She went straight back to the gate and returned to her chamber. (571–626)

Narcisus had raised a stag and they had pursued it all day. It was a burning hot day, for the sun was very high in the sky, and once midday had passed the youth was very hot. He left his companions in search of water to drink and came upon a fountain that was clear, sweet and wholesome. The grass that had grown all round it was tall and thick. He saw that the water was deep and inviting, and that the stream and the sand were clean. He dismounted by a marble block and tethered his horse to a tree, pleased to stay there. But when he tried to quench his thirst, he was heated by a different thirst, which caused him much greater distress. As he bent forward and drank, he saw in the fountain the reflection set opposite him. It seemed to him to be looking straight at him and he thought that it was a water nymph guarding the fountain. Love struck in no time! As the reflection remained there, and he stayed put and watched it in the fountain, he marvelled greatly at it and began to love it so much that he could not take his eyes off it. The more he looked, the more he liked it. He did not utter a word; rather did he keep quiet, fearing that if she heard him speak she would not wish to remain there any longer. So he looked at the reflection very intently, at the face and the body, which seemed to him to be so handsome. He admired the eyes, the hands and the fingers and was distraught and filled with anguish. He did not know what he was seeing, as the water played him false. He was praising himself, but did not realise it. It was his own beauty that he could see there, he was deceiving himself. This is the man who had been castigating love just now, and suddenly he has plunged himself into such agony. He begged Love for help, lamented, sighed and wept, but he was distracted by the single thought that he could neither keep silent nor dare speak. He lamented, then uttered a sigh and could not restrain himself from speaking. (627–78)

'Creature', he said, 'whom I can see in there. I do not know what to call you, whether you should be called a nymph, or whether you are a goddess or a fairy. Whoever you are, come on out and show me your whole body! You must not be too proud. Come on! Why are you drawing away? Why are you being haughty towards me? I am hardly less attractive than you. Many a time I have been begged for my love, and now I myself am seized by terrible ardour. Now I realise just what it was like for them and that it was right for them to lament. Why are you now hiding? Speak to me and come out here! You can easily pass through. There is no sea between us, just a little stretch of water, which is killing me. Alas! Can she hear what I have said? No, perhaps the water is too deep. By God, yes she does and she is replying. I perceive her lips moving, but I cannot hear what she says. The water prevents her voice from emerging so that I cannot hear her. Ah, alas! Why can I not hear her speaking? Why won't she come out and show herself? This is either great arrogance, or she does not want what I want, for when I smile I see her smile too, and when I sigh she sighs, then when I weep she does the same. She does not stop or do anything else, until I do something else. I can see the tears on her face, and I cannot tug my hair without seeing her doing the same. (679–716)

'But why does she do this? If she loved me, she would come out and show herself, unless she wants to mock me by doing this, or perhaps she is unable to come out to me. What shall I do? What could I say? At one moment I reflect, then I weep, then I want to smile, then I feel unwell, then I grieve, and then I do not know what I want. My heart is hot one moment and cold the next. What sort of cold am I feeling? What is happening when it is so hot outside and I feel cold inside? Now I recall what I have heard said: that such torment, such suffering and such an existence are the lot of those who become involved with Love. Is it Love then who treats me thus and makes me suffer sorrow and pain? It must be that I know nothing of Love, though I do know that he has enormous power and that he is troubling and tormenting me. That much I know and believe to be true, without any doubt, but where he comes from, or who he is, where he dwells, or where he may be seen, what people and what land he governs – all this I cannot know by myself. What business is it of mine to seek him out, or to try and find his land or country? If I were to ask for him, he would be very near. I feel him very energetic within me, so I do not need to seek him far away. (717–47)

Now I have seen how he operates, and now I think I know where he comes from. Until now I knew nothing about him! He was born on a mountain, amid the rocks of a savage land where there is permanent snow and ice. His body is hard, and so is his face, with a diamond-hard heart and iron veins. His abode is in hell. Whoever included him among the gods was not wise; rather he acted misguidedly. He had not looked carefully enough at his wicked heart and his cruelty. Gods do not do harm to people, but Love is always out to torment. He is wicked and harsh towards men of high rank and good to servants and rogues. I will never believe, whatever anyone may say, that he has any power in heaven. Now you are suddenly very learned about Love! Who taught you so much? Your heart? I do not think this can be so, that you should know so much without having a teacher. Love is the teacher who instructed me and who sets my body on fire and burns me. He teaches me all about his nature and torments me without restraint. Ah! Sweet creature that so sets me afire, if only you knew the torment and pain I suffer for you, you would come and speak with me. I am dying now and do not know what to do. Before I see the sun tomorrow, they will find me dead here, if I cannot have any comfort. Your heart is either very wicked or very cruel, for you readily look at me, as I understand from your expression, and yet you are unwilling to come out, when I beg you most gently to have mercy on me. Whatever I do, I see you do [the same]. Nothing could please me more. I have abandoned everyone for you and you have bent me to your will completely.' (748–92)

Thus he lamented and could not depart. He wanted to live or die there; no other outcome could please him. The sun had already set and he spent all night in pain. He stayed there till dawn without eating or drinking, and did not perceive his madness. As he wept and grieved intensely, his tears created ripples in the fountain, and because of the rippling water he could not see what he had seen before. 'Ah, alas!' he said. 'What has become of her? Where has she gone? Now I have lost her and am left here all alone, miserable, grieving and in anguish. Apart from Love, there is no living soul left here with me, I who would rather die quickly than live on for a long time in such pain.' (793–814)

Then he looked and saw the reflection reappear in the water. He smiled, and it seemed to him that she smiled back at him. That made him all the more upset and he kissed the water more than a hundred times. It seemed to him that she was very close and he could not restrain himself any longer. He reached out with his arms, expecting to take hold of her, but however much he tried to stretch out and embrace her he could neither hold her nor find her. Then he began to reflect and realised that he could not take hold of her; she was very close to him and did not move. Thus she escaped him and deceived him, and he thought she was a phantom. He regained his senses somewhat and realised that he had been deceived and loved a reflection. He rebuked himself and called himself a fool, yet he did not know what to do and could not withdraw his heart. He had lost his way and did not know how to escape or find his way back on to the straight path, for he was so inflamed with love that he could not turn away: the more he despaired, the worse the anguish became. One moment he tormented himself, the next he considered himself as dead, not knowing what he was saying or doing. (815–44)

'I know that what the soothsayer said is true. My death is near. This is the end for me, for I have got myself into a foolish situation. I can expect no hope from it, and I feel, believe and know for certain that I can expect nothing from it, and this increases my anguish and stokes the fire that burns within me. For at least my gaze used to be pleasurable and gave me great comfort. I thought I saw something or other in the reflection that deceived me and that might have done me some good. But now I know I see nothing and this makes my suffering worse. Now I am not getting a moment of peace, now I am not in love with a living soul, now I do not know what it is that I want. What kind of love is it that causes me grief, when I am in love and do not know what I want? The body and face I could see there I can find entirely in myself. I love myself: that is madness! Has such folly as yours ever been heard of? Alas! I can feel it, this pain is getting worse, and there is no one to whom I can complain. You, fields, you, meadows, here all around: in God's name, witness my grief! Lament for me and my beauty and say: "Alas that he was ever born, this child who endures such sorrow and is dying through great misfortune"! And you, forest, who spreads all around and who is so vast and ancient – you have long grown here and have seen many a love – tell me if you have ever witnessed such anguished love. Think and tell me. No you have not, by my faith, I know this for certain! (845–84)

'You gods, who judge the whole world, take pity on me! Why do you leave me languishing for so long? I would rather die. Ah! Alas! Beloved, how these gods are deaf! Why do none of them help me when they see me heading for such an end? They are not as propitious, it seems to me, as people used to say. Can they not do anything? People say this rightly! Since I invoke them all and beg them and they show me no mercy, I am entitled to conclude that they can neither harm nor help me. Where do these words come from? Alas! I must not think this, nor do I believe it. But you gods, forgive me, for I am speaking like a madman, like someone so seized by folly that I don't know why I languish, nor do I know what to ask for, except for what cannot be granted to me. And with me comes and goes the creature that causes me such grief. Everything I wish for is in me, and so I do not know why I am grieving. I am what I so long to be, yet I make myself languish. Since I have what I ask for, why do I not do as I wish with it? I do not know, for I love and am loved, and what I love loves me deeply in return and does not suffer any less, yet we cannot do anything about it. We? But I can, for I am alone. This love is not shared between two. Beg? What can I beg for? The thing that I love cannot help me or give me advice. There is no other outcome. I must die. (885–924)

'Alas! I lament but nobody hears me. My family knows nothing about it. What has happened to all my companions, who have lost me? I am far away from everyone and left all alone in this wood. I think that everybody hates me. Alas! Why is my mother not aware of this? She would come and lament and weep over me, and she could give me some comfort. Why has no one seen me who could lament for me and my beauty? Indeed yes, at least there was the maiden whom I found so beautiful the other day, and who proclaimed herself miserable and unhappy and begged me for my love. Now I can proclaim myself miserable, because I was unwilling to love her. Ah! Alas! How mean I was and full of great wickedness, and so heartless and ill-bred that there was no way that she could please me. Fair lord God, let her come now! Perhaps she could be of more use to me than my mother, father or sister, if I could transfer my heart to her and divert my feelings, so that I could forget this madness. For Love has so inflamed me that I am forced to love despite myself. But of one thing I think I can be certain: if my love knew where to take hold of me, and I were to see someone other than myself, I should not be in such a state. God! If by chance she were to come, she could now be sure that she would gain my love and release me from this sickness. It was right that misfortune should befall me when I would never listen to her!' (925–64)

As he spoke and rebuked himself, his heart gave out. He fainted three times and lost the power of speech. He opened his eyes and saw Dané, who arrived completely distraught, for Love had so inflamed her that she went to seek the youth, naked but for her mantle. He looked at her but said nothing, as he wanted to speak but could not. He pointed the fountain out to her, and the reflection that had deceived him. He reached out to her and moved his lips, opening his eyes as much as he could. It seemed to her that he was repenting. She looked at him and understood fully. She approached him without a word, tormenting herself with anguish. She kissed him, held him and fainted, then she came to, put her arms around him and embraced him, kissing his eyes and his face. 'Ah!' she said. 'Sweet love, how you are overwhelmed by death! You are trying to show me a welcome, yet you cannot speak to me. Alas! What an unhappy meeting, what a grievous embrace, such brief pleasure, such brief delight and such great anguish which is killing me! Alas! My prayer has killed him! Now there will be no more comfort for me and I must die and keep him company, for I much prefer death to life.' The youth died, his life ebbed away. The maiden drew nearer to him, holding him with such force that she made her soul depart from her body. That was Love's doing, which had overwhelmed her. Both of them died in this way. Let all other lovers take care that they do not die in the same manner! (965–1006)

Romance and Realism

20. The *Chastelaine de Vergi*

Introduction

The *Chastelaine de Vergi* (The *Châtelaine of Vergi*) is preserved in twenty-two manuscripts. Our translation is taken from MS Paris, BNF, fr. 837, as edited by Frederick Whitehead (his MS C).[1] In recent times this work has often been regarded as a short story or a short romance but there is no reason to deny it the designation of 'lay'. By the time this poem was written, no doubt well into the thirteenth century, the form and content of the lay had evolved, with fewer non-realistic elements than in earlier examples of the genre.[2] The author is unknown, but Jehan Renart, author of the *Lai de l'Ombre*, has been suggested.[3]

The tale recounts the tragic fate of two lovers at the court of the Duke of Burgundy. One of the lovers is a knight who frequents the duke's court and is much loved by the latter. The *châtelaine* is the duke's niece and she has granted her love to the knight on the condition that if he ever reveals it to anyone, it will immediately be withdrawn from him. The knight must make his way to his beloved's dwelling and watch for a little dog running through the garden as a sign that the coast is clear and that he can visit the lady and enjoy a night of love. This arrangement works well until the knight's frequent visits to court bring him to the attention of the duchess who, first with gestures and then with words, attempts to seduce him. Rebuffed, the duchess takes revenge by declaring

[1] For a full list and discussion of the manuscripts, see the edition by R. E. V. Stuip, pp. 31–47. Stuip bases his edition on MS Paris, BNF, fr. 375 (his MS A). See p. 11n2.

[2] For a discussion of the genre of the *Châtelaine de Vergi*, see Paula Clifford, *La Chastelaine de Vergi and Jean Renart: Le Lai de l'Ombre* (London: Grant and Cutler, 1986), pp. 9–12, 42–45.

[3] See Edwin E. Okafor, 'La Source et la structure de *La Chastelaine de Vergi*', *Francofonia*, 12 (1987), 65–77.

to her husband that the knight has spent the day trying to seduce her. She convinces the duke of the truth of this by pointing out that the knight does not seems to have a lover elsewhere. This accusation sets in motion a series of tragic events. At first, the duke refuses to accept the knight's protestation of innocence, then he gives him the opportunity to clear himself by naming his beloved (the duke has already noticed that his clothing and demeanour indicate that he is indeed in love with someone). On discovering that the knight's lover is his niece, he demands to accompany the knight on his next visit and, on doing so, realises that his wife has lied to him. But he makes the mistake of paying the knight too much attention at dinner and his wife, suspecting that something is not right, retires to bed, feigning illness. Despite her husband's reluctance to reveal the truth to her, the duchess finally wheedles it out of him. She then bides her time until she can speak to the *châtelaine*, and when the opportunity presents itself, at Pentecost, she taxes her with the training of the little dog, something that the other ladies present would not understand. Convinced that the knight has betrayed her, and that he no longer loves her, the *châtelaine* kills herself, pardoning him before she does so. When the knight eventually finds out what has happened, he runs himself through with a sword, and the duke, thanks to the testimony of a maiden who had overheard both the *châtelaine* and the knight, draws the sword from the knight's body and plunges it into his wife's head. The lovers are then buried together. Grief-stricken, the duke departs and, taking the cross, makes his way to the Holy Land, where he joins the Knights Templar.

The *Chastelaine de Vergi* is a tightly structured tale that deals with circumstances that lead to a tragic outcome for two lovers and for the society in which they live. Just as the *Lai de l'Ombre* shows how a love relationship can be formed, the *Chastelaine de Vergi* shows how a relationship can be destroyed, with tragic consequences. The organisation of the story revolves to a great extent around dialogue or monologues. The initial conversation between the knight and the duchess is followed by others between the duke and the duchess and between the duke and the knight. Then in the centre of the narrative occurs the meeting between the lovers themselves, during which they seem to be completely cut off from reality. This is followed in reverse order by conversations between the knight and the duke, the duke and the duchess, and finally, for the first time, between the duchess and the *châtelaine*. The two monologues, first by the *châtelaine* and then by the knight, both end in the speaker's death.

The time for talking is over and no further words are exchanged between the duke and the duchess, as the duke carries out his promise and kills his wife for failing to keep the secret he had entrusted to her.

All the words and actions in this poem relate to the love affair between the knight and the *châtelaine*. It is no surprise that the lovers wish to, or need to, keep their love secret, but one cannot but wonder why the *châtelaine* imposes on the knight what the text calls a 'couvenant' or 'couvenance' ('arrangement', 'condition', 'agreement', vv. 23, 274, 357, etc.). This states that at the very hour and on the very day that he reveals their love is revealed, he will lose both the love and the gift the *châtelaine* has made of herself (vv. 24–28). The revenge taken by the duke's wife for the knight's rejection of her sexual advances is often compared to what happens in Marie de France's *Lanval* when Lanval rebuffs Arthur's queen, so it is possible that the author is presenting the *châtelaine* as a fairy-type figure who requires that the love be kept secret and at the same time has the supernatural power to know when the 'couvenant' has been broken. If so, this would be the only non-realistic element in a narrative that otherwise never strays from the feudal and courtly values of contemporary society. Perhaps the lady has been reading about, or listening to, tales of the Other World, and fancies imposing on her beloved a stricture aimed at demonstrating her power over him.

When told of the love affair between the knight and his niece, the duke makes no comment about the unsuitability of the relationship in terms of birth and lineage. But he immediately wonders how the lovers have managed to communicate and meet. So is the lady married, like her counterpart in the *Lai de l'Ombre* (see below)? The *châtelaine*'s comment to the duchess that she did not want to dishonour her 'seignor' could indicate that she has her 'lord' (i.e. the Duke of Burgundy) in mind, but in Old French the term 'seignor' can also mean 'husband' (vv. 710–14). Perhaps it is telling that the duke relates 'the whole affair' (v. 929) to the assembled dancers, and the lovers are buried together in the same coffin. Would the duke humiliate the lady's husband in this way, and would a husband allow his wife to be buried with her lover?

Who is responsible for these deaths? The obvious answer is the duchess, as she makes advances to her husband's knight, falsely accusing him of attempted seduction. She uses her wiles to extract the details of the knight's love relationship from her husband and, after biding her time, employs veiled language to make the *châtelaine* aware that she knows her secret. But she is not the only candidate. The *châtelaine* does not help the situation by imposing the 'couvenant' on her lover, and when she finds out that it has been broken she immediately jumps to the false conclusion that the knight must have told the duchess and done so because he loves her. The duke also has an important role to play in the tragic outcome, as he breaks his promise to the knight – that he would not reveal the knight's secret to a living soul. After receiving proof of what the knight had told him, at dinner he foolishly makes a fuss of the knight in his wife's presence. Then, albeit under extreme pressure from his wife, he breaks his promise to the knight and tells her of the affair.

Is the knight himself the principal culprit for the tragic outcome? Even before he had been propositioned by the duchess, he had already partially broken the 'couvenant' by making it clear through his appearance and elegant dress that he was in love. Although lucid when it comes to the issue of whether or not to tell the truth to the duke, he fudges the issue by suggesting that he might be able to tell the truth and get away with it if his beloved does not get wind of what he has done. He then makes matters worse by crying, thus making it clear to the duke that he has something to hide. When the lovers meet in the lady's chamber, the knight fails to take the opportunity to broach the subject with her. Indeed, when they are together they address each other in a language that does not embrace the nitty gritty of everyday court life: 'My lady, my beloved, my love, my heart, my passion, my hope and everything I love ...' (v. 405ff.). The lovers speak the language of 'fine amor'. In her monologue the *châtelaine* twice makes an appeal to this form of perfect or pure love ('Ha! fine amor!' vv. 784, 808), addressing Love like a confidante. Perhaps the author is saying that this form of intense and all-consuming love has had its day, as it all too easily becomes caught in the snares of a nasty and hostile world. Surprisingly, when we reach the epilogue to the narrative, where we would expect some form of assistance with the knotty problem of guilt, the author merely tells us that his work is a cautionary tale of a tragedy that came about because the knight revealed something he should not have revealed, adding that we should all remember that it is sensible to keep love concealed. What we have here, even with three deaths in the closing stages of the narrative, is a return to one of the traditional principles of love, i.e. secrecy, without any recognition that it was the blindness induced by love itself that was the fundamental cause of the problem.

Further Reading

Clifford, Paula, *La Chastelaine de Vergi and Jean Renart: Le Lai de l'Ombre* (London: Grant and Cutler, 1986).

De Looze, Laurence, 'The Untellable Story: Language and Writing in *La Chastelaine de Vergi*', *French Review*, 59 (1985), 42–50.

Hunt, Tony, 'The Art of Concealment: *La Châtelaine de Vergi*', *French Studies*, 47 (1993), 129–41.

Maraud, André, 'Le Lai de *Lanval* et *La Chastelaine de Vergi*', *Romania*, 93 (1972), 433–49.

Payen, Jean-Charles, 'Structure et sens de *La Chastelaine de Vergi*', *Le Moyen Age*, 79 (1973), 433–59.

Translation

There are some who give the impression of being loyal and knowing how to keep a secret so well that it seems appropriate to put one's trust in them, and when it comes about that one reveals something to them, so that they know all about a love affair, then they spread the news throughout the land and make it a subject for laughter and jest. Thus it comes about that those who have revealed the secret end up losing the pleasure they had, for the greater the love the more afflicted are true lovers when one of them thinks that the other has said something that ought to have been kept secret. Often, such misfortune comes of this that of necessity the love has to come to an end in great pain and shame, as happened in Burgundy to a brave and bold knight and the Lady of Vergi, whom the knight loved so much that she granted him her love on condition that he knew that, at the very hour and on the very day their love was revealed by him, he would lose both the love and the gift she had made of herself. When this love was granted, they arranged that the knight would come to a garden every day, at the time she fixed for him, and would not stir from his hiding place until he saw a little dog running though the garden. Then, without delay, he would come into her chamber, knowing that at that time there would be no one there but the lady herself. (1–39)

They proceeded in this way for a long time and the love between them was tender and secret, as no living soul knew about it but them. The knight was handsome and elegant, and through his valour he became intimately acquainted with the duke who ruled Burgundy. He often visited court, so frequently that the duchess fell in love with him. She made her love so clear to him that, if he had not had his heart elsewhere, he could easily have noticed through her behaviour that she loved him truly. But whatever sign she gave, the knight showed no sign himself that he had noticed in any way at all that she was in love with him, to the extent that she suffered greatly. One day she spoke to him and addressed him in these words: 'My lord, you are handsome and brave, everyone says so, thanks be to God. You clearly deserve to have a beloved in such a high place that you would gain honour and advantage from it, for such a beloved would suit you very well.' (40–65)

'My lady', he said, 'I have not yet given any thought to this.' 'In faith', she said, 'a long wait could prove harmful to you, I believe. So I advise you to take a lover in a high place, if you see that you are well loved there.' He replied: 'My lady, in faith, I do not know why you are saying this, or what it means. I am not a duke or a count who should love so highly, and I am nowhere near to loving such a sovereign lady, even if I strove to do so.' 'Yes', she said, 'perhaps you are. Many greater marvels happen, and such a one will happen again. Tell me whether you are now aware that I have granted you my love, I who am a high-ranking, honoured lady.' He replied promptly: 'My lady, I was not aware of this, but I should like to have your love in sincerity and in honour. But may God protect me from such a love that on my part or yours would bring shame on my lord, for at no time and in no way would I undertake any wrong, such as acting unreasonably, churlishly or disloyally towards my lawful, natural lord.' (66–98)

'Fie!' said the woman, who was upset. 'Lord Trifler, and who is asking you to?' 'Ah, my lady, in God's mercy, I am fully aware of this, but I was just making a point.' She said nothing further to him, but in her heart she had great distress and displeasure, and she decided that if she could, she would have her revenge on him. She was greatly vexed, and that night, when she was in bed next to the duke, she began to sigh and then to cry. The duke immediately asked her what the matter was and ordered her to tell him straightaway. 'Certainly', she said. 'I find it very distressing that no high-born man knows who is faithful to him and who is not. Rather they show more kindness and honour to those who are traitors to them and yet none of them realises it.' 'In faith', said the duke, 'I do not know why you are saying this. But I am innocent of such a thing, because in no way would I have a traitor in my service, if I knew him to be so.' 'Hate then', she said, 'the man (and she named him) who all day long never stopped begging me to give him my love, and he told me that he had been of this mind for a very long time but had never before dared tell me. I made up my mind, fair lord, to tell you this at once. And it is possible that he has been thinking about this for a long time, because we have had no inkling that he has given his love elsewhere. As a reward for this, I beg you to look to your honour in this matter, as you know to be right.' (99–140)

The duke, to whom this seemed very upsetting, said to her: 'I will get to the bottom of this, and very soon, I believe.' That night the duke was distressed and did not sleep a wink because of the knight whom he loved and thought had wronged him, therefore rightly losing his love. For this reason, he spent the night awake. The next day he rose early and summoned to him the man whom his wife had caused him to hate, without him having done anything wrong. Now he spoke to him one to one; only the two of them were present: 'Indeed', he said, 'it is very distressing that, since you possess prowess and beauty, there is no loyalty in you! You have deceived me greatly, you whom I had long thought to be of good faith, loyal at least towards myself, because I have always loved you. I do not know where such a thought, one so treacherous, has come from, that you would entreat the duchess and beg for her love. You have acted with great treachery. One could not find any baser action. Get out of my land at once, for I banish you irrevocably and forbid and deny it to you utterly. Do not enter it in any way at all, because, if henceforth I should capture you, you can be assured that I would have you hanged.' (141–76)

When the knight heard this, he was inflamed with anger and wrath, so that all his limbs trembled, because he was mindful of his beloved, as he knew he could not enjoy her except by coming and going and frequenting the country from which the duke wanted him exiled. In addition, it was very hurtful to him that his lord should wrongly consider him to be a disloyal traitor, and he was in such discomfort that he considered himself dead and betrayed. 'My lord', he said, 'in God's mercy, do not ever believe or think that I would have been so bold. What you wrongfully accuse me of I never even thought of at any hour of any day. The person who told you this has done wrong.' 'It is no use your answering this charge,' said the duke, 'for there is no answer. She herself has told me in what way and in what fashion you begged her and beseeched her for her love as a dreadful traitor, and perhaps you said some things about which she has kept quiet.' 'My lady has said what pleases her,' said he who was very distressed. 'There is no point in your answering the charge.' 'Nothing I might say is of any use, yet there is nothing I would not do so that I would be believed, for nothing of this sort has happened.' (177–210)

'Yes it did, by my soul', said the duke, who was thinking of his wife, for he was convinced that she was telling the truth, as he had never heard anyone say that the knight loved anyone else. Then the duke said to the knight: 'If you are willing to pledge to me by your loyal oath that you will tell me truly what I ask of you, I would be certain through your words whether or not you had done what I suspect you of doing.' The man who wished and desired to rid his lord of the anger he unjustly felt towards him, and who feared the ruinous situation of abandoning the region in which lived the woman who pleased him most, replied that he would readily do what the duke had said. He did so because he had no inkling of what the duke was concerned about; nor did his suffering let him imagine what the duke wanted to ask him, other than about the act of begging for her love. He took an oath in this way and the duke accepted his pledge of faith. (211–39)

Immediately, the duke said to him: 'Be assured in pure truth that because I have loved you until now with a pure heart I cannot in any way give credence to any crime or shameful act on your part, such as the duchess relates to me. I would not have regarded it as true if it were not for one thing, which causes me to believe it and seriously suspect it. This is that when I look at your bearing, your elegant dress and other things one can very clearly deduce that you are in love with someone or other. Since no one knows of any maiden or lady with whom you are in love, I think it must be with my wife, who has told me that you have been begging her for her love. I cannot be deflected from this by anything that anyone could do, because I think that the affair is precisely this one, unless you tell me that you love passionately elsewhere, in such a way that you let me know, without any doubt, the entire truth of this matter. If you refuse to do so, get out of my land forthwith as a perjurer!' (240–67)

The knight did not know what to do, because the die was so precisely cast that on both counts he considered himself dead. For, if he told the pure truth, which he would do if he were to avoid perjuring himself, he considered himself dead; and if he committed such a wrong that he broke the covenant he had with his lady and beloved, he was sure he would lose her if she found out about it. And if he did not tell the duke the truth, he was a perjurer and a traitor to his word, and he would lose the land and his beloved. But the land did not matter to him, providing he retained his beloved, whom he feared losing more than anything else.[4] Because he then remembered the great joy and pleasure he had had in her arms and wondered how, if he betrayed her and lost her because of his wrongdoing, since he could not take her away with him, he could last without her. He was in a similar situation to the Chastelain of Coucy, who had nothing but love in his heart and said in a stanza of a song: 'In God's name, O Love, it is difficult for me to be without the sweet delight and the company and the favours that I used to be shown by her who was my companion and my beloved. And when I consider her innocent courtliness and the tender words she used to speak to me, how can my heart remain in my body? If it does not depart, it is indeed very perverse.' (266–302)[5]

The knight was in such anguish that he did not know whether to tell the truth or to lie and leave the country. While he was thus plunged in thought, not knowing which was best, because of the anguish he was experiencing, water from his heart came into his eyes. It ran down his cheeks, wetting his face. The duke was not pleased within his heart, for he thought that there was something he dared not reveal. Then the duke said to him swiftly: 'I can see that you do not trust me as much as you ought to. Do you think that, if you told me your secret in private, I would let anyone else know about it? Without fail, I should rather let my teeth be drawn out one by one.' 'Ah', he said, 'in God's mercy, my lord, I do not know what I should say, or what may become of me. But I would rather die than lose what I would lose if I had told you the truth, and it became known to her that I had confessed it any day of my life!' Then the duke said: 'I assure you, on my body and on my soul, and on the love and faith I owe you in return for your homage, that never in my whole

[4] The original text contains some remarkably complex sentences with a large number of subordinate clauses. The present note is positioned at v. 283 in the text, at the end of what is for the editor Frederick Whitehead a sixteen-line sentence (beginning in our translation at 'For, if he told the pure truth …'). We have divided it into three sentences.

[5] The *châtelain* of Coucy was a Picard *trouvère* named Guy de Thourotte, *châtelain* of Coucy-le-Château (Aisne). He died in 1202 during the Fourth Crusade. The poem we find in the *Chastelaine de Vergi* occurs with some textual variations in Gerbert de Montreuil's *Roman de la Violette*, vv. 4624–31 (ed. Douglas Labaree Buffum, Paris: Champion, 1928), and in full in the romance that takes his name, *Le Roman du Châtelain de Coucy et de la dame de Fayel*, by Jakemes (ed. John E. Matzke and Maurice Delbouille, Paris: Société des Anciens Textes Français, 1936).

life will the affair be related to any living creature, or any sign of it given, great or small.' (303–39)

In tears, the knight said to him: 'My lord, I will tell you about it. I love your niece of Vergi and she loves me, one cannot love any more deeply.' 'Now tell me then', said the duke, 'if you want to be shielded, did anyone apart from the two of you know about this affair?' The knight replied: 'No, no living creature'. And the duke said: 'That is not possible. How then did you manage this, and how do you know the time and place?' 'Upon my word, my lord, in a cunning way, which I will describe to you without holding anything back since you know so much about our affair.' Then he told him all about his comings and goings, and about the initial covenant and the way the little dog behaved. Then the duke replied: 'I ask of you that at your next agreed meeting you be willing to let me be your companion and go with you on this visit, for I want to know without any delay if your affair does operate like this. My niece will know nothing about it.' 'My lord', he said, 'I grant this, providing it does not worry or disturb you, and, know this, I will be going tonight.' The duke said he would go and that this would not inconvenience him, rather it would provide him with pleasure and distraction. (340–71)

They made arrangements with regard to the place where they would meet on foot. As soon as night fell, because the dwelling of the duke's niece was quite close to where they were, they made their way there until they reached the garden, where the duke did not have long to wait before he saw his niece's little dog, which came to the end of the garden and found there the knight who made a great fuss of him. At once the knight set off and left the duke behind, and the duke followed him to a point close to the window, from where he did not budge. He hid there as best he could. He was covered by a very large, broad tree as though by a shield, and he made every effort to conceal himself. From there he could see the knight on his way towards the chamber, and he saw his niece leaving the chamber and coming to meet him in a meadow outside. He saw and heard the joyful greeting she gave him with her mouth and her arms, as soon as she saw him: she rushed out of her chamber towards him and took him in her beautiful arms, kissing him more than a hundred times, before she addressed many words to him. (372–403)

He returned her kisses and embraces, saying to her: 'My lady, my beloved, my love, my heart, my passion, my hope and everything I love, be assured that I have had a great hunger to be with you, as I am now, every day since my last visit.' She replied: 'My sweet lord, my sweet friend, my sweet love, never since you were here has there been any day or any hour that the delay has not been distressing to me. But now I have no reason for sorrow, for I have with me what I desire, since you are here, hale and hearty, and you are very welcome!' He said to her: 'And you too are well met!' The duke, who had drawn very close to them, heard everything they said as they went in. He recognised his niece's voice very easily, and also her bearing, so that things were now beyond doubt, and he therefore regarded what the duchess had said as the words of a liar. This pleased him greatly, for he now saw that the knight had not committed any of the wrong of which he had suspected him. He spent the entire night there, while all the time the lady and the knight were in bed in the chamber, and without getting any sleep they lay together in such joy and such pleasure that it would be absurd for anyone to relate it, to speak of it or to listen to it, unless he himself aspired to such joy as Love gives to true lovers when it rewards their suffering. For he who does not aspire to such joy would not understand anything of it if he were to hear of it, since he does not have his heart set on Love, because no one would know in any way how much it means to have such joy, unless Love made him realise it. Such fortune does not come to everyone, for it is joy without grief, and pleasure and delight. But it is something that lasts only a short time, at least in the opinion of the lover who experiences it. So pleasing to him is the life he is leading that it will never last long enough, for if one night became a week, and a week became a month, a month a year and a year three, and three became twenty and twenty a hundred, when it came to an end he would rather that this night was just falling than dawn breaking. (404–60)

Such were the thoughts of the knight for whom the duke was waiting, for he had to leave before daybreak, and his beloved came to the door with him. As leave was being taken there, the duke saw the giving and returning of kisses, and he heard the deep sighs and the tears as they said goodbye. Many a tear was shed there and he heard arrangements being made for the next meeting. In such a way the knight departed and the lady closed the door. But, as long as she could still see him, she followed him with her beautiful eyes, since she could do no better. When the duke saw the door close, he set off at once and caught up with the knight, who was lamenting to himself about the night. As he said, for him it had all been too brief. Such were the thoughts and words of the woman he had left, to whom it appeared that her pleasure had been curtailed because of the night, and she had no praise for the dawn. The knight was at such a stage of thought and speech when the duke rejoined him, embracing and greeting him joyfully. Then he said to him: 'I promise you that I will love you forever and never again hate you, for you have told me the whole truth and have not uttered a word of a lie.' (461–96)

'My lord', he said, 'thank you. But in God's name I ask and beg you that it may please you to keep this secret, because I would lose my love, my joy and my ease, and without doubt die, if I knew that anyone else apart from you knew of it.' 'Say no more about this,' said the duke. 'Be assured that it will be well concealed, because it will never be spoken of by me.' They went along talking in this way until they reached the spot from which they had set off. And that day, when the time for the meal arrived, the duke made a greater fuss of the knight than he had ever done before, as a result of which, in truth, the duchess felt so much anger, distress and displeasure that she rose from the table and pretended deceitfully that she had been taken ill. She went to lie on her bed, where she had very little delight. When the duke had eaten, washed and feasted, he went to see her at once and had her sit up on the bed, ordering that no one should remain there apart from himself. The servants did his bidding at once, and the duke asked her straightaway how this illness had come about and what the matter was. (497–528)

She replied: 'So help me God. Just now, when I sat down to dinner, I did not expect that you would have as little sense and judgment as I saw you displaying when you cherished so dearly the man I told you about, who has done his best to bring shame and harm to me. And when I saw you making more of a fuss of him than before I was so upset and angry that I could not remain there.' 'Ah', said the duke, 'my sweet friend, be assured, I would not believe you or anyone else, because never in any way at all did what you told me actually happen. Rather do I know that he is quite innocent of it, and he never had any thought of doing this, so much have I learned about his situation. Do not ask me any further questions about this.' Then the duke left and she remained deep in thought. For as long as she lived she would not know an hour's peace until she had discovered more of the matter about which the duke had forbidden her to ask. She would never be put off by this prohibition, for in her heart she constructed a plan: if she waited until the evening when she had the duke in her arms, she would find out more about it. She was well aware that at such a time of delight, she had no doubt about this, she would accomplish her desire better than at any other time. (529–64)

For this reason, she restrained herself, and when the duke came to bed she withdrew to one side. She pretended not to like the duke lying with her, for she well knew that this was the way to get the upper hand over her husband, by feigning anger. Therefore, she behaved in such a way that provoked the duke into thinking that she was very upset. Without receiving more than a kiss from him, she said to him: 'You are very false, deceitful and disloyal, for you give the impression of loving me and yet you have never loved me for a single day. I have long been foolish enough to believe what you said when you told me on many occasions that you loved me with a loyal heart. But today I have realised that I have been deceived.' The duke replied to her: 'In what respect?' 'Upon my word', said the woman, who was planning to cause harm, 'you have just told me not to dare to ask questions about the matter you now know all about.' 'What are you referring to, my fair one, in God's name?' 'The fact,' she said, 'that he has told you lies and fabrication, and made you reach your present conclusion. But I am not interested in knowing this, because I have decided that it is of little use to love you with a loyal heart. For, whether it was good or bad, my heart saw and knew nothing that you did not know at once. And now I can see that you are concealing from me, if you please, all your thoughts. Be assured now, without any doubt, that I will never again give you my trust or my heart, in the way I have done in the past'. (565–608)

Then the duchess began to cry and to sigh, trying her very hardest. The duke took such pity on her that he said to her: 'My fair one, I would not suffer at any price either your distress or your anger but, be assured, I am not in a position to tell you what you want me to tell you without doing a great deal of harm.' She replied immediately: 'My lord, say nothing to me then, for I can see from your attitude that you have no faith in me to keep your secret. Be assured that I am amazed by this. You have never told me a secret that you have heard, great or small, that has been revealed by me. I tell you in good faith that this would never happen as long as I live.' When she had said this, she started to cry again, and the duke embraced and kissed her. He was distressed in his heart, in such a way that he could not refrain from revealing to her what she wanted to know. Then he said to her: 'Fair lady, I do not know what to do, upon my soul, for I have such trust and belief in you that I ought not to keep from you that anything my heart may know or hear. But, I beg you, do not say a word about this, and be assured, I say this to you now, that if I am betrayed by you, you will die as a result.' (609–43)

'I agree to this fully', she said. 'It would not be possible for me to do anything that would be harmful to you.' As he loved her, the duke believed her because of these words, and he thought that what she said was the truth. Then he told her the whole story about his niece, how he had learned it from the knight and about the hiding place in the garden, where there were only the two of them when the little dog came to them. He told her the truth about the knight's comings and goings, leaving out nothing of what he had seen or heard. When the duchess heard that the knight who had refused her love, loved someone less noble, she thought she was dead and humiliated. But she gave no sign of this. Rather did she promise the duke that she would keep quiet about this affair, otherwise he could hang her by a rope if she was the one to reveal it. Yet she was very anxious to speak to the woman she hated, from the very moment she knew that she was the lover of the man who had brought shame and pain to her, because, it seemed to her, he did not want to be her lover. She resolved that, if she saw the time and place, she would speak to the duke's niece and not stop short of including some poisonous remarks. (644–80)

But the duchess did not succeed in finding a suitable occasion or place until the following Pentecost came around, which was the next time the king held a plenary court and summoned all the ladies in the land, first and foremost his niece, who was *châtelaine* of Vergi. When the duchess saw her, at once her blood boiled, as she was the person she hated most in the whole world. But she knew how to conceal her feelings and made more of a fuss of her than she had ever done before. However, she was longing to reveal the great anger that was in her heart, and the delay was causing her a great deal of distress. For this reason, on the day of Pentecost, when the tables had been removed, the duchess took the ladies to her chamber so that they could get ready in privacy and come to the dance in their finery. Then the duchess, who saw her opportunity, could not hold back her words and said, as if jokingly: '*Châtelaine*, put your best clothes on, for you have a handsome and valiant friend.' The *châtelaine* replied simply: 'I do not know what friendship you are thinking of, my lady, in truth, for I have no desire to have a friend who is not completely in keeping with the honour I owe myself and my lord.' 'I accept this fully,' said the duchess, 'but you are a past mistress of the art of training the little dog.' (681–718)

The ladies heard what was said, but they did not understand its meaning. They returned with the duchess to take part in the dancing. The *châtelaine* remained behind, her heart in a turmoil of anguish and sorrow. Her whole body shuddered. She went into a dressing room, where there was a young maiden lying at the foot of the bed, but invisible to her. Grief-stricken, the *châtelaine* fell back on the bed, mourning and lamenting greatly. 'Ah! Lord God, have mercy!' she said. 'How can it be that I have heard my lady reproach me with the training of my little dog. No one can have told her that, I know full well, other than the man I used to love and who has betrayed me. He would never have told her unless he was on intimate terms with her and loved her without doubt more than myself, whom he has betrayed. I can clearly see that he does not love me, since he breaks his covenant with me, sweet God, and I loved him as much as anyone can love another person, in such a way that I could not think of anything else for a single hour, day or night! For he was my joy and my pleasure, he was my delight, he was my enjoyment, he was my solace, he was my comfort. How impossible it was for me to refrain from thinking about him when I could not see him! Ah, beloved, how has this come about? How can it have happened, that you have been so false towards me? I thought that you were more loyal to me, so help me God, than Tristan was to Iseut. I loved you more than half as much again, may God have pity on me, than I did myself. Never, earlier or later, or at any time, did I commit any crime, great or small, in thought, word or deed as a result of which you could have hated me or betrayed me so wretchedly as to destroy our love in order to love someone else, and to abandon me and reveal our secret. (719–71)

'Ah! Woe is me! Beloved, I am astonished, for my heart, so help me God, was never like this towards you. For, if God had given me the entire world, and even all heaven and its paradise, I would not have accepted them if it meant losing you. For you were my riches, my health and my joy, and nothing could distress me as long as my poor heart knew that your heart contained some love for me. Ah! True love! Who would ever have thought that this man would sin against me, a man who said, when he was with me and when I did all I could to accomplish his entire bidding, that he was mine completely and considered me his lady in both body and soul? He used to say this so tenderly that I believed him truly, and I would never have thought in any way that he could have found in his heart any anger or hatred towards me, either for a duchess or for a queen. Loving him was so good that I took his heart into myself as my own. I thought that he did the same, and that he regarded me as his lifelong beloved. For I know in my own heart that, if he died first, my love for him would be such that I would not last long after him. To be dead with him would be better for me than to live in such a way that I never again set eyes on him. (772–807)

'Ah! True love! So is it true that he has revealed our secret in this way, thereby destroying me? For, when I granted him my love, I made it a condition that he would lose me the very moment he revealed our love. Now that I have lost him first, after such suffering, and am without the man for whom I grieve, I cannot go on living, and do not want to do so. My life has no pleasure for me. Rather I pray to God to bring death to me and that, just as truly as I have loyally loved the man who has brought this upon me, he should have pity on my soul, and may he give honour to him who by his wrongful act has betrayed me and handed me over to death. I pardon him. My death holds nothing but sweetness for me, I believe, since it comes from him. When I recall his love, dying for him is not difficult.' Then the *châtelaine* fell silent, except that she said with a sigh: 'Sweet friend, I entrust you to God!' With these words she clasped her arms around herself. Her heart failed and her face became discoloured. She fainted in anguish and lay pale and colourless in the middle of the bed, dead and without life. (808–39)

Her beloved, who was enjoying himself in the hall and dancing in the round dance and other dances, was completely unaware of this. But nothing he could see there brought him any pleasure, since he could not see the woman to whom he had given his heart, and this surprised him greatly. He whispered in the duke's ear: 'My lord, how is it that your niece has been absent for such a long time and not come to the dancing? I do not know if you have hidden her away.' The duke, who had not noticed anything, looked at the dancing. He drew the knight by the hand and went straight to the chamber. When he failed to find her there, he requested and bade the knight to go and look for her in the dressing room, for in this way he wanted them to enjoy themselves inside it with embraces and kisses. The knight, who was deeply grateful to him, went into the dressing room, where his beloved was lying on her back on the bed, livid and drained of colour. As he now had the time and the opportunity, he embraced and kissed her at once. But he found that her mouth was cold and that she was very pale and stiff all over. From the appearance of her body, he could clearly see that she was stone dead. Aghast, he cried out immediately: 'What is this? Woe is me! Is my beloved dead?' The maiden who was lying at the foot of the bed jumped up and said: 'My lord, I believe that she is dead, for she has asked for nothing else since coming here, because of her grief over her beloved, about whom my lady taunted her and derided her about a little dog, and as a result of this her grief became fatal.' (840–81)

When the knight heard these words, indicating that what he had told the duke had caused her death, he lamented uncontrollably: 'Ah! Woe is me!' he said. 'My sweet love, the courtliest and the finest there ever was, and the most loyal, I have killed you like a disloyal scoundrel! It would have been right for this situation to turn against me, so that you would not have been harmed by it. But you have such a loyal heart that you took everything upon yourself first. But I will punish myself for the treason I have committed.' He drew forth from its sheath a sword that was hanging from a bracket and plunged it into his heart, falling on to the other body and bleeding to death. The maiden rushed out when she saw the lifeless bodies and was horrified by what she saw. She told the duke, whom she met, what she had heard and seen, keeping nothing back, how the matter had begun and even about the training of the little dog, of which the duchess had spoken. You can imagine how frantic the duke was! He went into the room at once and drew out of the knight's body the sword with which he had killed himself. He left immediately and at great speed went straight to the dance. Without further ado, he approached the duchess at once and carried out his promise, thrusting into her head the naked sword he was holding and doing so without speaking, so distressed was he. In the sight of everyone from the region, the duchess fell at his feet. Then the celebrations were greatly disrupted for the knights who were present and had been enjoying themselves greatly. (882–926)

In the hearing of all those who cared to listen, the duke immediately related the whole affair in the midst of the court. Then there was no one who did not weep, especially when they saw the two dead lovers, with the duchess close by. The court dispersed in great dismay, grief and sorrow. The next day the duke had the lovers buried in one coffin and the duchess in a separate place. But he was so grief-stricken at what had happened that no one ever heard him laugh again. He took the cross at once and went overseas, whence he never returned. He became a Templar. Ah! God! All this woe and upset happened because the knight had the ill luck to say something he should have kept to himself and which his beloved had forbidden him ever to speak of, as long as he desired to have her love. This cautionary tale tells us that one must conceal one's love so sensibly that it is constantly borne in mind that there is no advantage in revealing it, and that concealment is always best. He who does this fears no assault from base and treacherous busybodies who pry into the loves of other people. (927–58)

21. The *Lai de l'Ombre*

Introduction

The *Lai de l'Ombre* (*Lay of the Reflection*) is preserved in seven manuscripts: (i) S; (ii) A: Paris, BNF, fr. 837; (iii) B: BNF, fr. 1593; (iv) C: BNF, fr. 12603; (v) D: BNF, fr. 19152; (vi) F: BNF, fr. 14971; (vii) G: BNF, fr. 1553. Our translation is based on the edition of S by Alan Hindley and Brian J. Levy (their E). The author names himself in the epilogue as Jehan Renart (v. 953), who is also known as the author of the *Roman de l'Escoufle* (which Jehan mentions in the *Lai de l'Ombre*, vv. 22–23) and the *Roman de la rose ou de Guillaume de Dole*. Other texts, such as *Galeran de Bretagne* and the *fabliau Auberee*, have also been attributed to him.

A philandering knight is assailed by the goddess of Love because he has hitherto shown her insufficient homage. She has decided to make him feel her power and strength and to inflict worse anguish upon him even than experienced by the famous lover Tristan. Love implants in the knight's heart the name and beauty of a certain lady and he has no option but to go and visit her. Much of the interest in the tale lies in the couple's verbal jousting. Despite his protestations of love and his skilful use of the language of seduction, the knight makes little progress until he sheds tears. Shortly afterwards, he slips his ring on to her finger and then distracts her attention, so that he can ride off before she notices it. When lady does notice it, she calls him back to explain himself and to make him take back the ring. For if she kept it he would be able to call himself her lover. Although these are important stages in his quest for her love, victory is only achieved when he sits beside the lady on the edge of a well. He agrees to take back the ring, but only if he can dispose of it as he wishes and give it to his second-best girl. Intrigued by this, she returns the ring to him and he drops it on to the lady's reflection in the well. Filled now with emotion and passion, the lady gives the knight her love. They kiss and embrace beside the well, but the one remaining sport has to be postponed.

Actions speak louder than words in this work, which is called a lay in v. 38 and v. 52. The author likes to personify abstract concepts and he tells us that Prowess and Courtliness had elected to their domain this knight who is endowed with all the virtues of a true knight. His generosity astonishes his friends and he is noble, gracious, of good character and not at all conceited. In many of the lays we have seen, these qualities, allied to his outstanding eloquence, would be enough to win the lady with comparative ease. But the *Lai de l'Ombre* is seemingly one of the slightly later lays in which passion and eloquence are not enough to guarantee success. Lovers now come up against obstacles from the real world.[1] Here a major stumbling block for the knight is the lady's ability to counter whatever he says with a clever rejoinder. The lady is said to be courtly and wise, and she is far from being the first lady in a lay or romance to be described in this way. But here these qualities have hardened into a coping mechanism and the knight's courtly conceits are not enough to break down her resistance. Something more subtle and more innovative is required, not in words but in deeds, and after he has recovered from his tears of frustration, the knight hits on a series of four actions, revolving around a concrete object in the form of a ring: (i) he puts the ring on her finger, (ii) distracts her, (iii) takes the ring back, and (iv) drops it in the well. Both pairs of acts are described as the product of his intelligence (*sen*, vv. 572, 876) and his understanding of what is required in a courtly situation (*cortoisie*, vv. 565, 909).

As the lady points out at the end, it is a combination of fine words and pleasing actions that bring their two hearts together. In showing that success can be achieved in love, by means other than what had become to be regarded as the norm (that is, a clever, and perhaps deceptive, use of words), is Jehan Renart mocking courtly conventions, or is he just showing that things have moved on and that rhetoric is one of the casualties of this process? He certainly seems to be raising for a courtly audience the question of what courtliness is. For example, the knight complains to

[1] The author tells us in v. 41 that the lay was composed for the 'Eslit' ('Elected One'). This is probably a reference to Miles Châtillon-Nanteuil, to whom Jehan dedicated his romance *Le Roman de la Rose ou de Guillaume de Dole* and who was bishop *electus* of Beauvais from 1217 until he became bishop in 1222. This would suggest that the *Lai de l'Ombre* was written between 1217 and 1222.

the lady that on his arrival, her eyes welcomed him in a courtly manner, such that he had the right to expect that his protestations of love would be accepted and she would become his lover ('ami'). Her retort is that this is just presumptuousness on his part and a foolish interpretation of her innocent intention to be nice to him and honour him, nothing more (vv. 402–37). So where does courtliness lie? In a pleasant smile or an ingenious and spontaneous gesture? One thing is certain, Jehan probes such issues without recourse to any supernatural or folklore elements. The lady is as perfect as a fairy, but she is not one, and there are no magic devices or premonitory dreams to move the narrative forward. For the female members of the audience, it is not so much the wish fulfilment element that they will detect in the heroine, but the intellectual control she manifests and the superiority over her suitor that she retains until her true feelings are released by what she describes as the finest act of courtliness since Adam ate the apple (vv. 916–20).

Further Reading

Clifford, Paula, *La Chastelaine de Vergi and Jean Renart: Le Lai de l'Ombre* (London: Grant and Cutler, 1986).

Cooper, Linda, 'The Literary Reflectiveness of Jean Renart's *Lai de l'Ombre*', *Romance Philology*, 35 (1981), 250–60.

Kay, Sarah, 'Two Readings of the *Lai de l'Ombre*', *Modern Language Review*, 75 (1980), 515–27.

Monson, Don, 'Lyrisme et narrativité dans le *Lai de l'Ombre*', *Cahiers de Civilisation Médiévale*, 36 (1993), 59–71.

Translation

I do not wish to abandon the task of speaking well. Instead, I wish to use my talent for something other than idleness, for I have no desire to resemble those who in their idleness merely destroy things. But since I have the talent to create something of value, in word and deed, anyone who mocks this is churlish, since my courtliness reveals itself in an account of some pleasant affair, in which there is nothing insulting or harmful. He is a fool who knows a good story and abandons it because of some adverse comments. And if some fool pokes his tongue out at me behind my back, I permit him to do so, for I do not think that these days one can turn a cad into a nobleman any more than I can make this finger longer than the next one. It is better to be born at an auspicious hour than to be one of the great, as has long been said. Through Guillaume, who dismembered the kite and burned each and every piece of it, as the story reminds us, one can prove that I am telling the truth, for it is better for a man to have good fortune than to have family and friends.[2] A friend may die and, if you do not look after them, you can soon be deprived of possessions. If anyone invests his wealth foolishly, be aware that he soon wastes and squanders it. Afterwards, his folly becomes apparent, for he has spent his money beyond measure. But if as a result he makes better use of his talent and abandons his foolish ways, and misfortune leaves him alone, good fortune will soon have restored his prestige. It is for this that I have undertaken this lay, because I wish to display my talent by composing a good story and to bow to the eminence of the Bishop Elect.[3] It is a matter of great pleasure for me that his good will has chosen me to perform this delightful task: to put a good story into verse. People say, 'He who rows well comes to shore.' The man who reaches the shore from the high seas is foolish to rail against the sea. Kings and counts think more of him for not doing so. Now hear this tale that I wish to relate, if no one prevents me, and I will recount here the *Lay of the Reflection*. (1–52)

It is said that there was a knight along the borders of the Empire from Lorraine to Germany. I do not believe that from Châlons to Le Perche there is a man who has at his disposal such good qualities as this one, many of which resembled those possessed by Lot's son, Gauvain, as we call him. But I never heard his name and do not know whether he had one. Prowess and Courtliness had elected him to their domain, and all his friends were amazed by how lavishly he spent. But despite all his prowess you would not have found him too talkative or too conceited. He was not a man of great wealth, but he did know how to conduct his affairs. He knew just how to take money from one place and put it where it was lacking. No maiden or lady ever heard tell of him without esteeming him greatly, and he never made a determined effort to win a woman without being well received for he was, above all, noble, gracious and of good character. When he was indoors, anyone could do with him whatever they wished, but in battle they would have found him an entirely

[2] This is a reference to something that occurs in the same author's *Roman de l'Escoufle* (*The Romance of the Kite*).

[3] See p. 228n1.

different proposition. Once he had a helmet on his head, he was fierce, daring and courageous, and he was skilled at looking up and down the ranks in search of a joust. The knight I am telling you about had reached such a point that he wanted each week to have two Mondays.[4] God never made any knight who was as brave in arms as he was. He was not the sort to wear his summer clothing in winter, and he gave away more costly furs than someone with ten times his wealth. Every day he liked to have seven companions with him, or at least five, and he would never have anything in his hands that someone else could not have if they wanted it. He loved falconry when he had the opportunity, which is not something I despise. He was skilled in chess, fencing and other pastimes, even more so than Tristan. He lived a happy life for a very long time and was loved by many. He was handsome, fair in body, noble, lithe and fleet of foot. More courageous than he was handsome, he was everything a knight should be. (53–111)

At this precise moment, Love, who is both a man's mistress and his master, let fly at him, because she wanted to have the upper hand over him and receive her tribute for the great pleasure he had enjoyed in his lifetime from many a lady. As long as he was able to avoid doing so, he had never paid service or homage to her,[5] and because he did not acknowledge that he was her vassal and her bailiff, Love wanted him, when the time and place were right, to experience her power and her strength. For never did Tristan, who on Iseut's behalf was shorn as a fool with scissors, have a third of the travails he had until he made his peace with her. She shot an arrow at the knight that penetrated his body right up to its feathers, implanting in his heart the great beauty and the sweet name of a lady. Now he had to reject all others in favour of this one. Until then, because he had never loved any of them, his heart had left many a woman. But now he saw and realised without any doubt that he had to bring all his energy to bear for the purpose of serving this one, who appeared to him to be the very pearl of all beauty. Her sense, her graciousness and the great beauty of her fine features were, I believe, before his eyes night and day. No joy he experienced failed to irk him, except for that of thinking of her. Love

[4] This may be a reference to the fact that tournaments commonly began on a Monday, but it could simply indicate the active knight's enthusiasm for the week ahead.

[5] As mentioned above (p. 4n4), the gender of Love, when personified, varies from text to text. Here Love is clearly feminine.

hatched such a plot against him that he became fully acquainted with her powers. For he had never seen such a charming creature in female form, he said, and he had recourse to his eyes to corroborate the truth of what he said. 'Ah!' he said. 'I have been so miserly with myself and begrudged my affections so much. Now, through this woman, God wants to avenge the women who have experienced unrequited love for me. Certainly', said the man who was overcome by Love, 'I rue the day I held them in such low esteem. Love has now brought me to the stage at which she would have me know how powerful she is. For never was a peasant whose teeth were being pulled out by a barber in such a state of pain!' (112–61)

Such were his thoughts and words when he was alone. But he would never have willingly done things differently, for never was a man in such a sorry plight as Love had placed him. 'Alas!' he said. 'If I love her, what will happen if she does not love me? I do not know, and cannot see how I can go on living for a single day! Neither the pleasure of being away, nor that of remaining at home, can serve to relieve my pain. All I can do now is cherish those who go and visit her, for through this means many men have had joy and comfort from their ladies. If only this lady had made a noose around my neck with her two arms! All night long I dream that I am embracing her and that she has her arms tightly around me. Waking up breaks me from her embrace, just as I am on the point of enjoying the greatest pleasure, then I search throughout my bed, feeling for her beautiful body, which inflames and excites me. But, alas, "if you can't find, you can't catch"! This has happened many a time to me and to many others. Now I don't have any choice. I must go there, or send someone there, to beseech her, since it cannot be otherwise, to have mercy on me at last and in God's name, before I die, to take pity on my distress, thus preserving in her great kindness my life and my wits. There would be one less of her servants if she allowed me to die, so it is absolutely right that pity should issue forth from her heart and tenderness from her eyes. I think it would be better for me to go myself rather than to send someone else. "There is no one like oneself," as the saying goes, and no one else would go so willingly. It has often been said in the past that necessity and great suffering are good teachers. Now that I have drawn upon this saying to help me there is nothing for it but to go there and tell her that in her prison she has my heart, which has placed itself there willingly. It will never seek to escape, whatever the anguish it may suffer, until it enjoys the name of "lover". Kindness, pity and largesse should motivate her to grant me this.' (162–211)

He got ready to depart, taking with him no more than two companions. I do not know what else to tell you. He mounted his horse, together with six young servants, and rode along, happy and thoughtful, occupied by his thoughts and the road ahead. So that they would not realise the true motive for his journey, he deflected his companions' attention both from the road ahead and from his own intentions. He told them he was riding at full speed, thus keeping his thoughts and his route from them, until they reached the lookout post of the castle where the lady lived. Then the lord who was leading them said: 'Just look how beautifully situated this castle is!' He did not say this so much for the particular interest of the ditches or walls, as to find out if his good fortune had brought him to a high enough point for them to speak of the qualities of the lady he was going to see. They replied: 'You ought to be truly ashamed of yourself, for you have behaved badly in mentioning the castle to us before the beautiful lady, about whom everyone says that there is none so courtly or so beautiful in the kingdom. Hold your tongue,' they said. 'For if she knew how you had wronged her, it would be better for you to be captured by the Turks and taken off to Cairo!' (212–43)

The knight said immediately with a smile: 'Now, lords, gently does it! Don't be too hard on me, for I do not deserve to die. There is not a single castle I covet but this one. I would willingly spend five or six years in Saladin's prison, provided this castle were assigned to me in its present state, so that I had full control over it and everything within its walls.' They replied: 'You would be a true lord then.' But they did not understand from his words the cunning nature of what he was saying to them. The good knight did not say this for any other reason than to hear what they would say. Then he asked them if they wanted to go and take a look. 'What else could we do?' they said. 'On his travels a knight should never pass by a beautiful woman without seeing her.' He replied: 'I defer to your judgment, so I wish and recommend that we make our way there, since reason supports this.' Then each man turned his horse's head towards the gate, shouting 'To arms, knights!' a fitting cry for such a mission. (244–71)

With their horses on a tight rein they rode on, until they reached the fortress where they crossed a new outer bailey that was enclosed by ditches and palisades. The lord had slung his mantle to the side, off his chest, and also his very fine surcoat of scarlet silk trimmed with ermine and squirrel fur. Each one of them wore similar garments with white pleated shirts, together with chaplets of periwinkles and other flowers, and spurs of bright red gold. I do not know how they could have been more pleasingly dressed for a summer's day. They did not come to a stop anywhere until they reached the mounting block in front of the hall. Squires came down to each man's stirrups, as was right and proper. The seneschal of the dwelling saw them dismount in the courtyard, and he left the gallery where he had been standing and went to give the lady the news that the man she knew well through hearsay had come to visit her. The lady's face did not turn red from anger; rather it was because she was greatly amazed. She had just been having her hair plaited, seated on a bright red cushion, and now this lady of very great beauty rose to her feet. Her maidens threw around her shoulders a mantle of costly silk, thus enhancing the great beauty that Nature had bestowed upon her, as the story records. (272–306)

Although she intended to go and meet them, they were making such haste to see her that they entered her chamber before she had had time to leave it. From the way she greeted them she seemed happy that they had come. They too were very happy at the way she had come even just a short distance to meet them. The worthy and courtly lady wore a white shift of fine texture, which trailed more than a fathom's length behind her on the finely chopped rushes. 'My lord, welcome, and your two companions as well', said the lady (may this day be good for her, because she fully deserves it). His companions had spoken the truth when they said that she was not a lady to pass by. As they returned her greeting, all three of them were overcome by her beauty. (307–25)

With a smile she took the lord by the hand and led him to a seat. Now that he was seated beside her, he had achieved part of his ambition! His companions were very well bred. Without disturbing him, they sat down with two of her maidens on a chest covered with bands of copper. While they were enjoying themselves with the maidens and asking all sorts of questions, their good lord scarcely gave them a thought, being instead intent on his own affair. Because she was very wise and courtly, the noble, gracious lady was able to produce an intelligent rejoinder to whatever he said to her. He kept his eyes on her face constantly in order to gaze at her beauty. His heart, which had placed itself within her completely, rightly took his eyes as witnesses to the truth, for they bore good testimony to whatever his heart had promised him, and they had not deceived him in any respect. Her face and her expression gave him great pleasure. 'Fair, dear and very sweet friend', he said, 'for whom the strong feelings in my heart cause me to abandon all others and banish them from my thoughts, I have come to make you a gift of whatever strength and power I possess.

May I have joy from this, for there is nothing I love as much as you, if God forgives me and lets me accede in repentance to his mercy. This is the reason why I have come here, for I want to know this, so that kindness and pity can take hold of you, as there is a need for them to do so. Anyone who prays in church would do well to do so for those whose sole aim is to be a faithful lover.' (326–67)

'Ah, my lord, upon my soul', she said, 'what have you just said? I am astonished! Why do you speak in this way?' 'My lady', he said, 'I am telling the truth. You alone have power over me, more than any lady alive.' Her colour rose and quickened when he told her he was entirely hers. Then she said to him with great subtlety: 'Certainly, my lord, I cannot believe that such a handsome man as you could be without a mistress; no one would credit it. Your reputation would suffer from this and you would be thought less worthy – you being such a handsome man in body, hands, arms and everything else! You would easily be able to pull the wool over my eyes and make me think, in truth, of doing something that should not be done.' (368–87)

Her words stopped him in his tracks and upset his calculations, as he who taught me the story has given me to understand. He let himself be held on a tight rein, for there was nothing that would be more pleasing to him. If anyone else had scorned his love, he would have known just how to go about getting his own back, but he was so much in her power that he did not dare contradict her. So he began to address her again: 'Ah, my lady, have mercy, for pity's sake! My love for you has, without dissembling, made me disclose the suffering I am going through. Your words accord and correspond very poorly with your beautiful eyes, which just now greeted me better when I arrived, and more agreeably. You should realise that what they did was certainly an act of courtliness. For, since the time they were first able to see, your eyes have never seen any man who, this is the whole truth, would have been as willing as I am to become your vassal, without a word of a lie. My sweet lady, in your kindness, please put this to the test. Retain me as your knight and, when it pleases you, as your lover! For within a year and a half you will have made me such a worthy man, both in battle and inside the castle, and instilled so much good in me, that the name of "lover", God willing, could not be denied me.' (388–421)

'The presumption you are showing', she said, 'is doing you a great deal of good! All I intended by the way I looked was to act in a courtly and sensible manner. But foolishly you have given it a different interpretation, and this grieves me. If I were not so courtly, I would be very upset indeed by this. But it very often happens that, when a worthy lady behaves with courtliness and honour towards a knight, suitors then believe that they have achieved quite different aims! Through you I have proved this to be true; that is exactly the way you have understood it. You would have been better employed setting up a net outside for catching pigeons because, if the year and a half were as long as three whole years, you would not succeed, through any means you might employ, in making me as kind towards you as I was just now. A man should beware of counting his chickens before they are hatched!' (422–47)

Now the knight had no idea what he could do, whether it be in word or in deed, or what would become of him. 'My lady', he said, 'at least I cannot be worse off than I was before because of this. Pity and kindness are to be found in you, of that I have no doubt. No man who truly loved has ever failed to win his beloved in the end. I have set sail without a mast, in order to drown just like Tristan. Although I have been in full control of my own will for a long time, I have now reached the state where, if no mercy is shown me this night, I never expect to see another night, even if I get through this one. My heart has conspired against me by lodging itself in you without my permission to do so.' Chiding him a little, she said: 'I have never heard such a thing! We can leave things at that, because I can see that you are not joking. I still believed, by St Nicholas, that you were jesting.' 'Certainly, my lady, even if you were a poor abandoned serving girl, my beautiful, sweet honoured lady, I would never do such a thing.' (448–75)

Whatever he said or promised, nothing helped him win her favour, and he did not know what to do. His face turned bright red and tears rushed from his heart into his eyes, so that streaks of white and red moistened his cheeks. It now became apparent to the lady that her heart had not been playing tricks on her, and that, quite the contrary, as she now fully realised, he had often been in her thoughts, and not only at the present moment.[6] If she had joined him in his tears, this would have been very beneficial to her. She would never have imagined for a moment that he could be so distressed. 'My lord', she said, 'it would not be right for me to love you or any other man, for I have my very worthy lord,

[6] It is possible that what we have translated as 'her heart had not been playing tricks on her,' could be 'his heart had not been playing tricks on him.' The author used pronouns in a subtle and perhaps deliberately ambiguous way. See Sarah Kay, 'Two Readings of the *Lai de l'Ombre*', *Modern Language Review*, 75 (1980), 515–27.

who serves me and honours me very well.' 'Ah, my lady', he replied, 'how lucky he is! To do so must fill him with joy. But if Kindness and Pity were to take hold of you with respect to me, and Nobility too, never would anyone who sings or reads of Love think any the worse of you for it. On the contrary, you would be doing the world an honour if you were willing to love me. You could liken such a good deed to a pilgrimage to the Holy Land.' (476–505)

'Let me now leave your presence, my lord,' she said. 'All this is quite shameful! My heart does not permit or allow me to agree to it in any way. For this reason, it is a vain entreaty and I beg you to desist from it.' 'Ah, my lady', he said, 'you are the death of me. Mind you do not continue with this on any account, but do what is courtly and right. Retain me as your servant by means of a jewel, a belt or a ring, or take one of mine for yourself. I assure you that there is no service a knight could render a lady that I would not perform for you, even if it cost me my soul, so help me God. It would not take much for your sweet face and your beautiful features to retain me in your service. I am completely under your authority, with whatever strength and power I possess.' 'My lord', said the lady, 'I do not want you to have the praise without the profit. It has been common knowledge for a long time, and I am fully aware of it, that people think very highly of you. If I were to set you on the path to my love without my heart being in it, I would then be deceived,[7] and that would be an outrage. To be above reproach, if one can, is an act of true courtliness.' 'In order to save my life, you should be speaking quite differently,' he said. 'If you were to let me die unloved, that would be a blemish on you, and also if that beautiful face of yours, so full of candour, became my executioner; some swift solution should be found. Lady of beauty and mistress of all that is good, in God's name, see to this!' (505–46)

These fair, pleasing and elegant words caused her to lapse into deep thought and made her want to listen to his entreaties. She took pity on him and did not think his sighs were feigned, or the tears he had shed. Rather did she say to herself that he was being assailed by the force of Love, which was making him do all this, and that, if she rejected this one, she would never have such a noble lover. But the fact that before today he had never spoken of it came as a great surprise to her. On the other hand, along with these thoughts she had Reason nagging at her,

[7] It is not clear here whether the text is saying that the lady would be deceived ('deceüe') by the knight or that she would be misleading or deceiving him.

which was against her contemplating anything she would regret in the long run. To the man who was hanging on the outcome of the thoughts on which she had embarked, Love, who in many affairs of this kind has revealed how subtle and ingenious she is, came up with a very fine way of performing an act of great courtliness. While the noble lady was plunged in deep thought, he swiftly removed his ring from his finger and slipped it on to hers. Then he went on to perform an even more subtle act, breaking her train of thought so that she had no time to notice the ring on her finger. To make sure she did not observe it, he said: 'My lady, grant me leave! Rest assured that my power and my person lie entirely within your command.' (547–79)

He hurried away, followed by his two companions. No one but him knew the reason why he departed in this way. Sighing and deep in thought, he came to his horse and mounted. The woman on whom his restoration to happiness now depended said: 'Could he really be leaving? What is this? No true knight ever did such a thing! I would have thought that a whole year would have proved a good deal shorter than a day to him, providing he was still with me. And now he has left me so soon! Ah! What if I had given in to him in word or deed? The performance he has just put on for me is enough to make one suspect everyone one meets. If anyone had been convinced by his tears and his deceptive sighs, may the Holy Spirit preserve me, he would not have been the loser, and that is the least one can say.' (580–603)

Then she glanced down at her hands and caught sight of the ring. All her blood, right down to her little toe, drained away. Never had she been so startled or astonished by anything. Her face, which had been flushed, turned quite pale as a result. 'What is this?' she said. 'May God help me! I can see here the ring that belonged to him! I have my wits about me sufficiently to have seen it on his finger just now. Indeed I did, just a short while ago. Why did he place it on mine? He is certainly not my lover, and yet I believe he thinks he is. Now, in God's name, he is a past master of this art. I do not know who taught him. God, how did he bring about a situation where I, who am so observant, did not notice him slipping the ring on to my finger? Now he will claim that he is my lover. Indeed he will, I am sure of it. Will he be telling the truth? Am I his lover? No! It is no good him saying so. Rather I will call him back at once to come and talk with me, if he wants me to regard him as my lover. I will tell him to take the ring back. I do not think he will do anything offensive, if he does not want me to hate him. (604–35)

Then she ordered a mounted servant to be sent to her. Her maidens made him hurry so much that when he arrived he was already on horseback. 'My friend', she said, 'be on your way quickly! Spur after that knight and tell him, as he holds my love dear, not to proceed any further, but to come back immediately to speak with me about a matter that concerns him.' 'My lady', he said, 'I am confident I can carry out your bidding to perfection.' Then at full gallop he charged off after the knight, who was being tormented by Love with thoughts of the very woman who was sending for him. Within less than a league, he caught up with the knight and turned him back. Rest assured that he thought himself very fortunate to have been summoned to return, and he did not enquire of the messenger as to why he had been called back. The ring she had on her finger was the reason for this summons. The fact that she was anxious to see him was sufficient reason for him to change direction. On the way back, the squire became friendly with him. O God, how happy he would now have been to return, if it had not been for his grave concern that she wanted to give him back the ring. He said he would rather become a monk at Cîteaux than take it back. 'I cannot believe', he said, 'that she would offend me in this way.' The joy of returning hid the thoughts that were preying on his mind. (635–73)

He made his way back to the castle with his companions. The lady, who was in great distress and struggling with her feelings, came down from the hall, descending the steps one by one. Deliberately and of her own accord, she entered the courtyard to pass away the time with him. Shining on her finger, she caught sight of the ring she intended to give back to the knight. 'If he causes me any difficulty', she said, 'and refuses to take it back, I am not going to respond by grabbing him by his lovely head of hair. If I can manage to do so, I will bring him to the edge of this well and speak to him there. If he refuses to take it without causing a fuss, I will cut short the conversation very quickly. How? I will not be stupid enough to throw it down on to the path. Where then? In a place where no one will see it; that will be in the well, and that is no lie! Any gossip that might reflect badly on me will be nothing other than fantasy. Have I not lived with my husband for a long time without committing any wrong? If this man, through his chivalry and the sighs he has heaved before me, wants me to regard him as my lover at this first meeting, he would, if I were to agree to it, need to have deserved it far more rigorously than this.' (674–705)

At that moment the knight, unaware of all this, entered the inner ward of the castle. He saw walking across the courtyard the woman on whom he loved to gaze, and he quickly dismounted and ran over to her, just as a knight does towards his lady. Neither his two companions nor any occupant of the castle bothered him. He said: 'May good fortune shine today on my lady, whose servant I am and will always be'. This was the only earbashing she got from him. That day she had already heard many things that had affected her greatly. 'My lord', she said, 'let us go over there and sit by that well for our enjoyment.' Now, he said to himself, there was nothing that could harm his chances, since she had welcomed him so nicely. He now felt sure that through his ring he would have her love and her favour. But he was not yet far enough along the road for rejoicing. Before he could sit down next to her, he heard something that displeased him. 'My lord', she said, 'if you please, tell me, for pity's sake, this ring of yours that I hold here, why did you give it to me just now?' 'My sweet lady', he said, 'when I leave here, you will still have it. And I can tell you, believe me and do not think I am joking, that it is now worth half as much again for having been on your finger. If it pleased you, this summer my opponents would get to know my true worth if you accepted me as your lover and I accepted you as mine.' 'In God's name, there is no chance of that,' she said. 'Quite the contrary: I will never leave this castle again, so help me God, unless as a corpse, if you ever draw any fame or prestige from my love, and that is the way I see it. You are not on the right track, rather you have gone completely astray. Look here! I want you to have your ring, because I do not want anything to do with it.' (706–55)

Now the knight, who thought he had won the day, was filled with despair and misery. He said: 'My reputation would decline if this were all true. I have never known such joy that turned so soon to anguish for me.' 'How is that, my lord?' she said. 'Have I ever caused you any suffering or shame, I who have no ties to you through love or kinship? I am not doing you any great outrage in wanting to give you back the ring. In truth, taking it back is your only option, for I have no right to keep it, since I do not want to retain you as my lover. I would be wrong to do so.' 'God!' he said, 'if I were to plunge a knife into my thigh, it would not give me any more pain than I get from these words. Anyone who destroys and confounds what he has in his power is acting badly. The power of my love for you assails me so much and causes me such suffering. No woman on earth would fail to rue the day she insisted that I take back this ring. In truth, may God never grant me a happy end in heaven if I take it back. Instead, you will have it, and along with it I will leave my heart in your service, since there is nothing at your disposal that will serve you as perfectly as my heart and my ring together.' 'Do not speak to me about this again,' she replied. 'For then you would forfeit my friendship and my trust if you tried to force me to be consumed by passion for you against my will. It is your duty to take it back.' (756–94)

'No it is not.' 'Yes, it is. There is nothing more to be said. You are behaving in a very overbearing fashion, pestering me to the point where you are trying to force me to hold on to the ring against my will. Take it! I no longer have any wish to keep it.' 'Yes, you will.' 'No, I will not, in truth. Do you intend to force it on me?' 'No, my beloved, in truth. I am well aware that I do not have that power and it upsets me, so help me God. It is my belief that I would have no more disgrace or grief in my life if you bestowed a ray of hope on me, to give me comfort.' 'You might just as well dash your head against this mounting block as expect to succeed in this, and I advise you to take the ring back.' 'I have the impression that you are teaching me to go on repeating Renart the Fox tales.[8] I would rather have a hangman's noose strung around my neck than take it back. I do not know what more I can say, for there is just no question of my taking it back.' 'My lord', she said, 'I can clearly see now that this obstinacy of yours is the cause of all this, since nothing I say to you can get you to take the ring back. I now wish to beseech and beg you, by the great faith that you owe me, to take it back, insofar as you value your love for me.' (795–827)

Now there was, by the love of God, only one solution: either he had to take the ring back from her or he would consider himself disloyal or deceitful. 'God', he said to himself, 'which of these dilemmas is now the less damaging to me? I am well aware that, if I do not take it, she will say that I don't love her. Anyone who grasps a crust so hard that the crumb springs out of it has grasped too hard! What she has imposed on me has affected me so severely that it would not be to my advantage to leave it with her. In fact, I think my advantage and my honour lie in taking it back, unless I want to commit a very grave misdeed towards my

[8] The meaning of the knight's comment here is not clear. The text in the version of the story we are translating states literally: 'It seems to me that you are teaching me to sing of Renart,' that is, to recite tales of the famous medieval fox. However, other manuscripts of the lay have the name Bernart, rather than Renart, and this perhaps makes better sense (Bernart in the Renart stories is a tedious and sententious ass). The meaning in our manuscript may be 'to repeat something excessively'. But the situation is complicated by the existence of the expression 'to speak of another Bernart', which seems to have the meaning 'to change one's tune'. It is also possible that there is a pun here on the writer's own name, Jehan Renart.

noble, honoured lady, who has beseeched this of me in the name of my love for her and the great faith I owe her. Once it is back on my finger, it will remain hers, wherever it is. If I do her bidding, I can only gain honour from this. A man who fails to do his utmost in accordance with his beloved's wishes is not a true lover. Know this, he who neglects to do whatever he can does not love properly. I must make my actions conform to her wishes, for it cannot remain otherwise than according to what she desires.' (828–57)

He did not refer specifically to the ring as his or hers when he said to her:[9] 'My lady, I will take it with one proviso: that once your wishes have been accomplished I will do whatever I want with it, even though it has been on this finger of yours, which in my eyes is so beautiful.' 'I give you back the ring then with the understanding that you do just that.' Now this valiant knight's wits were not past their best or enfeebled. Wholeheartedly, and all aflame with love, he took the ring with deliberation and gazed at it tenderly. As he took it back, he said: 'A thousand thanks! For the gold has not become tarnished, as it has been on your beautiful finger.' She smiled at this, thinking that he was going to slip it back on to his own finger. But then he did something even more astute, and from it very great joy accrued to him. He leant over the well, which was only a fathom and a half deep, and did not fail to notice in the water, which was fine and clear, the reflection of the lady, who was the thing in the whole world he loved most. 'Know this once and for all', he said. 'I will not take it back with me. Instead, my sweet friend will have it, the one I love most after you.' 'Goodness', she said, 'there are only two of us here. Where did you find her so soon?' 'In God's name, the worthy and noble woman who is going to have it will soon be visible to you.' 'So where is she?' 'In God's name, there she is, your beautiful reflection that is waiting for it there!' He took the ring and held it out to her. 'Here you are, my friend', he said. 'Since my lady does not want it, you will take it without further ado.' The water rippled slightly when the ring fell into it, and as the reflection broke up he said: 'There you are, my lady, now she has taken it. My reputation has

[9] The meaning of the first part of this sentence is not clear. At first sight it appears to be saying that in his remark to her the knight does not use her name. But this would be odd as the lady's name is not given at any point in the text. It is also possible, as we have interpreted it, that he does not indicate in his reply whether the ring belongs to him or to her. But this is also a curious statement and there may be an error in the text.

been greatly enhanced now that this woman, who is your counterpart, has taken it away. If only there were a door or a gate down there! Then she could come up here and enable me to tell her how grateful I am for the honour she has done me.' (858–907)

O God! How lucky it was that he managed to perform such a courtly act! For nothing he had yet done had been so pleasing to the lady. Full of ardour and inflamed with passion, she gazed lovingly at him. Many things come to a man of great sense who performs a courtly act when there is a need for it. 'Just now this man was so far from my love and now he is so close! Never before or after, since Adam ate the apple, did anyone hit on such a fine act of courtliness! I have no idea where the idea came from when, for love of me, he threw his ring on to my reflection in the well. Now I should no longer, and cannot, deny him the gift of my love. I do not know why I am holding back, for no one has ever won love with a ring in such a fine and excellent way, or so richly deserved to have a beloved.' (908–29)

You may be sure that she did not wound him when she said: 'Fair, sweet beloved, these tender words and these pleasant deeds have placed your entire heart in mine, as has the gift you have made to my reflection in my honour. Now put my ring on your finger. Take it! I bestow it on you as your beloved, and I trust you will not regard it less highly than your own, even if it is inferior.' 'Lordship over the Empire would not have made me so happy!' he said. As far as they were able, they enjoyed themselves greatly on the edge of the well. The sweetness of the kisses with which they gratified themselves reached right to their hearts, and their fine eyes did not prevent them from speaking; quite the contrary. They had perfect freedom to indulge in the game that one plays with one's hands, yet avoiding the one that could not be, but will suit them very well! (930–51)

There is no need for Jehan Renart to devote any further thought to their affair. If there is nothing more to do, he can turn his attention elsewhere. For now that their wits and their love have brought their hearts together, they will both, I believe, manage to enjoy the one remaining sport. So, from now on, let nothing more be said about this. Here ends the *Lay of the Reflection*. Count, you who know your numbers![10] (952–62)

[10] There seems to be a pun here on two senses of the Old French verb *conter* 'count, reckon' and 'relate, recount' (from the Latin *computare*).

22. *Amours*

Introduction

Amours is preserved in only one manuscript: S. The last line of the lay contains the name Girart ('Girarz dira des lais avant'), but it is not entirely clear whether this is a reference to the author of the lay or to the clerk who is instrumental in recording the love affair recounted in the narrative. The author and the clerk could also be one and the same person.

An unnamed nobleman ('haut home', v. 10, etc.) visits a foreign country on business and meets there a lady of equal nobility. They fall in love at first sight. With little opportunity to be together they suffer the torments of love, to which they give vent in the form of monologues. The nobleman considers it unseemly to speak to the lady of his love, but, for her part, she tells him clearly of her feelings for him. Overjoyed, he declares his love for her, but no sooner have they got together than the nobleman is summoned to return home on urgent business. They pledge their hearts and love to each other, and after departing he devotes a lengthy monologue to the bond that unites them. The lady has told him that their two hearts are one and in learned fashion he examines the logic of this, explaining it as the equivalent of two streams that run together in such a way that they are inseparable. He decides to send the lady a love letter (*salut*) expressing his love, suffering and thoughts about their two hearts. His clerk is summoned to write the letter and a messenger takes it to the lady. When the messenger returns, we are provided with a detailed account of her reply, which leads to two more lengthy monologues by the nobleman, in the second of which he laments his delay in going to see her. So he sends her a further letter stating his intention to visit her. The lay ends with the nobleman waiting for a reply and Girart waiting to continue his tale when it arrives.

There is very little action in this lay. Beginning with the common 'boy meets girl' theme, the tale revolves principally around a series of conversations, personal thoughts and letters. Particularly notable are the forthrightness of the lady and the comparative timidity of the nobleman. It is she who makes the first move, telling him openly about her feelings for him; only then does he declare his love for her. When she replies to his first love letter, she begs him to come to her and provides a sensual description of the night they could spend together: they could hold each other all night long, flesh against flesh, so that she could feel his body and experience his pure, wholesome breath. Other lays in this collection contain examples of the power that female characters can exert over men, but this desire for the male body seems to go one step further and to fly in the face of conventional attitudes.

But this lay also contains some very traditional conceits. Especially prominent is the nobleman's comparison of their love to two streams from two regions that come together. One is sweet and clear, the other black and unpleasant, but when the water merges the two streams run together with only one colour, one name and one flavour (vv. 231–40). Then he worries about how two streams can unite if the lovers are apart, so he modifies the image to that of two vessels filled with water from confluent streams that are fed from the same source. Unsurprisingly, in the course of his thoughts the two streams become associated not just with the abstract concept of love, but with a specific part of the lovers' bodies, the heart. In the Middle Ages the heart was an extraordinarily versatile organ, being the seat of the emotions, consciousness and the intellect. When his heart came to hers, the nobleman says to himself, the two hearts were united and they ran together like the two streams. 'Never did our hearts break apart, or think of anything other than love, and they have only one thought and one name and they are one and the same thing' (vv. 246–49).[1] Other traditional love motifs in *Amours* are the eyes as the agents of love, the fire of love that ignites hearts and bodies, the dart of love that wounds and torments the lovers, the acts of trembling, shuddering and writhing through love.

[1] In the two lays that precede *Amours* in the present volume, the *Lai de l'Ombre* and the *Châtelaine de Vergy*, the heart is also of particular importance. See Glyn S. Burgess, 'The Role of the Heart in the *Lai de l'Ombre* and the *Chastelaine de Vergi*', in *Conjunctures: Medieval Studies in Honor of Douglas Kelly*, ed. Keith Busby and Norris J. Lacy (Amsterdam and Atlanta, GA: Rodopi, 1994), pp. 31–47. On the theme of the heart in *Amours*, see Elizabeth W. Poe, in Glyn S. Burgess and Leslie C. Brook, eds and trans., *The Old French Lays of Ignaure, Oiselet and Amours* (Cambridge: D. S. Brewer, 2010), pp. 214–16 ('*Amours* begins with the heart, ends with the heart and has the heart as its central theme', p. 216).

Structurally, the tale is divided into two parts: (i) the meeting between the lovers, their first thoughts about each other, the nobleman's need to return home, his thoughts once he has left her and the decision to get his clerk to write down his *salut* (vv. 1–292); (ii) the lady's reply, the nobleman's reaction and his decision to send his messenger to her again with another *salut* (vv. 293–518). As in the other lays in this section there are no supernatural figures here, and despite their traditional views on the nature of love both lovers have their feet firmly planted in reality. There seems to be no restrictive force that would prevent them in the longer term from enjoying a permanent relationship. Both lovers operate within a somewhat vague world, but their intelligence and independence would no doubt have impressed new urban audiences as well as old courtly ones.

Further Reading

Beston, John, 'The Role of the Secretary Girart in the Old French Lay of *Amours*', *Le Cygne*, third series, 2 (2015), 7–15.

Poe, Elizabeth W., '*Lai d'Amours* as *lai*', in '*Li Premerains vers*': *Essays in Honor of Keith Busby*, ed. Catherine M. Jones and Logan E. Whalen (Amsterdam and New York: Rodopi, 2011), pp. 357–68. See also the edition of *Amours* by Burgess and Brook, to which Poe contributed pp. 202–23 of the introduction.

Translation

Anyone wishing to portray the truth about love has to retrieve from his heart many an adventure and many a fine saying. But if there were ever fine talk of love, I ought to relate a fine tale about it, for I have fine material or this purpose, such as no one else has ever had.[2] What is its name? Shall I give it a name? No, I shall not. Why not? Because I do not wish to do so, that is all there is to it. (1–9)

[2] Our use of 'fine' (Old French *biau, bele*) four times in the first few lines of the translation reveals a liking on the poet's part for repetition. In the next few lines the concept of nobility is conveyed repeatedly, mainly by the terms 'haut(e)', 'hautement' and 'hautece'. A further example is the use of the motif of sweetness, which is conveyed by the terms 'douz/douce', 'doucement' or 'douçor' fourteen times in the passage vv. 318–77. Even more prominent in this lay is the recurrence of references to the heart, the first example of which occurs in v. 2 and the last in v. 505.

However, I want to relate to you a nobleman's adventure as it happened, and I want to tell you about him, his beauty, his manners and his military skills. Noble in honour, noble in riches, noble in lineage, noble in friends, God invested so much talent in him that no one alive could relate a tenth of it. About that there is no argument. In short, he is truly the noblest of men. But if I were to name him here and now, people would say that I was not telling the whole truth; rather I would be blamed for saying too little. For this nobleman the need arose, and many a nobleman experiences the same thing, to go travelling. He made himself ready and departed from his own land, as nobly as it was his duty to do so. This man travelled around on business, and the truth is that it came about that in the country to which he came there lived a very fine and noble lady. As far as Constantinople, there was no nobler lady than she. If the man to whom I am referring is noble above all gentility, she in her gentility is nobility surpassed, so that it seems to me that honour and gentility together, and also beauty, courtliness and knowledge – in other words, all the finest qualities a lady should have – resided in this lady, if words were not inadequate to describe her. So beautiful and so distinguished was she that there has taken up residence in her beautiful body, along with beauty of every kind, the most exceptional distinction. (10–46)

The nobleman stayed most contentedly in that region for many a day, until it happened very suddenly that in the region to which he had come an assembly was arranged and the noble lady came there as well, in such a noble fashion and just as would a woman in whom every virtue belongs and who has travelled very nobly. The nobleman, who had heard mention of the noble lady, needed no second bidding to attend. As soon as they saw each other, they focused their hearts and their bodies, along with their eyes, on gazing. Thus they stared at each other. And in the looks they bestowed on each other Love struck and seized hold of them, and the fire of love was kindled that burns and ignites hearts and bodies. Love, which has captured many people, pursued them, struck them and harried them. Each looked at, and became bound to, the other in this sweet blow. Then they approached one another to offer greetings but as these greeting were being, given people arrived from all sides, which gave them the opportunity only to complete them hastily, with a 'welcome' in return for 'God protect you.' Let me assure you that, if they had been able to find a spot where they had enough leisure to speak with each other, they would have greeted each other tenderly. So they loved each other passionately. One minute they separated, then came back together many a time in order to obtain solace, and they concealed the situation so completely that the lady, I do not doubt, had joy from her beloved and he from his. (47–84)

In this way Love had launched his attack and driven love into their hearts with the dart that killed and tormented them. She lamented and he grieved, she sighed and he trembled, saying: 'O God! What is assaulting me? What is the matter? I do not know. Yes I do, without doubt. I know well that Love is waging this battle against me. O God! What? Am I in love then? Yes, more than has ever happened before. With whom? With my lady, and there she is. My heart went to her just now, so she has it and, know truly, it is hers and she can have it forever. I shall never say anything to her. Shall I? How? I should be acting in very foolhardy fashion if I uttered such a lofty speech.' In this way he reproached himself and rebuffed her before she could rebuff him. (85–103)

For her part the lady, who was hurt by the blow, did not know what to say. Now she reproached herself, now she calmed down; now she felt reassured, now she was dismayed again; now she lamented once more, now she relaxed, more than a hundred times in a minute. Thus in this torment Love tormented her and asserted his right, until she said that straightaway she would go and speak to him. Then she repented. When she had gathered her thoughts together, she thought and said: 'O God! What would I say? It would be acting contrary to any other woman. I will not speak to him. I must remain silent. But this ill cannot leave me if he does not know of it, so let him know of it.' Love urged her to speak out, wishing to drag the words from her mouth. Whether to speak to him or to remain silent, that was the conflict within her, and Love pushed her so fast that she could not withstand him. So she went to speak with the nobleman, saying: 'My lord, be fully aware, without any doubt, that I should like to have your love and your friendship in this land, if it pleases you, and be truly aware that I am yours, do not doubt it.' He thanked her for this, just like a man who did not dare conceive, believe, think or expect that she would express any desire for his love. (104–35)

He thanked her tenderly for her words and replied: 'My lady, I grant you my love and my friendship without hesitation, for I would do for you whatever is in my power.' She replied immediately: 'What I am thinking, are you not thinking the same? Rather this is the state of things and I am telling you plainly that I love you passionately.' 'Passionately?' he said. 'Yes, indeed', she replied, and his heart was uplifted by this new joy. He rejoiced, then replied: 'My lady, I have never heard news that I liked so much. If I had dared, I would very willingly have said the same before you did so. I give myself to you, at your command, entirely and without reservation. In return I ask God that in time he should grant me such a noble gift as to return the favour, for that is the thing I most desire.' They had no further leisure to speak, but took leave of each other and then departed. However, as they left and separated, their eyes became more and more like crossbowmen. Their hearts urged them on, their desire made them stare, as Love provided an outpost for their vision and made them raise their heads, direct their eyes, utter sighs and shoot glances through which they struck and wounded each other. But in the end they were fully at peace, so much so that they considered themselves well rewarded. (136–69)

News came to the nobleman from afar to return home. His men needed to summon him on such an important matter that he could not refuse to go without doing wrong. He came to the lady in order to take his leave and he explained the whole situation to her, and she who could do nothing more about it could not have felt greater sorrow. The lady, who knew full well that he could not avoid making the journey, as this would turn to shame for him, and she did not want that to happen, spoke to her friend as a friend: 'Fair friend, you will be leaving and taking away my heart with you. It will go with you and yours will remain with me. Not that I have any fears in this respect, because both your heart and mine are as one, as they should be. Nothing could ever happen to separate my heart from yours. Wherever you go, you have my heart, never doubt it.' He replied: 'My love is completely yours, and my heart, my joy and my power. Know full well that I am yours, wherever I may be.' Thus each granted the other loyal love to be preserved. (170–201)

Not being able to detain him any longer, she gave him leave and he departed. He was very upset when he left his beloved, but he had to leave her. Then, when he thought of her, he said: 'O God! Help me now! What should I say? The one I loved most in the world is getting further away from me. Nothing in this can please me and I do not know what I should do. I am deprived of joy, for she has my joy. Lady at whom my heart rejoices, lady who is the most beautiful in the world, lady pure and without wickedness, lady with the finest manners, sweet beloved, who gave me your love without my asking for it, I cannot go against your words or forget in any way when you said that my heart and yours were one heart. Why was that said? How could such words come about through any authority, that two hearts could be one? And even if no one knows precisely how to do this, she did not say it for no reason; rather she thought it out carefully. If I had been able, I would very willingly have taken hers with me, but I do not think I could have done so. Could I? No, not for anything. Yet I think that I could do it. How could I? It seems to me that two streams from two regions could come together well, one sweet and clear, the other black and unpleasant. But when it happens that the water merges, that the two streams run together, they both have only one colour, only one name and only one flavour. Thus, when my heart came to hers, it could happen that our two hearts ran together, becoming united as they did so, just like the two streams that joined forces. Never did our hearts break apart, or think of anything other than love, and they have only one thought and one name and they are one and the same thing. (202–49)

'I think I have explained the meaning of this. Explained it? Yes, I have. No I have not, in faith! Now let the reason why be made known. Am I not here and she there, and do I have some of the heart and she some of it? How can a single heart be such that it can suffice for two? How? I will soon discover how. Have I not proved with the two streams, and explained the names of each, just how the two become one? Now let it be imagined that two vessels come to this stream to be filled. Now they are filled, now they are removed. In just this way our bodies drew on the heart, which is common to the body, and because of this the heart is only one. Indeed, I have proved it, I believe. I am referring to my lady and myself. No one can add any more to this in any way. We are two bodies with one heart.' (250–70)

Thus he lamented and said: 'My lady, to whom I belong without any doubt, I would not look for any other love, my sweet lady, and I would not refrain for any reason from sending you greetings. For in a *salut* [love letter] I must relate without any delay and make known the misery I have to suffer from the fine words you addressed to me.[3] You caused my heart such strife, my lady, as I wish to let you know.' The nobleman summoned his clerk to write down the *salut*, and he put his whole heart into describing the looks, the laments, the words, point by point, just as I have related them, and with the *salut* he set them all down in the book. The nobleman, who fully unburdened himself, sent it to her through his messenger. (271–89)

[3] On the tradition of the *salut*, a subgenre that functions as a love letter, and its use within *Amours*, see Poe, in Burgess and Brook, *The Old French Lays of Ignaure, Oiselet and Amours*, pp. 203, 206–08.

I will not continue this tale, whatever may happen, until the messenger returns. I have refrained from speaking until the return of the messenger, bringing me the material I need to relate further words. What does the messenger say? Now let him be heard. The lady sends greetings to her beloved and presents him with a written text that explains her wishes fully, saying: 'My friend, I can easily say this, that my heart cannot refuse to accept that you are my beloved. So much has my heart become united with yours that I am completely and utterly yours. You are completely mine, and I know without doubt that it would be impossible for me, without you, to experience any joy or laughter, however hard I tried. If you are in good health, then so am I. If you have no troubles, then I have none. If I have any grief, or hurt or pleasure, I wish to share it with you completely, without removing or taking any of it away.' (290–312)

Then she thanked him for the *salut* and said that it had filled her heart with great joy. She was greatly comforted by the sweet *salut*, which delivered her a blow that had struck her in the heart. But so sweetly had the sweet blow, by which she was wounded, tormented her that she thought herself well rewarded. Then she told him that she was very pleased with the proof that he had put forward as to how the two hearts become just one. She said that they came together very well, and this pleased her greatly and seemed good to her. She very much wanted the two hearts together to drink the sweet and wholesome love, of which the heart is the body's fountain. The lady, as a loyal friend, begs her friend, as a friend, to remember his friend and bring it about that she might see him, or otherwise the desire from such a long absence would kill her; this she tells him in truth. Then she said: 'I should like nothing better, fair friend, than to be in your arms, to experience joy and solace. For one whole night I would hold you, flesh against flesh, so that I could feel your body, and your sweet breath, sweet, pure and wholesome, which I desire to feel so much, and may God be willing to consent that in my arms, as my heart drives me to do, for comfort I could embrace your body, the most beautiful in the world. My lord, in order to bring about such joy, come and visit without delay the person who in sweet hope is awaiting your sweet arrival.' (313–53)

Hearing the sweet regrets and laments with which his sweet friend grieved, he sighed, trembled, shuddered and writhed, saying: 'In truth I am wrong, sweet, charming and lovely friend,' Then, sighing, he called upon her: 'O sweet friend, sweet sister, sweet of body, sweet of heart, sweet in all good manners, spice of all sweetness, fountain of all goodness, mirror of all beauties, noble above all nobility, rose of love, heaven of highness! Heaven of highness? O God, how? I must prove this, or otherwise nothing I say is of any value. In respect to both the heavens and the lady herself, it seems to me, so well have I studied my proofs, that just as up above the clouds heaven is higher than them all, in her case, just as honey is sweeter than gall, so too is her sweetness sovereign over all other women. Nor did God, who made all women, make any noble lady in the whole world that her nobility does not surpass; that is well known. Just as the sky makes the cloud more beautiful, so goodness makes my lady wiser in heart and mind, and I am not faint-hearted about this. God! How did my heart become so emboldened that I should love so highly? O God! She certainly has my heart. She wants it and she has it, without dividing it in any way. Let it be hers, I want it to remain hers. (354–91)

'My lady, however things turn out, I promise and grant you this: that you have a share of my heart and I a share of yours, in good, in evil, in sorrow and in joy. May God grant that I sport with you, for I wish to do so, and reason demands it. Why? Why? This question I will explain briefly and straightaway. With such a blow and in such a place, my lady, as you are wounded, I am wounded; that is a proven fact. For this reason, I must of necessity have some of the sorrow you are suffering, and it is right that I make clear who struck the blow from which the pain came, what the name of love's dart is, the dart that makes a person blanch, the dart that kills and grows cold, harming some and helping others. It is the one that kills and brings peace, the one that pierces hearts without a wound, the one that brings about every action that is appropriate for lovers, the dart that was felt by your heart. It wounded it, then returned to my heart and came in such rapid succession that it struck two hearts with one blow, such is the dart and so sharp is its point. The dart that awakens those who are asleep pierced me just where you are pierced. Dart of love, it is no surprise if you cause dismay to the disarmed, or that you bring about two wounds with one blow. Two wounds? How? What did I say? These two wounds, as I believe, are one wound, not two. Why? Because one single blow brought about the two wounds in one go and it was not necessary for one to enter both, and their whole infirmity must be restored to health by one cure, as no other cure can have any value. Because it is of necessity the case that one cure must be common to them and that the two wounds make only one.' (392–436)

There he stopped and was satisfied with this. After these sweet words she recalled his sweet arms, then she let her beloved know that she asked nothing more of God than to hold him in her arms. Then he grieved and lamented. He reflected and did not know what would happen. Then, when she came into his mind, he said: 'O God! There is such a delay. It is taking so long for her to have me, and for me to have her, held fast in both my arms! From so far away I cannot give her such a long embrace in my arms, but with my heart I embrace her. Embrace? How? Since our bodies have only one heart, because the two make one, our arms have embraced with our hearts so closely that they have embraced each other. Nevertheless, I do not doubt that I have a heart filled with joy and a body in a sorry plight, so that it could not enjoy anything I may hear of. Now my heart drinks so joyfully and is so bold, so happy and so grateful. My heart has become a great glutton, drinking and partaking of such joy, and it does not leave the body. Is not the heart then a glutton? Yes. It is a fault. If the body loses through its own fault what the heart has acquired and the heart seizes what it has hunted, do you then dare to say in any way that through the body the heart undergoes a loss? Yes. The heart inflames the body; the heart has jurisdiction over the body. (437–70)

Whatever the heart wants, the body grants, and since the heart controls the body completely, with nothing visible on the outside, why has the heart not then summoned the body and gone on summoning it? My heart has the right to cause me pain. I have behaved towards it like a cheat and let it down with a hundred faults. If the fault accuses me, why would my heart confess, because it has not gained anything by it? If I had believed my heart, I would have gone there, indeed some time ago, for never did my heart wrest desire from my body; rather it draws the two together. My heart said that, if I went to her, I would have complete solace, a full heart, a full body, full eyes and full arms. Heart, I will go to her, I grant you. Heart, I will do your bidding exactly. I hold fast to you. I have no desire to abandon you. No one should make a horse bound forward that does not want to run to the end. For he who begins and does not conclude is blamed for his activity. Heart, I begin and wish to carry out your intentions, and I will do so completely. Heart, I will never go against you. I hold fast to you without fail.' (471–99)

The nobleman immediately greeted his beloved and sent her a written message, so that she would know in truth and through what was written that he had taken heed of the proposal and pursued it, as a result of which the chase would never falter in his heart before he met with her. He would set off on his way at once, I have no doubt of this. This he explained point by point, for he never missed out a single word, just as I have related to you, and with the *salut* he sent all this to her. The messenger, who made his way to her, departed and this tale comes to an end, until the time when necessity brings back the messenger who took the letter. For if he returns and brings him news that differs from before, Girart will tell more of their exchange of lays. (500–18)

23. *Conseil*

Introduction

Conseil (*Advice*) is preserved in five manuscripts: (i) S (C in Grigoriu, Peersman and Rider); (ii) A: Paris, BNF, fr. 837; (iii) B: Paris, BNF, fr. 1593; (iv) D: Paris, BNF, Rothschild 2800; (v) E: Paris, BNF, Moreau 1729 (an incomplete eighteenth-century copy). Our translation is based on S, which is currently unpublished (an edition by Leslie C. Brook is forthcoming in the 2016 issue of *Le Cygne*). The recent translation by Grigoriu and Rider is based on A.

One Christmas Eve, at a large gathering in an unspecified plenary court, there is much talk of love. A powerful and wealthy lady present is being courted by three knights. Parting from them amicably, she approaches a knight she sees sitting alone. She tells him of her situation and asks his advice about which of the three is most suitable for her. First, he asks her to tell him about the respective qualities of the three knights. This she does briefly, relying on both her own observations and hearsay. The knight comments on each of the three suitors, condemning braggarts and slanderous talk and stressing the need for secrecy in love. But he refuses to choose between them, suggesting that she should seek advice from others and not rely simply on him. The lady is nevertheless impressed by the openness of his responses and the discussion is then prolonged by her request that he tell her more about the nature of love and how to keep it secret. The knight answers all her questions at length, dealing with both desirable and undesirable behaviour in men and women. Finally, she is so taken by his advice and obvious knowledge of the world that she gives him a belt she is wearing and asks him to present it to the man most suitable to receive her love. He puts the belt around his own waist and offers to be her companion in love. They become discreet lovers, and her wealth enables him to attend tournaments, which he often wins. After a time, the lady's husband dies and the couple are able to marry and live happily together.

Once the initial situation has been described, the main section of the lay consists of a discussion about love in which the knight warns against slanderers and gossips and advises the lady that, if she has a liaison, she should behave discreetly and resist the temptation to share her secret with anyone. He warns of the prevalence of slanderers, saying that while women should look closely at the nature of suitors they should be careful of hesitating too long when it comes to making their choice, lest in the meantime their beauty should fade. For, if a woman ends up failing to fulfil her desire for love, she will be condemned to hell, while those who succeed in doing so will achieve paradise, an idea graphically explored in the lay of *Trot*. It is therefore in a woman's interest to seek a companion in love. When the lady asks whether there is as much joy in love as she has heard, the knight replies with a speech of almost a hundred lines, affirming the lover's preference for the joy of companionship over all other material possessions (vv. 565–662). In giving her advice on the search for a companion in love, the knight implicitly recommends that she should try out various suitors until she finds the most suitable. The relationship the couple then forms will thus be based not on passion but on a shared attitude, and will lead to a socially acceptable relationship within a happy marriage. The lay illustrates the effectiveness of fair speech and at the end the narrator appears tacitly to hope that similar persuasion will help him in his own private life. When it comes to forming relationships, the knight's arguments demand hard-headed realism. At the close of the narrative an extramarital affair based on companionship becomes a successful marriage, but thanks only to the convenient death of the lady's husband.

Further Reading

Beston, John, 'The Psychological Art of the *Lai du Conseil*', *French Studies Bulletin*, 123 (2012), 26–28.

Brook, Leslie C., '*Omnia vincit rhetorica*: The *Lai du Conseil*', *Studi Francesi*, 44 (2000), 69–76.

Capusso, Maria Grazia, 'Contro la *bee*: spunti anticortesi nel *Lai du Conseil*', in *Figures du théâtre du monde: studi in onore di Giancarlo Fasano*, ed. Ana Maria Raugei (Pisa: ETS, 2005), pp. 51–65.

Maddox, Donald, 'Rewriting Marie de France: The Anonymous *Lai du Conseil*', *Speculum*, 80 (2005), 399–436.

Translation

Anyone who wishes to listen to fine words in French can learn a great deal from them, providing they are willing to retain them. This lay tells us without a word of a lie that one Christmas Eve, which is splendidly celebrated in many places, a great plenary court was held. Many different kinds of people had gathered there, and a large number of ladies, and also maidens, were there. Of the many people there, some were foolish, some wise and some worthy, and there was dancing, music played on viols and the reciting of romances. In many places there was talk of love, and both men and women in love were present; this was a very joyous feast. A wealthy and powerful lady was there whose love was frequently sought, as this tale tells us. Three knights wooed her every time they saw her and the lady left them without either granting or refusing her love to any of the three. From all three she parted amicably, thinking that this was the most advisable thing to do. (1–27)

The lady looked to one side and saw a knight sitting all alone. She addressed him straightaway and the knight jumped to his feet. When the lady summoned him, he came and sat down beside her. 'My lord, listen to what is on my mind,' said the lady. 'I will tell you and never lie to you about it. Three knights are wooing me and they keep on telling me they would like to have my undivided love. You understand the world, my lord,' she said, 'so tell me which one most deserves to be loved. Either the one who came first, the one who was the next to woo me, or the third and last of them?' 'Certainly', my lady, 'it should be the least common, the wisest, the worthiest, provided he is a pure-hearted lover. But you have not yet told me, sweet lady, so help me God, why I should be able to recommend to you the one whom you should love the most. So tell me about their qualities from start to finish, if you will.' 'Certainly', she said, 'gladly. The first is a knight who is brave, bold and very distinguished, but I have found him to be scatterbrained and a poor suitor. It seems to me that he has been badly brought up and badly educated. For he knows very little about the world and dresses inelegantly, and he is miserly and disagreeable; everyone bears witness to this. He is rich in both lands and possessions.' (28–65)

'It is common knowledge, my lady, that when he is well provided for, possessions cause a man to be called friend who would be very little loved if all his wealth were spent. But tell me what the others are like, my dear, sweet lady.' 'Indeed, gladly. One of the two is very handsome, but he is a little lacking in courage. He displays no valour with regard to arms, but in his person he is so handsome, so tall and so strong that he looks like a marvel, yet he is not worth a jot. The entire region bears witness to this. He is a nobleman with powerful allies, extensive lands and large holdings, but he takes very poor care of them. His neighbours do him harm, so that his vassals and his subjects suffer because of his failings. He is of very cowardly disposition, but is very handsome and elegant.' (65–87)

'All this makes him less than worthy, my lady, because he cherishes his own person since he can well afford to do so. What can you tell me about the third?' 'Certainly, he is courtly and amiable, and he is very well mannered, and be aware that he is very open about the fact that he is not a very rich man. He does not have many possessions, yet he behaves very nobly and conducts himself more elegantly than someone with three times as much as he has. He is not full of cares, but of delight and enjoyment, and he has never at any time wearied of displaying honour as best he can, in accordance with what wealth, possessions and resources he has. He is the least handsome and has the least amount of resources and inheritance, but he is widely recognised as wise by the men and women who have made his acquaintance. He knows how to dress very smartly and is not arrogant or irksome. I can tell you that things have not always gone the way he wanted them to go. Rather he has been at many a tournament on foot, which upset him, because his land had not yielded enough for him to buy horses. Yet I have also frequently heard it said that, at the end of the day, he has often been the winner on many a poor nag, because he had outdone the entire throng of knights who were present. I do not know what more to tell you about all three, except that with complete dominance the first one wants to have my love, and then the handsome one of necessity makes me recall his good looks. But I have forgotten to mention about him that, as I have heard tell, he is a braggart.' (88–129)

'Certainly, my lady, the fact that he had so much good in him makes things much worse. In my view a braggart has no right to true love and never will. He is not truly wise who has his love shouted from the rooftops, for in the same way as kindling is required to start a fire, in the forest or at sea, secrecy must accompany love, if anyone wants to have joy from it. He cannot enjoy it in any other way. And you, sweet lady, who wish to uphold love and preserve it, in God's name make an effort to keep secrets away from slandering braggarts. Such people, who are totally lacking in foresight, display a great deal of bombast. For this reason one should watch out for them, as love desires to be kept secret. Just as the dew climbs stealthily up a tree, and over the marble in a church, where it does not rain or blow a gale, in just the same way true love must pass through people without anyone perceiving a thing. For once love is perceived, it is betrayed and thwarted. And the third, how does he seek your love?' (130–59)

'Certainly, my lord, I could not recount this entire day how elegantly he woos me, with lays, letters and romances, but he has never confessed his love to me in person. Thus he constantly keeps things quiet, as if there were nothing to hide.' 'By the faith I owe you, my lady, he is right. He is wise and perspicacious, and he does not want to be thwarted by foolish, slanderous people; rather, it seems to me, he very wisely wants to affirm his pact. I will tell you how, my lady. If you wish to hold on to him, you can conceal it very well. If you have no desire to love him, he can conceal it and hide it, and he can very easily retreat and give the impression that he had never made any approach to you.' 'So, it seems to me, you are recommending this one to me more than the others.' 'My lady, by God in paradise, I make no judgment for you. But just as you desire it, choose a lover for yourself, because that is right. I could not say in a very long time anything that is, to my knowledge, hurtful, for he certainly commits an act of great folly who thinks he is wise in all things. You have told me about their habits and I am just one man. Now listen to what someone else says, and hear what they have to say to you. I say that a great advantage is enjoyed everywhere by a good knight, but this man's qualities are very mediocre, according to what you have told me about him. A handsome man who is bad, so help me God, fully deserves to be rejected, and yet he is often loved and coveted in many places. But he who is boastful is very poorly brought up, and that is great folly. For news never sleeps, rather it travels very swiftly from place to place. Many a country and many a region are reached by it in a very short time. A braggart laughs at what brings tears to the man who wishes to be a loyal friend. This is why I regard as well educated the third man who seeks your love wisely, and may God grant him as much honour and joy as can be accommodated in his heart, for it seems to me that he has prowess and knowledge combined.' (160–218)

'My lord', she said, 'it appears to me that you are giving your advice on this matter in accordance with your own feeling. But now teach me how to love and how I can keep it secret, if you please, correctly and properly, because I wish above all things to follow your advice. We have plenty of opportunity to make love bear fruit, but I am very fearful of the pains that I have heard one suffers from it.' 'Certainly, sweet lady, that is not true. From true love no harm comes, rather it comes from false and disloyal wretches who wish to deride love and are constantly more prepared to lie than a sparrowhawk is to fly. Of these people I cannot tell you a tale with a good beginning or a good end, for they are all constantly bent on bringing suffering into the world.' 'My lord, tell me what it means to deride love.' 'Gladly, my lady. He who, without any desire for it, begs for love wherever he goes and next day has no recollection of it, so that it seems to have been just a dream, such a man keeps his distance from the world. My lady, he who lives such a life, without cost, effort or pain to himself, wants to be loved in a hundred places.' (219–49)

'My lord, tell me what your opinion would be if ladies acted like this. Does each woman have more than one lover?' 'My lady, I will tell you my thoughts on this, certainly, if I am able and have sufficient knowledge. If there is a lady or a maiden, who is young, pleasing and beautiful, she will very soon be wooed by many men, and wooed in many ways. One man seeks her love through entreaties and another by sending messengers – such a man sends them to her and never goes himself, until the time comes when he finds out whether they have been received – and the third has a great desire to woo her but he does not dare, rather he just gazes at her. He is a lover through gazing. The fourth gets as close to her as he can, so that he can caress her, because in this way he intends to see if he will receive any mercy from her. The fifth tries a different approach with her. He serves her and gives her jewels, sending clasps, belts and rings to her, and if she accepts them he does not then expect to fail in any way, rather he expects to have a beloved. In just the same way a lady is approached by seven, eight, nine or ten suitors. She does not know which one is a faithful lover, nor does she know which one is more truthful. What can she do about it if she hopes that, when he woos her and shows her the way to love, each one does love her? (250–84)

'When she lies alone in her bed, thinking of the great delights of this world in which she is not sharing, Nature lies down next to her. One should not be surprised if Nature inspires a change of heart, and if she then shows a more favourable face to those who continue to woo her than to those who are not doing so. The slanderers who see this are very soon critical of her, and each one speaks his mind. One says that she is not wise, another calls her frivolous, a third says she is fickle, a fourth labels her two-faced. Thus people who have absolutely no idea about the world utter arrogant words, and in fact they lead frivolous lives, because by reason and nature a woman must be able to give a good response. A woman must be the bridge for the whole world's joy since we benefit from the many good things in her. We ought not to speak ill of her, but we all have need of a doctor to cure us of the ill that besets us, that is of the desire that comes over us to say outrageous and wicked things. We are all so filled with envy that we have ruined the world because of it, so that it has no power or strength, rather have all joy, contentment and tourneying gone to nought. (285–318)

'My lady, all good things have changed and all bad things have been improved, given roots and restored. To his shame and loss, many a man thinks he is of high repute. One should certainly not regard as a wise man the person who is intent on slander and who does not reflect on his own affairs before he slanders someone else's. When he sees that in himself there is nothing whatsoever to reproach, he should henceforth refrain from base utterances, for then he would not be without stain. My lady, he who could succeed in this would be better able to bring pleasure to the world. But very few are of such high repute. From Cologne to Paris, I do not think there are three men who, if anyone wished to take a close look at them, are so brave, so wise and so courtly that there is nothing in them to reproach. Therefore, my lady, it is necessary to be patient and listen to both the fool and the wise man, and many a time to tolerate wickedness. One cannot set everything to rights, my lady, or eradicate all evils. It would be necessary to wrack one's brains if one wanted to sort everything out. I tell you that I certainly do not know of anything other than good in women. But they do not all possess the same good sense; one knows more and another less. Thus the Sovereign Lord of this world created them to his liking.' (319–53)

'My lord, it is true, and for this reason it is my desire that if I have any wish to love I should be able to keep it secret. So tell me your thoughts on this. I beg you very tenderly, tell me what I must do to cover up my affairs more effectively.' 'Gladly, my lady, as best I can. Always set your heart and desire on serving and honouring God, and you should pay no heed to those who are full of baseness. Turn a deaf ear to them as soon as you become aware of their slander, and do not despise people because they have little money. Honour them in accordance with the sense and knowledge they possess. Be on good terms with the noble ladies in the region. Through this you will double your reputation, my lady, and if they trust you so much that they tell you about their affairs keep things completely secret and reprimand them for their follies. Chastise them without wickedness, so that for this reason they do not abandon either you or your companionship. Be kind and helpful to them, but keep your own intentions secret. Mind that neither stranger nor relative finds out about your affair, unless you need them to know of it. If any one of those who have the power to assist you has to know about it, never for this reason, or for any reason at all, make more of a fuss of her than of others in front of people. But, in private counsel with her, arrange your affair so well that no one could find any fault with it. For, my lady, slanderers will at once spot what is going on, and when people get together it is rare that no one detects any shameful behaviour. My lady, be mindful of the gaze that lingers in many places throughout the country and makes people stop and think.' (354–401)

'My lord, I do not know how to avoid this, because I am not aware of such a gaze.' 'My lady, this is some worthless folly that has permeated the region. It has spread far and wide, such that everyone has a large share of it. It stems from a futile desire by which many people are deceived, and I have very little regard for its value, for in my opinion it is worthless. It is right that I should explain to you what this gaze means. If there is a fun-loving woman who lives in a region, there will be knights gazing at her who will do nothing other than gaze, if they cannot find within themselves any sense, worth or courtliness through which to convey their thoughts or ever make them known to her. This is not because they are very knowledgeable. They are bewildered by their gaze, to the extent that when they have left her they very soon give an inaccurate account to those people with whom they are acquainted. Thus they waste all their youth until they become old and die. These men have nothing other than their gaze, my lady, and for the same reason I tell you that if there is a cheerful, happy and fun-loving knight travelling around the region, there will be gawping ladies there who will never have any pleasure from him. (402–35)

'These women plant gardens that yield no fruit. A lady who does this sort of thing is like the wild falcon that is hard to train. I will tell you why. The gentle one is considered plump, and the malicious one so base that it could never be haughty. At least this is true of what it achieves, which is nothing at all. The falconer carries the bird until a frost takes it by surprise and brings it to a swift death. A warm hen is of no use, for medicine is now too late and it cannot escape death. Thus the malicious one kills itself, because in it there is no pleasure or enjoyment. Many a woman who does not know how to train her heart to grab hold of a good thing if she sees it adorns her person with very fine clothes and cherishes herself. Thus her heart is in a state of desire from which she cannot escape. With such a gaze and such desire, she spends so many evenings and mornings that her beauty begins to fade until her youth has gone. Then she can say that in this gazing her beauty has been wasted. She has perhaps refused a man who was such that she would regret it if she could get not him back. (436–68)

'But what has gone is not coming back and her regrets have come too late, for she is now in the afternoon of life. Her vessels are ready in the harbour and their sails are already raised. She has said farewell to her youth. Her horse, without its bridle, carries her away. She has been betrayed by her tomorrows, and by the delays and the waiting. Then she makes the very greatest effort to cling on to her youth. But Nature cannot lie as it whisks her along, and the horse is not weary that carries her along so swiftly. Then she says that she was not wise when this or that man sought her love and she rejected them all. Alas! How sad that I ever made the acquaintance of the gaze that has betrayed and deceived me, and that I ever encountered my own great pride, now that I have nothing of what I want! I have never known what joy was.' Now I wish I could be burnt on a pyre! In this way the woman whose life passes without hope laments and complains. She has such expectations for the end of life, but I can tell you that her soul will not spend long on the scales. For if Scripture does not lie, she is going to take up residence in hell to remain there as her inheritance, from which she will never depart as long as Jesus Christ survives, who has neither ending nor beginning. My lady, I will now tell you how this woman can have paradise who has rejected the rewards of love, which is within her power. You have often heard tell, I believe, that everything works for good. Of this there is no doubt and it is all true. We will never be let down by this, and we will be judged according to how things turn out. (469–512)

'If a woman has greatly indulged her fancies and her desires, according to her will and pleasure, in secret and at leisure, and has pleasured her gracious body beneath the flower, beneath the fruit, beneath the leaves in enclosed gardens, in fine chambers, taking her delight and, by night and by day, her enjoyment with her arms around her beloved, thus, my lady, since I could say a great deal more about this if I wished, I must keep quiet about the rest. For, if you find sufficient sense in him, when you have your lover you should do with him what pleases you, just as others do who have wise and courtly lovers. Both men and women who do just the same, my lady, beg for mercy from Jesus, our Creator, when through old age or sickness they have to leave this world. Their misdeeds cause them to repent with such a pure and whole heart that Jesus Christ, he who is worthy and just and clearly shows us how things should be, generously pardons them all their sins. Longinus struck him with his lance, and at once he pardoned him because Longinus begged him for mercy out of sincere repentance. Yet I do not advise you to sin in such expectation, my lady, though I do dare to affirm to you that, if you remain in sin, you should never despair because of this, neither yourself nor anyone who hears this lay, because he goes very badly astray who thinks he is lost. This single sin condemns him more than any other he might commit. It would be of no use for the person who does not think he could achieve mercy to wear a hair shirt. God never forgets the sinner who begs for mercy when he abandons his folly; rather he welcomes him very joyfully.' (513–61)

'My lord, now tell me clearly if there is as much joy in love as I have always heard there is.' 'My lady, concerning joy I will tell you what I think and what I know. My lady, if there were a poor man without land and without resources who had been living in the world, a brave and valiant knight, without counsel and without succour, if a large tract of well-endowed land, my lady, at this point fell to his lot, he ought to be filled with joy and accept it very gladly. If he had as many counties and as large a kingdom as I could name, just as I am able to name them, then his joy ought to be doubled. My lady, now pay attention to the naming. If he were Lord of Touraine, Lord of Anjou, Lord of Maine, Count of Poitiers, Count of Brittany, King of Navarre, King of Spain, King of Morocco, King of Syria, and if he had the whole pagan world from end to end at his disposal, Constantinople and the power invested in its emperor, all the land surrounding it and the whole empire of Germany, Saxony, Russia and Sardinia, just as the sea divides it, so that there is nothing lacking in any way, Scotland, Wales and the entire land beyond England, and England and all its ports, where there are so many does and boars, Provence, as far as Gascony, and then Lorraine and Burgundy, and if France, throughout which I have travelled, were his private chamber, and other lands I could name, I would like to linger over them. So I wish to name them briefly, as I wish to conclude this advice. (562–606)

'Just as the heavens surround us, and as it rains and as it thunders, there would not be a full acre of land, as far as the world extends, nor any wood, river or sea, to be found, either by day or by night, without it being entirely in his domain, even if it were in various foreign places, my lady, and if he were fortunate enough that he could be everywhere without sailing and riding on his palfrey, with his men and all his company, taking all his people with him, in the same way as I could go one league today and two tomorrow, he could go to every point on his land, my lady, in one day from end to end and all around it, and it would not cause any harm either to himself or to all his people, no more than it does in this hall where we hear no evil gossip, he should then be content with this, without covetousness or theft, for he would have great joy and pleasure and would create fruit of many types, and he would have many dogs and birds.[4] He would be a great lord and a young nobleman. I cannot see or think how anyone could give more, nor wish more for one man, for he would finally have everything, except for eternal life, and may he have this if it is his wish, and love, because I do not want him ever to have any joy in his life, nor pain, suffering or hardship, nor desire or memories. (607–44)

'I say rather that he should not have, either from land or from wealth, or from everything I have mentioned to you, so much joy or pleasure, and this would not compare, my lady, with the pleasure from his beloved, when he has one who is wise and very pleasing, and able to fill his heart with joy and delight. A heart cannot glorify in either treasure or income, I can say this to you in truth, and you can clearly see this insofar as it does so for true love. The heart that is smitten with true love changes colour ten times each day. I do not know what more I can tell you. No joy can be compared to the heart that maintains true love. My lady, I will be severely reprimanded by slanderers when they hear this, but I am not afraid of those who understand, those who know what the term beloved means, thus I call upon them as supporters, and for them all to be my witnesses that love conquers everything and will do so, as long as the world lasts.' (645–70)

'My lord, you are very skilled in praising love. I never expected to find anyone in my whole life who could tell me so much about it. The man is a great fool who does not seek a lover in the expectation of such fulsome joy.' 'My lady, love does not deign to associate with those foolish and arrogant dandies, those envious slanderers who do not know how to enjoy love. My lady, such a man thinks he knows a great deal about the world, yet he does not know much about it.' 'My lord', she said, 'tell me now

[4] This remarkable sentence runs to twenty-seven lines in the original (vv. 603–33). This 'tour de force' forms a suitable climax to the exposition of love that impresses the lady.

if what I have heard tell is true, that love given freely is worse than that which is denied.' 'My lady, briefly and without delay I will tell you this very gladly. My lady, if a wise knight enjoys true love in a worthy place, when he has sufficient leisure and opportunity he and his beloved should come together as one, with shared contentment and joy, without denial or deception. This is what love and justice demand. If there is a lady or maiden who embarks upon a new love, at first she should hide her feelings from him in order to get to know the man whom she wishes to make her beloved. If she finds him to be foolish and troubled, she can leave him if she is able to do so, and if she cannot stop loving him, because she cannot separate her heart from him, she must, as far as she can, keep her feelings from him, in accordance with what love permits her to do. (671–705)

'If things are somewhat different because she loves a young man who, my lady, is embarking on his first love and knows nothing about it, it is right that she should draw him to her with a nice, alluring smile. She must be tender and kind until he becomes bold enough to burn with love for her. And when he is ardent and boiling hot, filled with longing and desire, then she should chastise him, instruct and teach him to the point where she wishes to have him, and then, if he is ever to pay attention to her, desire and longing will make him burn with love and she must create fear in him, in order to teach the youth how to keep things secret. For, unless they have been well trained in its use, young men are impetuous when it comes to speech. This is the way a woman must behave who wishes to enjoy the delights of love: reveal everything to the wise man, hide and conceal things from the fool, and teach and instruct the young man if she wishes to take him as her lover. My sweet lady, do not believe that it is true, no matter what anyone says, that rejected love is true love. Know well, such love freely given is of uncertain worth, which cannot prosper, so let it come to an end. He who wishes to speak reasonably and truthfully, in true love there must not be any trace of wickedness or denial. In joy, in contentment and in delight should a true lover and a loyal mistress spend their lives. This is what must be done, I believe, by a true mistress and a loyal lover.' (706–46)

The lady heard his words, which were so fine that she was forced to forget the entreaties of the other three. She saw that he was so wise and courtly, so well spoken and well-mannered that her heart became completely fixed on loving him without any regrets. She was kind and noble, and for some time she had heard it said that he was skilled at speaking eloquently of love. Now she wished to reveal to him the great wish and desire she had to grant him her love. This is what the lady said to the youth. 'I will tell you what you will do. You will take this belt I am wearing, which is made of silk and silver, and make a present of it according to your desire. Be careful how you use it and to whom you give my love. For you should know that he who wears the belt and to whom you give it will have my love.' He was wise and clever, worthy, courtly and perceptive. Very wisely he took the belt from around the lady's waist. 'My lady', he said, 'will you adhere to your plan fully, if it please God?' 'Indeed, my lord, above all things, just as a queen would do.' 'I take it as a fine gift and retain it for myself, as I have often heard it reported that he who sees the good and takes the bad is deliberately behaving like a fool. But I do not want to act in this way. Rather, my lady, I consider myself as your lover.' (747–84)

The lady, whom this pleased, granted it. He girded on the silk belt, happy, joyful and delighted. He was right to be so because never had such a fine present been given or granted. Since he was very forlorn and she a noble, wealthy lady with a husband who was base and mean, and because she had the entire land under her control, she often gave the knight many horses, palfreys or bridles, and he went to many tournaments, far and near. It often came about that in the evening he won the prize over all the others. Then he immediately attended a tournament in another place. He was contented and full of fun, and his companionship was most agreeable. Everywhere he went his friends were very high spirited. The lady easily found the money to pay for his very reasonable expenses. When he came to her dwelling, his stay was not announced, instead, just as he came, on horseback, he went secretly to his beloved, who was very happy about this. When the opportunity arose to have him with her, she had a great deal of what she desired. They were often in a beautiful chamber, enjoying fine dalliance together, many a night and many an entire day. This love was very well concealed, for no rumour or report of it got out. The whole region wondered how the knight managed to enjoy the splendid life he was leading. (785–822)

Thus they rejoiced in their love for a long time, until one day it came about that the lady's husband died. When his time came, he gave up his soul and was buried in the presence of many people. The lady, who had a noble heart and was learned and wise, brought together all her family and took and married her beloved. Thus his fine speech conferred on the knight this marriage, which elevated and honoured him and his whole family. You who listen to me, my lords, the *Lay of Conseil* [*Advice*] instructs you: he is a fool who takes a wrong path if the good one is to hand. Why do you not make use of fine speech as much as of slander? Does it not come from poor teaching? Yes, it is certainly from the foolish and the ill-bred. You well know that my lord Gauvain was the flower of chivalry. His courtliness was a great asset to him, as you have heard in many a fine tale. This *Lay of Conseil* comes to an end and relates that the man who is mean with good speech has too miserly a heart, providing he is not deaf or dumb. Slander is an envious morsel and it does no one any good. Avoid it at all cost, you who aim to succeed and who wish to enjoy love. A knight who did not want this adventure to be over has put this lay into French for us, in order to teach true lovers. He has done this as best he could, translating it word for word, but he is greatly astonished that he does not know how to advise himself about a love that has taken hold of him. Rather he says that he is just as overwhelmed as the man who spends his time gazing. Now let us ask God to bring him to a safe harbour and a safe passage, so that in the end he will consider himself to be wise. (833–70)

The Lay as History

24. *Haveloc*[1]

Introduction

Haveloc is preserved in two manuscripts: (i) H: London, College of Arms, Arundel XIV; (ii) P: Cologny-Genève, Bibliotheca Bodmeriana, Codex Bodmer 82. Our translation is based on P, as edited in our book *The Anglo-Norman Lay of Haveloc* (pp. 113–37). At 1,107 lines in H and 1,099 lines in P, *Haveloc* is the longest lay in our collection.

The setting of the lay alternates between Denmark and the East of England. King Arthur sails to Denmark in order to subjugate the land and exact a tribute from King Gunter, Haveloc's father. In the ensuing battle, Gunter is slain and his lands are given by Arthur to an unpopular usurper named Odulf. One of Gunter's vassals named Grim sets sail for England with his wife and Haveloc, but on the way the ship is attacked by pirates and Haveloc's mother is killed. In England Grim founds Grimsby and brings up Haveloc as his own child. But in due course he decides that Haveloc, who is not aware of his royal birth, should broaden his horizons by serving in a king's court. Haveloc makes his way to the court of the petty king Edelsi, who rules Lincoln, Lindsey and the surrounding areas. Haveloc is employed there as a scullion and displays great strength and skill in wrestling. At court he is known by the name Cuarant. Edelsi has a sister named Orwein who is married to a local king called Achebrit. The latter falls ill, but before he dies he asks Edelsi to look after his daughter

[1] In the MS P version, which we translate, the form used for the hero's name, in every case but one, is Aveloc. In our translation we have used the form Haveloc, found in MS H, by which the poem and its hero are traditionally known. We have also standardised Haveloc's other name as Cuarant, although different forms occur in the two manuscripts. Other personal names with variant forms are Achebrit, Edelsi, Gunter, Odulf, Orwein and Sigar Estal. See the Index of Proper Names in our edition of *Haveloc*, pp. 222–23.

Argentille and her lands and in due course to marry her off to the strongest man in the kingdom. The time comes for her to marry, but not wanting to lose control over her lands Edelsi marries her to Haveloc/Cuarant, whose immense strength qualifies him for her hand. The couple leave court and travel to Grimsby, where Haveloc discovers his true name and also that he is of royal birth and heir to Denmark. With the help of his father's former seneschal, Haveloc wins back his lands and subsequently returns to England, where he defeats Edelsi and thereby rules over Denmark and the lands belonging to his wife. Shortly afterwards, Edelsi dies and his lands too are handed over to Haveloc by Edelsi's barons, as there is no other rightful heir. Haveloc reigns for twenty years, during which time, as would be expected of him, he makes further conquests.

Although the author describes his composition as a lay, at the beginning (v. 21) and the end (v. 1097) of the narrative, *Haveloc* is not a typical lay. It is certainly not dominated by a love relationship, even if we are told that, after a difficult start to their marriage, love does develop between Haveloc and Argentille. *Haveloc* is dominated by social and political issues, the themes of kingship, land, power and inheritance being of particular importance. Six kings are involved in the narrative, three good (Gunter, Achebrit, Haveloc) and three bad (Arthur, Odulf, Edelsi). Odulf, for example, is described as 'always wicked at heart' (v. 35) and is said to have killed Gunter 'treacherously' (vv. 36, 595). Haveloc, on the other hand, constantly shows an interest in those around him, from helping to feed his foster brothers and the squires at court to challenging Odulf to one-to-one combat for the kingdom of Denmark, to prevent the common people from suffering unnecessarily. When the narrative reaches its conclusion, Haveloc is in a position to manifest his kindliness and generosity in three different kingdoms, those belonging originally to his father, to the father of his wife Argentille and to her uncle Edelsi. But the female members of the audience will not have failed to notice the contributions made by Argentille, for example her wheeze of fixing dead bodies on to stakes in order to give a false impression of the size of his army, which enables Haveloc to defeat the man who has usurped her lands.

All this does not mean that supernatural or folklore elements are absent from this lay. We are told that Gunter's seneschal is the custodian of a horn that can only be blown by the rightful heir to Denmark, and this does indeed turn out to be proof of Haveloc's credentials as long-lost king. The right to inherit the kingdom is also associated with another sign: a flame that emerges from the heir's mouth as he sleeps. A third non-realistic element is the hermit's power to interpret Argentille's dream and relate it to the future direction of the tale. Nonetheless, the lay reads in many ways like a piece of history, and it thus comes as no surprise that the earliest form of the tale is found in a chronicle, Geffrei Gaimar's *Estoire des Engleis*, dating from the 1130s.[2] Indeed, although efforts to establish the historicity of Haveloc and his actions have largely been fruitless, a legend developed around him that inspired a series of shorter versions of the story, in French, English and Latin (see Burgess and Brook, *The Anglo-Norman Lay of Haveloc*, pp. 39–46, 151–210). However, for the purposes of the present volume, *Haveloc* demonstrates the versatility of the genre of the lay.

Further Reading

Bradbury, Nancy Mason, 'The Traditional Origins of *Havelok the Dane*', *Studies in Philology*, 90 (1993), 115–42.

Fahnestock, Edith, *A Study of the Sources and Composition of the Old French Lai d'Haveloc* (Jamaica, Queensborough, New York: Marion Press, 1915).

Heyman, Harold E., *Studies on the Havelok-Tale* (Uppsala: Wretmans, 1903; repr. Whitefish, MT: Kessinger Publications, 2010).

Moll, Richard J., '"Nest pas autentik, mais apocrophum": Haveloks and their Reception in Medieval England', *Studies in Philology*, 105 (2008), 165–206.

Translation

One should gladly hear, relate and retain the noble actions of our ancestors and their acts of prowess and good deeds, imitating and remembering them so that worthy men will be improved. Acts of villainy and misdeeds, these ought to be the tales with which one should admonish them, for there is a very shameful need for this. May everyone pay heed, as if it were aimed directly at them. I will tell you very briefly the story of a powerful

[2] For a translation of the Haveloc episode in Gaimar's work (vv. 37–818), see Burgess and Brook, *The Anglo-Norman Lay of Haveloc*, pp. 138–48. See also *Geffrei Gaimar, Estoire des Engleis | History of the English*, ed. and trans. Ian Short (Oxford: Oxford University Press, 2009).

king and of many other barons whose names I will give you. I will relate the story to you. This king was called Haveloc and he also had the name Cuarant. I wish to tell you about him and recall his adventure, because the Bretons composed a lay about it and named it both *Haveloc* and *Cuarant* after him.[3] I will first tell you of his father: his name was Gunter and he was Danish. He ruled the land and was king. Arthur reigned at that time and he crossed the sea to Denmark, intending to make the land subject to him and to receive the king's tribute. He did battle with King Gunter and with the Danes, vanquishing them all. King Gunter himself was slain, along with many others from that country. Odulf, who was always wicked at heart, killed him treacherously. (1–36)

When Arthur had ended the war, he bestowed upon Odulf all the land and the homage of the barons; then he departed with his Britons. Partly through coercion and partly through fear, many people served Odulf. There were those who wished him harm and they were supported by Sigar Estal,[4] who was a worthy man and a powerful baron, very skilled in war. In his charge he had a horn that no man could sound unless he was, through his lineage, the rightful heir over the Danes, by heritage. Before King Arthur came and fought with the Danes, Gunter had a castle on the coast, strong and fair. It was well supplied with provisions and in it he had placed his wife and son. Their safety was entrusted to a baron from that region. His name was Grim and Gunter trusted him greatly; he had always been a loyal servant. Above all, he entrusted to him his son, whom he loved greatly. If anything happened to Gunter in the approaching battle, Grim should do his best to protect him and flee the country with him, so that he would not be captured, discovered or handed over to his enemies. The child was not very big, being no more than two years old.[5] All the time he was asleep a flame issued from him. It would come out of his mouth, so great was the heat that was in his body. Those in the land who knew about this regarded it as a great marvel. (37–76)

[3] Convention has it that this narrative and its hero are called Haveloc (Havelok is also found) but, as pointed out above, the form used in our base manuscript (P), with the exception of v. 856, is Aveloc.

[4] Forms of this name, which occurs three times in the text, differ across manuscripts. In P the name is Sigat Lestal (v. 44) and Sigar Estal (vv. 619, 642) and in H, Sigar Lestal (44, 631, 654).

[5] In the MS H version, Haveloc is said at this stage to be seven years old, which is less likely as we are told that he is hidden under his mother's cloak when they go aboard Grim's ship (v. 100).

After King Gunter, his men and his troops, had been killed, Odulf hated and expelled all those he knew Gunter had loved. The queen was very much afraid that he would seize their castle and kill the king's son, as was the good man who was guarding her. They lacked the power to defend themselves and were forced to adopt another plan. Grim had his ship prepared and fully stocked with provisions. He intended to flee the country in order to protect the rightful heir from death. He would take the queen with him for fear of the wicked king who had killed her husband and would swiftly dishonour her. When the ship was ready, he had his household, his stewards and his servants go aboard, and he escorted his wife and children. He put the queen into the ship; she was holding Haveloc beneath her cloak. Grim himself boarded next and entrusted them all to God in heaven. They weighed anchor and left the harbour, for they had a good breeze. They crossed the sea, but did not know in which direction to go in order to be able to protect their lord. That day misfortune befell them, for pirates came upon them, challenging them in terrifying fashion and attacking them very fiercely. Those on board the ship defended themselves, but their forces were limited; the pirates killed them all. They robbed and plundered the ship and the queen was killed on board. There were no survivors, great or small, except for Grim, who was known to the pirates. His wife and small children were also spared, and so was Haveloc. (77–120)

After they had escaped from the pirates, they rowed and sailed until they came to a harbour, where they left the ship to go on land. This was at Grimsby in the north. At the time I am telling about, there was not a single soul there, and no one frequented this harbour. Grim was the first to build a house there, and from him Grimsby takes its name. When he first arrived, he broke the ship in two. He stood the two ends upright and made his home in them. He went fishing, as he was accustomed to do, and bought and sold salt until he became well known and recognised there by the peasants. Many of them joined forces with him and took up quarters at the harbour, and because of the name they had heard they called the place Grimsby. The good man raised his lord, and his wife cherished him dearly. Everyone thought he was their son, for they did not know any different. Grim gave him a different name so that no one would recognise him. The child grew and flourished and he became stronger in body and limbs. Before he was very old, no one could have found any full-grown man who, if he had tried to wrestle with him, would not have been beaten by the youngster. He was very strong and powerful, enterprising and fiery. (121–56)

Grim, the worthy man who raised Haveloc, was exceedingly pleased to have the boy. But one thing distressed him: he was not being raised among the kind of people from whom he could in some way learn good manners and acquire wisdom. For Grim believed in his heart that Haveloc would still regain his heritage. He summoned him one day. 'Fair son', he said, 'listen to me. We live here in seclusion with fishermen and poor people who make a living through fishing. You know nothing of their trade. Here you cannot learn anything useful or ever make any money. Fair son, go to England in order to gain wisdom and learn to fight. Take your brothers with you. In the court of a powerful king, fair son, enter into his service. You are very strong, grown up and tall and you can bear a very great load. Make everyone like you and devote yourself to service where the opportunity arises, and may God grant you enough success that you can make some money there.' When the worthy man had pointed this out and provided him with new clothing, with some difficulty he made him depart; he took Gunter's two boys with him. (157–88)

The three of them thought they were brothers, just as their father had told them. They followed the straight path until they came to Lincoln. At the time I am alluding to, a king, whose name was Edelsi, held the land there under his control. He ruled Lincoln and the whole of Lindsey, the area towards the north, and also in his domain he had Rutland and Stamford. But he was Breton by lineage. At that time the kingdom over towards the men of Surrey was governed by another king. This king was called Achebrit and he was a very noble baron. He was married to Edelsi's sister – they were companions and friends – who was called Orwein, a noble lady. But they had no children, apart from just one beautiful daughter; Argentille was her name. King Achebrit fell ill with a very serious affliction and knew that he could not recover. He summoned Edelsi, entrusted his niece to him and handed over to him all his land. But first he made him swear and affirm, in the sight of his men, that he would bring her up loyally and look after her land for her until she reached the age at which marriage would be permitted. When the maiden had grown up, he should give to her, on the advice of his vassals, the strongest man he can find in the land. Then Achebrit handed over to him the fortresses, castles and cities, and he also gave him custody over his niece and his sister, together with all the men in the domain. But after Achebrit had passed away, the queen became ill. Her life too was soon over and she was buried beside her husband. (189–234)

I must now leave them, as I wish to deal henceforth with Haveloc. King Edelsi, who reigned at that time and ruled the two kingdoms, held a fine court with many people there. He often stayed in Lincoln and Haveloc came to his court. One of the king's cooks retained him in his service, because he saw that he was strong, tall and of very fine appearance. He could carry tremendous loads, cut firewood and carry water. After a meal he took charge of the dishes. That was the job he was given and whatever he could get hold of, a piece of meat or a complete loaf of bread, he very gladly gave it to the boys and the squires. He was so noble and kind that he wanted to bring pleasure to everyone. Because of his noble character they treated him like a fool, made fun of him and everyone called him Cuarant, for this was the word used by the Bretons in their language for a scullion. On account of his strength, the knights and the servants often brought him forward. Since they knew how strong he was, they made him wrestle in front of them with the strongest men they knew. He defeated them all, and if any one of them spoke ill of him he would tie him up with brute force, keep hold of him and punish him until he conceded and they were reconciled. The king himself had him wrestle very frequently in front of his men. Because of the strength he possessed the king regarded him as a great marvel. Ten of the strongest men in his household were no match for him, and a dozen men could not lift the load he was used to carrying on his own. (235–80)

Haveloc was at court for a good long time until there was an assembly, when the barons came to court who had held their lands from Achebrit and now held them from Argentille, the maiden who was his daughter. They addressed the king and made a request concerning his niece, who had now grown up and was tall and ready to bear children, that he should marry her to a man who could protect and help them, and that if he remained true to his oath he should support them loyally. The king heard what they said and the request they were making of him. He asked them for a delay and said he would take advice on this. He wanted to know and to ask to whom he should give her. He fixed a date with them and named the day, ordering them to return when he had taken advice. In this matter he was very astute. He spoke about this to his principal advisers and made his feelings plain to them. He asked for and sought their advice concerning those who were asking him to give his niece a husband who would protect both them and the land. But he would rather be at war than be dispossessed of the land. This is what the advisers said: 'Have her sent far away beyond the sea to Brittany and entrust her to your family. Let her become a nun in a convent and serve God all her life.' 'My lords', he said, 'I have decided to dispose of her differently. When King Achebrit died and entrusted his daughter to me, he made me swear an oath in the sight of his men, and vow that I would give her to the strongest man I could find in the land. I can acquit myself of this faithfully. I wish to give her to Cuarant, who is strong and very powerful. Those who have seen him know this. If there is anyone who opposes this or accuses me of baseness, I will put him in my prison and give her to this scullion.' (281–334)

This was the king's plan. On the day he had arranged with them, he made ready in his chambers one hundred and forty armed men from his household, for he was expecting a brawl in the place where she was to be given in marriage. The barons came to court and the king addressed them: 'My lords', he said, 'now listen to me, since you are assembled here. The other day when you came to see me, you made a request of me that I should give my niece a husband and entrust her land to him. You are well aware, and I remind you of this, that when Achebrit the king died he placed his daughter in my care and made me swear an oath that I would give her to the strongest man I could find in the kingdom. I sought hard and made so many enquiries that I have now found a strong man. I have a youth in my kitchen to whom I will give the maiden. His name is Cuarant. The ten strongest men in my household are no match for him and cannot withstand him in a fist fight or combat. The truth is that from here to Rome no man has such bodily strength. If I wish to keep my oath, I cannot bestow her otherwise.' When the barons heard that this was what he intended to do, they said openly among themselves that they would never tolerated it. Great blows were about to be exchanged when Edelsi summoned his armed men. He had his niece brought forward and married her to Cuarant. (335–74)

In order to disgrace and dishonour her, that night Edelsi made her lie next to him. When they were both brought to bed, she was very ashamed of him and he even more so for her sake. He lay face downwards and slept, not wanting her to see the flame that issued from him. But later they became so trusting of each other, both in their words and their expressions, that he loved her and lay with her as was his duty to his wife. On the night he first had relations with her he had such joy from it and loved her so much that he fell asleep and became oblivious. He lay on his back without turning over and the maiden slept, throwing her arm over her lover. She had a dream that she had gone with her husband over the sea into a wood. There they found a wild bear accompanied by foxes; the countryside was completely covered by them. They were on the point of attacking Cuarant when, from the other direction, they saw coming pigs and wild boars that defended him and protected him from the foxes. When the foxes were defeated, one of the boars with great strength approached the bear and attacked it, but Cuarant killed it and laid it low. The foxes, who were its companions, all came together towards Cuarant. They prostrated themselves before him, appearing to seek mercy, and Cuarant had them tied up. Then he intended to go back to sea, but the trees in the wood bowed down to him on all sides. The sea rose and the tide advanced right up to him; he was very much afraid. He saw two ferocious lions. They approached him and terrified him. They devoured the beasts in the forest, all those they found in their way. Cuarant was filled with dread, as much for his beloved as for himself. They both climbed up a tall tree for fear of the lions. But the lions came forward and knelt beneath the tree, seeming to show him affection and treating him as their lord. Through the entire wood there was such a great hue and cry that Argentille was awoken. (375–430)

She was very frightened by this dream, and then even more so by her husband, because of the flame she could see issuing from his mouth. She sat up and screamed so loudly that she awakened him. 'My lord', she said, 'you are on fire! Alas, you are all aflame!' He embraced her and drew her to him. 'My fair beloved', he said, 'why are you so frightened? Who has filled you with such dread?' 'My lord', she said, 'I had a dream. I will relate it to you.' She recounted it, explained it to him and told him about the fire she had seen issuing from his mouth. She thought that his whole body was on fire; that was why she had cried out. Cuarant comforted her: 'My lady', he said, 'do not be afraid of anything. This is very much to your advantage and to mine. The dream you have had can be explained tomorrow. The king is to hold his feast and he has summoned all his barons. There will be an abundance of meat and I will provide great joints of meat for the squires in large quantity and for the boys who have loved me greatly. The squires are the foxes as are the grooms, who are the lowliest of all. The bear was killed yesterday and put in our kitchen. The king has had two bulls baited and I take them to be the lions. The pots we can consider to be the sea. In them the fire makes the water level rise. I have explained the dream to you, so do not be afraid any longer. As to the fire that my mouth spewed out, I will tell you what it means: our kitchen will catch fire, I believe, and I will be struggling and perturbed when carrying our cauldrons and our pans and pots outside. But nevertheless I do not wish to lie. Fire always emerges from my mouth when I am asleep. I do not know why this happens to me and it troubles me.' (431–80)

The youngsters stopped talking about the dream and fell asleep. But when Argentille got up next morning, she related and explained the dream to a steward who was with her and had been raised by her father the king. He was very helpful to her and told her that in Lindsey there was a man who lived a holy life. He was a hermit and lived in the wood, and if she spoke to him he would tell her what the meaning of the dream could be, for he was a priest and God loved him. 'My friend', she said, 'I trust you fully. For the love of God, come with me. I wish to talk to the hermit, if you are willing to go with me.' He gladly agreed to go with her in secret. He put a cloak around her and took her to the hermitage. He had her speak with the holy man and explain what was on her mind with respect to the dream that had frightened her and her lord's mouth, out of which she had seen a flame coming but could not explain it. She begged and entreated him out of charity to counsel her and give her his advice and his opinion about this. The hermit uttered a sigh. He began to say a prayer to God and then interpreted the dream for her: 'My fair one', he said, 'what you dreamt about your husband, you will see it all happen. He was born of royal lineage and will yet have a great heritage. Many people will be subject to him. He will be king and you queen. Ask him who his father was, and if he has a brother or sister, then ask him to take you to their country. There you will hear the circumstances of his birth and who he is, and may God in heaven grant you strength and may he allow you to hear something that turns out to be of great advantage to you.' (481–528)

Argentille took her leave of him and the holy man commended her to God. She returned to her husband. Lovingly and in private she asked him where he was born and where his family were. 'My lady', he said, 'in Grimsby. I left them there when I came here. Grim the fisherman is my father, and Sebur, I believe, is my mother's name.' 'Beloved', she said, 'let us go and find them and let the king have the land he has wrongly deprived me. He has a mortal hatred for both you and me. I would prefer to be a beggar elsewhere than to be wretched among my own people.' Cuarant replied to her: 'My lady, we will be there very soon. I will gladly take you with me. Let us go and take leave of the king.' This they duly did that very morning and then set out on the road, taking with them Grim's two sons and going straight to Grimsby. But the worthy man had died, as had the lady who had raised them. But they found Kelloc, his daughter, who was married to a merchant. They greeted the husband and spoke to their sister. They asked about their father and about how their mother was faring. They were told that they were dead and the youngsters were filled with grief. Kelloc addressed Cuarant and asked him with a smile: 'My friend', she said, 'by your faith, this woman who is with you, who is she? She is very beautiful. Is she wife or maiden?' 'Wife', he said. 'King Edelsi, whom I have served for a long time, gave her to me recently. She is his niece, his sister's daughter, and a king's daughter of high lineage. But he has robbed her of her heritage.' Kelloc heard what he said and felt exceedingly sorry for him, as a king's son, and for his wife. She summoned her husband and on his advice asked him whose son he was, if he knew, and if he was acquainted with his family. He replied: 'Grim was my father, you are my sister and these are my brothers, who have come here with me. I know full well that you are our sister.' (529–86)

Kelloc said to him: 'That is not so. Keep it secret if I tell you. Have your wife come forward now and I will let both of you hear it. I will tell you whose son you are and relate the truth to you. Your father was Gunter the king, who was lord over the Danes. Odulf killed him treacherously when the Britons attacked him. King Arthur became an ally of Odulf and gave him Denmark. Grim, our father, fled and abandoned the land to save you. Your mother died at sea, for our ship was attacked by pirates who came upon us and killed most of our people. We escaped death and reached this port. We changed your real name and called you Cuarant. Your name is Haveloc, my friend. If you wish to go to that country, my husband will take you there and give you food and clothing. The other day it happened, less than a month ago, that he clearly heard that the Danes would like to have you among them, for the king is making himself much hated. There is a powerful man in the land against whom the king is constantly at war. He is called Sigar Estal and we advise you to go to him. He is married to one of your relatives, who is always unhappy because of you, since she cannot get any news of you. If you can get to them, you will yet have your heritage. Take your two young boys with you.' When she heard this, Argentille was filled with joy and she promised them faith and love. If God were to bring them any honour, she said, she would give them a rich reward. (589–631)

After this, there was scarcely any delay. They prepared their ship and their journey and crossed the sea to Denmark. When they had reached that land and disembarked, the merchant who had brought them there dressed them in new clothes. He then explained what they should do and which town they should head for, and he told them about the court of the seneschal, whose name was Sigar Estal. 'Haveloc', he said, 'dear friend, when you reach his land, go and take lodgings in his castle and eat at his table. Ask for hospitality out of charity. Take your wife with you. Seeing how beautiful she is, they will very soon ask you who you are and from which land, and who gave you such a wife.' They left the merchant and went on their way. They travelled and journeyed until they reached the city where the seneschal lived. They went straight to the castle and found the lord in his court. Out of charity they asked him to grant them hospitality and give them lodgings for the night. The seneschal agreed to this and sent them into the hall until it was time for dinner and everyone went to wash. The lord sat down to eat and had the three boys sit down, with Argentille next to her husband; they were served with great honour. The youths and squires who served at this meal gazed at the maiden and praised her beauty highly. Six of them went off to one side, and together they decided to take the youth's beloved away from him. If he became angry, they would beat him. (632–78)

When they rose from the meal, the youngsters went to their lodgings. The seneschal had them taken to a lodging house to rest. Those who had coveted the lady, who was very beautiful and well brought up, followed them down the street. They seized the youth's beloved and would have taken her off with them, but Haveloc obtained a sharp, heavy axe – I cannot explain the good fortune that one of them was holding and carrying it. Haveloc grabbed it off him and took his revenge, killing and slaughtering five of them. One of them escaped, his right hand cut off. A hue and cry arose in the city and Haveloc and his wife turned and fled. They ran to a church and went inside to seek refuge, closing and locking the door behind them. Haveloc climbed up the tower and the townsfolk surrounded them. They attacked them on all sides and he defended himself very well. He took hold of the stone from the top of the wall and threw it down vigorously. The news reached the seneschal's castle and it did not please him, because the man to whom he had given lodgings, and who had eaten at his table, had killed five of his men and maimed a sixth. He had gone into the church tower and the townsfolk had attacked him. They had assailed him very fiercely and he had defended himself very resolutely by hurling blocks of stone at them from the tower, maiming many and killing more. (679–718)

The nobleman demanded his horse and ordered all his knights to accompany him to the skirmish that had arisen in the town. First he went to the church and saw Haveloc being so successful that he was making them all draw back; they were all afraid of being struck by him. The seneschal went forward and saw how big and tall Haveloc was, with a noble body and fine stature, long arms and broad hips. He looked at him very closely and was reminded of his lord, King Gunter, whom he had loved so much. He uttered an anguished sigh. This man looked just like him in face, height and build. The seneschal brought the attack to a halt and forbade anyone from proceeding with it. He called out to the youth: 'Do not throw any more, my friend,' he said. 'I can guarantee your safety. Speak to me, explain to me and tell me why you have killed my men in this way and which of you was in the wrong.' 'My lord', he said, 'I will tell you and not lie to you in any way. When we left after the meal we had with you just now, we headed straight for our lodgings. As we left your dwelling, the scoundrels pursued us, intending to seize my wife and lie with her in front of me. I grabbed one of their axes and defended myself and her. It is true that I killed them, but I did so in self-defence.' (719–56)

When he heard about their arrogance, the seneschal replied to him: 'My friend', he said, 'come forward and do not be afraid of anything. Tell me where you were born and mind you do not conceal it from me.' 'This is what one of my friends tells me: that I was born in this country and a powerful man from this country, by the name of Grim, raised me. After the kingdom had been conquered, and my father had been killed, together with myself and my mother he fled because of my father's death, taking with him a great deal of gold and silver. We were at sea for a long time and were attacked by pirates. They killed my mother, but I survived, as did the good man who brought me up and loved me dearly. When our ship had docked in a wild region, the good man built a house there. He was the first to live there and he found enough food for us by selling salt and fishing. Later so many people lived there that a town and market developed. Because he was called Grim, the town's name is Grimsby. When I was grown up, I left him and worked in King Edelsi's household for the cooks in the kitchen. He gave me this maiden. She is related to him. I do not know why he brought us together. I took her away from the land and have now come to look for my family. I do not know where to find any of them because I cannot name a single one.' (757–96)

The seneschal replied to him: 'Dear, sweet friend, tell me your name.' 'I am called Haveloc, my lord, and was called Cuarant when I was at the king's court and worked in the kitchen.' The nobleman thought hard. In his heart he remembered that the king's son, whom Grim had taken away with him, had the same name. He came close to acknowledging him, but nevertheless was still doubtful. Making him a pledge of safety, he took him to his castle, together with his wife and his two companions – he called them his prisoners – and that day had them very well served. At night they slept in his chamber. When the youngsters were in bed, he sent one of his close advisers to find out whether the flame issued forth from Haveloc when he slept. The nurse who had raised him had often reported to him that this happened while he was sleeping, without the fire doing him any harm. Haveloc was very weary and fell asleep straightaway. From the very moment he went to sleep, fire issued from his mouth. The steward was very frightened and went to tell his lord, who thanked God that he had found the rightful heir. He summoned his scribes to write and seal letters. He entrusted them to his messengers and sent them to his allies, his vassals and his relatives. (797–835)

The next day he assembled a large number of people, all those who lived in the land and who hated King Odulf. In the morning he had the baths heated and Haveloc was bathed and washed. He dressed him in costly garments, and also his wife, who was with him. He took them into the hall. Haveloc was very much afraid because of the large number of people he saw there. Be aware that that the youth was fearful that, because of the men he had killed, it was the custom of that land for someone to be served in this way, being bathed, washed and dressed. Then he would be judged for his crime and put on trial. It was no wonder that Haveloc was afraid. He grabbed a large axe – it was hanging from a hook in the palace – and grasped it in both hands. He would defend himself vigorously if they intended to try him or hang him. The seneschal looked at him, drew him towards him and kissed him. 'My lord', he said, 'do not be afraid, give me back that axe. Do not worry, I tell you. I pledge you my loyalty.' Haveloc gave him back the axe and he put it back on the hook. He had him sit down on one side, with his wife seated next to him. The seneschal called his steward and asked him for the king's horn, saying that they would try it, to find out whether they could sound it. To the man who could sound the horn he would give his golden ring. In the hall there was not a single knight, sergeant, youth or squire who did not put the horn to his mouth, but not one of them caused it to make a sound. The seneschal took the horn and placed it in Haveloc's hands. 'My friend', he said, 'now try and see if you can sound it.' Haveloc replied: 'My lord, I do not know how to do this. I have never touched a horn and would not like to be laughed at. But since you command it of me, I will put the horn to my mouth and, if I can, I will sound it.' Haveloc rose to his feet and prepared to blow the horn. He sounded the horn with such force that it could be heard a long way off. It was regarded as a great marvel by those who were in the house. (836–94)

The lord called to them and presented him to everyone at the same time. 'My lords, this is the reason I have summoned you, for God has visited us again. Here is our rightful heir. You should be overjoyed at this.' First of all, he divested himself of his cloak and knelt before Haveloc. He became his vassal and swore to him that he would serve him loyally. The others followed suit, each one most willingly. After they had acknowledged him, they all became his vassals. The news spread; it could not be concealed for long. Those who heard it flocked from all sides, rich and poor. They made him their overlord and dubbed him a knight. The seneschal, who was a worthy man and a good vassal, helped him so much that he assembled a huge army. He informed King Odulf by letter that he should hand his land over to him and depart swiftly. When he heard this, King Odulf mocked and scorned him a great deal, saying that he would do battle with him. He gathered men from all sides and the youth for his part also had a large number of men. On the day they had arranged between them, when the armies were assembled and prepared for battle, Haveloc saw the common folk, who had come to his aid. He did not want them to be killed, so he sent word to Odulf through his allies that he would do battle with him, man to man, and that if he won everyone would submit to him and would all serve him as their lord. There was no reason why those who were blameless should die because of this. The king did not dare to refuse him. He had all his men disarm and Haveloc on his side did the same. The king was very keen for them to come together, so that his opponent would be captured or destroyed. The men clashed and attacked each other like lions. Haveloc possessed great strength and he struck King Odulf with an axe he had brought with him, laying him low; he never rose again. He killed him there in front of his men, who all cried in a loud voice: 'My lord, have mercy and do not let us die, for we will serve you willingly.' They all committed themselves to Haveloc and he pardoned them fully. (895–956)

After this act, he received the kingdom that had belonged to his father. The Danes made him their king and all his neighbours submitted to him. He established peace in the land and punished evildoers. He loved and greatly cherished his wife, for she had served him well. Earlier she had been in great despair, but now God had comforted her. Once Haveloc had become a powerful king, he ruled the kingdom for more than three years, amassing an enormous amount of treasure. Argentille advised him to cross the sea to England in order to regain her heritage, from which her uncle had driven her out and wrongfully disinherited her. The king said he would do whatever she advised. He had his fleet prepared and his men and his army summoned. When he had prepared his journey, he did not delay long. When there was a breeze, he set sail and took his queen with him. Haveloc had four hundred and eighty ships filled with men. They carried arms and provisions, wine and wheat, meat and fish. They rowed and sailed until they arrived at Charlfleet. They set up camp on the seashore and searched for food in the countryside. Then, on the advice of his Danes, the noble king sent word to Edelsi, telling him to surrender the land that Achebrit had ruled, which has been promised to his niece and from which he had disinherited her. If he refused to hand it over to her, he would capture it. The messengers came to the king and found him inflexible and arrogant. They gave their message to him and he laughed at it and scorned it. He replied to them with great arrogance: 'I have heard remarkable news,' he said, 'about Cuarant, that cook of mine, whom I raised in my household, that he will come and demand my land. I will have my cooks joust with him with trivets and cauldrons, and with pans and pots.' (958–1010)

The messengers departed and informed their lord of the response the king had made to them, and about the date he had fixed with them when the two armies would meet and engage in battle. Before the day they had chosen, Edelsi summoned his allies and all those he could assemble, so that no one was left behind. The troops gathered in Tetford and made ready to attack. King Edelsi was the first to arm himself and he mounted an iron-grey horse. He went to survey his enemies, to see how many men they had. When he had seen the Danes, with their pennants and their shields, he did not think of cauldrons, or of pans and pots, with which he had threatened them. Instead, he withdrew and told his men what they should do and how they should join battle. The combat between them was fierce, lasting until evening. Many of the Danes were killed and many others seriously wounded. They were at breaking point when the darkness made them part. Haveloc was very angry because of the men he had lost. If the queen had allowed it, he would have retreated with his Danes and returned to his ship. Because of a stratagem she promised would work, by which he could conquer his enemy, the king remained behind and trusted her. All night long he had stakes cut, and pointed at each end. They fixed the dead men on them and positioned them among the living, forming them into two detachments, with axes raised on their shoulders. (1011–54)

In the morning, when it became light, King Edelsi got ready to commence battle, as did all his knights. But when they saw their opponents, all their flesh crept. The company of dead men they saw on the plain was fearsome. For each man they had they saw seven on the other side. The king's counsellors told him it would be of no use to fight. The Danes had increased in number, but he had lost many of his men. He should give the lady what was rightfully hers and make peace before matters got worse. The king had no other choice but to accept this argument. On the counsel of his closest advisers, he made peace with the king of the Danes, pledging his loyalty to him and giving him hostages. He restored to him all the land that Achebrit had ruled over when he was alive. The Danes were lords and masters from Holland [in Lincolnshire] to Colchester. When he reached Colchester, Haveloc held his feast in the city. He received homage from the barons and restored their heritages to them. Once this had been done, King Edelsi lived for no more than a fortnight. He had no heir who was as rightful as Haveloc and his wife. The barons accepted them and handed over cities and castles. Haveloc held in his power Lincoln and all of Lindsey. He reigned and was king for twenty years, making many conquests through his Danes. People everywhere spoke well of him. In remembrance of him, the ancients composed a lay about his victory, so that it would be remembered for evermore. Here ends *Haveloc*. (1055–99)

Bibliography

Editions

The first edition given is the one used for the translation in the present volume.

N.B. References to the *Lais* of Marie de France are to the edition by Alfred Ewert (Oxford: Blackwell, 1944; repr. with introduction and bibliography by Glyn S. Burgess, London: Bristol Classical Press, 1995).

Amours

Ed. Glyn S. Burgess and Leslie C. Brook in *The Old French Lays of Ignaure, Oiselet and Amours* (Cambridge: D. S. Brewer, 2010), pp. 199–251.

Ed. Gaston Paris in 'Un lai d'Amours', *Romania*, 7 (1878), 407–15.

Aristote

Ed. Glyn S. Burgess and Leslie C. Brook in *Henri de Valenciennes, Aristote*, Liverpool Online Series, Critical Editions of French Texts 16, 2011. <https://www.liverpool.ac.uk/modern-languages-and-cultures-languages/french/liverpool-online-series/>

Ed. Alain Corbellari in *Les Dits d'Henri d'Andeli*, Classiques Français du Moyen Age 146 (Paris: Champion, 2003), pp. 73–90. This edition contains diplomatic transcriptions of all six manuscripts of this lay.

Ed. Maurice Delbouille in *Le Lai d'Aristote de Henri d'Andeli* (Paris: Les Belles Lettres, 1951).

Ed. T. B. W. Reid in *Twelve Fabliaux* (Manchester: Manchester University Press, 1958), pp. 70–82.

Chastelaine de Vergi

Ed. Frederick Whitehead in *La Chastelaine de Vergi* (Manchester: Manchester University Press, 1944).

Ed. Jean Dufournet and Liliane Dulac in *La Châtelaine de Vergy* (Paris: Gallimard, 1994).

Ed. R. E. V. Stuip in *La Chastelaine de Vergi, édition critique du ms. B.N. f. fr. 375 avec introduction, notes, glossaire et index* (The Hague and Paris: Mouton, 1970), pp. 73–113. This edition is based on MS A and contains diplomatic editions of the other manuscripts of the lay.

Conseil

Ed. Leslie C. Brook, forthcoming in the 2016 issue of *Le Cygne*.

Ed. Brînduşa Elena Grigoriu, Catharina Peersman and Jeff Rider in *Le Lai du Conseil*: *Critical Edition*, Liverpool Online Series, Critical Editions of French Texts 18, 2013. <https://www.liverpool.ac.uk/modern-languages-and-cultures-languages/french/liverpool-online-series/>

Ed. Albert Barth in '*Le Lai du Conseil*: Ein altfranzösisches Minnegedicht. Kritischer Text mit Einleitung und Anmerkungen', *Romanische Forschungen*, 31 (1912), 799–872.

Cor

Ed. C. T. Erickson in *The Anglo-Norman Text of Le Lai du Cor* (Oxford: Blackwell, for the Anglo-Norman Text Society, 1973).

Ed. Philip Bennett in *Mantel et Cor: deux lais du XIIe siècle* (Exeter: University of Exeter, 1975), pp. 43–63.

Ed. Margherita Lecco in *Robert Biket, Il corno magico* (Alessandria: Edizioni dell'Orso, 2004).

Ed. Nathalie Koble in *Le Lai du Cor et Le Mantel mal taillé*: *les dessous de la Table Ronde* (Paris: Éditions Rue d'Ulm, 2005), pp. 18–91.

Desiré

Ed. Glyn S. Burgess and Leslie C. Brook in *French Arthurian Literature IV: Eleven Old French Narrative Lays*, with the collaboration of Amanda Hopkins for *Melion* (Cambridge: D. S. Brewer, 2007), pp. 11–81.

Ed. Margaret E. Grimes in *The Lays of Desiré, Graelent and Melion: Edition of the Texts with an Introduction* (New York: Institute of French Studies, 1928; repr. Geneva: Slatkine, 1976), pp. 48–75.

Ed. Nathalie Koble and Mireille Séguy in *Lais bretons (XIIe–XIIIe siècles): Marie de France et ses contemporains, édition bilingue établie, traduite, présentée et annotée* (Paris: Champion, 2011). Contains an edition of *Desiré*, based on MS S, with a parallel French translation, pp. 638–95.

Ed. Prudence Mary O'Hara Tobin in *Les Lais anonymes des XIIe et XIIIe siècles: édition critique de quelques lais bretons* (Geneva: Droz, 1976), pp. 157–205. Tobin's edition has been reprinted with a parallel French translation in Alexandre Micha, *Lais féeriques des XIIe et XIIIe siècles* (Paris: GF-Flammarion, 1992) and by Walter Pagani, *Lais anonimi bretoni dei secoli XII e XIII: introduzione, bibliografia, traduzione con testo a fronte* (Pisa: Servizio Editoriale Universitario di Pisa, 1984).

Doon

Ed. Burgess and Brook in *French Arthurian Literature IV*, pp. 245–75 (see *Desiré* above).

Ed. Burgess and Brook in *Doon and Tyolet: Two Old French Narrative Lays, Edited and Translated*, Liverpool Online Series, Critical Editions of French Texts 9, 2005, pp. 10–42. <https://www.liverpool.ac.uk/modern-languages-and-cultures-languages/french/liverpool-online-series/>

Ed. Tobin in *Les Lais anonymes*, pp. 31–33 (see *Desiré* above).

Espervier

Ed. Glyn S. Burgess in 'The Lay of *Espervier*', in *The Medieval Imagination: Mirabile Dictu. Essays in Honour of Yolande de Pontfarcy Sexton* (Dublin: Four Courts Press, 2012), pp. 34–44.

Ed. Gaston Paris in '*Le Lai de l'Épervier*', *Romania*, 7 (1878), 1–21.

Espine

Ed. Burgess and Brook in *French Arthurian Literature IV*, pp. 199–241 (see *Desiré* above).

Ed. Tobin in *Les Lais anonymes*, pp. 255–88 (see *Desiré* above).

Graelent

Ed. Burgess and Brook in *French Arthurian Literature IV*, pp. 351–412 (see *Desiré* above).

Ed. Margaret E. Grimes in *The Lays of Desiré, Graelent and Melion*, pp. 76–101 (see *Desiré* above).

Ed. Nathalie Koble in *Lais bretons (XIIe–XIIIe siècles)* (see *Désiré* above). Contains an edition of *Graelent*, based on MS S, with a facing French translation, pp. 774–823.

Ed. Tobin in *Les Lais anonymes*, pp. 83–1253 (see *Desiré* above).

Ed. Russell Weingartner in *Graelent and Guingamor: Two Breton Lays* (New York and London: Garland, 1985), pp. 2–39.

Guingamor

Ed. Burgess and Brook in *French Arthurian Literature IV*, pp. 143–95 (see *Desiré* above).

Ed. Margherita Lecco in *Lais di Guingamor, Tydorel, Tyolet* (Alessandria: Edizioni dell'Orso, 2015). The edition of *Guingamor*, with a parallel Italian translation, is found on pp. 29–53.

Ed. Nathalie Koble and Mireille Séguy in *Lais bretons (XIIe–XIIIe siècles)* (see *Désiré* above). Contains an edition of *Guingamor* with a parallel French translation, pp. 696–741.

Ed. Tobin in *Les Lais anonymes*, pp. 31–33 (see *Desiré* above).

Ed. Russell Weingartner in *Graelent and Guingamor*, pp. 42–75 (see *Graelent* above).

Haveloc

Ed. Glyn S. Burgess and Leslie C. Brook in *The Anglo-Norman Lay of Haveloc: Edition and Translation* (Cambridge: D. S. Brewer, 2015). Edition and translation based on MS H, with MS P in an Appendix.

Ed. Alexander Bell in *The Lai d'Haveloc and Gaimar's Haveloc Episode* (Manchester: The University Press, 1925). Edition based on MS P.

Ignaure

Ed. Burgess and Brook in *The Old French Lays of Ignaure, Oiselet and Amours*, pp. 7–113 (see *Amours* above).

Ed. Martina Di Febo in *L'amante prigioniero* (Alessandria: Edizioni dell'Orso, 2002).

Ed. Rita Lejeune in Lejeune in *Renaut [de Beaujeu], Le Lai d'Ignaure ou Lai du Prisonnier* (Brussels: Palais des Académies; Liège: H. Vaillant-Carmanne, 1938).

Lai de l'Ombre

Ed. Alan Hindley and Brian J. Levy in *Jehan Renart, Le Lai de l'Ombre*, with a translation and introduction by Adrian P. Tudor, Liverpool Online Series, Critical Editions of French Texts 8, 2004. <https://www.liverpool.ac.uk/modern-languages-and-cultures-languages/french/liverpool-online-series/>

Ed. Joseph Bédier in *Le Lai de l'Ombre par Jean Renart* (Paris: Firmin-Didot, 1913; repr. Johnson Reprint Corporation, 1971). An early but still influential edition. Edited from MS A.

Ed. Félix Lecoy in *Jehan Renart, Le Lai de l'Ombre* (Paris: Champion, 1979). Edited from MS A.

Ed. John Orr in *Jehan Renart, Le Lai de l'Ombre* (Edinburgh: Edinburgh University Press, 1948). Edited from MS E.

Ed. Margaret E. Winters in *Jehan Renart, Le Lai de l'Ombre: Edited from Manuscript E [B.N. nouv. acq. fr. 1104]* (Birmingham, AL: Summa Publications, 1986).

Lecheor

Ed. Burgess and Brook in *French Arthurian Literature IV*, pp. 279–97 (see *Desiré* above).

Ed. Burgess and Brook in *Three Old French Narrative Lays: Trot, Lecheor, Nabaret*, Liverpool Online Series, Critical Editions of French Texts 1, 1999, pp. 47–72. <https://www.liverpool.ac.uk/modern-languages-and-cultures-languages/french/liverpool-online-series/>

Ed. Tobin in *Les Lais anonymes des XIIe et XIIIe siècles*, pp. 347–58 (see *Desiré* above).

Mantel

Ed. Glyn S. Burgess and Leslie C. Brook in *French Arthurian Literature V: The Lay of Mantel* (Cambridge: D. S. Brewer, 2013).

Ed. Philip Bennett in *Mantel et Cor: deux lais du XIIe siècle* (Exeter: University of Exeter, 1975), pp. 3–39.

Ed. Nathalie Koble in *Le Lai du Cor et Le Mantel mal taillé: les dessous de la Table Ronde* (Paris: Éditions Rue d'Ulm, 2005), pp. 54–91.

Melion

Ed. Amanda Hopkins in Burgess and Brook in *French Arthurian Literature IV*, pp. 415–66 (see *Desiré* above).

Ed. Margaret E. Grimes in *The Lays of Desiré, Graelent and Melion*, pp. 102–22 (see *Desiré* above).

Ed. Amanda Hopkins in *Melion and Biclarel: Two Old French Werewolf Lays. Edited and Translated*, Liverpool Online Series, Critical Editions of French Texts 10, 2005. <https://www.liverpool.ac.uk/modern-languages-and-cultures-languages/french/liverpool-online-series/>

Ed. W. Horak in '*Lai von Melion*', *Zeitschrift für romanische Philologie*, 6 (1882), 94–106.

Ed. Nathalie Koble and Mireille Séguy in *Lais bretons (XIIe–XIIIe siècles)* (see *Désiré* above). Contains an edition of *Melion* with a parallel French translation, pp. 824–63.

Ed. Tobin in *Les Lais anonymes*, pp. 289–318 (see *Desiré* above).

Nabaret

Ed. Burgess and Brook in *French Arthurian Literature IV*, pp. 469–80 (see *Desiré* above).

Ed. Burgess and Brook in *Three Old French Narrative Lays: Trot, Lecheor, Nabaret*, Liverpool Online Series, Critical Editions of French Texts 1, 1999, pp. 75–88. <https://www.liverpool.ac.uk/modern-languages-and-cultures-languages/french/liverpool-online-series/>

Ed. Tobin in *Les Lais anonymes*, pp. 359–64.

Narcisus and Dané

Ed. Penny Eley in *Narcisus et Dané*, Liverpool Online Series, Critical Editions of French Texts 6, 2002. <https://www.liverpool.ac.uk/modern-languages-and-cultures-languages/french/liverpool-online-series/>

Ed. Mario Mancini in *Il lai di Narciso* (Parma: Pratiche Editrice, 1989).

Ed. Emmanuèle Baumgartner in *Pyrame et Thisbé, Narcisse, Philomena: trois contes du XIIe siècle français imités d'Ovide* (Paris: Gallimard, 2000), pp. 84–153.

Ed. Raymond Cormier in *Three Ovidian Tales of Love (Piramus et Tisbé, Narcisus et Dané, and Philomena et Procné)* (New York and London: Garland, 1986), 87–177.

Ed. Margaret M. Pelan and N. C. W. Spence in *Narcisse (poème du XIIe siècle)* (Paris: Les Belles Lettres, 1964).

Ed. Martine Thiry-Stassin and Madeleine Tyssens in *Narcisse, conte ovidien français du XIIe siècle: édition critique* (Paris: Les Belles Lettres, 1976).

Oiselet

Ed. Burgess and Brook in *The Old French Lays of Ignaure, Oiselet and Amours*, pp. 117–96 (see *Amours* above).

Ed. Suzanne Méjean-Thiolier and Marie-Françoise Notz-Grob in *Nouvelles courtoises occitanes et françaises* (Paris: Le Livre de Poche, 1997), pp. 426–48.

Ed. Lenora Wolfgang, *Le Lai de l'Oiselet, an Old French Poem of the Thirteenth Century: Edition and Critical Study* (Philadelphia, PA: American Philosophical Society, 1990).

Piramus and Thisbe

Ed. Penny Eley in *Piramus et Tisbé, Edited and Translated*, Liverpool Online Series, Critical Editions of French Texts 5, 2002. <https://www.liverpool.ac.uk/modern-languages-and-cultures-languages/french/liverpool-online-series/>

Ed. Emmanuèle Baumgartner in *Pyrame et Thisbé, Narcisse, Philomena: trois contes du XIIe siècle français imités d'Ovide* (Paris: Gallimard, 2000), pp. 22–81.

Ed. Francesco Branciforti in *Piramus et Tisbé* (Florence: Olschki, 1959).

Ed. Raymond Cormier in *Three Ovidian Tales of Love (Piramus et Tisbé, Narcisus et Dané, and Philomena et Procné)* (New York and London: Garland, 1986), pp. 3–82.

Tydorel

Ed. Burgess and Brook in *French Arthurian Literature IV*, pp. 301–48 (see *Desiré* above).

Ed. Margherita Lecco in *Lais di Guingamor, Tydorel, Tyolet* (Alessandria: Edizioni dell'Orso, 2015). The edition of *Tydorel*, with a parallel Italian translation, is found on pp. 55–74.

Ed. Nathalie Koble and Mireille Séguy in *Lais bretons (XIIe–XIIIe siècles)* (see *Desiré* above). Contains an edition of *Tydorel* with a parallel French translation, pp. 742–73.

Ed. Tobin in *Les Lais anonymes*, pp. 207–26 (see *Desiré* above).

Trot

Ed. Burgess and Brook in *French Arthurian Literature IV*, pp. 483–508 (see *Desiré* above).

Ed. Burgess and Brook in *Three Old French Narrative Lays: Trot, Lecheor, Nabaret*, Liverpool Online Series, Critical Editions of French Texts 1, 1999, pp. 15–44. <https://www.liverpool.ac.uk/modern-languages-and-cultures-languages/french/liverpool-online-series/>

Ed. Tobin in *Les Lais anonymes*, pp. 335–46 (see *Desiré* above).

Tyolet

Ed. Burgess and Brook in *French Arthurian Literature IV*, pp. 85–140 (see *Desiré* above).

Ed. Burgess and Brook in *Doon and Tyolet: Two Old French Narrative Lays, Edited and Translated*, Liverpool Online Series, Critical Editions of French Texts 9, 2005, pp. 50–109. <https://www.liverpool.ac.uk/modern-languages-and-cultures-languages/french/liverpool-online-series/>

Ed. Margherita Lecco in *Lais di Guingamor, Tydorel, Tyolet* (Alessandria: Edizioni dell'Orso, 2015). The edition of *Tyolet*, with a parallel Italian translation, is found on pp. 75–100.

Ed. Tobin in *Les Lais anonymes*, pp. 227–53 (see *Desiré* above).

Further Reading

Students of the lays in this volume will find many pertinent items in the bibliographies established for the Lais *of Marie de France by Glyn S. Burgess:* Marie de France: An Analytical Bibliography *(London: Grant and Cutler, 1977; Supplement No. 1, 1986; Supplement No. 2, 1997; Supplement No. 3 (Woodbridge: Tamesis, 2007)). For the lays in this volume, see Glyn S. Burgess,* The Old French Narrative Lay: An Analytical Bibliography *(Cambridge: D. S. Brewer, 1995). The following items are of special interest for the study of the lay as a genre. For further bibliography, see the editions used for the translations in this volume and the further reading sections at the end of each introduction.*

Aubailly, Jean-Claude, *La Fée et le chevalier: essai de mythologie de quelques lais féeriques des XII*^{e} *et XIII*^{e} *siècles* (Paris: Champion, 1986).

Baader, Horst, *Die Lais: zur Geschichte einer Gattung der altfranzösischen Kurzerzählungen*, Analecta Romanica, 16 (Frankfurt am Main: Klostermann, 1966).

Beston, J. B., 'The Nonceltic French *lais*', in *Proceedings and Papers of the Sixteenth Congress of the Australasian Universities Language and

Literature Association Held 21–27 August 1974 at the University of Adelaide, South Australia, ed. H. Bevan *et al.* (Sydney: AULLA, 1974), pp. 300–08.

Boyd, Matthieu, Elizabeth W. Poe and Joseph M. Sullivan, 'What is a Lay?', *Le Cygne*, third series, 1 (2014), 21–35. Contains separate studies of the term *lai* and equivalents in Celtic, Occitan and German texts.

Braet, Herman, 'Les Lais "bretons": enfants de la mémoire', *Bibliographical Bulletin of the International Arthurian Society*, 37 (1985), 283–91.

Bromwich, Rachel, 'Celtic Dynastic Themes and the Breton Lays', *Études Celtiques*, 9 (1960–61), 439–74.

Bullock-Davies, Constance, 'The Form of the Breton Lay', *Medium Aevum*, 42 (1973), 18–31.

Burgess, Glyn S., 'Chivalric Activity in the Anonymous Lays', in *L'Imaginaire courtois et son double*, ed. Giovanna Angeli and Luciano Formisano (Naples: Edizioni Scientifiche, 1992), pp. 271–91.

———, 'Marie de France and the Anonymous Lays', in *A Companion to Marie de France*, ed. Logan E. Whalen (Leiden and Boston: Brill, 2011), pp. 117–56.

———, 'The Old French Narrative Lay: A Guide to Manuscripts, Editions, and Translations', *Le Cygne*, third series, 1 (2014), 37–54.

De Caluwé, Jacques. 'L'Autre Monde celtique et l'élément chrétien dans les lais anonymes', in *The Legend of Arthur in the Middle Ages: Studies Presented to A. H. Diverres by Colleagues, Pupils and Friends*, ed. P. B. Grout et al. (Cambridge: D. S. Brewer, 1983), pp. 55–65.

Donovan, Mortimer J., *The Breton Lay: A Guide to Varieties* (Notre Dame, IN and London: University of Notre Dame Press, 1969).

Dubost, Francis, *Aspects fantastiques de la littérature narrative médiévale (XIIème–XIIIème siècles)* (Paris: Champion, 1991).

Field, Rosalind, 'Romance as History, History as Romance', in *Romance in Medieval England*, ed. Maldwyn Mills, Jennifer Fellows and Carol M. Meale (Cambridge: D. S. Brewer, 1991), pp. 163–73.

Fleuriot, Léon, 'Les Lais bretons', in *Histoire littéraire et culturelle de la Bretagne*, ed. J. Balcou and Y. Le Gallo, 3 vols (Paris and Geneva: Champion – Slakkine, 1987), I, pp. 131–38.

Foulet, Lucien, 'Marie de France et les lais bretons', *Zeitschrift für romanische Philologie*, 29 (1905), 19–56, 293–322.

Frappier, Jean, 'Remarques sur la structure du lai: essai de définition et de classement', in *La Littérature narrative d'imagination, des genres littéraires aux techniques d'expression (colloque de Strasbourg, 23–25 avril, 1959)* (Paris: Presses Universitaires de France, 1961), pp. 23–29; repr. in *Du Moyen Age à la Renaissance: études d'histoire et de critique littéraire* (Paris: Champion, 1976), pp. 15–35.

Gallais, Pierre, *La Fée à la fontaine et à l'arbre: un archétype du conte merveilleux et du récit courtois* (Amsterdam and Atlanta, GA: Rodopi, 1992).

Gosman, Martin, 'Le Statut descriptif de la dame aimée dans les lais dits "féeriques"', in *Amour, mariage et transgressions au Moyen Age: actes du colloque des 24, 25, 26 et 27 mars 1983, Université de Picardie, Centre d'Études Médiévales*, ed. D. Buschinger and A. Crépin (Göppingen: Kümmerle, 1984), pp. 203–13.

Guillet-Rydell, Mireille, 'Nature et rôle du mariage dans les lais anonymes bretons', *Romania*, 96 (1975), 91–104.

Harf-Lancner, Laurence, *Les Fées au Moyen Age: Morgane et Mélusine, la naissance de fées* (Paris: Champion, 1984).

Hoepffner, Ernest, 'Marie de France et les lais anonymes', *Studi Medievali*, new series, 4 (1931), 1–31.

——, 'The Breton *lais*', in *Arthurian Literature in the Middle Ages: A Collaborative History*, ed. Roger Sherman Loomis (Oxford: Clarendon Press, 1959), pp. 112–21.

Jodogne, Omer, 'L'Autre Monde celtique dans la littérature française du XIIe siècle', *Académie Royale de Belgique, Bulletin de la Classe des Lettres et des Sciences Morales et Politiques*, fifth series, 46 (1960–61), 584–97.

Jones, Rosemarie, *Love in the romans d'antiquité*, MHRA Dissertation Series 5 (London: The Modern Humanities Research Association, 1972). Contains chapters on *Piramus and Thisbé* and *Narcisus and Dané.*

Kallaur, M., 'Une reconsidération du portrait dans les lais médiévaux', in *Le Portrait littéraire*, ed. K. Kupisz, G.-A. Pérouse and J.-Y. Debreuille (Lyon: Presses Universitaires de Lyon, 1988), 15–23.

Kroll, Renata, *Der narrative Lai als eigenständige Gattung in der Literatur des Mittelalters: zum Strukturprincip der Aventure in den Lais* (Tübingen: Niemeyer, 1984).

Lee, Charmaine, 'Dinamica interna della narrativa breve antico-francese', *Medioevo Romanzo*, 8 (1981–83), 381–400.

Lefay-Toury, Marie-Noëlle, *La Tentation du suicide dans le roman français du XIIe siècle* (Paris: Champion, 1979). Contains material on *Piramus and Thisbé* and *Narcisus and Dané.*

Llamas-Pombo, Elena, 'Beauté, amour et mort dans les Ovidiana français du XIIe siècle', in *Le Beau et le laid au Moyen Age* (Aix-en-Provence: Université de Provence, Centre Universitaire d'Études et de Recherches Médiévales d'Aix, 2000), pp. 337–50. Contains material on *Piramus and Thisbé* and on *Narcisus and Dané.*

Pagani, Walter, 'Prologhi e epiloghi des *lais* anonimi bretoni', in *Studia in honorem Prof. M. de Riquer*, 4 vols (Barcelona: Quaderns Crema, 1986–91), IV, pp. 571–91.

Paris, Paulin, '*Lais*', *Histoire Littéraire de la France*, 23 (1856), 61–68, 833.

Payen, Jean-Charles, 'Le Lai narratif', in *Typologies des sources du Moyen Age occidental*, fasc. 13 (Turnhout: Brepols, 1975), pp. 31–63.

——, 'Lai, fabliau, *exemplum*, roman court: pour une typologie du récit bref aux XIIe et XIIIe siècles', in *Le Récit bref au Moyen Age: actes du colloque des 27, 28 et 29 avril 1979*, ed. D. Buschinger (Amiens: Université de Picardie, Centre d'Études Médiévales; Paris: Champion, 1980), pp. 7–23.

Régnier-Bohler, Danielle, 'Figures féminines et imaginaire généalogique: étude comparée de quelques récits brefs', in *Le Récit bref au Moyen Age: actes du colloque des 27, 28 et 29 avril 1979*, ed. D. Buschinger (Amiens: Université de Picardie, Centre d'Études Médiévales; Paris: Champion, 1980), pp. 73–96.

Sims-Williams, Patrick, 'Shrewsbury School MS 7 and the Breton Lays', *Cambrian Medieval Celtic Studies*, 60 (2010), 39–80.

Smithers, G. V., 'Story-Patterns in some Breton Lays', *Medium Aevum*, 22 (1953), 61–92.

Suard, François, 'Le Fils dans les lais anonymes', in *Le Récit bref au Moyen Age: actes du colloque des 27, 28 et 29 avril 1979*, ed. D. Buschinger (Amiens: Université de Picardie, Centre d'Études Médiévales; Paris: Champion, 1980), pp. 57–73.

Tobin, Prudence Mary O'Hara, 'L'Elément breton et les lais anonymes', in *Mélanges de langue et de littérature françaises du Moyen Age et de la Renaissance offerts à Charles Foulon, II, Marche Romane*, 30 (1980), pp. 277–86.

Williams, Harry F., 'The Anonymous Breton Lays', *Research Studies*, 32 (1964), 76–84.

Index of Proper Names

Personal and geographical names found in the twenty-four lays are listed here along with the relevant page numbers.